A GUIDE TO GOOD REASONING

A GUIDE TO GOOD REASONING

David C. Wilson
UCLA

Boston Burr Ridge, IL Dubuque, IA Madison, WI
New York San Francisco St. Louis
Bangkok Bogotá Caracas Lisbon London Madrid Mexico City
Milan New Delhi Seoul Singapore Sydney Taipei Toronto

McGraw-Hill College 

A Division of The **McGraw-Hill** *Companies*

A GUIDE TO GOOD REASONING

This book is printed on acid-free paper.

1 2 3 4 5 6 7 8 9 0 DOC/DOC 9 3 2 1 0 9 8

ISBN 0-07-070738-3

Editorial director: *Phillip A. Butcher*
Sponsoring editor: *Sarah Moyers*
Developmental editor: *Alexis Walker*
Senior marketing manager: *Daniel M. Loch*
Project manager: *Christina Thornton-Villagomez*
Production supervisor: *Michael R. McCormick*
Freelance design coordinator: *Gino Cieslik*
Supplement coordinator: *Rose Hepburn*
Compositor: *Carlisle Communications, Ltd.*
Typeface: *10.5/13.5 Janson Text*
Printer: *R. R. Donnelley & Sons Company*
Cover Credit: *Tate Gallery, London/Art Resource, NY*
Nicholson, Winifred. Moonlight and Lamplight, 1937. Tate Gallery, London, Great Britain.

Author Photography: *Author photograph by Justin Warren and courtesy of the Daily Bruin*

Library of Congress Cataloging-in-Publication Data

Wilson, David C. (David Carl), 1951–
A guide to good reasoning / David C. Wilson.
p. cm.
Includes bibliographical references and index.
ISBN 0-07-070738-3 (alk. paper)
1. Reasoning. I. Title.
BC177 .W56 1998
160—dc21 98-45471
CIP

http://www.mhhe.com

To Sita

ABOUT THE AUTHOR

DAVID C. WILSON is a philosopher and administrator at UCLA, where he began teaching courses in reasoning more than fifteen years ago. He received degrees from the University of Georgia, the University of Illinois, and UCLA before earning his Ph.D. in philosophy from UCLA. His research and teaching interests include the theory of knowledge and the philosophy of religion.

PREFACE

Several things are, I hope, distinctive about *A Guide to Good Reasoning*. They fall into two main categories—the practical and the intellectual.

The book's chief *practical* advantage is that it gradually unfolds for the student a single simple system—what amounts to a checklist of steps for clarifying and evaluating any argument. There is a standard format for *clarifying* the argument and a list of things to achieve in the clarification. And, there is a standard format for *evaluating* the same argument and a list of things to achieve there. The book also provides a handy test for clarifying ("imagine the arguer over your shoulder") and for evaluating ("imagine a reasonable objector over your shoulder"). Useful features abound in support of this practical approach: highlighted guidelines at regular intervals, glossaries, and copious real-life exercises and examples. I have tried hard to achieve the additional practical advantage of writing the book in a clear and inviting style.

The major *intellectual* advantage is that the book does not treat critical thinking as a grab bag of tips and topics—that is, not merely as fodder for a course in "reasoning appreciation." Rather, it treats it as a philosophical subdiscipline—*applied epistemology* is probably the best term for it—in which all the tips and topics fit together sensibly. The theory behind it is a simple one: good reasoning is ultimately a matter of cultivating intellectual virtues—of developing habits of thought that are conducive to knowledge. And this can best be done by cultivating skill in clarifying and evaluating arguments. Topics as diverse as definition, equivocation, truth, fallacies, deduction, and induction all fit naturally and coherently into such a system. This is not at the forefront of the book—my aim is to teach a skill, not a philosophical subdiscipline—but it is there. In addition, even though the book is written not for philosophers but for college freshmen, I have tried hard to maintain high standards of intellectual respectability throughout.

Several things *not* found in most such books are found here. There is an emphasis on judgmental heuristics, the quick and dirty shortcuts that psychologists have shown we constantly use in our reasoning. Intellectual virtues—especially intellectual honesty—are stressed, since cultivation of these virtues is ultimately the path to good reasoning. Conversational implicature (which, to make it easier on the students, I rename *conversational implication*) plays a significant part in the discussion of clarifying arguments. And I assign a prominent role to "conversational relevance" (failures of which include missing the point and begging the question) as a merit of arguments on a par with soundness and clarity.

On the other hand, a few things found in most similar books are not found here. Argument diagramming (numbering sentences in a passage and connecting them appropriately with arrows) is displaced by the simple procedure of outlining an argument in standard clarifying format. Symbolic logic is not here because it belongs in a different course; nor are truth tables, since they do not reliably describe language as we ordinarily use it. Categorical syllogisms are only briefly treated, given that they are exceedingly rare in real life.

On almost every page I have resisted the temptation to provide a philosophical defense of the terms and strategies adopted there. This is a guide to good reasoning, not a grand unified theory of good reasoning. To adapt a line from Daniel Dennett, I am mainly trying to offer students some training in reasoning first aid, so they'll know what to do until the doctor of philosophy arrives.

Many people have contributed significantly to this book. It would not exist without David Kaplan, who invented UCLA's critical reasoning course in the 1970s, invited me to teach it (again and again), and imparted to me a vision for what the course—and consequently the book—ought to be. The book has benefited immeasurably from the suggestions of those who have served as my teaching assistants or have taught their own courses with these materials. Carol Voeller merits special praise for her extraordinary help, as does Amy Kind, who wrote the superb *Instructor's Manual.* Many others are in this group: Adeofe Adeleke, Don Brown, Ron Condon, Keith DeRose,

Simon Evnine, Bill Fitzpatrick, Roger Florka, Gary Gleb, Steve Gross, Dan Guevara, Yoram Gutgeld, Martin Hahn, Lisa Halko, Matt Hanser, Julie Heath-Elliot, Del Kiernan-Lewis, Andreas Koch, Maryann Kooij, Rob Koons, John Mandeville, Frank Menetrez, Adele Mercier, Laurie Pieper, Gary Rawnsley, Sam Rickless, Josie Rodriguez-Hewitt, Marco Ruffino, Joseph Vaughan, Jon Wilwerding, and Eric Wing. I am also indebted to David Rivette, and to the countless students who have shaped the book by their participation in the course.

This book would, likewise, not exist without Dorothy Raymond of McGraw-Hill. When she couldn't sell me her company's textbook on this subject, she sold me on writing one I liked better. I owe much to the remarkable McGraw-Hill editors, who have shown professionalism, intelligence, and patience throughout the project. Cynthia Ward began by establishing a matchless standard; Sarah Moyers and Alexis Walker matched it. I am also grateful for the assistance they brought in from elsewhere—Vicky Nelson made a big difference, as did their team of reviewers: David W. Benfield, Montclair State College; C. J. Cassini, Barry University; Leonard Berkowitz, Pennsylvania State University, York; Thomas Feehan, College of the Holy Cross; Ricardo Gomez, California State University, Los Angeles; Arnold Johanson, Moorhead State University; Robert Kirkpatrick, University of Southwestern Louisiana; Michael Levin, City University of New York, City College; Richard Miller, East Carolina University; Walter H. O'Briant, University of Georgia (who may not recall that in the early 1970s he gave me a *B*, probably better than I deserved, in my only undergraduate philosophy course); Michael F. Patton, Jr., University of Montevallo; George Rainbolt, Georgia State University; Robert G. Wengert, University of Illinois at Urbana-Champaign; Nancy E. Shaffer, University of Nebraska at Omaha; Peter Chad Finsterwald, Boston University; Frank C. Williams, Eastern Kentucky University; Arnold Wilson, University of Cincinnati; Sara Worley, Bowling Green State University; and Michael Wreen, Marquette University.

Dave Wilson

BRIEF TABLE OF CONTENTS

TABLE OF CONTENTS

PART ONE

REASONING AND ARGUMENTS

CHAPTER ONE

Good Reasoning

The life according to reason is the best and the pleasantest, since reason, more than anything else, is human. This life therefore is also the happiest.

—Aristotle, *Nicomachean Ethics*

Rational, adj. Devoid of all delusions save those of observation, experience, and reflection.

—Ambrose Bierce, *The Devil's Dictionary*

TOPICS

Good Reasoning
Good Arguments
How We Normally Reason
Intellectual Virtues
How This Book Can Help

GOOD REASONING

You *know* the answers to many of the questions you care about, but you merely have opinions about many others. What is the difference between knowledge and opinion? Why is it that you now know, for example, that your teacher is highly competent, even though at one time this was only your opinion? The answer has partly to do with your level of confidence; although once you believed it tentatively, you now believe it with assurance. But there is a deeper difference: you now have better reasons for believing it. You have read her student evaluations, talked to many of her former students, maybe even taken a class from her yourself. There might still be some remote chance that she will disappoint you. (If it does turn out that you have been misled, you will conclude that it was merely an opinion all along—that you *thought* you knew that she was highly competent, but you never *really* knew it.) But, from where you now sit, your reasons are so good that you do justifiably claim it as knowledge and not as mere opinion.

So an important difference between knowledge and mere opinion is the quality of your reasons. Your ***reasons*** are what you depend on in support of what you believe—regardless of whether you consider what you believe to be knowledge or mere opinion. There are many rough synonyms for *reasons: evidence, warrant, justification, basis, grounds, rationale,* and—the term we will rely on most heavily—*premises.*

This book pays a great deal of attention to reasons, but it is ultimately concerned with something more. The title is not *A Guide to Good Reasons;* it is *A Guide to Good Reasoning.* Typically, reasons are something you have, while reasoning is something you do. The term ***reasoning*** refers here to the attempt to answer a question by thinking about reasons, as in the sentence *He stood in the polling booth, reasoning one last time about the relative merits of the two candidates.* **Good reasoning** is the thinking most likely to result in your having *good* reasons for your answers—and, thus, the sort of thinking most likely to give you knowledge rather than mere opinion.

Good reasoning, as Ambrose Bierce hints in the lead quotation, does not guarantee anything. Even with the best of reasoning you might still end up with a false belief and thus fail to have knowledge. Consider those before the time of Copernicus who believed that the sun orbited the Earth. Given the limited information available to them, there was nothing wrong with their reasoning. But their belief was false, and thus they did not *know* that the sun orbited the Earth. But the fallibility of good reasoning is no basis for rejecting it. There is simply no infallible substitute for it. And it is by continuing to reason well in the presence of new information that you learn that some of your beliefs are false—for example, that it is actually the Earth that orbits the sun.

Aristotle, in the other lead quotation, may be overenthusiastic in saying that good reasoning leads to the best, pleasantest, and happiest life. Some people might benefit from concentrating a little less on reason and a little more on friendship and human kindness—though, Aristotle might reply, the *right* use of reason—*good* reasoning—would tell them just that! Good reasoning does make an enormous contribution to a good life. For answering the questions you care about, knowledge is better than mere opinion and, thus, good reasoning beats bad reasoning.[1]

> *Guideline.* Use good reasoning if you want to *know* the answers to the questions you care about.

GOOD ARGUMENTS

Arguments

Arguments are the means by which we express reasons in language. So arguments will be the chief focus of this book. Chapter 2 will provide a more detailed account of arguments and their component parts. For now, consider the following brief definitions. An ***argument*** is a series of statements in which at least one of the statements is offered as a reason to believe another. A ***premise*** is a statement that is offered as a reason, while a ***conclusion*** is the statement for which reasons are offered.

Here is a typical everyday argument. Suppose you realize that you've broken out in hives and you wonder aloud what happened. I try to solve it for you as follows:

> Look at those hives! You only break out like that when you eat garlic—so there must have been garlic in that sauce you ate.

This argument provides two closely related reasons to believe its conclusion. The conclusion is this:

> *Conclusion:* There was garlic in the sauce you ate.

[1]Good reasoning may not guarantee that your belief is true; but it at least means that it is *justified*—another worthy goal.

The reasons, or premises, are these:

Premise one: You have hives.
Premise two: You get hives when you eat garlic.

Here is a slightly more elaborate argument from *The Panda's Thumb* by Stephen Jay Gould. Gould wonders whether a larger animal, in order to be as smart as a smaller animal, must have the same ratio of brain size to body size; his answer is as follows:

> As we move from mice to elephants or small lizards to Komodo dragons, brain size increases, but not so fast as body size. In other words, bodies grow faster than brains, and large animals have low ratios of brain weight to body weight. In fact, brains grow only about two-thirds as fast as bodies. Since we have no reason to conclude that large animals are consistently stupider than their smaller relatives, we must conclude that large animals require relatively less brain to do as well as smaller animals.

Gould expresses in language his reasons for believing his answer to the question—that is to say, he has provided us with an argument. The answer, his conclusion, is this:

Conclusion: Larger animals require relatively less brain to do as well as smaller animals.

And his reasons, or premises, are these:

Premise one: In comparing smaller types of animals to larger types of animals, brains increase only about two-thirds as fast as bodies.
Premise two: Larger animals are not consistently stupider than their smaller relatives.

Good Arguments

Four things are required of a good argument. First, the premises must be ***true***—that is, the premises must correspond with the world. Typically, this can be decided about each premise independently, without paying any attention to the other premises or to the conclusion. So, the garlic argument would be defective if, say, contrary to its first premise, you *didn't* have hives. Gould's argument would be defective if, say, contrary to its second premise, larger animals were consistently stupider than smaller ones.

Second, the argument must be ***logical***—that is, the premises must strongly support the conclusion. They must make it reasonable for you to believe the conclusion. This can normally be decided without paying any attention to whether the premises or conclusion are true. Suppose the conclusion to the garlic argument were *There was pepper in the sauce you ate*, or that Gould's conclusion were *Larger animals require relatively more brain to do as well as smaller animals*. It would then not matter whether the premises were true, or, for that matter, whether the conclusions were true. The arguments would be flawed anyway, since the premises, as stated, clearly do not support such conclusions. Regardless of whether the premises are true, the arguments would not be logical.

Truth and logic are the most important merits of arguments. If an argument has both merits—if its premises are true and it is logical—then it is ***sound***. But if it is defective in even one of these two ways, it is ***unsound***.

Third, the argument must be ***conversationally relevant***—that is, the argument must be appropriate to the conversation, or to the context, that gives rise to it. Conversations—between two people, between author and audience, or even between arguer and imaginary opponent—generate questions, and arguments are typically designed to answer such questions. In the garlic argument I am interested in the question, *Why do you have hives?* But suppose I had misunderstood your question in the noisy restaurant; you hadn't yet noticed that you had broken out in hives, and what you actually wondered aloud was why you had *chives*, since you had ordered your baked potato plain. My argument may still be perfectly sound—with true premises and good logic—yet it is now clearly defective, since it misses the point. This is not the only kind of conversational irrelevance. In Gould's argument, suppose he answered the question asked, but in doing so had adopted this as his premise:

> Larger animals require relatively less brain to do as well as smaller animals.

But this, of course, is identical to his conclusion! Gould would be offering as a premise the very thing that, in this particular conversation, is in question. Even if this premise were true, and even if the logic of the argument were good, the argument would be defective; for Gould would be helping himself to the answer without offering any reason for it.

Fourth, the argument must be ***clear.*** This means the language in which the argument is expressed must not thwart the decisions about whether the premises are true, whether the argument is logical, and whether it is conversationally relevant. Gould, for example, uses the phrase *bodies grow faster than brains.* This could mean, on the one hand, that as any *individual* grows, its body grows to its full size more rapidly than its brain grows to its full size. This, of course, is false. But, on the other hand, *bodies grow faster than brains* could mean that as you progress along a scale from smaller-bodied animals to larger-bodied animals, the brain size of the animal does not increase at the same rate as does the body size. The context makes it clear that this is what Gould means, and, since I have good reason to accept Gould's expertise in this field, I readily accept it as a true statement. If we did not have the context that Gould does provide, we would not be able to decide whether this sentence was true or false, for it would not have the merit of clarity.

Three of the requirements are kinds of *fit:* the fit of the premises with the world (truth), the fit of the conclusion with the evidence (good logic), and the fit of the argument with the conversation (conversational relevance). And the fourth requirement is that it must be possible to tell whether these three kinds of fit exist (clarity).

Guideline. Look for the following four merits in any argument: true premises, good logic, conversational relevance, and clarity.

The Merits of Arguments

1. True premises
2. Good logic
3. Conversational relevance
4. Clarity

The first two constitute *soundness.*

Arguments Are Models of Reasoning

Arguments are important for reasoning because part of their function is to provide *models*, made of words, that represent reasoning—verbal models that are especially designed to allow thinking to be examined and evaluated.

Keep in mind that a model contains only selected features of the object or event that it represents. An engineer who wants to design a car with reduced wind drag, for example, creates a model of the car for use in a wind tunnel. The model, however, represents only the external surfaces of the car and ignores such things as tread design, upholstery, and sound system.

Similarly, even a very good argument drops some of the features of reasoning, because it is usually not necessary to represent all the surrounding activities, such as the actual thought processes that produced it or the flash of insight that gave rise to the ideas behind it. Nor is it usually necessary to represent every piece of marginally relevant information. What matters most to the quality of the reasoning are the conclusion and the chief reasons behind it; and these are the features that arguments ordinarily display.

Throughout this text, we will be looking most closely at *arguments as they are found in the language of daily life*. As we shall see, these arguments are seldom offered *solely* as models of reasoning; they are usually also designed to persuade. One concern of this book is to learn how to *clarify* such arguments—to reduce them to their essential elements—so that most of what does not bear on good reasoning drops out.

HOW WE NORMALLY REASON

Edmund Halley, later to be immortalized by the comet named after him, once asked Isaac Newton how he knew a certain law of planetary motion. Newton replied, "Why I've known for years. If you'll give me a few days, I'll certainly find you a proof of it."

Reflect for a moment on how *you* think. Do you deliberately, meticulously work out the proofs for everything you believe? If you are like Sir Isaac Newton and the rest of us, you do so rarely. You have too many questions, too much evidence, and too little time to consciously construct perfect arguments for every belief. Perhaps you typically *have* many reasons for your beliefs, but it may not always be necessary—or even possible—for you to consciously think them through. You *intuitively* use your reasons, consciously using only a variety of quick-and-dirty shortcuts to finding the answers. When, for example, you arrive at a store at 6:05 P.M. and find the windows dark, you conclude the store is closed without consciously reasoning to this conclusion. The similarity of this experience to others—not a meticulously constructed argument—convinces you that you will not be able to buy a new shirt that night. We will refer to these as ***shortcuts in reasoning***. A more formal term is *judgmental heuristics*. (*Heuristic* is closely related to the word *eureka*, which is Greek for "I found it!" According to legend, Archimedes shouted "Eureka" as he ran naked through the streets of ancient Athens, having hit upon an important idea while in the bathtub.)

Some Common Shortcuts in Reasoning

You will find many of these shortcuts familiar, and you will see that often more than one shows up in the same bit of thinking.

First, there is the ***vividness shortcut*** (or what psychologists call the *availability heuristic*). You probably tend to rely heavily on whatever information is the most vivid. This can be a good thing; it is partly why, when deciding whether you should cross the street, you pay more attention to the screaming siren of the oncoming fire engine than to the walk signal (and thus avoid being flattened). But the most vivid information will not *always* lead you to the correct conclusion. For example, your single disastrous experience with an unreliable Hoover might lead you to conclude that Hoovers are inferior vacuum cleaners, though you have also read a page full of monotonous statistics in *Consumer Reports* showing that they are among the best. If you based your purchasing decision on your single unpleasant (but unforgettable) experience, you might rule out a perfectly acceptable appliance.

Second, you probably tend to rely on quickly noticed similarities between the familiar and the unfamiliar. If you liked James Cameron's *Aliens*, for example, you might expect to like his later movie, *Titanic*, as well. This is the ***similarity shortcut*** (or what psychologists term the *representativeness heuristic*). This often works well to lead you to the correct conclusions, but significant dissimilarities may also exist between two partly similar things. You might expect, for example, a new acquaintance with a German accent to be good at math because your college math professor spoke with a similar accent. Too often you will be disappointed in this kind of expectation.

And third, you probably tend to preserve beliefs you have previously adopted. Believing that you do better on exams after a good night's sleep, you would probably not carefully reevaluate that belief before you decide to go to bed reasonably early the night before you take a critically important exam. This tendency, which we call the ***conservation shortcut***, is often appropriate; after all, you did have good reasons for your belief if you were reasoning well when you first adopted it. Sometimes, however, this tendency persists even when evidence for the belief has been discredited. If, for instance, you were told that a co-worker had taken credit for your project, you may find yourself continuing to mistrust your co-worker even after you discover that the person who told you was lying.

Shortcuts in Reasoning: Judgmental Heuristics

1. *Vividness*—relying on the most vivid information.
2. *Similarity*—relying on similarities between the familiar and the unfamiliar.
3. *Conservation*—preserving previously adopted beliefs.

Having Reasons without Thinking about Reasons

In some cases, the thinking that leads us to arrive at a belief has nothing to do with our reasons for the belief. For example, 19th century chemist Friedrich Kekule was pondering the 40-year-old question of the structure of the benzene molecule when, slipping into a dream, he saw a roughly hexagonal ring in the flames of his fireplace. It dawned on him: *the benzene molecule is hexagonal.* Seeing the shape in the flames gave him the idea; that was a part of his *finding* the shape of the benzene molecule. But he did not consider the dream to be a *reason* to believe that the benzene molecule was hexagonal. Neither he nor anyone else would have concluded that the benzene molecule was square if Kekule had dreamed a square shape in the flames instead. The reasons that Kekule had for the belief only had to do with how well the theory of the hexagon fit the evidence he had accumulated. Getting an idea is one thing. Having support for the idea is quite another.[2]

In other cases, beliefs just seem to happen with no conscious consideration of the question. You look at your watch and you believe it is noon, or

[2]This is sometimes described as the distinction between the *context of discovery* (those things that contribute to the discovery of some belief) and the *context of justification* (those things that provide reasons for the belief).

you glance out the window and believe it is raining, or you read the business headlines and believe that the Dow rose 27 points. An important reason you have for believing these sorts of things is your belief that *this source of information is normally reliable*—although that reason never actually crosses your mind.

The reasons that you have for believing something may be very different from what you were thinking about when the belief occurred to you. These reasons are what, in the end, matter most—not the activity that gets you there.

EXERCISES Chapter 1, set (a)

For each passage below, state the shortcut that is probably being used and explain how it has apparently failed or succeeded.

Sample exercise. Two psychologists write, "The present authors have a friend who is a professor. He likes to write poetry, is rather shy, and is small in stature. Which of the following is his field: (a) Chinese studies or (b) psychology?" Most people, they say, answer that it must be Chinese studies.

—Richard Nisbett and Lee Ross, *Human Inference*

Sample answer. Similarity. For most people, the description is more similar to the mental image that they have of an Asian scholar than of a psychologist. But this is likely to lead to a mistake, since psychology is a huge field of study, especially compared to Chinese studies, and there are surely far more small, shy, and poetic psychologists than Asian scholars (even if a larger proportion of Asian scholars are like this). Further, the two psychologists are more likely to know other psychologists than they are to know professors of Chinese studies.

1. When I was in the market for a used car, I commented to a friend that there were far more cars parked on the street with "For Sale" signs on them.
2. Subjects in an experiment watched a series of people take a test—multiple choice, 30 problems, and each problem roughly equal in difficulty. By design, the test taker always solved 15 problems; but in some cases most of the 15 were solved early in the test, in other cases most were solved late. When the problems were solved early, the test takers were judged by the subjects to be more intelligent than when the

problems were solved late, and they were credited with solving more problems than they actually had solved.

3. "We had the sky up there, all speckled with stars, and we used to lay on our backs and look up at them, and discuss about whether they was made or only just happened. Jim he allowed they was made, but I allowed they happened; I judges it would have took too long to *make* so many. Jim said the moon could 'a' *laid* them; well, that looked kind of reasonable, so I didn't say nothing against it, because I've seen a frog lay most as many, so of course it could be done. We used to watch the stars that fell, too, and see them streak down, Jim allowed they'd got spoiled and was hove out of the nest."

—Mark Twain, *Adventures of Huckleberry Finn*

4. Subjects in an experiment were asked to discriminate between real and fake suicide notes. They were periodically told during the experiment whether their performance was average, above average, or below average. Afterward, the experimenters explained convincingly to each subject that the feedback they had been given was unconnected to their performance—that the feedback had been randomly decided before they had even started. Nevertheless, the subjects' answers to a final questionnaire showed that they continued to evaluate themselves as good at this sort of task if the feedback had been positive and bad at it if the feedback had been negative—even though that feedback, the only evidence they had, had now been discredited.

—Richard Nisbett and Lee Ross, *Human Inference*

EXERCISES Chapter 1, set (b)

Come up with examples, either invented or actual, of the use of each of the three shortcuts—vividness, similarity, and conservation—in everyday situations.

INTELLECTUAL VIRTUES

Chances are that your thinking typically follows shortcuts that run along grooves deeply worn into your mind. It probably isn't possible to eliminate them. Nor is it desirable. Successful living in this complicated world demands shortcuts, and these particular ones probably often do serve you well—but almost certainly could serve you better.

What *is* possible and desirable is that you develop other grooves that run just as deep—habits of thinking that can help you get to the right destination even when you do take shortcuts. These are ***intellectual virtues,*** that is, habits of thinking that are conducive to knowledge, habits that make it more likely that the answers you arrive at are well reasoned. Three virtues are especially important—the virtues of *critical reflection*, *empirical inquiry*, and *intellectual honesty*. The path to good reasoning is the cultivation of these three habits.

> *Guideline.* To become a good reasoner, cultivate intellectual virtues—that is, habits of thinking that are conducive to knowledge.

The Virtue of Critical Reflection

In *The Lyre of Orpheus*, novelist Robertson Davies describes the mental clutter of one of his characters as follows:

> He had discovered, now that he was well into middle age, that . . . his mental processes were a muddle, and he arrived at important conclusions by default, or by some leap that had no resemblance to thought or logic. . . . He made his real decisions as a gifted cook makes soup: he threw into a pot anything likely that lay to hand, added seasonings and glasses of wine, and messed about until something delicious emerged. There was no recipe and the result could be foreseen only in the vaguest terms.

I do not propose that there *is* a recipe. But if his muddle sounds familiar to you, you can do *something* to introduce a bit more order. You can cultivate the virtue of ***critical reflection,*** that is, the habit of asking what the arguments are for your beliefs and whether those arguments are sound, clear, and relevant.

This is termed *critical reflection* since it requires *reflection* to answer the first part of the question—to detect what your reasons actually are—and it requires *criticism* to answer the second—to evaluate those reasons to determine how sound, clear, and relevant they are.

This is not a question that should or could be asked for *every* belief you adopt. But it is always appropriate to ask it when the question is important to you and when time allows. (In addition, it is often appropriate when your view is challenged.) When deciding what sentence to utter next in a casual conversation, conscious critical reflection is not called for—in fact, it could seriously impede the progress of your chat. When, on the other hand, you must decide where to attend college or what career to pursue, critical reflection can make the difference between a good choice and a poor one. Consciously engaging in critical reflection when it *is* appropriate helps to cultivate the habit so that your instincts are sharpened for those cases when you cannot consciously do it.

Reasoning is in some ways like snowboarding or speaking a foreign language. Often you can do it well by doing it instinctively—with no conscious thought of any formal principles. Nevertheless, it is possible to formally state what you must do to do it well, just as in how-to-snowboard videos or grammar books for a language. And spending a certain amount of time drilling—*consciously* applying the formal principles to the activity—means that on other occasions you will do it more successfully. Cultivating the virtue of critical reflection—the habit of expressing and evaluating arguments in words—means that when you must reason instinctively (i.e., when you do not have the time to express and evaluate the arguments), you will reason more successfully.[3] You will continue to use shortcuts like vividness, similarity, and conservation, but they will take you in the wrong direction much less often.

Guideline. To reason more successfully, cultivate the virtue of critical reflection—that is, develop the habit of asking what the arguments are for your beliefs and whether those arguments are sound, clear, and relevant.

The Virtue of Empirical Inquiry

Another important intellectual virtue is the virtue of ***empirical inquiry***, the habit of seeking out new evidence from the world around you in order to better answer your questions. (The word *empirical* means *having to do with sense experience*—that is, having to do with information gathered by seeing, hearing, tasting, smelling, or feeling.)

[3]What it also means (and in this way, fortunately, it is unlike speaking a foreign language or snowboarding) is that when you reason *less* instinctively—when you take the time to express and evaluate the arguments—you will often reason even *more* successfully.

Let us say you are puzzled by a certain senator's support for legislation that would open large tracts of previously protected wetlands to development. Upon critical reflection you might conclude that you have no good answer to the question, *Why does she support this legislation?* Many at this point are tempted to take the easy way out and adopt one of many possible unsupported answers. *The only way to explain the senator's support for that legislation is that she's being paid off by industry/running for president/insensitive to her constituents/stupid*—take your pick.

If you don't care a great deal about the question, then, with such meager evidence, simply admit that you don't know. But if you really do want to know the answer, this is where empirical inquiry comes in. Empirical inquiry is the patient collection of whatever additional information is required to come up with a *good* answer. It includes such activities as making observations, setting up experiments, studying, doing research, and talking to experts, thereby gathering *new* evidence—new reasons—which must then be formulated into arguments and subjected to critical reflection.

Inquiry into the question of the senator's support for the legislation might show that she acted on the testimony of a number of impartial experts who stated definitively that the wetlands had been misidentified as such, and that they had no particular environmental importance. While you might still disagree with the senator's decision, your inquiry will at least have provided a good answer to your question about her motivations.

> *Guideline.* To find good answers to your questions, cultivate the virtue of empirical inquiry—that is, develop the habit of seeking out new evidence from the world around you.

The Virtue of Intellectual Honesty

If you are like most people, you sometimes don't do what you ought to do—simply because you don't want to. Physical exercise is easy to skip when you're tired, busy, or just feeling lazy. To keep at it, you have to continually remind yourself of the goal—good health and all the benefits it brings—and get in the *habit* of pursuing it. Similarly, to reason well, it is important that the habits of *doing* the right thing—critical reflection and empirical inquiry—are combined with consistently *wanting* the right thing. And the right thing to want, in the case of good reasoning, is *knowledge of the truth*. The virtue of ***intellectual honesty*** is the habit of wanting, above all, *to know* *the truth* about the questions you care about. To sincerely ask a question is to want to know the truth about the question; to want something other than knowledge of the truth is to be insincere in asking the question—that is, it is to be intellectually dishonest.

In early 1986, the National Aeronautics and Space Administration (NASA) was under an enormous amount of pressure. It had been more than 15 years since it had triumphantly put Neil Armstrong on the moon. NASA's next major triumph was supposed to have been the space shuttle. It would fly as many as 60 times a year, NASA had predicted, thereby providing increasingly cheap transportation and an inexpensive platform for an array of scientific experiments. But it had not worked out that way. In 1985, due to a variety of technical glitches, there had been only five launches. NASA's leaders were desperate for success. They viewed the approaching launch of the space shuttle Challenger, scheduled for January 28, with a strong sense of determination.

The rest of the story is well known. When engineers at Morton Thiokol (where the rocket boosters for the shuttle had been built) heard that Cape Canaveral temperatures were below freezing, they were alarmed. They feared that the O-rings that sealed the fuel containers on the boosters were not resilient enough to maintain a perfect seal in the cold. They notified their top managers, who notified NASA: the launch must be postponed until the arrival of warmer weather. But NASA officials refused to be convinced; reconsider your recommendation, they told Morton Thiokol, in a way that suggested future NASA business might otherwise go elsewhere. Morton Thiokol management finally caved in, overrode the engineers, and told NASA what NASA wanted to hear. NASA now had the evidence it needed to support the belief it wanted, and the schedule would be kept. Thiokol's engineers, watching anxiously on TV, feared the shuttle would explode on the launching pad. As it cleared the pad, one of them whispered, "We dodged a bullet." A few seconds later seven astronauts plummeted to their deaths.[4]

NASA officials were concerned about whether it was safe to launch the Challenger. But their chief desire, it seems, was not to know the truth, but to get whatever evidence it took to support the answer they wanted. They were not intellectually honest.

This virtue shows up most clearly as the willingness to consider any answer to a question so long as it is reasonable—that is, so long as the evidence

[4]This account is drawn largely from "The Truth about Lies," an episode of *The Public Mind* with Bill Moyers.

for the answer holds some promise. This does *not* mean that you should never confidently hold onto your beliefs in the face of opposing evidence; you *should* remain confident when the weight of the evidence is clearly on your side. It *does* mean that you should cultivate the habit of seriously considering the opposing evidence even if you do confidently hold to your own answer. The virtue is not in drifting wherever the winds blow, but in being ready to test the winds in case they do warrant a change of course.

Intellectual honesty is displayed by the professor who sincerely grants that his star student may have identified a crucial error in his famous book, by the scientist who takes seriously an easily concealed experimental anomaly, by the politician who carefully reconsiders her own widely advertised bill on the grounds that legislation offered by the opposing party just might better address the social problem, and by the police officer who wonders whether the light really might have been yellow. We might just as easily term this virtue *open-mindedness*—openness to *all* reasonable answers—or *impartiality*—partiality to *no* particular answer except on the basis of reasonableness.

The corresponding vice, intellectual dishonesty, entails a disregard for knowing the truth. It can be characterized as *close-mindedness*—being closed to the consideration of some reasonable answers—or *dogmatism*—being committed to an answer with no regard for its reasonableness or the reasonableness of the alternatives.

Intellectual honesty does not by itself produce good reasoning. But it does put you in the correct frame of mind to evaluate all relevant arguments and to seek further evidence if need be—that is, to practice the virtues of critical reflection and empirical inquiry.

> *Guideline.* To lay the foundation for good reasoning, cultivate the virtue of intellectual honesty—that is, develop the habit of wanting, above all, to know the truth about the questions you care about.

The Major Obstacles to Intellectual Honesty

Three of the biggest impediments to intellectual honesty are self-interest, cultural conditioning, and overconfidence.

Intellectual dishonesty often occurs when the desire to know the truth is overridden by self-interest. *Wishful thinking* is what we often call it. This was the problem in the case of the space shuttle Challenger. But many cases of self-interest aren't nearly so dramatic. Suppose it is spring, the Monday after daylight-saving time has gone into effect. As always, you get into your car at 6:30 A.M. to drive to your early class. But today, because of the time change, you must turn on your headlights. By the time you get to school the sun is up. You go to class, and midway through the first lecture it hits you—you forgot to turn off your headlights! But with a full day of classes and your part-time job, you will have no chance to walk all the way back to the parking lot to turn them off. Your mind races. You squeeze out the thought that you can't remember turning them off and tell yourself that you surely clicked them off instinctively. Yes, you reassure yourself, you turned them off. Your desire is not above all to know the truth about the question, *Did I turn off my headlights?*, but to arrive at your preferred answer. You succeed and don't think of it again until late that night when you are wondering where you can find some jumper cables.

Another obstacle to intellectual honesty is *cultural conditioning*. It is usually easy for us to find examples of this in other cultures (or in other segments of our own culture), but much harder to find them in our own. Our own views are familiar, comfortable, and do not seem to call out for special scrutiny. They are *ours*, after all. *Women are inferior. Slavery is acceptable. The prevailing religion is true.* All of these have been clung to uncritically only because the believer's training and environment make the beliefs seem so right.

Self-interest and cultural conditioning are not the only impediments to honesty. It sometimes is hindered by *overconfidence in the power of good reasoning* to deliver knowledge of the truth. If you are like most of us, you sometimes get the wrong answer, even when your reasoning is flawless. It is always possible that you are mistaken, and forgetting that possibility can be the first step toward close-mindedness and dogmatism.

Consider science, often held up as the paragon of good reasoning. Scientists have repeatedly and confidently offered their definitive answers to many questions, including, for example, *How large is the universe?* Note this partial record, measured in earth radii.

Scientist	*Date*	*Universe in Earth Radii*
Ptolemy	AD 150	20,000
Al Farghani	9th century	20,110
Al Battani	13th century	140,000

Levi ben Gerson	14th century	159,651 billion
Copernicus	1543	7,850,000
Brahe	1602	14,000
Kepler	1609	34,177,000
Kepler	1619	60,000,000
Galileo	1632	2,160
Riccioli	1651	200,000
Huyghens	1698	660,000,000
Newton	1728	20 billion
Herschel	1785	10,000 billion
Shapley	1920	1,000,000 billion
Current value	Now	100,000 billion

—Derek Gjertsen, *Science and Philosophy* (London: Penguin, 1989), p. 42.

Science itself looks honest here—always willing to revise in the face of new evidence. But we are not talking about the intellectual virtue of disciplines (like science), but the intellectual virtue of human beings (like individual scientists, or you and me). The lesson is that even when good scientists reason well about the physical world, their conclusions are subject to revision in the face of additional evidence; and they can be guilty of a sort of dishonesty if they become overconfident in their conclusions. Surely many conclusions reached by nonscientists like you and me are at least as susceptible to revision.

Intellectual honesty requires that you be always aware of the possibility that you might be wrong. And the alternative to your current answer is not necessarily another answer. The alternative may be that there is, as yet, no good answer.

The good reasoner is critically reflective, empirically inquisitive, and intellectually honest.

Guideline. To enhance intellectual honesty, be especially wary of the influences of self-interest, cultural conditioning, and overconfidence.

Some Intellectual Virtues: Habits of Thinking That Are Conducive to Knowledge

1. *Critical reflection*—asking what the arguments are for your beliefs and whether those arguments are sound, clear, and relevant.
2. *Empirical inquiry*—seeking out new evidence from the world around you to better answer your questions.
3. *Intellectual honesty*—wanting, above all, to know the truth about the questions you care about.

EXERCISES Chapter 1, set (c)

For the scenarios below, describe ways in which each of the intellectual virtues appears to be lacking.

1. You take a course in an area that is new to you and work harder than you have ever worked in your life on the term paper. The professor returns it with a D+, commenting that you should come to his office to talk to him about how you can improve. Although he has provided copious notes in the margins, you do not even look at them, charging out of the classroom and complaining to your friends, "He's been against me since the first day of class! I had no chance to do well on this paper!"
2. Your new roommate is from another country and follows a religion you have never heard of. You treat your roommate's observances of the religion with respect, but privately remain convinced that your religion is the right one. You have never really thought much about it, but it is what you have always been taught, and it just seems right to you. Surely your roommate is mistaken.
3. Trofin Denisovich Lysenko had a stranglehold on Russian biology from 1934 to 1964. What he lacked in scientific talent, Lysenko more than made up for in political know-how. Early in his career, Lysenko hit upon the idea that winter wheat could be converted into spring wheat by exposing it to cold and then planting it in springtime. The seeds from that wheat, he believed, would not need to be converted into spring wheat; they would have already become spring wheat by virtue of inheriting the "vernal" characteristic acquired by the previous generation. But he had

no good evidence that acquired characteristics could be transmitted to offspring, and the view flew in the face of modern biology.

But Lysenko managed to convince Stalin, and later Kruschev, that only his view of biology conformed to Marxist political ideology. Through his influence, textbooks were altered and biologists who tried to do real biology were persecuted and imprisoned. Thus insulated from contrary evidence, Lysenko's beliefs about biology were secure and his ambitions were realized. Soviet agriculture faced crisis after crisis during the middle years of the 20th century, but until Lysenko's death in 1964, it was unable to benefit from the agricultural advances of modern biology.

—Jeremy Bernstein, *Experiencing Science*

4. Jake McDonald dreamed of getting rich. Although he had no money, he had a plan: find the right existing business, buy it with a loan from the seller, pay off the loan with income from the business, and sell franchises. He was sure he could make it happen; he was just sorry that his name had already been used.

   After a year of searching, he was confident he had found his ticket to riches right around the corner from his apartment. It was a pizza place with a difference. Aptly named Take and Bake Pizza, its made-to-order pizzas were unbaked. He was in love with it! Prices were lower because the business required less equipment and less space (no ovens) and needed fewer employees (no cooks). Customers would have a shorter wait for delivery and, since they would bake it at home, would never have to eat it cold. Best of all, the owner wanted to sell. And, well, Jake's name did fit it so perfectly.

   He could hardly contain his enthusiasm. As he went to sleep every night, his mind was filled with images of Jake's Take and Bake stores in mini-malls across America. True, the sketchy records the owner showed him suggested that cash flow was barely covering expenses, but that could be corrected with aggressive marketing.

   Jake's girlfriend, however, was skeptical. There's still a wait for the pizza while you bake it yourself, she pointed out. And don't most people who call Domino's want to avoid even the trouble of turning on the oven, properly preheating it, and listening for the timer? The real competition, she suggested, could be the grocery and convenience stores; they are surely capable of stocking fresh unbaked pizzas daily and selling them even cheaper than Take and Bake. And finally, she wondered, if the current income was barely covering expenses, how did Jake propose to pay for the marketing campaign?

Jake ignored her and made the deal. After all, he had scored over 1500 on his SAT, and she hadn't even gone to college. Six years later, while on the way home from his job as a cook at McDonald's, Jake stopped off at one of the 7-Elevens she now owned to buy a fresh unbaked pizza for dinner.

5. "Stepan Arkadyevich had not chosen his political opinions or his views—these political opinions and views had come to him of themselves—just as he did not choose the shapes of his hat and coat, but simply accepted those that were being worn. . . . If there was a reason for his preferring liberal to conservative views, which were held also by many of his circle, it arose not from his considering liberalism more rational, but from its being in closer accordance with his manner of life. The liberal party said that in Russia everything was wrong, and indeed Stepan Arkadyevich had many debts and was decidedly short of money. The liberal party said that marriage was an institution quite out of date, and that it stood in need of reconstruction, and indeed family life afforded Stepan Arkadyevich little gratification, and forced him into lying and hypocrisy, which were so repulsive to his nature. The liberal party said, or rather allowed it to be understood, that religion was only a curb to keep in check the barbarous classes of the people, and indeed Stepan Arkadyevich could not stand through even a short service without his legs aching, and could never make out what was the object of all the terrible and high-flown language about another world when life might be so very amusing in this world. . . . And so liberalism had become a habit of Stepan Arkadyevich."

—Leo Tolstoy, *Anna Karenina*

HOW THIS BOOK CAN HELP

You may already be pretty good at reasoning. You got through childhood and adolescence, which means that you successfully answered many critical questions, such as *Where's the food?* and *Where's the shelter?* You got through most of this introductory chapter; perhaps you even found some mistakes in it. But for something as valuable as good reasoning, pretty good should not be good enough. What can this book do to help you reason better?

At a minimum, it can draw your attention to things you already instinctively know about reasoning, thereby putting you in a better position to use that knowledge. Very few of the concepts in this book will be new to you. But many of them will get a name for the first time and will be explained in such a way that their significance for reasoning is clearer. Like the title character of Moliere's *Bourgeois Gentleman*, who is amazed to learn that for most of his life he has "been speaking *prose*, and didn't know a thing about it," for most of your life you may have been reasoning according to certain guidelines without knowing what they were called or even being fully aware of them.

But this book should do more than that. It gradually unfolds a systematic approach to clarifying and evaluating arguments, with the focus on soundness, clarity, and relevance. And it contains many examples of real-life arguments on which you can practice this systematic approach, thus gaining a great deal of practical experience in following the book's guidelines.

When I first learned to type, I was temporarily cursed with the habit of mentally typing out my every conversation. When students first work on these exercises, they sometimes find that they cannot read the newspaper or talk to a friend without mentally clarifying and evaluating every argument. But the curse is eventually lifted, and it is replaced with the blessing of better reasoning. The philosopher Gilbert Ryle, comparing formal logic to real-life reasoning in "Formal and Informal Logic," notes:

> Fighting in battle is markedly unlike parade-ground drill. . . . None the less the efficient and resourceful fighter is also the well-drilled soldier. . . . It is not the stereotyped motions of drill, but the standards of perfection of control, which are transmitted from the parade ground to the battlefield.

And management expert Peter Drucker tells of his boyhood piano teacher's stern words: "You will never play Mozart the way Arthur Schnabel does, but there is no reason in the world why you should not play your scales the way he does." You may never reason like Aristotle or Newton, but by applying yourself to these exercises you can expect to more fully develop the same fundamental habits of mind and to become a better reasoner for it.

SUMMARY OF CHAPTER ONE

Reasoning is the attempt to answer a question by thinking about reasons. Good reasoning requires *having good reasons for what you believe*, and good reasons can best be expressed in good arguments. So good arguments are crucially important to good reasoning.

An argument is a series of statements in which at least one of the statements is given as reason for belief in another. A *good* argument is an argument that is sound—that is, the premises are true and the conclusion follows logically from the premises—and one that is also relevant to the conversation and clear.

We don't usually think by means of carefully constructed arguments, but by means of various quick-and-dirty shortcuts, or judgmental heuristics. For example, we tend to rely on the most vivid information, we tend to infer on the basis of similarity, and we strongly favor preexisting beliefs. These tendencies are not to be entirely discarded but are to be tempered by the cultivation of other habits—by the cultivation of intellectual virtues.

One important intellectual virtue is the virtue of critical reflection—the habit of asking (when both time and the significance of the question warrant it) what the argument is for each belief and whether that argument is sound, clear, and relevant. Another is empirical inquiry—the habit of seeking out evidence from the world around us. And a third virtue is intellectual honesty—the habit of wanting, above all, to know the truth about the questions we ask; this virtue enables us to express and evaluate arguments unencumbered. The good reasoner is critically reflective, inquisitive, and honest.

GUIDELINES FOR CHAPTER ONE

- Use good reasoning if you want to *know* the answers to the questions you care about.
- Look for the following four merits in any argument: true premises, good logic, conversational relevance, and clarity.
- To become a good reasoner, cultivate the intellectual virtues—that is, habits of thinking that are conducive to knowledge.
- To reason more successfully, cultivate the virtue of critical reflection—that is, develop the habit of asking what the arguments are for your beliefs and whether those arguments are sound, clear, and relevant.
- To find good answers to your questions, cultivate the virtue of empirical inquiry—that is, develop the habit of seeking out new evidence from the world around you.

- To lay the foundation for good reasoning, cultivate the virtue of intellectual honesty—that is, develop the habit of wanting, above all, to know the truth about the questions you care about.
- To enhance intellectual honesty, be especially wary of the influences of self-interest, cultural conditioning, and overconfidence.

GLOSSARY FOR CHAPTER ONE

Argument—a series of statements in which at least one of the statements is offered as reason to believe another.

Clear argument—an argument in which it is possible to tell whether the premises are true, whether the logic is good, and whether the argument is conversationally relevant.

Conclusion—the statement that reasons, or premises, are offered to support.

Conservation shortcut—preserving previously adopted beliefs as a shortcut in reasoning. This can be helpful but is not always supported by the evidence.

Conversationally relevant argument—an argument that is appropriate to the conversation, or the context, that gives rise to it; it does not miss the point or presuppose something that is in question in the conversation.

Critical reflection—asking what the arguments are for what you believe, and whether those arguments are sound, clear, and relevant.

Empirical inquiry—seeking out new evidence from the world around you to better answer your questions.

Good reasoning—the sort of thinking most likely to result in your having good reasons and, thus, the sort of thinking most likely to give you knowledge.

Intellectual honesty—wanting, above all, to know the truth about the questions you care about.

Intellectual virtues—habits of thinking that are conducive to knowledge by making it more likely that the answers you arrive at are well reasoned.

Logical argument—an argument in which the premises strongly support the conclusion—that is, the premises make it reasonable to believe the conclusion.

Premise—a statement offered as a reason to believe the conclusion of an argument.

Reasoning—the attempt to answer a question by thinking about reasons.

Reasons—whatever you depend on in support of what you believe, regardless of whether you consider your belief to be knowledge or mere opinion. Words that mean more or less the same thing are the following: *premises*, *evidence*, *warrant*, *justification*, *basis*, *grounds*, and *rationale*.

Shortcuts in reasoning—quick and practical ways of arriving at answers to your questions that do not involve organized arguments. More formally called *judgmental heuristics. Heuristic* is closely related to the word *eureka,* which is Greek for "I found it!" According to legend, Archimedes shouted "Eureka" as he ran naked through the streets of ancient Athens, having hit upon an important idea as he bathed.

Similarity shortcut—relying on a quickly noticed resemblance between the familiar and the unfamiliar as a shortcut in reasoning. This can be helpful, but is not always supported by the evidence. Also called the *representativeness heuristic.*

Sound argument—an argument that both is logical and has true premises.

True statement—a statement that corresponds to the world.

Unsound argument—an argument that has at least one false premise or is illogical (or both).

Vividness shortcut—relying on whatever information stands out most in your mind as a shortcut in reasoning. This can be helpful but is not always supported by the evidence. More formally called the *availability heuristic.*

CHAPTER TWO

What Makes an Argument

"An argument isn't just contradiction."
"Can be."
"No it can't. An argument is a connected series of statements intended to establish a proposition."
"No it isn't."
"Yes it is."

—Monty Python, *The Argument Clinic*

TOPICS

Statements: The Building Blocks of Arguments
Statements That Offer a Reason for Belief
Statements That Do Not Offer a Reason for Belief
Implicit Statements
Complex Arguments

The goal of this chapter is to look closely at arguments so that you will be able to identify them and to pick out their premises and conclusions. As we saw in Chapter 1, arguments are models of reasoning that allow reasoning to be examined and evaluated. They are important because good reasoning is the way to get good answers to the questions you care about.

According to the definition provided in Chapter 1, an argument is a series of statements in which at least one of the statements is offered as reason for belief in another. This definition applies to a ***simple argument;*** later in this chapter we will cover complex arguments, which link simple arguments together into chains.

Any statement, whether explicit or implicit, that is offered as a reason is a ***premise*** (sometimes spelled *premiss* by the British). As we saw in Chapter 1, we can also refer to premises as *evidence, warrant, justification, basis, grounds,* or *rationale.* The statement for which the reason is offered is the ***conclusion.*** There must be at least one premise (but there is no upper limit) and, in a simple argument, there is exactly one conclusion.[1]

Let's look more carefully at two pieces of the definition: what statements are, and what it is to offer a reason for belief.

STATEMENTS: THE BUILDING BLOCKS OF ARGUMENTS

Statements are sentences that can be true or false.[2] Most of the sentences in this book and most of the sentences you speak are statements. Here are two concrete examples:

> Eleanor Roosevelt was one of the most prominent first ladies in history.
> A water molecule is made up of two hydrogen and two oxygen atoms.

Both of these statements *can* be true or false. The first is true, while the second is false.

[1]In formal logic, logicians include as a degenerate case one-line arguments, with no premise at all. For our concerns, which are practical, it is inappropriate to call them arguments.

[2]Philosophers debate what a *statement*, used in this sense, really is—that is, what it *is* that is true or false. Some say that it is a concrete object, namely, a *sentence*. Some say that it is an abstract object—the *meaning* of the sentence; this stays the same regardless of which actual sentence is used to concretely express it. And some say that it is an event—an *utterance*—the actual speaking or writing, the *stating*, of the statement. For practical purposes we are operating with the first definition.

The following four sentences do not count as statements for our purposes:

Oh, to be at the beach this afternoon!
Speak into the microphone.
Are you now or have you ever been a member of the Communist party?
I promise to return the money on Tuesday.

Read each of these and ask yourself if it is true or false. You will see that they aren't quite like the sentences about water molecules and Eleanor Roosevelt. The first of the four can be sincere or insincere; the second can be obeyed or disobeyed; the third can be answered yes or no; and the fourth can be kept or broken. But none of them can be true or false.

EXERCISES Chapter 2, set (a)

For each of these four nonstatements, create a new sentence at least loosely about the same topic that *is* a statement. (There could be many correct answers for each sentence.)

Sample exercise. Oh, to be at the beach this afternoon!
Sample answer. The beach will be crowded this afternoon.

1. Oh, to be at the beach this afternoon!
2. Speak into the microphone.
3. Are you now or have you ever been a member of the Communist party?
4. I promise to return the money on Tuesday.

The Form and the Function of Statements and Other Sentences

Statements typically exhibit a certain *form.* The usual form of a statement includes a subject—such as *water molecule*—and a property, or a trait, attributed to that subject—such as being *made up of two hydrogen and two oxygen atoms.* (More rarely, statements assert an identity instead of attributing a property; that is, they assert that two different names pick out the same thing, as in the sentence *Santa Claus is St. Nick.*)

Statements, in addition, fulfill a certain *function,* namely the ***declarative*** function of conveying information. The statement *Eleanor Roosevelt was one* *of the most prominent first ladies in history* conveys information about a historical figure; as noted above, we can usually evaluate this information, depending on our store of knowledge or our commitment to researching it, as either true or false.

Sentences that are *not* statements serve a wide variety of other nondeclarative functions. Some sentences are ***exclamatory***—that is, they function to express strong and sudden emotion, as in the sentence:

> Oh, to be at the beach this afternoon!

Some sentences are ***imperative***—that is, they direct others to action. The following sentence is imperative:

> Speak into the microphone.

Others are ***interrogative***—that is, they serve to ask a question. Consider, for example, the following:

> Are you now or have you ever been a member of the Communist party?

Still other sentences serve a ***performative*** function; by *asserting* certain things under the right circumstances, they enable you thereby to *do*, or perform, those things. Examples include:

> I promise to return the money on Tuesday.
> I resign from this committee.
> I apologize for what I said.
> I categorically deny all allegations.

A single sentence can serve more than one function. This means that a sentence *not* in the form of a statement might nevertheless function as a statement. Note the following question:

> Don't you know that I love you?

It is not in the form of a statement, but of a question—its form, then is interrogative, not declarative. But in the right circumstances it can function both to ask and to tell. So it not only serves its explicit interrogative function, but it also serves a declarative function—that is, it also functions as a statement.

Here is a sentence that might be thought to serve all five functions:

For the last time I ask you to tell me your name!

On a fairly generous interpretation, you might find these functions:

Declarative, since it conveys the information that this is the last time.
Exclamatory, since it expresses strong emotion—exasperation, to be specific.
Imperative, since it directs another person to action.
Interrogative, since it asks for your name.
Performative, since by virtue of asserting "I ask," I do ask.

Often you need to know more about the context to determine whether a sentence is serving as a statement. It is often necessary to see a larger section of the passage in which it is written, or to hear a larger part of the conversation in which it is spoken, or to know more in general about the circumstances surrounding the expression of the sentence. Suppose, for example, you are asked, *Is the beach pleasant this afternoon?* Some possible answers might be:

Oh, to be at the beach this afternoon!
Is the beach *pleasant* this afternoon?
Whatever you do, go to the beach this afternoon.
Yes.

None of these sentences is cast in the form of a statement. And in other contexts each might function quite differently. In this context, however, each sentence is clearly intended to serve the same declarative function as the statement,

The beach is pleasant this afternoon.

For identifying arguments, what matters most is the *function* served by the sentences; so, in defining an argument as a series of statements, the term *statement* is meant to include sentences that function declaratively, whether they take that form or not.

Guideline. For the purpose of identifying arguments, consider a sentence a statement if it serves a declarative function.

Five Functions Served by Sentences

1. *Declarative*—conveys information.
2. *Exclamatory*—expresses emotion.
3. *Imperative*—directs others to action.
4. *Interrogative*—asks a question.
5. *Performative*—does things by virtue of saying them.

Only those sentences serving a declarative function count as statements.

EXERCISES Chapter 2, set (b)

Identify the form and function of each of the sentences below. Where you can see more than one function, briefly explain each. Assume there is nothing unusual about the context.

Sample exercise. Please remember that this is a sonata for piano, not pianist.
—Mieczyslaw Horszowksi, rebuking one of his students.

Sample answer. Form is imperative. Function is imperative (telling to remember) and declarative (giving information about playing it).

1. Didn't you hear that class was canceled?
2. I now pronounce you man and wife.
3. How could he say that and expect us to believe him?
4. Hooray for the Tigers!
5. "The real liberator of women in America is the free enterprise system." —Phyllis Schlafley
6. "Just say no." —Nancy Reagan
7. "This is the best story ever written." —W.H.D. Rouse, in his preface to Homer's *Odyssey*
8. "All the news that's fit to print." —slogan of the *New York Times*
9. "Don't leave home without it." —slogan of American Express
10. "To succeed in this world, you have to change all the time." —Sam Walton, *Sam Walton: Made in America*

EXERCISES Chapter 2, set (c)

(*i*) Make up a sentence in each of these forms, then (*ii*) explain how it might be used to serve the declarative function.

Sample exercise. Performative.

Sample answer. (*i*) I promise to be home on time. (*ii*) Suppose you ask me, "Will you or will you not be home on time tonight?" I might reply "I promise to be home on time" in part to communicate the declarative *I will be home on time.*

1. Interrogative
2. Exclamatory
3. Imperative
4. Performative

EXERCISES Chapter 2, set (d)

Consider the declarative sentence *The price is too high.* Provide four other sentences that are not in declarative form that serve the same declarative function. Use at least two different nondeclarative forms.

STATEMENTS THAT OFFER A REASON FOR BELIEF

The Reason Need Not Be Good

What matters in identifying an argument is not whether the premise *succeeds* in supporting the conclusion, but whether it is *intended* to support it—whether, as our definition puts it, a statement is *offered* as a reason to believe another statement. When the premise succeeds in supporting the conclusion, that can make it easier to see that it is an argument. But success is not what *makes* it an argument.

The story is told of a professor, walking across campus, who stops a student to ask, "Excuse me, in what direction am I headed?" When the bemused student replies, "North," the professor smiles and says, "Ah, then I've had my lunch." It is hard to see how the premise *I am headed north* supports the conclusion *I have had my lunch*, but he considers it a reason, and that makes the series of statements an argument.

Or consider the account of Denis Diderot, 18th century French intellectual and atheist, who in 1773 was staying at the Russian court in St. Petersburg, where he entertained and educated the nobility. Fearing that Diderot was undermining their religious faith, Catherine the Great commissioned Leonhard Euler, the most distinguished mathematician of the time, to debate him publicly. Euler, so the story goes, began with this argument.

> A squared minus B squared equals A minus B times A plus B; therefore, God exists. Reply!

Diderot, we are told, left the court abruptly amid the laughter of the audience, confined himself to chambers, demanded safe conduct, and promptly returned to France. It is hard to see how Euler's premise about A and B has any connection to the conclusion that God exists, but it is *offered* as a reason, and so we take the series of statements as an argument.

It may be that in the professor's or Euler's case there really is a worthwhile argument waiting to be appreciated once we figure out what the implicit premises are. Perhaps the professor's routine is so invariable, and his autopilot so effective, that he feels confident in deducing his past action from his present direction. Perhaps Euler believes that mathematical truths cannot be true unless there is a God to make them true. But in other cases the argument is clearly beyond redemption. Members of the Israel Antiquities Authority were incensed when the Huntington Library in southern California decided to release to the public its photographs of the Dead Sea Scrolls, breaking the authority's 40-year monopoly over the scrolls. The *Los Angeles Times* reports:

> Bruce Zuckerman, the acting director of the Ancient Biblical Manuscript Center, said he was concerned that someone might depict the Dead Sea Scrolls on T-shirts. Because of such a disrespectful possibility, Zuckerman would preserve the secrecy imposed by the team of editors that has controlled access for the last 40 years.

Not only is the danger of disrespectful T-shirts a terrible reason for preserving secrecy (should we suppress photographs of Gandhi and Mother Theresa as well?), but also it is doubtful that it is Zuckerman's *real* reason. Nevertheless, he offers it as a reason for believing his conclusion, and that is enough to count the series of statements as an argument.

Guideline. Count it as an argument even if the reasons offered seem clearly to be bad ones.

Inference Indicators

Given the frequent absence of good reasons for belief, what tells us that an argument is even being offered? Perhaps the best sign of an argument is the presence of an ***inference indicator***, a term that frequently signifies the presence of an ***inference***—that is, of movement from premises to conclusion. (An old-fashioned word for inference indicator, *illative*, comes from a form of the Latin word for *infer*.)

Note this hasty bit of reasoning by Christopher Hitchens in *Harper's*:

> *Since* it is obviously inconceivable that all religions can be right, *the most reasonable conclusion is* that they are all wrong.

The highlighted terms suggest that a reason for belief is being offered, and they help us to figure out where the premise is (after the word *since*) and where the conclusion is (after the words *the . . . conclusion is*).

Some other inference indicators that introduce a premise are highlighted in the sentences below:

> *Since* you said it, it must be true.
> *Because* he is being so sweet, you know he's about to ask for money.
> Spring is coming early, *for* the crocuses are already in bloom.
> I can tell that she will accept the job offer; *my reason is* that I heard her talking to a moving company yesterday.
> I think that the butler did it, *on account of* his fingerprints on the weapon.

A common pitfall in identifying indicators is to suppose that *if* is an inference indicator that introduces a premise. Suppose, for example, I say,

> If the Dow Jones Industrial Average doubles this week, then you will be rich.

This looks a bit like an argument in which the premise is *The Dow Jones Industrial Average doubles this week* and the conclusion is *You will be rich.* But this argument—*You will be rich, because the Dow Jones Industrial Average will double this week*—expresses much more confidence about your imminent wealth than the sentence *If the Dow Jones Industrial Average doubles this week, then you will be rich.* Premises are held to be true by the arguer. But an arguer who uses *if* is not asserting that what comes between *if* and *then* is true but is only asking us to suppose for the moment that it is true. I am not offering you a reason to believe you will be rich (unless in a separate sentence, I do, without the *if*, state that the Dow will double this week). It is true that if–then statements do occur often in arguments (Chapter 11 is devoted to such arguments), but these statements can be either premises or conclusions. So, *if* is not useful as an inference indicator that introduces a premise.

The following are examples of inference indicators that introduce the conclusion:

> You said it, *therefore* it must be true.
> He is being sweet; *thus*, you know he's about to ask for money.
> The crocuses are already in bloom; *consequently*, spring is coming early.
> I heard her talking to a moving company yesterday; *it follows that* she will accept the job offer.
> These are the butler's fingerprints; *hence* the butler did it.

In addition, two old-fashioned inference indicators are left over from the days when Latin was the dominant European academic language. *Ergo* is the Latin term for *therefore*, as in the sentence *You said it, ergo it must be true.* And *Q.E.D.* is the acronym for the Latin phrase *quod erat demonstrandum* (or, *which was to be demonstrated*); it is placed *after* the conclusion, as in, *You said it. It is true. Q.E.D.*

The list of inference indicators is seemingly endless; we have covered only a few of the most common ones. Note a less conventional one in this statement:

> Rastafarians smoke the herb "ganga" or marijuana as part of their religious rites, citing Psalms 104:14: "He causeth the grass to grow for the cattle, and herb for the service of man."

Citing is the inference indicator here. What we *cite* is typically support, so the term indicates that the premise is coming up—the premise (true or false) that the Bible approves of the use of marijuana.

Guideline. When possible, identify premises and conclusions by the location of inference indicators.

Some Inference Indicators

BEFORE PREMISES	BEFORE CONCLUSIONS
Since	Therefore
Because	Thus
For	Hence
My reason is	So
On account of	Consequently
The justification is	What this justifies is
Is confirmed by	Confirms
It follows from	It follows that

EXERCISES Chapter 2, set (e)

Construct a simple argument using each of the following inference indicators. State in each case whether it introduces a premise or a conclusion.

Sample exercise. is confirmed by.

Sample answer. That he is impractical is confirmed by the fact that he never bought car insurance. (It introduces a premise.)

1. it follows that
2. confirms
3. the justification is
4. on account of
5. so
6. for

EXERCISES Chapter 2, set (f)

Identify the inference indicator in each of the following short passages and state whether it introduces the premise or the conclusion. *Two of the passages do not have an inference indicator* (these two are not arguments). Identify them as well.

Sample exercise. "I do not want war, but if it is forced upon me I will win because I have always won." —Napoleon to the Russian ambassador

Sample answer. Because; introduces the premise.

1. The gauge is low, so we're low on gas.
2. My sense that he doesn't like me was confirmed by his refusal to talk to me at the party.
3. The way he is dragging his feet shows that he isn't in very good shape.
4. The recent crime statistics in the newspaper are my reason for believing that my neighborhood is safe.
5. Jesus loves me, this I know, for the Bible tells me so.
6. The church-burnings are intended to cripple the spiritual lives of thousands of blacks. But amid the destruction they persist, showing that a church exists in its people, not in a wooden frame or pulpit.
7. "The saddening syllogism of Marshall Herff Applewhite and his followers seems to have gone like this: we think that an alien spaceship is trailing the comet; observation through a capable telescope shows no such spaceship; therefore, let's get rid of the telescope." —*New Yorker*
8. "Because normal two- to four-celled embryos have no differentiated organs or nervous systems, they cannot be harmed by cloning or other research manipulations." —John Robertson, *Chronicle of Higher Education*
9. "Still obsessed by thoughts of death, I brood constantly. I keep wondering if there is an afterlife, and if there is will they be able to break a twenty." —Woody Allen, *Without Feathers*
10. "If you believe the doctors, nothing is wholesome; if you believe the theologians, nothing is innocent; if you believe the soldiers, nothing is safe." —Lord Salisbury, at the end of the 19th century
11. "Fiercer far than the light which beats upon a throne is the light which beats on a presidential candidate, searching out all the recesses of his past life. Hence, when the choice is between a brilliant man and a safe man, the safe man is preferred." —James Bryce, *The American Commonwealth*, 1888

12. When asked how he could justify getting confessed murderers off, Texas criminal lawyer Percy Foreman said, in his rolling tones, "Mah fees are their punishment." —Henry Rothblatt, *That Damned Lawyer*

When There Are No Inference Indicators

Arguers don't always supply inference indicators to help you find your way around. This leaves you in the dark if the logic of the argument is bad—that is, if there is no plausible connection between premises and conclusion. But otherwise, you should still be able to make your way.

Bernie Smith, a train buff who manages a model railroad store in Kansas City, was asked about the possibility that cabooses might be eliminated from trains for economic reasons. He offered this argument:

> I think they should keep the cabooses. What's a train without a caboose? People are used to seeing a red caboose tagged on the end and someone waving at them.

Without inference indicators in Bernie Smith's argument, how are you to find the premises and conclusion?

Here is a helpful, but not foolproof, suggestion. In the absence of inference indicators *look for the most controversial statement in the argument; it is usually the conclusion.* Then test it out either mentally or on a piece of paper by placing the word *therefore* in front of the statement. If it sounds right in this form, you've found the conclusion. This often works because arguments typically use the *familiar* as grounds for accepting the *new.* Premises are usually easier to accept than the conclusion, since the premises are not supposed to be what is in question; the conclusion is. The conclusion, presumably, becomes plausible because it follows from the already plausible premises.

This technique is easy to apply to Bernie Smith's argument. There's nothing surprising about this statement:

> People are used to seeing a caboose at the end of the train.

But this one is less obviously true:

> They should keep the cabooses.

And it sounds right if we insert *therefore* in front of it; it, then, is the conclusion.

Here's another argument with no inference indicator, provided by an aide to the senator and astronaut John Glenn when Glenn was running for president. The aide, speaking anonymously to reporter Morton Kondracke about whether Glenn would make a good president, said this:

> It's great to have Glenn with you. He's indefatigable when he homes in on one issue. But he doesn't see the forest or even the trees, only branches and twigs. He's a responder and not a leader. He has no coherent vision. He would be a symbol, not a man of substance. He would not be a good president.

Our technique of looking for the most controversial statement is not as useful here. Because our knowledge of Glenn's political capability is probably limited, it is hard to tell whether any of the statements is substantially more controversial than the others. But arguments, as already noted, often occur in the context of answering questions. This suggests another technique: *look in the wider context for the question being asked; the argument's conclusion is usually a proposed answer to that question.* In this case, the wider context is a media interview in which the aide was asked whether he believed that Glenn would be a good president. Glenn's aide is giving reasons for his answer:

> John Glenn would not be a good president.

And, again, inserting *therefore* in front of it does sound right. That statement is the conclusion.

Notice that the conclusion is the first sentence in the caboose example; in the John Glenn example, it is the last. First and last are the two places where a conclusion is most likely to be found, though it could, in principle, be found anywhere.

> *Guideline.* When there are no inference indicators, look for the most controversial statement in the argument; if one can be readily identified, it is usually the conclusion.

Guideline. When there are no inference indicators, look in the wider context for the question being asked; the proposed answer to it is usually the conclusion.

EXERCISES Chapter 2, set (g)

For each argument below, identify the conclusion. If there are inference indicators, identify them, and state whether they introduce premises or conclusions.

Sample exercise. Definitions cannot, by their very nature, be either true or false, only more useful or less so. For this reason it makes relatively little sense to argue over definitions. —Peter Berger, *The Sacred Canopy*

Sample answer. Conclusion: It makes relatively little sense to argue over definitions. Inference indicator: for this reason (referring to the reason that has just been given), introduces the conclusion.

1. You aren't my real mother. Documents in the Hall of Records show that I was adopted.
2. Everybody expects the band to come back on stage for an encore, since in their other concerts they have always saved their old hits for the finale.
3. I'm sick of hearing my friends telling me to get a life and to spend my time somewhere besides video arcades. Hey, I have a life. As long as I'm living, I have a life.
4. What's that shimmering on the highway? Well, there is no water in this desert. It's got to be a mirage.
5. Dade County, which includes Miami, is the best place in America to be a criminal. It has the nation's worst crime rate and does the laziest job of putting criminals behind bars. —*Miami Herald*
6. "We're waste managers," said the CEO of Chem Waste. "So, if the business moves to more services and processing, we'll move with it." —*Forbes*
7. Those who oppose euthanasia buttress their case by pointing to the rare patients that have been given up for dead but inexplicably

survived. —*U.S. News and World Report* (Note that this passage contains an argument, but does not advocate it—it merely reports on it.)

8. "We are describing the first one of a new phylum," Higgins says. "If Loricifera is not a new phylum, then it must be assigned elsewhere, and there is no satisfactory elsewhere for it." —*Science News*
9. "I believe in turning our attention to things of importance—to questions that may by some possibility be solved. It is of no importance to me whether God exists or not. I exist, and it is important to me to be happy while I exist. Therefore, I had better turn my attention to finding out the secret of happiness, instead of trying to ascertain the secret of the universe." —Robert Ingersoll, *Ingersoll: Immortal Infidel*
10. "I believe there will be a new crusade with Jesus Christ as the commander-in-chief who will bring our nation back to greatness," he continued. Wickstrom, head of the fundamentalist and paramilitary group Posse Comitatus, went on to say that the targets of the crusade would be Jews, "so they better get the hell down to Brazil or anywhere else that will have them." —*Los Angeles Times*

STATEMENTS THAT DO NOT OFFER A REASON FOR BELIEF

Now that we have determined what it is that makes an argument, let's look at a few things that do not. We will here rule out three of the many kinds of statements that sometimes look as though they may be arguments, but are not: mere assertions, mere illustrations, and mere explanations.

Mere Assertions

Arguments are probably far more common than you have previously thought, but you should not expect now to find arguments in *everything* you hear or read. Most forms of communication are in part an attempt to influence beliefs, but they do not always use arguments to do so, nor should they. A journalist, for example, is not typically expected to *argue* that unemployment is down; a teacher does not normally argue that *agricola* is the Latin word for *farmer*; and I need not argue that I was born in California and did most of my growing up in Georgia. Merely asserting such things—just *saying* them—is usually good enough to get others to believe them.

In other cases, however, ideas are asserted without reasons—sometimes with great fervor—and it *isn't* good enough. Note this passage from a speech by Robert Ingersoll, 19th century American orator and lawyer:

> I do believe in the nobility of human nature. I believe in love and home, kindness and humanity. I believe in good fellowship and cheerfulness, in making wife and children happy. I believe in good nature, in giving to others all of the rights that you claim for yourself. I believe in free thought, in reason, observation, and experience. I believe in self-reliance and in expressing your honest thought. . . . Above all, I believe in liberty.

There is no argument here, no reason offered in support of the beliefs Ingersoll expresses. This does not mean that his beliefs are immune from evaluation; as we will see in Chapter 9, there is much to be said about how to evaluate statements that are not themselves argued for. But they are not to be evaluated as arguments.

> *Guideline.* If a series of statements is merely an attempt to influence belief without offering reasons, do not count it as an argument.

Mere Illustrations

Passages intended merely to illustrate a point might also look a bit like arguments. But they would normally be *bad* arguments; and, as we will see in the discussion of the principle of charity in Chapter 3, it is usually preferable to take them as good illustrations rather than as bad arguments. There are usually clues to mere illustrations, such as *for example*, *for instance*, and *is illustrated by*. I am providing a verbal picture, not making an argument, if I say, "Charlie Parker is a good example of the fine line between artistic genius and insanity." Similarly, Mark Twain provides us with this in *Pudd'nhead Wilson:*

> There is no character, howsoever good and fine, but it can be destroyed by ridicule, howsoever poor and witless. Observe the ass, for instance: his character is about perfect, he is the choicest spirit among all the humbler animals, yet see what ridicule has brought him to. Instead of feeling complimented when we are called an ass, we are left in doubt.

The ass is not trotted out as reason to *believe* the first sentence, but as a way of making its point more vivid. It is better to take the passage merely as an illustration, not as an argument. As the old Yiddish saying puts it, "*For example* is no proof."

The distinction between mere illustration and argument is not always clear-cut. Suppose you overhear this remark:

> White Southerners are racists. Take David Duke.

Is this an *argument*, generalizing from a premise about a single case, David Duke, to a conclusion about an entire population, white Southerners (an important sort of argument called *inductive generalization* that will be covered later in the book)? Or is it merely an illustration? There is no clear way in this case to tell. You could probably tell if you heard more of the conversation. If the listener, for example, had just said, "I don't understand exactly what you mean. What sort of racism do you have in mind?" then it is clearly an illustration. But if the listener had just said, "Why should I accept such a sweeping indictment of a huge part of our population?" then it is clearly an argument. For this would make it clear that the speaker is offering a reason for belief.

> *Guideline.* Do not count a series of statements as an argument if it merely offers an attempt to make a statement easier to understand—that is, if it is a mere illustration. Terms like *for example, for instance,* and *is illustrated by* typically introduce mere illustrations.

Mere Explanations

Often reasons are given to provide *a causal explanation of some state of affairs,* not to offer reason for belief in some statement. If I point to my watch and angrily say, "Because you couldn't read the darn map, we're going to be late," my statement is not providing a reason to believe we are late; we both already know that. I'm merely identifying the cause of our being late. Consider this explanation:

> In the 19th century, British jurists sought to modify the laws permitting a husband to "chastise his wife with any reasonable instrument" by dictating that the instrument be "a rod not thicker than his thumb." Hence the rule of thumb.

This passage points to the cause behind the existence of the phrase *rule of thumb*. It does not offer a reason to believe that such a phrase exists; it is a commonly used phrase and no fluent English speaker doubts its existence. The first sentence of the passage is not a premise; it refers to a *cause*. And the second sentence is not the conclusion; it refers to the *effect*. The passage is not an argument; it is a mere causal explanation.

Terms that serve as inference indicators can also occur in mere explanations (where they are no longer inference indicators). *So* and *hence*, for instance, are used in the two preceding examples not to indicate movement from premise to conclusion, but movement from cause to effect. The same goes for inference indicators that typically introduce premises. A psychologist, for example, asks this on a talk show:

> Did you ever wonder why people are more likely to laugh out loud when they are with others than when they are alone? Because, among other things, laughing announces "I got it," and in an empty room, they'd be announcing to nobody.

The psychologist is not providing us with a *reason to believe* that we more readily laugh out loud when we are with others; he assumes that we already know it or that we'll recognize it by reflecting briefly on our own experience. When we do realize it, it strikes us as curious. Why would it make any difference whether the room is empty or not? This leads to the explanation offered in the passage, with *because* used to introduce a cause—the fact that laughter functions as a signal to others that a joke has been understood—not a premise.

There is one way in which premises in arguments are sometimes the opposite of the causes in mere causal explanations. In arguments, recall, the movement from premises to conclusion is typically from the familiar to the new. But in mere explanations, the movement from cause to effect is often from the new to the familiar—*from*, for example, the surprising and unfamiliar origin of a phrase in British law (the cause) *to* the well-known everyday phrase *rule of thumb* (the effect).

> *Guideline.* Do not count a series of statements as an argument if it offers merely a causal explanation of a state of affairs. If the statements show the familiar following from the new, and if the new is not offered as a reason to believe the familiar, it is probably a mere explanation.

Some Attempts to Influence Beliefs That Are Not Arguments

1. Mere assertions
2. Mere illustrations
3. Mere explanations

EXERCISES Chapter 2, set (h)

None of the passages below is an argument. Study each one, satisfy yourself that it is not an argument, and state which of the three it is: mere assertion, mere illustration, or mere explanation.

Sample exercise. "A recent report in *Advertising Age* tells how English-speaking visitors to Tokyo are amused by Pocket Wetty premoistened towelettes, Green Piles lawn fertilizer, Cow Brand shampoo, Shot Vision television sets, Kitchy soup mix, More Ran tea cakes, Trim Pecker trousers, and Creap, an artificial coffee creamer. Calpis is not bovine urine, but a soft drink. Nail Remover is actually a fingernail cleaner. The reason for the odd names is usually a lack of marketing research." —*Psychology Today*

Sample answer. Mere explanation.

1. The car wouldn't start because it was out of gas.
2. The first company to market a new product isn't always the company that makes all the money. Take Apple Computers, for example.
3. Year in and year out, the people who succeed are those who work the hardest, regardless of their talent. I urge this view upon you with all of my heart.
4. "When a given name is in the long form, it is often set aside in social use for a less proper version, but it is rare that someone legally named Frank will go around calling himself Francis. This illustrates that formal names are often the starting point for shorter forms, but the reverse is not true." —Daniel Dorff, *Verbatim*
5. "Question to the UCLA Chancellor: The conference Board of Associated Research Councils has recently released its survey results

which ranked UCLA in the top five universities in the country. What factors do you think contribute to this kind of academic success? Answer: The basic reason is the quality of the faculty. It is also a tribute to the support that the University has been given by the state of California, the people of California, and the Los Angeles community. This support has provided increased research teaching opportunities and facilities." —*UCLA Monthly*

6. "I don't like depressing pictures. I don't like pestholes. I don't like pictures that are dirty. I don't ever go out and pay money for studies in abnormality. I don't have depressed moods and I don't want to have any. I'm just happy, very happy." —Walt Disney
7. "Stanley Fish's essay, 'The Unbearable Ugliness of Volvos,' chastises professors for their masochistic refusal to admit . . . that they like the money and the perks. 'In the collective eye of the academy,' he writes, 'sloppiness, discourtesy, indifference, and inefficiency are *virtues*, signs of an admirable disdain for the mere surfaces of things, a disdain that is itself a sign of a dedication to higher, if invisible, values.' This explains the Volvo, the professor's car of choice, which by its very ugliness signals that the academic is ambivalent about nice things, Mr. Fish writes." —*Chronicle of Higher Education*
8. "Our capacity for identification and sympathy goes out most readily to non-human characters. Think of Bambi or the Little Engine That Could. Melville intended Moby-Dick to be the symbol of universal evil, and instead we find ourselves rooting for him against one-legged Captain Ahab." —*New Yorker*
9. "I don't know where the thought came from or how it struck me, yet all at once I said to myself, 'But God doesn't exist!' It's quite certain that before this I must have had new ideas about God and that I had begun solving the problem for myself. But still, as I remember very well, it was on that day and in the form of a momentary intuition, that I said to myself 'God doesn't exist.' It's striking to reflect that I thought this at the age of eleven and that I never asked myself the question again until today, that is to say for sixty years." —Simone de Beauvoir quoting Jean Paul Sartre, *Harpers*
10. "My pedagogy is hard. What is weak must be hammered away. In my fortresses of the Teutonic Order, a young generation will grow up before which the world will tremble. I want the young to be violent, domineering, undismayed, cruel. There must be nothing weak or

gentle about them. The free, splendid beast of prey must once again flash from their eyes. I want my young people strong and beautiful."
—Adolf Hitler, *Mein Kampf*

EXERCISES Chapter 2, set (i)

Take the topic of taxes and construct statements of the following sort.

Sample exercise. Mere explanation.

Sample answer. Because the politicians cannot control their spending, taxes have to go higher and higher.

1. Mere assertion
2. Mere illustration
3. Mere explanation
4. Simple argument

Arguments and Explanations Sometimes Overlap

As we have seen, any series of statements could potentially be used as an argument if at least one of the statements were offered as reason to believe another. So even a series of statements offered as a causal explanation could at the same time be used as an argument—and thus would no longer be a *mere* causal explanation. The cause could be the premise, or the cause could be the conclusion. There is nothing tricky to worry about. The standard rule continues to apply: a statement is the conclusion if a reason is being offered to believe it. And the tips for identifying it are no different: it is probably the conclusion if it answers the question being asked in the broader passage; if it is the least familiar, most controversial, of the statements; or if *clear* inference indicators point to it.

Here is an example of a cause as a conclusion from Alan Abelson, a financial reporter for *Barron's*, written on one of his more lighthearted days:

> Very often a company comes to market with an initial public offering, boasting a classy record of earnings growth. Then, the very next year, profits take a strange tumble. Obviously, logic impels us to the conclusion that the reason profits took a tumble was because the company went public.

There is clearly a causal explanation here; the tumble in profits (the effect) results from the company's going public (the cause). But there is also an argument; note the clear inference indicator *logic impels us to the conclusion that.* The conclusion—*Profits often fall because companies go public*—includes the cause. And the premises include the effects—*Profits often fall the year after companies go public.* The effects, Abelson suggests, give us evidence of a particular cause. Arguments of this sort—*explanatory arguments*—are quite common and will be covered in depth in Chapter 16.

On the other hand, here is an example of a cause as a premise, found in *Manage*, a magazine geared toward business executives:

> Today's doctors tell us that a hearty laugh is great exercise. When you emit an explosive guffaw, they say, your diaphragm descends deep into your body and your lungs expand, greatly increasing the amount of oxygen being taken into them. At the same time, as it expands sideways, the diaphragm gives your heart a gentle, rhythmic massage. That noble organ responds by beating faster and harder. Circulation speeds up. Liver, stomach, pancreas, spleen and gall bladder are all stimulated—your entire system gets an invigorating lift. All of which confirms what that sage old Greek, Aristotle, said about laughter more than 2,000 years ago: "It is a bodily exercise precious to health."

This argument offers a reason to believe the conclusion,

> Laughing is good exercise.

Note the inference indicator *confirms*, which precedes the conclusion. But at the same time the premises offer a causal explanation—of what *causes* laughter to be good exercise. (Even, apparently, in an empty room.) So this passage serves both as argument and explanation, with premises doubling as causes and conclusion as effect.

Use of cause as premise is most obvious when the effect being explained is itself a belief. Suppose I say the following:

> I believed it was murder because the coroner's report said so.

In a case like this, there seems to be hardly any difference between saying that the coroner's report caused me to believe it was murder and saying that the statement *The coroner's report said so* serves as a premise for the statement *It was murder.* It is both an argument and a causal explanation. It would be quite a different matter had I said:

> I believed that it was murder because my enemies put me under a magic spell.

This explains what caused the belief, but makes no mention of any reason I had for believing it (presumably I had no reason). So it is merely a causal explanation, not an argument.

> *Guideline.* Count causal explanations as arguments when they also offer a reason for belief—whether the effect is offered as reason to believe the cause, or the cause is offered as reason to believe the effect. In such cases they are not *mere* explanations.

EXERCISES Chapter 2, set (j)

Determine whether each of the following includes an argument or is a mere explanation. Defend your answers.

Sample exercise. I saw him treat person after person with respect. That forced me to change my mind, and to believe that he was a decent person after all.

Sample answer. Includes an argument, since his treatment of others is cited as a reason to believe he is a decent person.

1. Pushing this button causes that red light to flash.
2. You can tell that pushing this button causes that red light to flash, since—look—it flashes every time I push the button, but otherwise it is unlit.
3. What caused all the dominoes to fall down? Well, the first domino hit the second one, the second hit the third, and so on—thus, all the dominoes fell down.
4. Why should I believe that all of the dominoes will fall down? Well, the first one will hit the second one, the second will hit the third, and so on—thus, all the dominoes will fall down.

IMPLICIT STATEMENTS

This chapter expands on the definition of a simple argument as a series of statements in which one of the statements is offered as reason for belief in another. We have seen how sentences not cast in the declarative form can still function as statements, hence as building blocks of arguments. Sometimes, too, arguments rely on ***implicit statements,*** statements that are not spoken or written in any form but are implied or assumed. Note the following argument reported in the obituary of Roy Sullivan, who had killed himself with a shotgun:

> Roy Sullivan, a retired forest ranger, was hit by lightning seven times and survived. He was baffled by his misfortune and speculated that the chemical makeup of his body in some way attracted lightning. "I don't believe God is after me," he told an interviewer. "If he was, the first bolt would have been enough."

At the end of the passage, Sullivan offers an argument to rule out the explanation that God was after him. (Assume that he means what most people mean by *God*—that he is an all-powerful being.) His conclusion is this:

> God is not after me.

And his stated reason—his premise—is this:

> If God were after me, the first bolt of lightning would have killed me.

But there is another reason that must be combined with this one to get to the conclusion—an unexpressed and thus implicit premise—that Sullivan obviously assumes:

> The first bolt of lightning did not kill me.

It would have been silly for him to state it—after all, Sullivan was alive when he offered the argument.

An arguer can have many reasons for leaving a premise or conclusion implicit. Sullivan's is the most common one—he considers the premise so obvious that there is no need to express it, since it would be pedantic or insulting to do so. But this is not the only possible reason. The arguer may not have thought through the argument carefully enough to be aware of the assumption. Or the arguer, fully aware of the assumption, may be suppressing it to deceive you.

Note the example of a Burger King commercial from many years ago:

> The bigger the burger, the better the burger; the burgers are bigger at Burger King.

In this case it is the *conclusion* that is implicit:

> The burgers are better at Burger King.

This is advertising, so a good guess is that a marketing motive lies behind it. Perhaps they think that if you help yourself to the conclusion, you're more likely to help yourself to a Whopper.

An argument with an implicit premise or conclusion is called an ***enthymeme.*** (This word comes from the Greek roots *en* for *in* and *thumos* for *mind;* an enthymeme, then, is an argument that leaves a premise or conclusion behind, *in the mind.*) For the purpose of clarifying and evaluating, implicit statements should be considered just as much a part of an argument as explicit ones.

> *Guideline.* Consider any premise or conclusion that is assumed by the arguer, but not expressed, as part of the argument.

EXERCISES Chapter 2, set (k)

Identify the implicit premise or conclusion in each of these arguments.

Sample exercise. "Every man who attacks my belief . . . makes me uneasy; and I am angry with him who makes me uneasy." —spoken by Johnson in Boswell, *Life of Samuel Johnson*

Premise: Every man who attacks my belief . . . makes me uneasy.
Premise: I am angry with him who makes me uneasy.
Conclusion: ?

Sample answer. I am angry with anyone who attacks my belief.

1. Son to father: "Dad, the nicer the father the more generous he should be with allowances—and you're the nicest father I know."

   Premise: The nicer the father the more generous the father should be with allowances.
   Premise: You're the nicest father I know.
   Conclusion: ?

2. Daughter to father: "We've been waiting for a windy day to fly the kite. So we should go fly it right now."

   Premise: We've been waiting for a windy day to fly the kite.
   Premise: ?
   Conclusion: We should go fly the kite right now.

3. Geoffrey Hellman, a longtime writer for the *New Yorker*, tells of how he wrote many pieces on "spry oldsters" and was asked to write a second story on Charles C. Burlingham as Burlingham approached his hundredth birthday. As Hellman tells it, "I called him up, and he begged off. He said he didn't care for publicity and that he was delighted that my previous article on him had not been published. 'But it was,' I said. 'Sent you a proof and we ran it several years ago.' 'No, you didn't,' he said. 'I tore it up and threw it in the scrap basket.'" —Brendan Gill, *Here at the New Yorker*

   Premise: Burlingham tore up the proof and threw it away.
   Premise: ?
   Conclusion: Burlingham prevented the first story from being published.

4. "After Vice President Spiro Agnew resigned in disgrace in 1973, there was much speculation about whom Richard Nixon would nominate as Agnew's replacement. Gerald Ford had advance word that he was the man, but it was strictly confidential. As one reporter tells it, in the afternoon, Barber Conable had told Ford on the House floor that he was going back to Rochester that night to make a speech instead of going to the scheduled presentation of the new vice president. 'You might want to be there, Barb,' Ford said.

" 'The only reason I'd go there is if it's you,' said Conable. . . . 'I'll only go if you ask me.'

" 'I'm asking you,' Ford said.

" 'Can I draw any inference from that?' Conable said with a smile.

"Ford smiled back, 'I'm asking you.' "

—Richard Reeves, *A Ford, not a Lincoln*

Premise: The only reason Ford would invite Conable was if Ford was the new vice president.
Premise: Ford invited Conable.
Conclusion: ?

5. Musicologist H. Wiley Hitchcock predicts that in a couple of centuries, the music of Charles Ives and Aaron Copland will still be listened to, but not the music of the Ramones. Hitchcock is quick to add that this is not a value judgment but a prediction based on a practical notion: "The Ramones can be listened to but the music cannot be performed except by the Ramones. Notated music—music that is written down—can always be performed."

   Premise: Notated music can always be performed.
   Premise: ?
   Premise: ?
   Conclusion: In a couple of hundred years, the music of Charles Ives and Aaron Copland—but probably not of the Ramones—will still be performed.

6. "If I were in my right mind, I would retire," said George Allen after failing to coach his team to victory in the title game. "He hasn't retired," quipped a sportscaster.

   Premise: If George Allen were in his right mind, then he would retire.
   Premise: George Allen did not retire.
   Conclusion: ?

7. Joe Portale, former Lakewood, Ohio, high school football player, claims New York Yankees' owner George Steinbrenner violated NCAA regulations while recruiting him to play for the University of Florida in 1976. Steinbrenner denies any wrongdoing in recruiting

Portale. "No way," Steinbrenner said. "That would be wrong." —*Los Angeles Times*

Premise: It would be wrong for Steinbrenner to violate NCAA regulations.
Premise: ?
Conclusion: Steinbrenner did not violate NCAA regulations.

8. "Our ideas reach no farther than our experience: we have no experience of divine attributes and operations: I need not conclude my syllogism: you can draw the inference yourself." —David Hume, *Dialogues Concerning Natural Religion*

Premise: We cannot have an idea of anything we do not experience.
Premise: We do not have any experience of God.
Conclusion: ?

COMPLEX ARGUMENTS

So far our concern has been solely with simple arguments. ***Complex arguments*** link together simple arguments, so that the conclusion of one serves as a premise for the next. *Judge, this man is a well-established member of the community, so he will not flee the country. Thus, you should release him on his own recognizance.* Usually, the conclusion of the final simple argument—such as *He should be released on his own recognizance*—is the ***main conclusion.*** Properly speaking, the main conclusion is the most important one, the one that answers the question being asked in the broader passage. Conclusions that provide a link between the simple arguments—such as *He will not flee the country*—are termed ***subconclusions.*** Complex arguments can be made up of any number of simple arguments and thus may have any number of subconclusions.

In *Of Property* John Locke argues:

The materials of nature (air, earth, water) that remain untouched by human effort belong to no one and are not property. It follows that *a thing can become someone's private property only if he works and labors on it to change its natural state.* From this I conclude that whatever a man improves by the labor of his hand and brain belongs to him, and to him only.

Pay special attention to the second sentence, which is italicized. It is a subconclusion, since it is offered both as a conclusion (*it follows that* indicates that the second sentence is supported by the first) and as a premise (*from this I conclude* comes immediately after it). The statement for which it is offered as a premise is the main conclusion of the complex argument.[3]

Complex arguments occur often, and we will look at examples from time to time, but simple arguments will be our major concern. If you know how to evaluate simple arguments, you know how to evaluate a series of simple arguments.

> *Guideline.* Count a series of statements as a complex argument when the conclusion of one simple argument serves as the premise for another simple argument.

EXERCISES Chapter 2, set (l)

In the following complex arguments, identify the subconclusions and the main conclusion.

Sample exercise. Three brothers were arrested for disorderly conduct on Christmas Eve after they scuffled with the man posing as St. Nicholas at a children's Mass. The brothers describe themselves as fundamentalist Roman Catholics. They said they objected to St. Nick's presence because, "Santa is not real, therefore he is a lie. Therefore he does not belong in church." —Associated Press

Sample answer. Subconclusion: Santa is a lie. Conclusion: Santa does not belong in church.

1. Don't be silly—you can never become president of the United States. Your official papers show that you were born in Russia. It follows from

[3]Some authors consider a cluster of independent arguments offered for the same conclusion to be complex arguments of another sort. If arguments are independent, however, they should be evaluated independently as simple arguments; these so-called convergent arguments, then, will not be a feature of this text. Likewise, some authors consider arguments with more than one conclusion to be complex arguments. But if the conclusions are indeed independent of one another, then the passage really contains two arguments—to different conclusions—that share the same premises. These, too, should be evaluated independently as simple arguments.

that, of course, that you were not born in the United States. But only those born in the United States can become president.

2. Police officer to suspect: "Eyewitnesses place you at the scene of the crime. Therefore, you lied about your whereabouts at the time. I'm afraid that means that we must consider you a suspect."
3. Teacher to student: "Your work this term was very impressive. It convinces me that you are a prime candidate for our graduate program. And, since all of our graduate students are on full fellowships, you should expect to have funding for your schooling next year."
4. "I have been admitted to the bar in London. That makes me a lawyer. I am—in your terms—colored. So, there is at least one colored lawyer in South Africa." —Mahatma Gandhi in the film *Gandhi* (replying to the challenge "There are no colored lawyers in South Africa.")
5. "Twain makes an odious parallel between Huck's being 'enslaved' by a drunken father who keeps him locked in a cabin and Jim's legal enslavement . . . [so] Twain does not take slavery, and, therefore, black people seriously." —Julius Lester, *Mark Twain Journal*
6. "Woman is incapable of forming clear judgments, so the distinction between true and false means nothing to her. Thus women are naturally, inescapably, untruthful. . . . On this account . . . they do not enter the moral realm at all. Woman simply has no standard of right or wrong. And, as she knows no moral or logical imperative, she cannot be said to have a soul, and this means she lacks free will. From this it follows that women have no ego, no individuality, and no character. Ethically, women are a lost cause." —account of Otto Weininger's views from Ray Monk, *Wittgenstein: The Duty of Genius.* (There are five or six subconclusions in this passage, depending on how you count them.)
7. "But the power of Marxism cannot be explained solely by his theories; for these were at least partially limited by his 19th-century experience, and they have been superseded by the considerable development of the social science. The power of Marxism must therefore be located to a considerable degree in its religious impulse and its moral protest." —Paul Kurtz, *Free Inquiry*
8. "God, who prescribes forbearance and forgiveness of every fault, exercises none himself, but does exactly the opposite; for a punishment which comes at the end of all things, when the world is over and done with, cannot have for its object either to improve or to deter, and is

therefore pure vengeance." —Arthur, Schopenhauer, *The World as Will and Idea*

EXERCISES Chapter 2, set (m)

Each of the next two passages has two conclusions, but in each case they are conclusions to two different simple arguments (with shared premises), not a single complex argument. Identify the two conclusions.

1. "There is a famous scene in the *Confessions* (Book IV) where Augustine saw Ambrose reading without speaking, without even moving his lips. Augustine was amazed! Two conclusions can be reached: by the fifth century A.D. literacy had worked its way into culture and this literacy was rare." —D. M. Dombrowski, *Teaching Philosophy*
2. "I got hooked on opera when I was 14. It is an addiction that I've never for a moment regretted. But, wholly unguided as I was, I developed some curious misapprehensions for which I've paid ever since. One of them was the notion that it takes superhuman brains and talent to write an opera. Ergo, operettas are composed by people with only average brain and talent who are unable to aspire to opera, and 'musicals' are written by brainless, talentless opportunists who cater to the most vulgar tastes." —David Greene, *Musical Heritage Review*

EXERCISES Chapter 2, set (n)

Some of the following passages contain arguments; others do not. If a passage does not contain an argument, identify it either as a mere assertion, a mere illustration, or a mere explanation. If it does contain an argument, identify the conclusion.

1. "Every pitcher should know, from the first day of spring, that after covering first base to take a throw, the next move is always to turn to the left quickly and face the infield. Why? So that if there's a fast runner on second base he can't score on a routine ground out." —Thomas Boswell, *How Life Imitates the World Series*
2. "One of the fundamental axioms of physics, embodied in what is known as Fourier's law of heat conduction, is that heat flows from the warmer parts of a body to the cooler ones. It can therefore be inferred that since the temperature increases with depth in the earth's

crust, there is a flow of heat outward from the earth's interior." —Henry Pollack and David Chapman, *Scientific American*

3. "Actually, I like convention food. I like it for the same reason I like airplane food; it's made of real food, but it's softer, shinier, and sweeter. Also, everybody gets the same thing and you never know what you're having until it's served, if then: the thrill of the unknown." —David Owen, *Harper's*
4. Since Defense Secretary McNamara (who had become president of Ford just when the disastrous Edsel was being brought out) promoted inefficient ideas like the TFX airplane, slowed progress by halting LeMay's B-70 bomber, analyzed everything for cost instead of charging ahead, and favored unilateral disarmament, he *must* have been responsible for the Edsel. Longtime political opponent Barry Goldwater glued the Edsel charge to McNamara's back for life. —Deborah Shapley, *Promise and Power: The Life and Times of Robert McNamara*
5. "Early dinosaur reconstructions were not terribly accurate. A horn put on the snout of Iguanodon in its earliest reconstructions, for example, was later shown to be a spike-like thumb bone."[4] —*Science News*
6. "Of course, there are reasons why academics write in this barbarous way. If they were to use the language that is natural to them, and to express the thoughts and feelings that are really theirs, the result would be so stunningly banal that no one would dream of employing them in a university. It has become necessary to write gibberish to gain promotion." —Roger Scruton
7. "That beavers react aggressively to the presence of a trespasser's scent mound was demonstrated in another experiment. D. Muller-Schwarze and fellow researchers introduced alien mounds into the territories of two beaver colonies. . . . As soon as the resident animals got a whiff of the foreign odors, they began hissing. . . . One of them summoned up courage to mount the bank and cancel out the unwanted scents with a blast of his or her own excretions." —Hope Rydeh, *Lily Pond: Four Years with a Family of Beavers*
8. "I am of the opinion that the Bible is the most remarkable book I have read in the English language. I am of the opinion that the au-

[4]This prompted paleontologist George Gaylord Simpson to write that ". . . the animal thus thumbed its nose at its first reconstructor."

thors and the editors of the Bible were the first nonreligionists: that the Bible has nothing to do with religion; that the religionists have purloined the camouflage used by the authors and have made of the camouflage the substance of their power over people." —letter to the editor, *Free Inquiry*

9. "I think robots appeal to us because we want slaves, and since people always want to be set free, we'll settle for one that is made of polyurethane and whose brain is a silicon chip. That way we don't get any complaints." —Jack Smith, *Los Angeles Times*
10. "If external circumstances determine behavior, then punishment is still needed to curb crime. A home-grown example of this principle is the small California ghetto community of East Palo Alto, which was once the 'murder capital' of the country in terms of its murder rate per capita. A year later, the murder rate was down drastically, as were other violent crimes. It put more cops on the streets and more criminals behind bars." —Thomas Sowell, *Forbes*
11. "The Western concepts embraced by the traditional liberal arts education made a tremendous contribution to intellectual history. Yet certainly their universality is compromised by ethnocentrism. It is only natural, for instance, that Western ideals should lead one to assume the cultural primacy of Europe over Asia, and such an assumption clearly lacks universal validity." —Yasusuke Murakami, *Japan Echo*

SUMMARY OF CHAPTER TWO

Sentences vary according to their forms and their functions. Statements—which are sentences that can be true or false—function to convey information. And their form is typically that of a subject and a trait attributed to that subject; an example is the statement *The beach is pleasant today.* Other types of sentences differ in their forms and functions in ways that mark them as imperative, interrogative, exclamatory, and performative. Sentences that are not in statement form might nevertheless function as statements—that is, they might communicate information; an example is the sentence *Oh, to be at the beach this afternoon!*

A simple argument is a series of statements in which at least one of the statements is offered as reason for belief in another. The statements offered as reasons are the premises. The statement for which the reasons are offered is the conclusion. Inference indicators are helpful in identifying the premises (e.g., *because* . . .) and the conclusion (e.g., *therefore* . . .). In the absence of inference indicators, the conclusion can usually be identified either by looking for the most controversial claim in the passage or by looking for the answer to the question being asked.

A series of statements can count as an argument even if some of the statements are implicit and even if the reasons are bad. On the other hand, statements merely asserted with conviction do not count as arguments, because they supply no reason to believe them. Nor do mere illustrations (which might make an idea easier to understand, but do not straightforwardly aim to convince us that we should believe it). Nor do mere causal explanations. In a mere explanation, a cause is often offered to explain an effect that is typically *already* believed to exist; this differs from an argument, in which a premise is offered to justify belief in a conclusion that may not already be believed to be true. Sometimes, however, explanations and arguments do overlap.

A complex argument is a series of connected simple arguments in which the conclusion of one simple argument serves as the premise of another and is thus a subconclusion.

GUIDELINES FOR CHAPTER TWO

- For the purpose of identifying arguments, consider a sentence a statement if it serves a declarative function.
- Count it as an argument even if the reasons offered seem clearly to be bad ones.
- When possible, identify premises and conclusions by the location of inference indicators.
- When there are no inference indicators, look for the most controversial statement in the argument; if one can be readily identified, it is usually the conclusion.
- When there are no inference indicators, look in the wider context for the question being asked; the proposed answer to it is usually the conclusion.
- If a series of statements is merely an attempt to influence belief without offering reasons, do not count it as an argument.
- Do not count a series of statements as an argument if it merely offers an attempt to make a statement easier to understand—that is, if it is a mere illustration. Terms like *for example*, *for instance*, and *is illustrated by* typically introduce mere illustrations.

- Do not count a series of statements as an argument if it offers merely a causal explanation of a state of affairs. If the statements show the familiar following from the new, and if the new is not offered as a reason to believe the familiar, it is probably a mere explanation.
- Count causal explanations as arguments when they also offer a reason for belief—whether the effect is offered as reason to believe the cause, or the cause is offered as reason to believe the effect. In such cases they are not *mere* explanations.
- Consider any premise or conclusion that is assumed by the arguer, but not expressed, as part of the argument.
- Count a series of statements as a complex argument when the conclusion for one simple argument serves as the premise for another simple argument.

GLOSSARY FOR CHAPTER TWO

Complex argument—a series of two or more simple arguments, in which the conclusion of one argument serves as a premise for the next. Complex arguments can be made up of any number of simple arguments, and thus may have any number of subconclusions.

Conclusion—the statement for which the reason is offered. Each simple argument has exactly one conclusion.

Declarative function—the function of conveying information. An example of a sentence with this function is *Eleanor Roosevelt was one of the most influential first ladies in history.*

Enthymeme—an argument with an implicit premise or conclusion. This word comes from the Greek roots *en* for *in* and *thumos* for *mind;* an enthymeme is an argument that leaves a premise or conclusion behind, *in the mind.* For the purposes of clarifying and evaluating, the implicit statements should be considered just as much a part of an enthymematic argument as the explicit ones.

Exclamatory function—the function of expressing emotion. An example of a sentence with this function is *Oh, to be at the beach this afternoon*!

Imperative function—the function of directing others to action. An example of a sentence with this function is *Speak into the microphone.*

Implicit statements—statements that are not spoken or written in any form, but are relied on by the arguer as a part of the argument.

Inference—movement from premises to conclusion. Also, sometimes simply a synonym for *simple argument.*

Inference indicator—a term that indicates movement from premise to conclusion. Also called an *illative*. Examples are *because*, which introduces premises, and *therefore*, which introduces conclusions.

Interrogative function—the function of asking a question. An example of a sentence with this function is *Are you now or have you ever been a member of the Communist party*?

Main conclusion—the most important conclusion of a complex argument, the one that answers the question being asked in the broader conversation.

Performative function—the function of doing, or performing, something by the very act of asserting it under the right circumstances. An example of a sentence with this function is *I promise to return the money on Tuesday*.

Premise—any statement that is offered as a reason for belief in another statement. (Sometimes spelled *premiss* by the British.) We alternatively refer to premises as the *evidence, warrant, justification, basis, grounds*, or *rationale*. There must be at least one premise in an argument, but there is no upper limit.

Simple argument—a series of statements in which at least one of the statements is offered as reason for belief in another.

Statement—a sentence that can be true or false. It functions to convey information. Its form, typically, includes a subject and a trait that is attributed to the subject.

Subconclusion—in a complex argument, the conclusion of one simple argument that also serves as premise for the next simple argument.

PART TWO

CLARIFYING ARGUMENTS

CHAPTER THREE

A Framework for Clarifying

Everything that can be thought at all can be thought clearly. Everything that can be said can be said clearly.

—Ludwig Wittgenstein, *Tractatus Logico-Philosophicus*

Duchess: Do, as a concession to my poor wits, Lord Darlington, just explain to me what you really mean.
Lord Darlington: I think I had better not; nowadays, to be intelligible is to be found out.

—Oscar Wilde, *Lady Windermere's Fan*

TOPICS

The Process of Clarifying
The Principle of Loyalty
The Principle of Charity
The Straw Man Fallacy

Clear arguments are arguments that can be evaluated. But arguments in everyday life are often lacking in clarity; so before you evaluate an argument, you will be asked to engage in the process of *clarifying*. This chapter is concerned with the clarifying process and with two principles that regulate it, the principle of loyalty and the principle of charity.

THE PROCESS OF CLARIFYING

If you are preparing to evaluate an argument, the first order of business is ***clarifying***. This means you should make sure the argument is expressed as clearly as possible, so that it is as easy as possible to tell whether the premises are true, whether the logic is good, and whether the argument is relevant to the conversation. Clarifying requires two procedures, performed at the same time: outlining the argument in standard format and paraphrasing the argument.

Standard Clarifying Format

As we saw in Chapter 2, when an argument is expressed in ordinary English it is not always obvious which statement is the conclusion and which statements are the premises. The standard clarifying format that we use in this text provides a simple way of making it obvious which is which. When an argument is outlined in this format, the premises (including any premises that may also serve as subconclusions) are numbered and listed immediately above their conclusion, while the main conclusion is indicated not by a number, but by *C*, for *Conclusion*. (This provides a simple way of referring to the elements of the argument in your evaluation.) All conclusions—including subconclusions if the argument is complex—are preceded by ∴ in the left margin.[1] Implicit statements are enclosed in square brackets, but otherwise treated like all other statements in the argument.

Standard Clarifying Format

1. Premises numbered above their conclusion.
2. Main conclusion identified as *C*.

[1]Another common way of designating a conclusion is to draw a horizontal line between the last premise and the conclusion. This leaves no simple and clear way, however, of indicating subconclusions if the argument is complex.

3. All conclusions (main conclusion and subconclusions) preceded by ∴ in the left margin.
4. Implicit statements in brackets.

Consider this modest argument from the *Miami Herald:*

> Dade County, which includes Miami, is the best place in America to be a criminal. It has the nation's worst crime rate and does the laziest job of putting criminals behind bars.

Once we have identified the conclusion (the first sentence) and the premises (each half of the second sentence), it can be painlessly put into standard clarifying format, as follows:

1. Dade County has the nation's worst crime rate.
2. Dade County does the laziest job of putting criminals behind bars.

∴ *C.* Dade County is the best place in America to be a criminal.

That's all there is to it.

Let's take a slightly more complicated example. Can subliminal messages in rock music have an effect on the listener? Anthony Pellicano, a forensic audio specialist, testified for CBS Records in the case against rock band Judas Priest. He gave this argument:

> The volume at which alleged auditory subliminal sounds are produced is not loud enough to cause the eardrum to vibrate. If the eardrum does not vibrate then the message cannot be sent to the brain. "The subliminal argument has absolutely no basis in fact," Pellicano concluded.

Here is the argument in standard clarifying format (with minimal paraphrasing).

1. The volume at which alleged auditory subliminal sounds are produced is not loud enough to cause the eardrum to vibrate.
2. If the eardrum does not vibrate then the message cannot be sent to the brain.

∴ *C.* The subliminal argument has absolutely no basis in fact.

This outline makes plain which statements are the premises—1 and 2—and which is the main conclusion—*C*.

Suppose Pellicano, the forensic audio specialist, had finished his remarks with the following additional assertion:

> So Judas Priest is innocent.

We would then outline the entire passage as a complex argument, as follows:

1. The volume at which alleged auditory subliminal sounds are produced is not loud enough to cause the eardrum to vibrate.
2. If the eardrum does not vibrate, then the message cannot be sent to the brain.

∴ 3. The subliminal argument has absolutely no basis in fact.
∴ ***C*. Judas Priest is innocent.**

The revisions are highlighted. Note that 3 is now a subconclusion; as such, it is not only the conclusion to 1 and 2, but it is also the premise for the new main conclusion, *C*.

This does not *completely* clarify the argument. Note that the arguer clearly is inferring from premises 1 and 2 that *the message cannot be sent to the brain*—and that this is the immediate reason for his assertion that the subliminal argument has no basis on fact. If we include that implicit statement—as a subconclusion—the outline takes the following form.

1. The volume at which alleged auditory subliminal sounds are produced is not loud enough to cause the eardrum to vibrate.
2. If the eardrum does not vibrate, then the message cannot be sent to the brain.

∴ **[3. The message cannot be sent to the brain.]**
∴ 4. The subliminal argument has absolutely no basis in fact.
∴ *C*. Judas Priest is innocent.

Revisions are again highlighted. There are other implicit premises in the argument (you might think for yourself about what might be implicitly assumed between 3 and 4), but this is enough to illustrate the format. This format sets the stage for evaluation of the argument, which should follow.

Guideline. Outline each argument in standard clarifying format.

EXERCISES Chapter 3, set (a)

Outline each of the following arguments in standard format. There is no need, at this point, to attempt to paraphrase or supply implicit statements. Don't assume that every sentence in each passage is a premise or conclusion.

Sample exercise. "For a scrapbook of the Truman senatorial campaign, Fred Canfill kept clipping the local papers along the way. One item dated August 3, from an unidentified paper, acknowledged that Judge Truman was no orator, but then this was an argument in his favor since there was already too much oratory in the United States Senate."—David McCullough, *Truman*

Sample answer.

1. Judge Truman was no orator.
2. There was already too much oratory in the United States Senate.

∴ *C.* Judge Truman was the better candidate in the senatorial campaign. (Paraphrased from the expression "in his favor")

1. "When, at the time of the moon landing, a woman in rural Texas was interviewed about the event, she very sensibly refused to believe that the television pictures she had seen had come all the way from the moon, on the grounds that with her antenna she couldn't even get Dallas." —Richard Lewontin, *New York Review of Books* (Stick to clarifying here—resist the urge to evaluate this as a good or bad argument.)
2. "'The real object of sports writing', says a friend of mine who does it, 'is to keep readers away from the horrors in the rest of the paper.' Thus sports continues its rounds as the Magnificent Evasion, since it also keeps us away from the bad news at home and in one's own psyche."—Wilfred Sheed, *Harper's* (Look for more than one premise here—inference indicators are there to help you.)
3. "Japanese still tend to think in terms of personal relationships and subjective circumstances in their business dealings. Thus an

agreement between a Japanese and a foreign businessman should be reduced to its basic elements, and each point thoroughly discussed, to make sure each side understands and actually does agree to what the other side is saying."—Boyne De Mente, *The Japanese Way of Doing Business*

4. "Says Buntrock of Chem Waste, 'We're waste managers, so we have to help our customers manage their waste. So if the business moves from a quantity function to more services and processing, we'll move with it.'"—*Forbes*

Paraphrasing the Argument

It is usually necessary for you to paraphrase the argument at the same time you are organizing it into standard clarifying format. This means that, to achieve clarity, you must reword the argument, highlighting what matters most in determining the merits of the argument—in determining whether the premises are true, the argument is logical, and the argument is conversationally relevant. Why is this usually required? There are at least two reasons. First, arguers often find it hard to make themselves understood, despite the best of intentions. And, second, their intentions are almost always to do more than merely to make it easy to evaluate their reasoning. They almost always have a *rhetorical* purpose as well; that is, they intend to persuade.

Rhetoric is aptly defined by W. V. Quine in *Quiddities* as "the literary technology of persuasion." It can help or hurt the argument's clarity. It helps when it is used to make good arguments easy to accept *on their own merits.* But it hurts when, as Quine puts it, those who use it place "the goal of persuasion above the goal of truth . . . , disregarding every discrepancy while regarding every crepancy." In this chapter and the next three, you will find dozens of examples of the use (and misuse) of rhetoric. Your aim in paraphrasing should be to get rid of what is incomprehensible or misleading, whether intentional or not, so that the only thing that *could* be persuasive about the argument is the quality of the reasoning.

> *Guideline.* Paraphrase each argument for greater clarity as you are outlining it in standard clarifying format.

Procedures in the Clarifying Process

1. Outline in standard clarifying format.
2. Paraphrase for greater clarity.

THE PRINCIPLE OF LOYALTY

When clarifying an argument it is essential that you be guided by the ***principle of loyalty***, which says that your clarification should aim to remain true to the arguer's intent. This principle does *not* say that you should feel fondness for the arguer or that you have any obligation to try to defend the argument. It applies *before* you decide how much you like the argument; its point is strictly to ensure that the clarified argument you go on to evaluate is the arguer's argument.

Let's look at a simple example in which a paraphrase achieves greater clarity, but at the same time violates the principle of loyalty. *Forbes* magazine describes a group of New York University economists who set out to find out how our spending patterns would be affected if we had absolutely no way of knowing what our income would be or what the interest rates on our credit cards would be. The economists argued for the following conclusion:

> If the income and interest rate processes are sufficiently stochastic, then consumption eventually grows without bound.

For those of us who are not professional economists, this needs some clarification. *Forbes* lightheartedly chides the economists for their obscure writing and suggests that their conclusion really amounts to the simple truism,

> The more you have the more you spend.

The *Forbes* paraphrase is definitely clearer. No doubt about it. But there is a new problem: it isn't the authors' conclusion any more. *Stochastic*, as used by the economists, means *unpredictable*. So, despite the obscurity of their prose, you can see that they are *not* talking about consumers who have more and more income, but consumers who don't know what their income will be. A more loyal paraphrase, then, is this:

> The more uncertain you are of how much you have, the more you spend.

This, too, is clearer than the original. But it has the additional virtue of capturing what the economists seem to have had in mind. It is *their* conclusion, and thus accords with the principle of loyalty. In sum: it is a good idea to paraphrase when it clarifies the point—but not in such a way that it *changes* the point.

> *Guideline.* In your clarification, remain true to the arguer's intent.

The Arguer over Your Shoulder

A useful book on writing style by Robert Graves and Alan Hodge is titled *The Reader over Your Shoulder*. Its guiding principle is this: always write as though the reader were peering over your shoulder, insisting that everything you write be easily understood. We can adapt this advice for our purposes: when you clarify, always imagine *the arguer over your shoulder*. That is, clarify as though the arguer is always there, looking over your shoulder, insisting that you stick with the point, ready to say, "No, no, that's not at all what I had in mind."

When you fail to do this, the results can be uncomfortable. Note this retort from one of the great philosophers of our time, W. V. Quine, to a lengthy critique of some of his views by one of the great linguists of our time, Noam Chomsky:

> Chomsky's remarks leave me with feelings at once of reassurance and frustration. What I find reassuring is that he nowhere clearly disagrees with my position. What I find frustrating is that he expresses much disagreement with what he thinks to be my position.

Of course, when arguers are unclear they must bear some of the blame for a disloyal rendering of their views. Still, we must do our best to ensure that the argument we are evaluating is indeed the arguer's. Imagining that you are under the watchful eye of the arguer can serve to keep you in line.

> *Guideline.* Imagine that the arguer is looking over your shoulder to ensure that your clarification is true to the arguer's intent.

Consider Both What the Arguer Says and What the Arguer Does Not *Say.*

An obvious way to find out the arguer's intent is to note carefully what the arguer says. This focuses your attention on ***logical implication***, or what we sometimes informally call the *literal* meaning of the sentence. The logical implications of a statement are those things that absolutely must be true if the statement is true; if they were not true, there would be no imaginable way in which the statement could itself be true. Suppose you call me on the telephone and I almost immediately say to you, "I'm already very late for a meeting on another part of campus." Some of the things *logically implied* by this remark are:

I'm already very late for a meeting on another part of campus.
I'm on campus.
The campus has more than one part.
The other meeting is scheduled to have already started.

These are simply part of what I mean by the words I have used.

There are, however, many related things that *could* be false even if the statement is true; thus, they are not logically implied. These include:

The meeting has actually already started. (Everyone could be late, for example, or the building could be locked.)
I plan to attend the meeting. (I could be late even if I intend to be absent.)
I am expected at the meeting. (It could be open to everyone on campus, and thus perhaps no one would miss me.)

Logical implication surely does not cover all that I intend to communicate to you by my remark. This leads to a less obvious piece of advice: note carefully what the arguer *does not say*. This focuses your attention on ***conversational implication***—what I want you to believe, over and above the literal meanings of my words, when I express a sentence. You draw these implications on the basis of broader customs that we all follow that govern the use of certain sorts of expressions under certain circumstances. Normally if I say to you when you call, "I'm already very late for a meeting on another part of campus," what I'm *most* concerned about letting you know is,

I can't talk to you right now.

This is no part of the literal meaning of the terms I have used—that is, it is not logically implied. Rather, it is conversationally implied. Based on your experience in a lifetime of conversations, you realize that I would normally have no reason to tell you that I was late for a meeting unless I wanted you to understand that I could not talk to you right now.

Suppose, to provide another example, I recommend that you write a friend of mine to ask her advice about a job. You ask for her address and I reply, "It's somewhere in Dallas." You immediately understand that I intend to communicate the following:

> I do not know her exact address.

This is not a logical implication; it does not follow from the meanings of the terms I have used. But you instinctively understand that, under these conditions, I surely would have given you the exact address had I known it. My reason for not giving it to you must be that I did not know it.

Note that *conversation* is used here broadly to mean an interchange of ideas, whether spoken, written, or thought. Obviously, something I say to you in a face-to-face dialogue is part of a conversation. But in the larger sense of conversation, something I write in this book is also a part of a conversation, since it is aimed at a certain audience that I hope will understand it and react to it in certain ways.

To provide an example of written conversational implication, in the 1920s newspaper magnate William Randolph Hearst was out to make the mayor of New York look bad. So Hearst planted a reporter for his New York newspaper, *The New York American*, to slyly ask this question at a mayoral press conference: "Mr. Mayor, Mr. Hearst wants to know if you have a corrupt motive in supporting the Remsen Gas Bill?" The angry mayor ejected the reporter, and was further enraged to see this headline in the next day's *New York American:*

> Mayor Does Not Deny That He Has A Corrupt Motive In Supporting The Remsen Gas Bill.

The headline is literally true and does not logically imply anything that is false. But the conversational implication is that the mayor *admits* that he has a corrupt motive in supporting the Remsen Gas bill. And this is indeed false. Note that since conversational implication is another means of communicating, it is another means of lying.

Figures of speech—rhetorical devices—are especially noteworthy in considering conversational implication. They include cases in which conversational and logical implications actually conflict with one another, and conversational implication wins. (It must always win, since what you are clarifying is always the use of a sentence in a particular conversational setting—and the broader conversational context is what I, as the speaker or writer, use to indicate my intentions in using that sentence.) If I say, "Her mind is a steel trap," one of the logical implications is that her mind is a mechanism made out of steel that opens and closes and is designed for catching animals and not for thinking. In most conversational contexts (except for, perhaps, a bizarre piece of science fiction) this is so obviously false that you instinctively realize that I could not intend it, but that my real, unspoken, intent must be to draw attention to important similarities between her mind and a steel trap. So, in cases of metaphor such as this, it is *only* the conversational—and *not* the logical—implications that capture my intentions.

In Chapter 2 we covered sentences that are not in statement form—questions, commands, or even fragments, for example—but that nevertheless function as statements. *Oh to be at the beach this afternoon*! for example, though in the form of an exclamation, in many contexts also serves that same function as the declarative *I want to go to the beach this afternoon*. This is a further example of conversational implication. We understand that they are intended as statements, even if their form does not logically mark them as such. Likewise with implicit statements in arguments; sometimes they are logically implied, but usually the implication is conversational. When, for example, the daughter says to her father, "We've been waiting for a windy day to fly the kite, so we should go fly it now," her implicit premise is "Today is a windy day." This premise isn't logically implied by anything she says; rather, it is part of what she intends to communicate over and above the literal meanings of the statements she expresses. It is conversationally implied.

Unfortunately, we are not infallible interpreters of conversational implications. During much of my career as a student I worked as a waiter. I learned quickly that when a customer asked for a steak *raw*, the customer really meant *extremely rare*—until the day came when I delivered a very rare steak to a customer who complained, "But this steak isn't raw; it's been on the grill." And so it had. I now saw that I should, in this case, have been concerned only with the logical implications of his order. It did not take long to properly prepare his new steak.

Guideline. Look for indications of the arguer's intent both in what is said and in what is not said—that is, in both the logical implications and the conversational implications.

Types of Implications

1. *Logical implication*—the literal meanings of the words.
2. *Conversational implication*—what is intended above and beyond the literal meanings of the words.

Consider the Broader Context of the Argument

Almost every argument has a broader context, and the more you know about its broader context the more likely you are to correctly understand the intent of the arguer. Perhaps you can discover the circumstances under which the argument was offered, thereby better understanding its conversational implications. Perhaps you are able to examine a larger chunk of the passage in which it was written or listen to a larger portion of the conversation in which it was spoken. Perhaps you are able to learn more about the argument's author. Sometimes, of course, little such information is available. But when it is, you should take full advantage of it.

Guideline. Look for indications of the arguer's intent in the broader context.

EXERCISES Chapter 3, set (b)

Identify the given implications in each of the exercises below as either *logical* or *conversational.* Come up with a reasonable example of the other kind of implication in each case.

Sample exercise. Shopper to a store clerk: "I can't find your orange juice." Implication: Shopper is interested in buying orange juice.

Sample answer. Conversational implication. Logical implication: I can't find your fresh orange juice.

1. Instructor to student: "You cannot pass this class unless you turn in your final paper." Implication: The final paper is a class requirement.

2. Narrator on television documentary: "This series would not have been possible without the generous assistance of the Brady Corporation." Implication: The corporation funded the documentary.
3. Character in film, to his on-screen romantic interest: "I couldn't live without you." Implication: He loves her.
4. Politician to journalist: "I have never done anything illegal while in office." Implication: He could have done something illegal before he was in office.
5. Customer to car salesman: "This car is great, but it's overpriced by at least $2,000." Implication: Customer would be willing to make a deal at a lower price.

EXERCISES Chapter 3, set (c)

State a conversational implication (*not* a logical implication) of each expression below. Assume that the circumstances in each case are not unusual. In some cases you might imagine more than one conversational implication.

Sample exercise. From a review of a musical performance:
Miss X produced a series of sounds which corresponded closely with the score of "Home Sweet Home."—from a lecture by philosopher Paul Grice

Sample answer. Miss X did not sing well.

1. In a letter of recommendation for a student who is looking for a job in philosophy, the only evaluative comment is this: "I've never had a student who made fewer mistakes in spelling or grammar."
2. Said to a waiter in a restaurant, hungrily pointing to another table that was just served: "Our party got here before they did."
3. After your rich friend refuses to lend you some money, you say: "You're the sort of friend I can depend on."
4. In a textbook: The answers to the exercises are in the back of the book. (Hint: What does this conversationally imply about whether they are also at the end of each chapter?)
5. In response to your request for a phone number, I say: "I think you can find it through Directory Assistance."
6. After the first mate went on a binge, he found the next day that the captain had written in the ship's log, "The first mate was drunk tonight." When challenged by the first mate, the captain said that he

entered it in the log "because it was true." The next day the captain saw that the first mate had made the following entry in the log: "The captain was not drunk tonight."

7. Q. Did you ever stay all night with this man in New York?
A. I refuse to answer that question.
Q. Did you ever stay all night with this man in Chicago?
A. I refuse to answer that question.
Q. Did you ever stay all night with this man in Miami?
A. No.

—*Humor in the Court*, Mary Louise Gilman

THE PRINCIPLE OF CHARITY

The other important principle guiding the clarifying process is the ***principle of charity***, which requires that you adopt the paraphrase that makes the arguer as reasonable as possible.

It is often easy to interpret an argument in a way that makes it an obviously bad argument. But it may be possible to interpret the same argument in another way that is much more reasonable. When the history professor mentions "Columbus's voyage of *1942*," should you call it a gross error or forgive it as a slip of the tongue? When the newly elected senator claims she received 60 percent of the vote when the exact figure is 59.8 percent, should you charge her with distortion or interpret her as meaning *roughly* 60 percent? The principle of charity says to adopt in each case the second interpretation—the one that makes the speaker more reasonable.

This principle has a single purpose: *to enable you to be loyal to the arguer's intent.* Most people *are* fairly reasonable most of the time. So you are more likely to get it right if you choose the more reasonable interpretation. There is a chance, of course, that you will get it wrong. If you do get it wrong because you were being too charitable, the result is not so bad. The arguer might wish to thank you for improving on the original argument. And you can benefit from evaluating a better argument.

Guideline. Assume the interpretation that makes the arguer as reasonable as possible.

The Golden Rule of Clarifying

There is a fairly straightforward way of applying the principle of charity. Imagine yourself in the same circumstances as the arguer, and imagine that *you* have spoken or written the same unclear words. What are *you* likely to have intended by them? How would you want to be understood? We might term this the golden rule of clarifying: paraphrase others as you would have them paraphrase you.

Consider the simple instructions on the back of an ordinary bottle of shampoo:

> Wet hair, lather, rinse, repeat.

At first glance this seems clear enough. But think about it for a moment. Are you really being told that after you wet your hair, lather, and rinse the first time you must then repeat *all three steps*? Suddenly the instructions aren't so clear. But you know what they mean—after all, you might quite reasonably say exactly the same thing, and you know what *you* would mean if you said it. You would mean this:

> Wet hair, lather, rinse, then lather again—your hair is already wet now—and then rinse again.

In addition, you know that you don't repeat the *repeat* step and perform the procedure endlessly! (Much of this is a matter of conversational implication.) The words weren't perfectly clear, but you were instinctively able to clarify by using the principle of charity.

Notice that usually (but not always) applying this principle results in *selecting the interpretation that is most likely to make the argument sound.* When you see that there are two plausible interpretations of an argument, one with good logic and one with faulty logic, charity will normally point toward the one with good logic. Likewise, when one of the premises could be understood in a way that makes it true or in a way that makes it false, charity will normally point toward the paraphrase that is true.

But this is not *always* the case. In many circumstances a perfectly reasonable person might offer an unsound argument. Consider, for example, the following excerpt adapted from the writings of William Emerson, an 18th century disciple of Sir Isaac Newton's:

> Unlike those who went before him, Newton admits nothing but what he gains from experiments and accurate observations. *It is a mere joke to talk of Newton's philosophy being overthrown.* He will always, therefore, be regarded as the greatest scientist of all.

Look only at the highlighted sentence, which serves as a premise for the final sentence. Surely Emerson does not mean that it is *literally* a joke to talk of Newton's philosophy being overthrown; this claim would make the premise obviously false. Let us, therefore, charitably allow that Emerson's real point (which follows by conversational implication) is this:

> Newton's philosophy will never be overthrown.

But notice that this paraphrase is still false, for Newton's "philosophy" has indeed been overthrown—by Einstein's. But it was not unreasonable for Emerson to hold to this view; if I had been in the same circumstances—two centuries before Einstein and amazed at Newton's brilliant successes—this is what *I* would have meant had *I* written the same sentence. So it is a charitable paraphrase, even though clearly false.

You will not always be able to arrive at the arguer's true intent by this technique. You may be stymied for any of several reasons. The arguer might simply express the argument too badly. The arguer might not know the arguer's own true intent. Or it might be that there isn't enough context available to be confident of the arguer's intent. In addition, even when it is possible to arrive at the arguer's true intent, there may be several equally good ways of clearly paraphrasing it. *Newton will remain preeminent in the field of natural philosophy* or *No scientist will ever disprove Newton's philosophy* would also be acceptable paraphrases of Emerson's statement above, for example.

Thus, there is seldom a single correct way of paraphrasing an argument, all others being wrong. It does not follow, however, that anything goes. It is usually possible to determine what is likely to be closer and what is likely to be farther from the arguer's intent, and what is a clearer and what is a more obscure way of expressing it.

Guideline. Ask what you probably would have meant had you expressed the same words under similar circumstances.

EXERCISES Chapter 3, set (d)

There is a problem in interpreting each of the following passages. Explain the problem and indicate the more charitable interpretation. The difficulty is highlighted.

Sample exercise. "Noziere was a self-confessed young murderess of the thirties whose case became notorious largely because, having killed *her father*, she then complained of incest. Since she was almost certainly *not his daughter*, this seems rather hard cheese."—Derek Malcolm, *Manchester Guardian*, (cited by Malcolm Acock, *Informal Logic Examples and Exercises.)*

Sample answer. Appears to be contradictory—she is almost certainly not her father's daughter. Presumably the reviewer means that she killed her *purported* father, but was almost certainly not his *real* daughter.

1. A classified ad reads: AUTO REPAIR SERVICE. Free pick-up and delivery. Try us once and you'll *never go anywhere* again.
2. "An accomplished swimmer who has only one hand was disqualified from a local swimming event because he failed to touch the end of the pool with both hands. Greg Hammond, 16, placed second in a men's 100-meter race at swimming championships last weekend in Narooma. . . . But officials reluctantly disqualified him after an appeal was lodged pointing out that international rules specify that swimmers must finish *by touching the pool with both hands.* Hammond was born with a right arm that ends just below his elbow."—*Los Angeles Times* (This has to do with charity toward those who wrote the law, not toward the swimmer—though in the end each produces the same result.)
3. "It was Feshbach who, two years ago, first disclosed an increase in Soviet infant *morality.*"—*Daily Herald* of Wausau-Merrill, Wisconsin
4. "St. Luke tells of the shepherds going to the *manager.*"—from the program for a Christmas candlelight service at Connecticut College

5. Classified ad: And now, the Superstore—unequaled in size, unmatched in variety, unrivaled *inconvenience.*
6. In a Paris hotel elevator: Please leave your *values* at the front desk.
7. "The logical *man* is *always* self-righteous and therefore *inhuman* and therefore wrong, while the reasonable man suspects that perhaps he is wrong and is therefore *always* right."—Lin Yutang, *The Importance of Living*

THE STRAW MAN FALLACY

It can be very tempting to interpret an argument so as to make it an easy target. But, unless the bad argument is clearly what the arguer intends, this is contrary to the principles of loyalty and charity. Yielding to this temptation results in a well-known fallacy. ***Fallacies*** will be mentioned often throughout this text; they are defined simply as the easiest-to-make types of intellectual mistakes. The easy-to-make mistake, in this case, is the ***straw man fallacy.*** This fallacy is so named because a straw man is a lightweight construction of one's own devising, much easier to knock down than a real man.

In an article from *Creation/Science* titled "The Impossible Voyage of Noah's Ark," Robert Moore argues against creationists who defend the literal truth of the biblical account of Noah's ark. His central point against them is this:

> Nearly every defender of the Noah story argues that the interior of the ark could have held literally hundreds of standard-sized railroad stock cars and thus was quite roomy. But they ignore the federal law which requires a train on a long haul to stop every 28 hours, to unload the stock, to feed and water them, and to give them a five-hour rest period. This may be just a minor inconvenience to American ranchers, but it would have been quite impossible for Noah. The fact that every creationist has triumphantly trotted out his train statistics, yet overlooked this decisive flaw, demonstrates once again the sloppiness of creationists' research.

At first glance, Moore seems to be saying that the creationist account must be mistaken *because their account would put Noah in violation of federal law*—surely an unacceptable infringement for such a godly man as Noah! In standard clarifying format, it might look like this.

1. If the story of Noah's ark were true, then Noah would've had to violate federal law.
2. Noah would not have violated federal law.

∴ C. The story of Noah's ark is not true.

We can defend this paraphrase—after all, doesn't Moore say that the "decisive flaw" is that "they ignore the federal law"? And it would be fun to critique that premise by reminding Moore that, to the best of our knowledge, that particular federal law was not in place in the year 3000 B.C.—thus, premise 1 is obviously false.

But because it is so easy to knock it down, we should ask whether we might have missed the point. What else might Moore mean by his words, however clumsily he has put it? How would *we* want to be interpreted had we written those words? Probably as saying that the creationist account must be mistaken *because the very factors that later gave rise to the federal law would have made Noah's voyage impracticable and perhaps even cruel.* This is a harder point to dispute, makes the argument more interesting, and is almost certainly what Moore has in mind. The improved—more charitable and thus more loyal—outline might look like this:

1. If the story of Noah's ark were true, then Noah would've had to treat the animals in a way that was cruel and probably fatal.
2. Noah would not have treated the animals in a way that was cruel and probably fatal.

∴ C. The story of Noah's ark is not true.

The straw man fallacy is a fallacy that has to do with *conversational relevance.* Suppose I adopted the "straw man" version of Moore's argument. My own argument against his first premise would be sound: my premise (that no federal law was in place in 3000 B.C.) would be true and my conclusion (that Noah, thus, did not violate federal law) would logically follow. But *my* argument would nevertheless be defective for the simple reason that it would be conversationally *irrelevant.* It would miss the point. It would be offered in the context of evaluating Moore's argument but would actually be an evaluation of another argument, not Moore's.

Arguments that commit the straw man fallacy miss the point in a very specific way—they miss it by making the target easier than it really is. They form a species of a broader sort of ***fallacy of missing the point,*** traditionally termed the *fallacy of ignoratio elenchi.* This broader fallacy, which includes the straw man fallacy, consists in this: apparently addressing the question at issue while actually addressing some other question.

(*Elenchi* is from a Greek term for *cross-examination*; so this might be said to be the fallacy of ignoring—*ignoratio*—the question that is being asked—the *elenchi*).

Many arguments occur in a context where there is a definite question being considered. Perhaps the arguer has set out an explicit agenda or—perhaps there is a dialogue between two arguers. When the argument you are evaluating occurs in such a context, you should be prepared to consider in your evaluation not only whether it is sound, but also whether it commits a fallacy of conversational relevance.

The procedure of clarifying and evaluating, as elaborated in this book, is usually part of a dialogue with the arguer and thus usually occurs in such a context. (Sometimes the dialogue is nothing more than an internal dialogue with yourself, as you reason alone about answers to your own questions.) Be especially careful that you do not commit this fallacy as you attempt to clarify the argument you intend to evaluate.

Guideline. Ask whether your paraphrase makes the argument too easy to attack. If it does, then you are violating the principle of charity and committing the straw man fallacy (which is a version of the fallacy of missing the point).

EXERCISES Chapter 3, set (e)

Outline each of these arguments in standard clarifying format. Where appropriate, paraphrase in accordance with the principles of loyalty and charity.

1. "Paleontologist R. Bakker presented evidence, based on the stride and leg length of some dinosaurs, that their walking speed averaged about 3 miles per hour—about four times as fast as that of present-day lizards and turtles, and comparable to the speeds of moose, deer, bull and other warm-blooded animals. Because the average cruising speed reflects an animal's metabolism, Bakker argues that many dinosaurs were warm-blooded."—*Science News*
2. It is said that Socrates had his character read by one of the first professional physiognomists, Zopyrus. As the story goes, Zopyrus de-

scribed Socrates, that wisest of men, as "stupid and thick-witted because he had not got hollows in the neck above the collarbone" and added that he was, among other vices, addicted to women.

3. "Psychics can perform as readily across the Atlantic as they can over the dinner table. To a physicist like Einstein this was most surprising. Accordingly, he wrote to a correspondent in 1946, 'but I find it suspicious . . . that the distance of the subject from the cards or from the "sender" has no influence on the result. This is, a priori, improbable to the highest degree, consequently the result is doubtful.'"—Derek Gjertsen, *Science and Philosophy* (Outline Einstein's argument.)
4. "Acheson and Senator Robert Taft were both members of the governing body of Yale University. An important difference of opinion arose over the question of whether all undergraduate students should be required to take a course in mathematics. When Senator Taft argued that he had never taken a course in mathematics and, therefore, saw no reason for others to do so, Acheson quietly said: 'The defense rests.'"—Paul H. Nitze, *Tension between Opposites* (Outline the argument that *Acheson* seems to have in mind.)
5. "Ocean temperature is now virtually the same as it was in the 1940s. Since two-thirds of the buildup of CO_2 has taken place since 1940, the MIT data blow all of the global warming forecasts into a cocked hat."—*Forbes*

SUMMARY OF CHAPTER THREE

An argument must be clarified before it is evaluated. This process requires that you do two things concurrently: that you outline the argument in standard format, so that it is clear exactly which statements are premises and which are conclusions; and that you paraphrase it, so that any negative effects of rhetoric and other distracting language are minimized. The point is to express the argument as clearly as possible so it is as easy as possible to tell whether the premises are true and whether the logic is good.

Two general principles regulate clarifying. The principle of loyalty requires that your paraphrase remain true to the arguer's intent; this can be aided by imagining the arguer watching over your shoulder. And the principle of charity, which is a way of getting at the arguer's intent when the context is not helpful, requires that your paraphrase always assume that the arguer is as reasonable as possible. One way of doing this is to consider how you would want to be paraphrased if you had said the same thing under similar circumstances.

If you fail to be loyal and charitable, you may be offering an argument of your own that commits a fallacy of relevance. The fallacy of missing the point (also known as the fallacy of *ignoratio elenchi*) is committed when the argument you evaluate is not the arguer's argument. The straw man fallacy is a certain sort of missing the point—the fallacy of setting up a version of the argument that is easy to knock down.

GUIDELINES FOR CHAPTER THREE

- Outline each argument in standard clarifying format.
- Paraphrase each argument for greater clarity as you are outlining it in standard clarifying format.
- In your clarification, remain true to the arguer's intent.
- Imagine that the arguer is looking over your shoulder to ensure that your clarification is true to the arguer's intent.
- Look for indications of the arguer's intent both in what is said and in what is not said—that is, in both the logical implications and the conversational implications.
- Look for indications of the arguer's intent in the broader context.
- Assume the interpretation that makes the arguer as reasonable as possible.
- Ask what you probably would have meant had you expressed the same words under similar circumstances.
- Ask whether your paraphrase makes the argument too easy to attack. If it does, then you are violating the principle of charity and committing the straw man fallacy (which is a version of the fallacy of missing the point).

GLOSSARY FOR CHAPTER THREE

Clarifying—ensuring that the argument is expressed as clearly as possible so it is as easy as possible to tell whether the premises are true, whether the logic is good, and whether the argument is relevant to the conversation.

Conversational implication—what the speaker or writer wants the audience to believe, over and above the literal meanings of the words that are expressed. These implications are drawn on the basis of broader customs that we all follow that govern the use of certain sorts of expressions under certain circumstances.

Fallacy—an easy-to-make type of intellectual mistake.

Fallacy of missing the point—conversational fallacy that errs by answering the wrong question. Also known as the fallacy of *ignoratio elenchi. Elenchi* is from a Greek term for *cross-examination*; this might be said to be the fallacy of ignoring (*ignoratio*) the question that is being asked (the *elenchi*).

Logical implication—those things that must be true if the statement is true; if they were not true, there would be no imaginable way in which the statement could be true. Logical implications have to do with the *literal* meaning of the statement.

Principle of charity—requires that you adopt the paraphrase that makes the arguer as reasonable as possible. This principle provides a way of aiming for the arguer's intentions when the context is unhelpful and thus is subordinate to the principle of loyalty.

Principle of loyalty—requires that your clarification aim to remain true to the arguer's intent. Imagine that the arguer is looking over your shoulder.

Rhetoric—principles of persuasive writing or speaking. Rhetoric can help or hurt the argument's clarity. It helps when it is used to make good arguments easy to accept on their own merits.

Straw man fallacy—uncharitably representing an argument or position in a way that makes it too easy to attack. This is a variety of the fallacy of missing the point. This fallacy is so named because a straw man is a lightweight construction of one's own devising, much easier to knock down than a real man.

CHAPTER FOUR

Streamlining

His reasons are as two grains of wheat hid in two bushels of chaff; you shall seek all day 'ere you find them.

—William Shakespeare, *The Merchant of Venice*

"When you come tomorrow, bring my football boots. Also, if humanly possible, Irish water spaniel. Urgent. Regards. Tuppy."
"What do you make of that, Jeeves?"
"As I interpret the document, sir, Mr. Glossop wishes you, when you come tomorrow, to bring his football boots. Also, if humanly possible, an Irish water spaniel. He hints that the matter is urgent, and sends his regards."
"Yes, that's how I read it, too. . . ."

—P. G. Wodehouse, "The Ordeal of Young Tuppy"

TOPICS

Paraphrasing Only with Statements
Eliminating Unnecessary Words
Neutralizing Slanted Language

Streamlined objects, like airplanes or torpedoes, have had nonessential features removed so that those features will not impede movement. The ***streamlining*** of arguments has the same purpose. Nonessential features of the argument are removed so that they will not get in the way of evaluation. Streamlining is one important aspect of paraphrasing. Not every passage needs to be streamlined before it can be evaluated—take, for example, the letter from Mr. Glossop in the lead quotation. But many are closer to Shakespeare's two grains of wheat in two bushels of chaff—they are far easier to evaluate if you first discard the chaff.

PARAPHRASING ONLY WITH STATEMENTS

In everyday language—as noted in Chapter 2—arguments often include expressions that are not in statement form, but that nevertheless function as statements. It is necessary to reword these sentences so that in your clarification they are in statement form.

Practical reasoning provides an important opportunity for this sort of paraphrasing. Practical reasoning is concerned with reasons for *doing* things. I might, for example, deliberate over reasons that bear on whether to move to a new town, or I might give you reasons for changing your major. But conclusions like *Move to a new town* and *Change your major* could not be true or false (though they could be wise or foolish, followed or ignored). They are in imperative, not declarative, form. Notice, however, that reasons offered for *doing* something are also reasons offered for *believing* something—believing, namely, that it should be done. Imperative sentences, then, should be paraphrased to statements such as *I should move to a new town* or *You should change your major.* Either of these statements can be true or false.

Consider this cheerful argument:

> Be glad of life because it gives you the chance to love and to work and to play and to look up at the stars.

The explicit premise, based on the inference indicator term *because,* is this:

1. Life gives you the chance to love and to work and to play and to look up at the stars.

And the conclusion, apparently, is *Be glad of life*. But—so that we're working with sentences that can be true or false—it should be paraphrased as the statement:

∴ *C.* You should be glad of life.

Rhetorical questions—questions that do not call for an answer, but rather assert something—also should be paraphrased as statements, since, phrased as they are in interrogative form, they cannot be true or false. Consider this little passage from Raymond Smullyan's *This Book Needs No Title:*

> But that doesn't seem to bother him! As he says, "Why should I worry about dying? It's not going to happen in my lifetime!"

The explicit premise is this:

1. Dying is not going to happen in my lifetime.

But the conclusion *Why should I worry about dying?* must be paraphrased, since, as a question, it cannot be true or false. A much clearer version of the conclusion is this:

∴ *C.* I should not worry about dying.

Fragments—partial sentences—can also function as statements, and when they do should be paraphrased accordingly. For example, look at this tongue-in-cheek passage from Ambrose Bierce:

> In his great work on *Divergent Lines of Racial Evolution*, the learned Professor Brayfugle argues from the prevalence of this gesture—the shrug—among Frenchmen, that they are descended from turtles and it is simply a survival of the habit of retracting the head inside the shell.

The explicit premise of this argument doesn't even appear as a complete sentence. It is easy to find it—the inference indicator *argues from* makes it clear that a premise is coming next. But all that comes next is the series of prepositional phrases *from the prevalence of this gesture—the shrug—among Frenchmen*. So, the fragment must be converted into a statement, namely:

1. The shrug is prevalent among Frenchmen.

The conclusion, of course, is this:

∴ *C.* Frenchmen are descended from turtles.

It goes beyond the scope of this book to judge whether this is true or false.

Remember that the ultimate aim of reasoning is to know the truth. Premises and conclusions will not be true if they *cannot* be true; and they cannot be true if they are not statements.

> *Guideline.* Include only statements in your clarification. If a premise or conclusion is expressed as a partial sentence or a nondeclarative sentence, paraphrase it as a statement.

Paraphrase These Expressions as Statements

1. Imperatives that conclude practical reasoning.
2. Rhetorical questions.
3. Fragments.

EXERCISES Chapter 4, set (a)

In each of the following passages, paraphrase the highlighted portion in statement form.

Sample exercise. "I was dismayed, in fact, when talking recently to a group of aspiring young writers to discover that none of them had read Mr. DeVries and that they had indeed hardly even heard of him. *Which is their loss,* of course, for his works make up a shelf of some of the funniest books written in America during the last 30 years."—Thomas Meehan, *New York Times Book Review*

Sample answer. Aspiring young writers who have not read Peter DeVries have been deprived of something valuable.

1. "*Beware,* for I am fearless and therefore powerful."—Mary Shelley, *Frankenstein*

2. On the TV screen: a white-haired woman sits in an overstuffed chair and says, "All this talk of cutting Social Security is really making me nervous. *How can I be so sure Barney will do the right thing by us older people?* She smiles. "Because he's my son."—ad for Barney Frank for Representative
3. "*Go in through the narrow gate,* because the gate to hell is wide and the road that leads to it is easy, and there are many who travel it. But the gate to life is narrow and the way that leads to it is hard, and there are few people who find it."—Matthew 7:13-14
4. "Barry Setterfield was alone one night when the Lord invisibly entered his room and spoke to him. They argued about creation for four hours. When Setterfield awoke next morning, he was a creationist, but he whispered one lingering doubt: If the earth is young, as the Bible says, how can we see distant galaxies? Instantly the Lord replied aloud, '*What makes you think the speed of light is constant?*'"—*Skeptical Inquirer*
5. "In Newport, realtors play nearly religious roles. They deliver their clients to terrestrial glory. '*What is wrong with hedonism?*' the broker asked. '*What is wrong with clear-skinned people raising their children and living athletically? What responsibility do these people have to those who live elsewhere?*'"—Steve Oney, *California* (not an argument)
6. "But isn't $2,700 for a 50-inch TV set too steep for most people's budgets? Goldberg is ready for that one, too. '*If you sell somebody a mountain cabin, a boat, or a piano, how much enjoyment are they really going to get out of it, compared to something like this that they will use every day?*'" —*Forbes*

ELIMINATING UNNECESSARY WORDS

Eliminating Discounts

Often an arguer acknowledges possible objections to the argument and explicitly sets aside those objections. That is to say, arguers *discount* possible objections to the argument. Discounts are best understood in contrast to premises. As we have seen, premises are statements the arguer offers as *supporting* the conclusion. ***Discounts*** are statements the arguer offers as *not* *undermining* the conclusion, but discounts are typically neither premises nor conclusions and should usually not be included in your clarification.

Suppose I really want you to read a certain book. I might say to you, "Look, I know that you don't have much time for fiction nowadays and I admit that the reviews have mostly been negative. But you should read it anyway. It will give you more insight into yourself than anything else you've ever read." My conclusion is *You should read the book.* By pointing out the poor reviews and your lack of time, I surely am not giving reasons *for* reading it; these would normally be reasons for *not* reading it.

I achieve, however, at least two important things. First, I make it less likely that you misunderstand my meaning. Otherwise you might think, "Perhaps he means some *other* book, since he must know *that* book got terrible reviews." So discounts help in the *interpretation* of the argument. Second, I make it less likely that you underestimate how thoroughly I have considered my argument and how serious I am about it. Had I not mentioned the two possible objections, you might have supposed I did not know about them and that I might well give up my argument upon learning about them. As a result of my mentioning them, you are probably less likely to raise those objections yourself. Discounts help to frame the dialogue—they are *conversationally* useful.

But they do not normally have any bearing on the logic of the argument. Being reminded that you have little time to read and that the reviews have been bad does not provide you with a reason to read the book I recommend. So you should look to discounts to help you understand the arguer's intent, but you should normally not include them in your clarification.

Guideline. Exclude discounts from your clarification of the argument.

EXERCISES Chapter 4, set (b)

Rewrite each of the following short arguments, adding one discount but otherwise leaving it the same.

Sample exercise. You need the money and the hours are good, so you should go ahead and take the job waiting tables.

Sample answer. Even though you never were very good with people, you need the money and the hours are good, so you should go ahead and take the job waiting tables.

1. I think you should buy your mother an answering machine, since you never get any credit for the times you call and she isn't in.
2. My high school biology teacher was better than my college biology teacher, since he really cared about us students.
3. Because of all the cultural diversity, Louisiana is a great state to live in.
4. The tax system should be reformed—it's so complicated that nobody can understand it.
5. Women are much more attuned to people's feelings, so they make better doctors than men.

Discount Indicators

The best clues to the presence of discounts are ***discount indicators*** (sometimes also called *adversatives*, since they indicate a nonsupportive, or adversarial, relationship). In the previous argument I urged, "*but* you should read it anyway." *But* is perhaps the most common discount indicator. It typically points backward to discount the previous clause. Other backward-pointing discount indicators are illustrated in the brief passages (not arguments) below:

I woke up with a fever. I decided, *however*, that I should go to work.
It rained all day. *Nevertheless*, we had a wonderful time.

Other discount indicators typically point forward to discount the clause that immediately follows. These include:

In spite of the great care I took, I managed to put my foot in my mouth.
Although it cost far more than we expected, we bought the stereo system anyway.
Regardless of how hard you have worked, we have to fire you.

Note that in clarifying an argument, you are to eliminate not only the indicator term but also the entire discounted clause. Consider the following passage adapted from Charles Peirce:

> Though those who claim to know everything there is to know about science seem to me comical, I highly respect them, for they make up the majority of those who have anything interesting to say.

The first clause—that those who think they know everything about science are comical—is discounted by the forward-pointing *though*. The argument comes next:

1. Those who claim to know everything about science make up the majority of those who have anything interesting to say.

∴ C. Those who claim to know everything about science are worthy of respect.

The discounted clause is not a part of the argument, so it is eliminated from the clarification.

These terms are not perfectly reliable indicators of the presence of discounts; sometimes they merely introduce a negatively stated premise—for example *We are either plants or animals; however, we are not plants, so we are animals*. This may be clarified as follows:

1. We are either plants or animals.
2. We are not plants.

∴ C. We are animals.

Although it is introduced by the term *however*, the statement *We are not plants* is essential to the support of the conclusion. It is not merely a "statement that does not undermine the conclusion," as it would be were it a mere discount.[1] Before eliminating the presumed discount, be sure the argument can function without it.

Guideline. Use discount indicator terms to identify discounts, making sure it is a discount rather than a negatively stated premise or conclusion.

[1] *But*, in particular, is frequently used to introduce premises in mathematical arguments.

Some Discount Indicators

BACKWARD-POINTING	FORWARD-POINTING
But	In spite of
However	Despite
Nevertheless	Although
Nonetheless	Though
Yet	Regardless of
Still	Notwithstanding

EXERCISES Chapter 4, set (c)

Identify the discount and the discount indicator in each of the following passages (many of which are not arguments).

Sample exercise. The following is an excerpt from a letter from Mozart to his father shortly after Mozart left Paris:

Le Gros purchased from me the two overtures and the sinfonia concertante. He thinks that he alone has them, but he is wrong, for they are still fresh in my mind, and as soon as I get home, I shall write them down again.

—*Musical Heritage Review*

Sample answer. Discount: He thinks that he alone has them. Indicator: but. (Note that the discount is important here for making clear the conclusion *He is wrong to think that he alone has them.*)

1. "It's illegal," said a 17-year-old computer student. . . . "But it's fun." The teenager was talking about stealing computer programs.—television interview
2. "*Gandhi* won the Oscar, but I doubt that many men will hold Mahatma Gandhi up to their sons as a role model, even though his non-violent methods liberated an entire nation without bloodshed."—*Los Angeles Times* (Note: there are two discounts in this passage.)

3. "Ours may be an age of reason—or at least high-tech reducibility—but belief in the irrational, the occult, and the supernatural seems almost as persistent and pervasive today as it was in the Middle Ages."—James Cornell, *Psychology Today*
4. "American music may now be good enough to be judged by the highest standards, but the standards themselves, it can be argued, are still set in Europe."—Christopher Lasch, *Harper's*
5. "Although the United States remains the largest single market for telecommunications equipment, with approximately $15 billion in sales last year, the non-U.S. market is now almost twice as large. Moreover, the non-U.S. market is growing more rapidly."—Huey Lewis, *The Real World War*
6. "Dreams are not to be likened to the unregulated sounds that rise from a musical instrument struck by the blow of some external force instead of by a player's hand; they are not meaningless, they are not absurd; they do not imply that one portion of our store of ideas is asleep while another is beginning to wake. On the contrary, they are psychical phenomena of complete validity—fulfillments of wishes."—Sigmund Freud, *The Interpretation of Dreams*
7. "Roger Sessions and Elliot Carter are composers of undoubted stature. Charles Ives is a most intriguing 'original.' Up to this point in its history, however, American music has been of an essentially provincial character. In support of this, let me point out that the great symphony of the 'new world' is by Dvorak."—George Steiner, "The Archives of Eden," *Salamagundi* (Dvorak was not an American; he was a great Czech composer whose *New World Symphony* was written while in America and in honor of America. Sessions, Carter, and Ives are prominent American composers.)
8. "Those very scenes of stark sexual despair are the tip-off to what's wrong with the movie. They are so strong that they deserve to be in a movie that is sincere, honest and true. But *Blue Velvet* surrounds them with a story that's marred by sophomoric satire and cheap shots. The director is either denying the strength of his material or trying to defuse it by pretending that it's all part of a campy in-joke."—Roger Ebert, *Chicago Sun-Times*

Eliminating Attitude Indicators, Report Indicators, and Inference Indicators

Another item to eliminate in the streamlining process is the ***attitude indicator***, which indicates the arguer's attitude of either belief or disbelief toward a statement. Philip Howard writes in *Verbatim*,

> I believe that the criticism of the *Oxford English Dictionary* for neglecting spoken English is largely mistaken. It seems to me that a new word or new use is written down somewhere almost as soon as it is coined.

Without any paraphrasing, the conclusion of Howard's argument would have to be expressed in this way:

> I believe that the criticism of the *Oxford English Dictionary* for neglecting spoken English is largely mistaken.

But surely Howard's argument is not about *himself* (which it would be if *I* were the subject of this conclusion); it is an argument about a certain criticism of the *Oxford English Dictionary*. The conclusion of the argument, then, should really be paraphrased thus:

> The criticism of the *Oxford English Dictionary* for neglecting spoken English is largely mistaken.

I believe that merely expresses Howard's attitude toward the conclusion—an attitude of belief. *It seems to me that* works exactly the same way with his premise. The clarified version runs as follows:

1. A new word or new use is written down somewhere almost as soon as it is coined.

∴ *C*. The criticism of the *Oxford English Dictionary* for neglecting spoken English is largely mistaken.

There are many other such attitude indicators, including the following:

I think that
Everybody knows that
It is clear that

The rule for paraphrasing these terms is simple: drop them in favor of simply stating what is believed, what is thought, what everybody (presumably) knows, or what is (presumably) clear.

Other terms express an attitude of *disbelief.* Famed biologist Ernst Mayr describes in *Animal Species and Evolution* how he lived with a tribe of Papuans in the mountains of New Guinea.

> These superb woodsmen had 136 names for the 137 species of birds I distinguished (confusing only two nondescript species of warblers). That Stone Age man recognizes the same entities of nature as Western university-trained scientists refutes rather decisively the claim that species are a product of the human imagination.

Refutes rather decisively the claim that is the attitude indicator, indicating an attitude of disbelief. Others include:

I deny that
I doubt that
It is wrong to suppose that

Drop these terms in favor of the *negation* of the statement that is disbelieved, refuted, denied, doubted, or wrongly supposed—that is, in favor of the disbelieved statement with *it is not the case that* or *it is false that* in front of it. The statement that Ernst Mayr disbelieves—the one that he says is decisively refuted—is:

Species are a product of the human imagination.

The negation of this statement—and the conclusion of his argument—is:

It is not the case that species are a product of the human imagination.

You could have expressed the same thing more smoothly by the statement,

Species are *not* a product of the human imagination.

This sort of negation is usually acceptable in your paraphrase, so long as you do it with care. But there are traps to avoid. Suppose, for example, you want to write the negation of *Every student will pass the course.* Here you have to be wary. *Not every student will pass the course* is acceptable, but *Every student will not pass the course* can mean something altogether different—namely, that every student will fail. If you are in any doubt, it is always safe to mechanically write *It is not the case that. . . .*

Note that attitude indicators, whether they indicate belief or disbelief, can reflect varying degrees of confidence in one's attitude. Some terms—call them *hedges*—suggest tentativeness on the arguer's part; these include:

Perhaps
Probably
Apparently
It seems that
I have my doubts whether
I suspect that

Other terms—call them *assurances*—suggest confidence on the arguer's part; these include:

Certainly
Everybody knows that
Clearly
Obviously
I categorically deny that

Phrases like *I believe that* can be either assurances or hedges, depending on whether we stress the *I* or the *believe.*[2]

Often an argument is expressed as a report of someone *else's* attitude, an attitude that the reporter may or may not agree with. In *Fads and Fallacies in the Name of Science*, for example, Martin Gardner writes:

> In essence, Gall and his disciples argued that human personality consisted of a number of independent, inborn mental "faculties," each of which was localized in a part of the brain. The larger the size of each region, the stronger the faculty. Consequently, an examination of skull bumps would reveal a person's character.

[2]Stress on *I* usually indicates assurance while stress on *believe* usually indicates a hedge. In some contexts, however, stress on *believe* indicates assurance: "I refuse to give multiple choice tests, since I *believe* in essay exams."

There is an argument in this passage; but the writer is reporting it, not arguing it. The phrase *Gall and his disciples argued that* is the ***report indicator***, the term that shows the argument is being reported by, but is not necessarily embraced by, the speaker or writer. It too should be eliminated from the clarification. Here is a brief clarification of the explicit portion of the argument:

1. Human personality consists of a number of independent, inborn mental "faculties," each of which is localized in a part of the brain.
2. The larger the size of each region, the stronger the faculty.

∴ *C.* An examination of skull bumps reveals a person's character.

Finally, inference indicators should be eliminated from your final clarification. Terms such as *because* and *thus* are very useful in distinguishing between premises and conclusions, but they are no longer useful once the argument is in standard clarifying format. The format itself clearly indicates which statements are premises and which are conclusions.

Guideline. Eliminate attitude indicators, which are indicators of belief or of disbelief; insert a negation at the beginning of disbelieved statements. Also eliminate report indicators and inference indicators.

EXERCISES Chapter 4, set (d)

Eliminate the attitude, report, and inference indicators from the passages below. If there is an argument, clarify it.

Sample exercise. Descartes argued that because God is not a deceiver, our clear and distinct perceptions of the world around us must be true.

Sample answer.

1. God is not a deceiver.

∴ *C.* Our clear and distinct perceptions of the world around us must be true.

1. "Is this evidence that the stress level in the ground in Southern California is building back to the point where there will be another great

earthquake?" Lindh asked in an interview. "The answer is probably yes."—*Los Angeles Times* (No argument to be clarified.)

2. "Babies with a common and often devastating birth defect, spina bifida, are much less likely to be paralyzed if they are delivered by Caesarean, a study has found."—*New York Times* (No argument to be clarified.)
3. "Kuznetsov became a creationist because in his mind there was no other recourse after he lost his faith in evolution. . . . But, he said, he is not against teaching the theory of evolution 'because it exists—but I don't believe evolution exists.'"—Associated Press (There are two separate arguments—one in each sentence. There is also a discount to be eliminated.)
4. "I stopped believing in Santa Claus when I was six. Mother took me to see him in a department store and he asked for my autograph."—Shirley Temple (Though there is no inference indicator, there is an argument.)

Eliminating Repetition

Repeating part of an argument in the same or different words is often rhetorically effective. But it has no use in your clarification of the argument. When there is such repetition, pick the best alternative—or make one up—and say it once. Pick the alternative that is clearest, most loyal, and most charitable.

In *The Natural History of Nonsense*, for example, Bergen Evans writes,

> The civilized man has a moral obligation to be skeptical, to demand the credentials of all statements that claim to be facts, for a refusal to come to an unjustified conclusion is an element in an honest man's religion.

His argument can be simply clarified:

1. A refusal to come to an unjustified conclusion is an element in an honest man's religion.

∴ *C.* The civilized man has a moral obligation to be skeptical.

This paraphrase eliminates from the conclusion the clause *to demand the credentials of all statements that claim to be facts*, since it seems to amount to another way of saying *to be skeptical.* The two clauses do not mean exactly the same thing, but nothing important seems to turn on the difference. You must rely on the context in deciding whether the statement or phrase is being repeated in different words for rhetorical effect or whether the arguer really has a different point to make. In most cases, it is easy to tell.

There is an exception to the *eliminate repetition* guideline. If an argument repeats—perhaps in disguised form—a premise as the conclusion, then you must repeat it in your clarification. As already mentioned in Chapter 1, these arguments usually commit the fallacy of begging the question.

> *Guideline.* Eliminate repetition of statements and phrases that do not add to the argument; use whatever expression best captures the arguer's meaning.

EXERCISES Chapter 4, set (e)

Paraphrase to eliminate the repetition and, where there is an argument, clarify it.

Sample exercise. "With digital images there is no difference between an 'original' and a copy. Since 'discrete states *can* be replicated precisely,' a digital image that is 'a thousand generations away from the original is indistinguishable in quality from any of its progenitors. A digital copy is not a debased descendent but is absolutely indistinguishable from the original.'"—*Art in America*

Sample answer.

1. Discrete states can be replicated precisely.

∴ *C.* With digital images there is no difference between an "original" and a copy. (Note that the conclusion is stated in the passage in *three* different ways.)

1. Salesman: There's never been anything like this widget. It's one of a kind. First thing of its kind on the planet. So you shouldn't pass it up!
2. They have the highest payroll and the best players. No doubt about it, the Yankees will win the pennant. They'll take home all the marbles this year.

3. "My teacher told me: 'Always question authority,'" said Paul Grugin, 22, one of two dozen young people interviewed by the *New York Times* in Columbus, Ohio. "You can question authority," he added, but in doing so, "you can burden authority." So, he said, let the authorities make their decisions: "Let them authoritate."—*New York Times* (There is also a discount.)
4. "Proponents of molecular computers argue that it is possible to make one because biological systems perform those processes all the time. Proponents of artificial intelligence have argued for years that the existence of the brain is proof that it is possible to make a small machine that thinks like a brain. It is a powerful argument. Biological systems already exist that compute information in a better way than digital computers do."—*Los Angeles Times* (There are also various indicators to be eliminated.)
5. "Surely also there is something strange in representing the man of perfect blessedness as a solitary or a recluse. Nobody would deliberately choose to have all the good things in the world, if there was a condition that he was to have them all by himself. Man is a social animal, and the need for company is in his blood. Therefore the happy man must have company, for he has everything that is naturally good, and it will not be denied that it is better to associate with friends than with strangers, with men of virtue than with the ordinary run of persons. We conclude then that the happy man needs friends."—Aristotle, *Ethics*
6. "So death, the most terrifying of ills, is nothing to us, since so long as we exist, death is not with us; but when death comes, then we do not exist. It does not then concern either the living or the dead, since for the former, it is not, and the latter are no more."—Epicurus, "Letter to Menoeceus"
7. "Amidst all this bustle 'tis not reason, which carries the prize, but eloquence; and no man needs ever despair of gaining proselytes to the most extravagant hypothesis, who has art enough to represent it in any favourable colours. The victory is not gained by the men at arms, who manage the pike and the sword; but by the trumpeters, drummers, and musicians of the army."—David Hume, *Treatise of Human Nature* (Not an argument, so no need to also clarify it. In your paraphrase of the passage, also eliminate the discount.)

Eliminating Wordiness

> In the early 1800s a leading logic text sagely warned, A very *long* discussion is one of the most effective veils of Fallacy; . . . a Fallacy which when stated barely . . . would not deceive a child, may deceive half the world if *diluted* in a quarto volume.

This has been adapted to the realm of corporate annual reports to shareholders and dubbed the *windbag postulate*. "The chairman's verbosity," say the authors of an article in one business magazine, "increases in direct proportion to the severity of the company's problems."

Usually the diluting material should have never been there in the first place. When this is the case, says philosopher Max Black, "The abuse involved is a kind of converse of the emperor's clothes—too many clothes and no emperor." We can thank famed sociologist Thorstein Veblen for unintentionally providing this marvelous example in *The Theory of the Leisure Class:*

> In an increasing proportion as time goes on, the anthropomorphic cult, with its code of devout observances, suffers a progressive disintegration through the stress of economic exigencies and the decay of the system of status. As this disintegration proceeds, there come to be associated and blended with the devout attitude certain other motives and impulses that are not always of an anthropomorphic origin, nor traceable to the habit of personal subservience. Not all of these subsidiary impulses that blend with the bait of devoutness in the later devotional life are altogether congruous with the devout attitude or with the anthropomorphic apprehension of sequence of phenomena. Their origin being not the same, their action upon the scheme of devout life is also not in the same direction. In many ways they traverse the underlying norm of subservience of vicarious life to which the code of devout observances and the ecclesiastical and sacerdotal institutions are to be traced as their substantial basis.

H. L. Mencken offers up a nifty paraphrase of this passage (probably sacrificing some loyalty for the sake of humor) remarking that Veblen's real point is this:

> Many people go to church not because they are afraid of the devil but because they enjoy the music and like to look at stained glass, the potted lilies, and the reverend pastor.

Mencken adds this, for good measure:

> This highly profound and highly original observation might have been made on a postage stamp, thereby saving a good deal of wasted paper.

Eliminate wordiness, save a tree.

Extra words do not necessarily mean bad writing. Note this gem by Robert Herrick:

> Come, let us go while we are in our prime,
> And take the harmless folly of the time.
> We shall grow old apace, and die
> Before we know our liberty.
> Our life is short, and our days run
> As fast away as does the sun;
> And as a vapor or a drop of rain
> Once lost, can ne'er be found again;
> So when or you or I are made
> A fable, song, or fleeting shade,
> All love, all liking, all delight
> Lies drowned with us in endless night.
> Then while time serves, and we are but decaying,
> Come, my Corinna, come, let's go a-Maying.

There is an argument of sorts in this verse, directed to Corinna. Herrick surely could have put it much more succinctly. Its most straightforward paraphrase is something like this:

1. We have one short life, which is passing fast.

∴ *C.* We should enjoy it now to the fullest.

Of course, Herrick's goal is art. Ours is a certain sort of clarity—the sort that will better allow us to tell whether statements are true or false and whether they are logically connected to one another. The result is not always pretty.

> *Guideline.* Eliminate wordiness that does not contribute to the argument's clarity.

NEUTRALIZING SLANTED LANGUAGE

Statements convey information. Depending on the words chosen for the job, they can also influence the emotional reaction to that information. When Henry Louis Gates applied to Yale in 1969, he wrote, "My grandfather was colored, my father was Negro, and I am black." Twenty-five years later, in the preface of his *Colored People: A Memoir*, he addresses his two daughters:

> In your lifetimes, I suspect, you will go from being African Americans, to "people of color," to being, once again, "colored people." (The linguistic trend toward condensation is strong.) I don't mind any of the names myself. But I have to confess that I like "colored" best, maybe because when I hear the word, I hear it in my mother's voice and in the sepia tones of my childhood.

There is no substantial difference in the information that each of the terms communicates; the major difference is in the emotional reaction it is likely to arouse. A skillful writer or speaker chooses language with this in mind—dressing approved statements in positive language and disapproved statements in negative.

Influencing emotions is an important and legitimate use of language. But it can sometimes cause trouble in arguments by illegitimately ***slanting*** the argument—that is, by unjustifiably aiming it toward the audience's emotions rather than the audience's reason.

Janet Novack, for example, argues in a *Forbes* article against including self-esteem studies as a part of the elementary school curriculum. She describes such studies as among the "new politically correct fads" that are pushing out more traditional subjects because of the need to satisfy "do-gooders who want their touchy-feely subject taught."

This description certainly communicates information: liberals favor self-esteem studies (they are "politically correct"); there is much current interest in them (they're "fads"); they are promoted by those with a concern for society (the "do-gooders"); and they emphasize relationships (they are "touchy-feely"). But this information by itself doesn't seem to be enough to establish that self-esteem studies have no place in elementary schools.

Such a negative conclusion is nevertheless hard to resist, due to the negative emotions aroused by Novack's choice of terms. Her terms suggest—though probably do not logically imply—the following about self-esteem studies: they are based on dogmatism (they are "politically correct"); they will not stand the test of time (they are "fads"); they are promoted by those who do not consider the broader consequences of their actions (the "do-gooders"); and they are mindless (they are "touchy-feely").

Not only do these terms sway the emotions, but also no argument is given for the *legitimacy* of a negative emotional reaction, and success in winning us over to the conclusion depends, at least in part, on that reaction. Thus it counts as slanted language. Because such language can impede honest critical reflection about the information, it is best to eliminate it from your clarification of the argument.

It is often difficult and sometimes impossible to find a completely neutral way of communicating information. We saw, for example, that *those with a concern for society* is more neutral than *do-gooders*. And so it is, but the phrase *those with a concern for society* seems to have a slant to it—but now in the positive direction. In such cases, my best advice is to prefer the more neutral language even if it is not perfectly neutral.

Sometimes slanted language is blatant. An Associated Press item reports that, in a poll regarding the American presence in Lebanon,

> A razor-thin 48%–47% plurality thought that "the Marines should be withdrawn." But in the same poll, by a 55%–39% margin, they agreed with the contention that "after being occupied for a long time by Syria, Israel, and the PLO, Lebanon needs help from the U.S., including the presence of U.S. Marines to help Lebanon re-establish control of its own country."

The two claims in quotation marks are substantially the same. But at least 7 percent of those polled had a different answer when the terse statement about withdrawal of troops was replaced by more sympathetic—and more slanted—words about Lebanon's need for help.

But in other cases the slant can be remarkably subtle. Consider the following scenario described by Kevin McKean in *Discover:*

> Threatened by a superior enemy force, the general faces a dilemma. His intelligence officers say his soldiers will be caught in an ambush in which 600 of them will die unless he leads them to safety by one of two available routes. If he takes the first route, 200 soldiers will be saved. If he takes the second, there is a one-third chance that 600

soldiers will be saved and a two-thirds chance that none will be saved. Which route should he take?

Researchers have found that most people favor the first route, reasoning that it's better to save those lives that can be saved than to gamble when the odds favor even higher losses. But what about the following scenario?

The general again has to choose between two escape routes. But this time his aides tell him that if he takes the first, 400 soldiers will die. If he takes the second, there is a one-third chance that no soldiers will die, and a two-thirds chance that 600 soldiers will die. Which route should he take?

In this case, most people favor the second route. The first route involves the certain death of 400 men. At least with the second route there is a one-third chance that no one will be killed. And even if the general loses this gamble, his casualties will be only 50 percent higher.

As you may have noticed, these are not two different scenarios but two descriptions of the same scenario. Researchers find that even when people realize this, they often continue to recommend contradictory actions for the general. It just sounds smart to do something that will certainly save 200 men and stupid to do something that will certainly sacrifice 400—even if the two, in the end, amount to the same thing.

Guideline. When slanted language has not been argued for, and when there is more neutral wording available, eliminate slanted language in favor of more emotionally neutral language.

EXERCISES Chapter 4, set (f)

Clarify each argument, following all rules for paraphrasing. Focus on using emotionally neutral language.

Sample exercise. "Mr. Murdrick's article is worthless to anyone who might want to know something about *A Susan Sontag Reader*. For it is a personal polemic of witless and barely intelligible sneers compiled by a self-serving oaf."—letter to the editor, *Harper's*

Sample answer.

1. Mr. Murdrick's article is hard to understand and aims to serve only his own interests.

∴ *C.* Mr. Murdrick's article is not informative about *A Susan Sontag Reader.*

1. The fat cat Republicans have one passion—to make their bank accounts bigger, no matter how much suffering it causes all of the decent folks of our society who through no fault of their own happen to be poor and underprivileged. So, whatever you do, don't vote for those self-centered, callous parasites.
2. Murdering unborn babies is no better than murdering born ones. So, don't let the pro-choice people fool you—they're really pro-murder.
3. "Down in Austin, Tex., when some nutcake poisons to death a 500-year-old oak tree, he's arrested. The news reports advise that for this tree-trashing the man could be sentenced to life in prison on this felony charge of criminal mischief because he had a previous conviction for burglary. Life imprisonment for tree-murder? Give us a break! Violent criminals all across this country commit far more serious 'criminal mischief' than offing an oak and they never spend one day in the slammer. This is moral insanity."—John Lofton, *Los Angeles Times*
4. "Hardly a master and miss in all the land but must be pulling and snivelling out French, and capering like a French goat. So go, goatish and apish as you are, and dangle at the heels of goats and apes!"—James Gilchrist, "Reason, the True Arbiter of Language," arguing in the early 19th century that the British should resist the influence of the French language on English
5. "There's no future to nuclear energy because Three Mile Island taught everybody what some of us already knew: that nuclear power plants are time bombs ready to melt down. And even if nuclear power plants were safe, which they aren't, there's still the potentially more dangerous nuclear waste problem. But you don't care about waste, Dan. You're content to wallow in the short-term profits the corporate pigs reap for themselves. But unlike real pigs, the corporate animals haven't learned that you don't excrete where you eat, and that their ra-

dioactive excrement will be with us for 250,000 years. That's one pile you just can't flush down the toilet, Dan."—Jane Curtin to Dan Ackroyd, on "Saturday Night Live's" "Point-Counterpoint"

6. "Undeniably, the wanton torment and destruction of animals, plants, bacteria, viruses, and plasmids is simply intolerable, whatever the excuse. I find it inconceivable that physicians pledged to the Sanctity of Life, my own parents included, could have brought themselves to consign untold millions of innocent bacteria to an excruciating death, having once witnessed their agonized contortions through a microscope. The lesson to us all: ban antibiotics."—letter to the editor, *Journal of the American Medical Association*
7. "Commenting on Donald Trump's confirmed suggestion that he might consider building the world's tallest skyscraper on the hotel site he recently acquired, Lotery says: 'Wilshire is no place for such overwrought ego statements. A huge high-rise would overwhelm the humane scale of the boulevard, which we at UIG consider its prime urban virtue.'"—*Los Angeles Times*
8. "Miss Manners is always so puzzled to hear well-meaning people rattling on about not wanting to inhibit the naturalness of their children. Why not, pray? Repressing the dear things, an activity of bygone days that was known as child-rearing, can only improve the state of the world."—Judith Martin, *Miss Manners' Guide to Rearing Perfect Children*

Things to Eliminate When Streamlining

1. Nonstatements (paraphrase as statements).
2. Discounts and discount indicators.
3. Attitude indicators.
4. Report indicators.
5. Inference indicators.
6. Repetition.
7. Wordiness.
8. Slanted language (neutralize it).

EXERCISES Chapter 4, set (g)

Paraphrase the arguments below by outlining them in standard clarifying format and following all of this chapter's streamlining guidelines.

Sample exercise. What remained of the great library at Alexandria is believed to have dwindled slowly between 415 and 624. Many scholars and historians, including both Gibbon and Durant, doubt the claim that Muslims destroyed the library around 624, since by that time there was nothing left to destroy. Civilization thus entered a dark age of ignorance, disease, and superstition.—Ronald Mohar, *Free Inquiry*

Sample answer.

1. By 624 the library at Alexandria had dwindled away.

∴ *C.* The Muslims did not destroy the library at Alexandria in 624. (Note the repetition of the premise in the passage; also note that the last sentence of the passage is not part of the argument.)

1. "Robert Merton has shown that almost all major ideas arise more than once, independently and often virtually at the same time—and thus, that great scientists are embedded in their cultures, not divorced from them. Most great ideas are 'in the air,' and several scholars simultaneously wave their nets."—Stephen Jay Gould, *The Panda's Thumb*
2. "'Usually, when we try to solve a problem, we force our minds to follow a certain train of thought, but those preconceived notions are the ones that don't lead to a solution to a problem that requires some creative approach,' says Klinger. 'In contrast, daydreams follow their own directions, often quite contrary to the expectations of our conscious logic, and this is probably what enables them to give birth to creative ideas.' So the next time you catch yourself daydreaming, and you're not driving in heavy traffic or operating a nuclear power plant, don't stop yourself. Let your mind wander. You never know how much happier you'll be until you daydream about it."—Joseph Alper
3. "Jeffrey Potter, a friend of Jackson Pollock, is claiming that Naifeh and Smith have, in their film on Pollock, infringed his copyright on his oral biography of Pollock, *To a Violent Grave.* Naifeh and Smith, who are both lawyers, say that Potter has no copyright interest because his book is formed entirely of quotations. 'You have no copyright interest in what other people have said to you,' Smith said."—*Los Angeles Times*

4. "Exposing psychic fraud is not, alas, a lucrative career. Steiner works as a CPA to support his hobby. 'The people who claim to have the power are the ones who get the money,' he says. 'If I convince you that I am a psychic, you'll pay me a lot of money to help you with your problems. But if I convince you that all that's a fraud, you don't need me.'"—*Science*
5. "For over thirty years the West has been encouraged to accept the fiction that Philby alerted his fellow spies for 'old boy' or compassionate reasons. Yet informed people know that friendship and compassion are not included in the survival kits of intelligence professionals who are at mortal risk in the field. Such human reactions are excess baggage in the secret world. The obvious conclusion is that the KGB has successfully protected its most valuable agent. In all probability Big Mole is now a highly respected member of the foreign-policy establishment."—letter to the editor, *Harper's*
6. " 'Dave Lowry could have escaped,' the Lone Ranger said. 'There were a number of times when he could have shot me from ambush. He didn't do it, even though he knew that it would mean freedom. And there was a time when I was trapped by a landslide. Dave saved my life. He didn't have to do that. He could have ridden off and left me there to die. But, instead, he saved my life, though he knew I would go on and capture him. Does that sound like the act of a hardened killer?'"—Fran Striker, *The Lone Ranger on Powderhorn Trail*
7. "Finally, what of Tertullian who claimed that 'the Son of God died' was worthy of belief because 'it was absurd'; that 'He was buried and rose again' was 'certain because it was impossible'?"—Richard Swinburne, *Faith and Reason*
8. "It is immediately obvious that not all necessary truths are known a priori; for there are necessary truths . . . that are not known at all, and *a fortiori* are not known a priori."—Alvin Plantinga, *The Nature of Necessity*

SUMMARY OF CHAPTER FOUR

Streamlining is a very important part of the clarification process. Be sure to paraphrase as statements all nonstatements that function as part of the argument. These include imperatives when they serve as the conclusion to practical reasoning, rhetorical questions, and fragments. You should also strive to eliminate all unnecessary words. These include discounts, attitude indicators, report indicators, inference indicators, repetition, and any sort of nonessential wordiness. Finally, you should neutralize slanted language.

GUIDELINES FOR CHAPTER FOUR

- Include only statements in your clarification. If a premise or conclusion is expressed as a partial sentence or a nondeclarative sentence, paraphrase it as a statement.
- Exclude discounts from your clarification of the argument.
- Use discount indicator terms to identify discounts, making sure it is a discount rather than a negatively stated promise or conclusion.
- Eliminate attitude indicators, which are indicators of belief or of disbelief; insert a negation at the beginning of disbelieved statements. Also eliminate report indicators and inference indicators.
- Eliminate repetition of statements and phrases that do not add to the argument; use whatever expression best captures the arguer's meaning.
- Eliminate wordiness that does not contribute to the argument's clarity.
- When slanted language has not been argued for, and when there is more neutral wording available, eliminate slanted language in favor of more emotionally neutral language.

GLOSSARY FOR CHAPTER FOUR

Attitude indicator—indicates the arguer's attitude of either belief or disbelief toward a statement. *I believe that* and *I deny that* are examples.

Discount indicator—indicates a nonsupportive, or adversarial, relationship between statements rather than a supportive one. *But* and *despite* are examples. Sometimes also called *adversative.*

Discount—a statement the arguer offers as not undermining the conclusion. Discounts are typically neither premises nor conclusions and should usually not be included in your clarification.

Report indicator—shows that the argument is being reported by, but is not necessarily embraced by, the speaker or writer. *So-and-so argues that* is an example.

Slanting—unjustifiably pointing a premise or conclusion toward the emotions rather than the reason of the audience.

Streamlining—removal of nonessential features of the argument so they will not get in the way of the evaluation process. It is one important aspect of the paraphrasing procedure.

CHAPTER FIVE

Specifying

Clearness and precision usually go together, though one may be clear without being precise . . . or precise without being clear. . . . Ideally, clearness is precision with due courtesy for one's audience.

—Brand Blanshard, *Four Reasonable Men*

Sydney Smith once described how two women used to lean out of their windows, on opposite sides of the street, and argue with each other. "They will never agree," he said, "for they are arguing from different premises."

—Lionel Ruby, *The Art of Making Sense*

TOPICS

Semantic Ambiguity and the Fallacy of Equivocation
Syntactic Ambiguity and the Fallacy of Amphiboly
Generality
Vagueness
Emptiness

When language is not specific enough, it too often gives rise to misunderstanding. An important part of the clarifying process is ***specifying***—that is, paraphrasing in a way that narrows the range of possible things that an expression can mean, thus increasing the clarity of the argument. Perfectly specific language is not always achievable or even desirable, but increased specificity often makes it easier to understand an argument and thus to tell whether it is sound and conversationally relevant.

SEMANTIC AMBIGUITY AND THE FALLACY OF EQUIVOCATION

Ambiguity occurs when an expression has more than one possible meaning and it is not clear which meaning is intended. We will pay special attention to two types of ambiguity: semantic and syntactic.

At the height of the American Civil War, Abraham Lincoln gave a speech that included this parable:

> The shepherd drives the wolf from the sheep's throat, for which the sheep thanks the shepherd as a liberator, while the wolf denounces him for the same act as the destroyer of liberty, especially as the sheep is a black one. Plainly the sheep and the wolf are not agreed upon a definition of the word liberty; and precisely the same difference prevails today among us human creatures, even in the North, and all professing to love liberty. Hence we behold the processes by which thousands are daily passing from under the yoke of bondage, hailed by some as the advance of liberty, and bewailed by others as the destruction of all liberty.

To the slave, illustrated by the black sheep, *liberty* means "for each man to do as he pleases *with himself*, and the product of his labor," Lincoln went on to explain. But to the slaveholder, illustrated by the wolf, *liberty* means "for some men to do as they please *with other men*, and the product of other men's labor." In Lincoln's parable the word *liberty* is an example of ***semantic ambiguity***—that is, it is a term that has more than one plausible meaning and it is not entirely clear which is intended. A semantically ambiguous term may be also described as *equivocation*, since different things are being called (. . . *vocation*) by the same (*equi* . . .) name.

Ambiguity exists only when there is lack of clarity about which meaning is intended; the mere presence of a term with more than one possible meaning does not count as ambiguity if the context makes it clear which is intended. Lincoln, for example, uses the word *love* in his parable, a word that can have a romantic or a nonromantic meaning. The context makes it clear that the romantic meaning is not intended (we don't love liberty in that way!), so the term *love* is not semantically ambiguous in this passage.

When clarifying an argument, follow this simple guideline for any sort of ambiguity: eliminate the ambiguity—by paraphrasing with terms that are not ambiguous. This assumes there is enough information in the context for you to be confident that you can apply the principle of loyalty; if not, then apply the principle of charity.

Lexical Ambiguity

As we have seen, semantic ambiguity most often occurs when there is more than one meaning of a term and it is unclear which is intended. When the multiple meanings are due to different *definitions* of the term, this sort of semantic ambiguity is sometimes termed ***lexical ambiguity***—indicating that a lexicon, or dictionary, might define the term in more than one way.

The notorious wit Dorothy Parker, for example, was laughing at the clownish antics of another guest at a dinner party. Her companion, an overeducated snob, was disdainful. "I'm afraid I can't join in the merriment," he said. "I can't bear fools." "That's queer," replied Parker. "Your mother could."

Our pleasure in her quick riposte arises at least partly because the word *bear* is, if only for a moment, semantically ambiguous. Two of the word's definitions are at issue. The snob's remark, rendered unambiguous, would be "I can't tolerate fools." Parker's would be, "Your mother could give birth to them." (If Parker had concerned herself with disambiguation, she would not be remembered today as a humorist.)

More subtle examples are easy to find. Monetary measures, for example, sometimes mean something different depending on the year—and in some economies, depending on the month or the day! A 1999 dollar is worth less than a 1990 dollar; so, a statement such as "Your house is worth $100,000" might be ambiguous if it is unclear when it was uttered. The ambiguity of such statements is eliminated with qualifiers such as "in 1999 dollars."

In "What Pragmatism Means" American philosopher William James recounts a discussion with some friends about whether one of them was going around a squirrel. The squirrel was on the trunk of a tree; as one of James's friends circled the tree the squirrel also circled the tree, keeping itself hidden behind the tree as the man circled. His friend had gone around the tree and the squirrel was on the tree—that much was certain. But had his friend gone around the squirrel? Here is James's solution:

> "Which party is right," I said, "depends on what you practically mean by 'going around' the squirrel. If you mean passing from the north of him to the east, then to the south, then to the west, and then to the north of him again, obviously the man does go around him, for he occupies these successive positions. But if on the contrary you mean being first in front of him, then on the right of him, then behind him, then on his left, and finally in front again, it is quite as obvious that the man fails to go round him, for by the compensating movements the squirrel makes, he keeps his belly turned towards the man all the time, and his back turned away. Make the distinction, and there is no occasion for any further dispute."

The term *going around* is not normally ambiguous in this way, since the two ways of going around usually amount to the same thing; I doubt that any dictionary would be so precise as to offer these as alternative definitions of the term. Nevertheless, it was this subtle lexical ambiguity that was baffling James's friends.

> *Guideline.* Eliminate lexical ambiguity by replacing or qualifying the ambiguous terms with unambiguous definitions.

EXERCISES Chapter 5, set (a)

For each of the following sentences, state at least two possible definitions for the lexically ambiguous term, then rewrite it in a way that eliminates the ambiguity. There is not enough context provided to decide which is actually meant, so simply take your pick as to which way to disambiguate.

Sample exercise. I'll meet you at the *bank*.

Sample answer. Financial institution or side of river. "I'll meet you at the river bank."

1. I wasn't expecting a strike.
2. You need to practice driving.
3. The entire group gave her a hand.
4. We had a ball last night.

Referential Ambiguity

Semantic ambiguity sometimes occurs not because a term has more than one definition, but because it has more than one referent—that is, because there is more than one thing that might plausibly be picked out by a term. This sort of semantic ambiguity is sometimes called ***referential ambiguity***. It is said that Croesus, the king of Lydia in the 6th century B.C., consulted the oracle at Delphi about whether to attack Cyrus and the Persians. The oracle pronounced, "If Croesus went to war with Cyrus, he would destroy a mighty kingdom." Croesus charged ahead, was swiftly crushed by Cyrus, and returned bitterly to the oracle to complain. The ancient Greek historian Herodotus offered this analysis of the situation:

> But regarding the prophecy that was given to him, Croesus should not complain about it. He should have sent and asked whether the god spoke of Croesus's or Cyrus's kingdom. But Croesus did not understand what was said, nor try to; so he should blame only himself now.

In the oracle's pronouncement there was no confusion about how to define the word *kingdom;* but it was unclear to which kingdom it referred, and on that account the term was semantically ambiguous.[1] (There is another term that could possibly be referentially ambiguous in the same utterance of the oracle: in *he would destroy a mighty kingdom,* the pronoun *he* could refer to Cyrus or Croesus.)

Proper names sometimes get us into the same trouble. In my graduate student days I often worked as a teaching assistant in introductory

[1]It might be tempting to identify these sorts of ambiguities as syntactic rather than semantic, because rearranging the order of the words can disambiguate. But this is a mistake. The rearrangement does not provide an alternative grammatical interpretation of the sentence; it simply suggests a different referent for the ambiguous term.

philosophy courses that enrolled hundreds of students. A professor lectured to the multitude; the teaching assistants taught the same students in smaller groups and graded their work. Early one quarter we met with the professor to coordinate our grading of an assignment. Another TA and I discovered that we had each received work from an Eloi Castro: same name, similar handwriting, similar quality of work. Aha! He was trapped in the old undergraduate trick of turning in work to more than one TA, so that he could find out who was the easier grader and switch to that TA's section. We set out to confront him . . . only to find that there were two Eloi Castros. One name, two people who could be referred to by it, and insufficient information to make the distinction resulted in semantic ambiguity.

The English language often uses italics, underlining, or quotation marks to avoid referential ambiguities. These conventions, unfortunately, are not entirely standard and are useless in spoken English. But they can be helpful. Consider these sentences:

> *Turtle Beach* will get your mind off your worries.
> Turtle Beach will get your mind off your worries.

The convention of italicizing titles makes it clear that only the second sentence asserts that the place named Turtle Beach will divert you from your worries. (The first sentence, however, remains ambiguous, since it is not clear whether the title refers to the book or to the movie.) But this convention, we have seen, is not entirely regular; underlining or quotation marks are sometimes substituted for italics, depending on the sort of title and the medium (in handwriting and typewriting, for example, we normally use a combination of quotation marks and underlining; some newspapers use quotation marks exclusively).

Sometimes we wish to use words to talk about words. To do this, we must employ the word we're talking about; for example:

> *Life* is short.

After all, it's only four letters long. But I might express the same words to talk about life; for example:

> Life is short.

After all, it's only three score and seven years.

The difference between these two sentences is commonly termed the ***use-mention distinction.*** Ordinarily, we *use* words—as in the second sentence. But when we talk about the word itself (rather than what the word talks about), then we *mention* it—as in the first sentence. When it is unclear which we are doing, the lack of clarity has to do with whether the word is or is not referring to itself; thus, it can count as referential ambiguity. This ambiguity is usually eliminated by the use of either italics or quotation marks to indicate the mention of a word; thus, the ambiguity occurs more often in speech than in writing. (Since in this text I am using italics rather than quotation marks to indicate that a word is being mentioned, there is still a possible ambiguity in the first sentence—you might wonder whether I mean to say that a certain word or a certain magazine is short.)

If referential ambiguity arises because the arguer has failed to use the appropriate marks—or because the argument is spoken, not written—then be sure to eliminate the ambiguity by introducing these conventions into your clarification of the argument. Not all referential ambiguity can be eliminated by such conventions. When necessary, supplement the ambiguous term with an unambiguous name or a definite description that uniquely picks out the intended item; for example:

For *Eloi Castro*, substitute *The Eloi Castro who is a student of Andrew Hsu's.*
For *Turtle Beach*, substitute *the book Turtle Beach.*

Guideline. Eliminate referential ambiguity by using conventions such as italics, underlining, or quotation marks and, if necessary, by supplementing the ambiguous terms with names or definite descriptions.

EXERCISES Chapter 5, set (b)

For each of the following sentences, state at least two possible referents for the referentially ambiguous term, then rewrite it in a way that eliminates the ambiguity. There is not enough context provided to decide which is actually meant, so simply take your pick as to which way to disambiguate.

Sample exercise. Jennifer gave Carissa's Social Security number to *her* new employer.

Sample answer. Jennifer's new employer or Carissa's new employer. Jennifer gave Carissa's Social Security number to Carissa's new employer.

1. Time really confuses me sometimes.
2. Her favorite expression is way cool.
3. Look—Jack is wearing sunglasses; if his father doesn't recognize him, he is going to be really upset.
4. I thought Melrose Place was beautiful.

Elliptical Ambiguity

"I heard you finally finished your book last summer. I never knew you were such a slow reader!" In this remark *finished* is, if only briefly, semantically ambiguous. But it is not because of two different definitions or because of two different things it might refer to. It is because of two possible expressions that have been omitted. At first we assume that you finished *writing* it and later that you finished *reading* it. Since such omissions are termed ellipses, this sort of confusion is best termed ***elliptical ambiguity.*** Eliminate the ambiguity by supplying the omitted expressions—instead of *I finished my book last summer,* write *I finished reading my book last summer.*

> *Guideline.* Eliminate elliptical ambiguity by supplying the omitted expression.

Some Types of Semantic Ambiguity

1. Lexical ambiguity
2. Referential ambiguity
3. Elliptical ambiguity

An expression can be ambiguous in more than one of these ways.

EXERCISES Chapter 5, set (c)

Each passage below includes at least one semantically ambiguous expression. Paraphrase to eliminate any ambiguity, and state whether it is lexical, referential, or elliptical. Expressions are not necessarily ambiguous in only one way—though you need to point out only one plausible way. (If it isn't clear which way to disambiguate, state all the plausible alternatives.)

Sample exercise. "Robber Holds Up Albert's Hosiery"—headline in the *Buffalo Evening News*"

Sample answer. Robber burglarizes a store named Albert's Hosiery. There are two ambiguities: "holds up" is lexically ambiguous; "Albert's Hosiery" is referentially ambiguous.

1. "In biblical times, a man could have as many wives as he could afford. Just like today." —Abigail Van Buren (Presumably, something is being omitted about when the man has the wives.)
2. In a church: Would parishioners please note that the bowl to the rear of the church that says "For the sick" is for monetary contributions only.
3. "Outside of a dog, a book is man's best friend. Inside of a dog, it's too dark to read." —Groucho Marx
4. "Lawmaker Backs Train Through Iowa." —headline in the *Des Moines Register*
5. "INFANCY, n. The period of our lives when, according to Wordsworth, 'Heaven lies about us.' The world begins lying about us pretty soon afterward." —Ambrose Bierce, *Devil's Dictionary*
6. "God is alive and well in Fresno. The former Terrill Clark Williams, 42, a writer and former broadcaster, became God in the eyes of the law Tuesday when Superior Court Judge Charles Hamlin signed the official decree of name change. 'It's something I've wanted to do for a long, long time,' God said. 'As a writer I was convinced that words are man's most powerful tool, and by changing my name to God, I am demonstrating the power of God.' It wasn't easy for Williams to become God. 'I couldn't get a lawyer anywhere to handle the court petition because they said no judge would sign it,' he said. . . . God is a bachelor living by himself." —*Los Angeles Times*
7. "Q: And lastly, Gary, all your responses must be oral. OK? What school do you go to?

   "A: Oral.

   "Q: How old are you?

   "A: Oral."

   —*Humor in the Court,* Mary Louise Gilman
8. "An anonymous reader takes issue with the note that Jim Thorpe, an African American, led the U.S. Open at Merion in 1981. 'You young fellows probably don't know it, but Jim Thorpe was an Indian,' he

said. 'And I don't think he was still alive in 1981.' Yes and no, depending on which Jim Thorpe you have in mind. The golfing Jim Thorpe, 44, is a regular on the PGA Tour. Jim Thorpe, the all-around athletic legend, died in 1953."—*Los Angeles Times*

9. "Longaville: I desire her name.
   "Boyet: She hath but one for herself; to desire that were a shame."
   —Act 2, Scene 1, of Shakespeare's *Love's Labours Lost*
10. *Harry Truman was the 32nd president of the United States.* Disambiguate the preceding sentence in light of the information in the following letter, written by Harry Truman and archived in the *Forbes* American history autograph collection. He is writing to complain about his being referred to as the 33rd president:

    > In reply to your letter, I am the 32nd man who has been President of the United States. Mr. Eisenhower is the 33rd. The Hearst Publications started the wrong numbering program. They do that by counting Grover Cleveland twice. If Grover Cleveland is to be counted twice then every man who served two terms should be counted twice. Sincerely yours, Harry Truman.

The Fallacy of Equivocation

Eliminating ambiguity puts you in a better position to tell whether a premise is true, since it puts you in a better position to tell what the premise means. But it can also help you avoid disasters in assessing the logic of an argument. Good logic means that the conclusion follows from the premises, quite apart from whether the premises are true. Here's a "textbook" example, expressed in standard clarifying format.

1. Only man is rational.
2. No woman is a man.

∴ *C.* No woman is rational.

At a glance, not only does each individual premise look plausible, but also the logic looks good—that is, it looks as though the conclusion follows from the premises. It appears as though the argument is sound. But how could a sound argument have such a silly conclusion? The answer is that the argument is *not* sound, but only appears to be. This appearance of soundness is created because an ambiguous expression shifts its meaning from its first use to its second use. The first premise is plausible only if *man* means *human* (i.e., "mankind"), but the second premise is plausible only if it means *male.* This is an example of the ***fallacy of ambiguity***—when an argument appears to be successful because of an ambiguous expression that shifts in meaning. More specifically, this is the ***fallacy of equivocation***—that is, a fallacy of ambiguity in which the ambiguity is a semantic one.

The paraphrase of the *No woman is rational* argument, thus, is not yet complete, because we must eliminate the ambiguity. There is no context provided for this argument, thus no way of determining exactly what the arguer means. The question I must ask, according to the principle of charity, is *What paraphrase would make the argument the most reasonable?* There are two ways of doing this. One way is to make the premises of the argument as reasonable as possible. Call this the *reasonable-premises* approach. Here is such a paraphrase (the disambiguated term is in italics):

1. Only *humans* are rational.
2. No woman is *male.*

∴ *C.* No woman is rational.

The premises seem reasonable, but the conclusion does not follow from the premises. Eliminating the ambiguity in this way makes it clear that the argument is unsound.

The other way of doing it is to make the logic of the argument as reasonable as possible. Call this the *reasonable-logic* approach. You could then eliminate the ambiguity in this way:

1. Only *humans* are rational.
2. No woman is *human.*

∴ *C.* No woman is rational.

Or you could adopt this variation:

1. Only *males* are rational.
2. No woman is a *male.*

∴ *C.* No woman is rational.

Each of these paraphrases produces an argument that is logically successful but each has a false premise (in the former version, *No woman is human;* in the latter, *Only males are rational*).

While either the reasonable-premises or the reasonable-logic approach is acceptable, I recommend the reasonable-premises approach. Recall from Chapter 3 that one way of thinking about the principle of charity was to ask, *What might I have meant if I had uttered these words?* Making the premises reasonable comes closer to answering this question. I don't offer a rigid rule here because once the ambiguity is eliminated, arguments that commit a fallacy of ambiguity will typically prove to be defective regardless of which approach is adopted. As we saw in the example above, if you disambiguate for reasonable premises, the logic will typically be ridiculously bad; but if you disambiguate for reasonable logic, the premises will typically be preposterous.

No one is fooled by the *No woman is rational* argument. But much subtler ones abound. Several years ago a major university was trumpeting a 25 percent increase in the size of its library holdings during a four-year interval, catapulting it to the rank of third-largest among the nation's university libraries. Various publications reported an account that might be clarified as follows:

1. Four years ago the university's libraries had 4,000,000 volumes.
2. This year the university's libraries had 5,000,000 volumes.

∴ *C.* The university increased its holdings by 25 percent in the last four years.

It seems doubtful that the university would be lying about the premises (it would be too easy for someone to publicly embarrass the school); and the conclusion apparently follows—mathematically and thus logically—from the premises. But there nevertheless is a problem; two different definitions of the term *volume* are being used. While browsing through the stacks of this university's main research library, someone overheard one library worker comment to another that they had for the first time begun including free government publications in their count. If this is so, then *volume* is semantically ambiguous, and the argument is better clarified as follows (using the reasonable-premises approach):

1. Four years ago the university's libraries had 4,000,000 volumes (not including free government publications).
2. This year the university's libraries had 5,000,000 volumes (including free government publications).

∴ *C.* The university increased its holdings by 25 percent in about four years.

With the elimination of ambiguity for both occurrences of *volume*, the appearance of logical success is gone.

Later in the book you will be expected to follow each clarification with a full-fledged evaluation. One important thing to note when you evaluate the logic of an argument like this is that it has committed the fallacy of equivocation.

In general, it is a good idea to be especially attentive when an argument's premises seem plausible and the conclusion seems to follow from the premises, yet the conclusion strikes you as preposterous. There are many reasons this can happen. The preposterous conclusion might even be true! Nevertheless, in such cases look hard for a fallacy of ambiguity. It is often the culprit.

Guideline. If the apparent success of an argument depends on a shift in the meaning of a semantically ambiguous term, you should say in your evaluation that the argument commits the fallacy of equivocation. (You will also need to point out that it has either false premises or bad logic, as described above.)

EXERCISES Chapter 5, set (d)

Each argument below commits the fallacy of equivocation. Clarify according to all guidelines so far introduced; pay special attention to disambiguation in order to provide the most reasonable premises.

Sample exercise. "Just tell me, said Dionysodorus, have you a dog?
"Yes, and a very bad one, said Ctesippus.
"Has he got puppies?
"Very much so, he said, as bad as he is.
"Then the dog is their father?
"I have seen him myself, he said, on the job with the bitch.
"Very well, isn't the dog yours?
"Certainly, he said.
"Then being a father he is yours, so the dog becomes your father. . . ."
—Plato, Euthydemus

Sample answer.

1. The dog is a father.
2. The dog is yours (possessed by you).

∴ *C.* The dog is your (relative to you) father.

1. I'm required for my biology class to write a term paper on the belly of a frog. There isn't much space, of course, on the belly of a frog. So it is going to be difficult to satisfy this requirement. (Disambiguate by filling in what is missing after the word *on* in the first sentence.)
2. I recently read that most traffic accidents occur within five miles of your home. That's a good reason for you to move to a new neighborhood more than five miles from your home. (Focus on the word *your.*)
3. A blindfolded man stands against a stone wall, in front of a firing squad—all attired in academic caps and gowns. One of the academics explains to a bystander: "It's publish or perish, and he hasn't published." —cartoon in the *New Yorker* (*Perish*, of course, is the ambiguous term here.)
4. "The Toronto Blue Jays had drawn 2,139,313 through 46 dates, an average of 46,507, which projects to 3,767,058 in attendance, a total that would break the Dodgers' major league attendance record of 3,608,881, set in 1982. The Dodgers would argue that they sold more than 3.8 million tickets that year, but the National League's announced totals include only turnstile admissions. The American League announces total sales, including no-shows. On the other hand, the Blue Jays would argue that the Dodgers' 3.6-million turnstile total of '82 includes complimentary admissions." —*Sporting News* (Clarify and evaluate the argument in the first paragraph that Toronto would break the *attendance* record.)

SYNTACTIC AMBIGUITY AND THE FALLACY OF AMPHIBOLY

Newspaper columnist Jack Smith puzzled over the following passage he found in a book called *The Christian Couple:*

> We discovered . . . that good sex doesn't happen automatically. The pleasure and fulfillment of sex involves more than two people sleeping together in the same bed.

The columnist adds: "The question that arises, of course, is how many people does it take in a bed to make good sex?"

The phrase *more than two people sleeping together in the same bed* is ambiguous, but not because it includes an expression with more than one meaning. (The term *sleeping together* can be semantically ambiguous, but not here.) The puzzle is whether the author is saying that good sex requires more than two people or that good sex requires more than sleeping together in the same bed. The problem is strictly a grammatical one: whether *more than* modifies *two* or *sleeping*. This is ***syntactic ambiguity***—the sort of ambiguity that occurs when the terms of an expression have more than one plausible grammatical relationship to one another, and when this results in lack of clarity about what the expression means. It is also called *amphiboly*, from a Greek word for a special net that could be cast on both sides of the boat, thereby catching twice as many fish—or meanings.

The guideline for paraphrasing syntactic ambiguity is the same as for semantic ambiguity: when there is syntactic ambiguity, and when it is possible to tell from the context what the arguer probably intended, then eliminate the ambiguity by rewriting the offending expression in an unambiguous way. Sometimes it requires only a comma or a reorganization of the phrases in the sentence. Our initial example might be paraphrased in the following way:

> Pleasure and fulfillment in sex involves two people doing more than sleeping together in the same bed.

A syntactic ambiguity in the United States Constitution was the focus of much debate in the early years of the history of America. Article I, Section 8, sometimes known as the "general welfare clause," states:

> The Congress shall have power to lay and collect taxes, duties, imposts and excises, to pay the debts and provide for the common defence and general welfare of the United States.

Supporters of a strong central government argued *that provide for the . . . general welfare* was the object of the infinitive *to . . . collect taxes.* On this interpretation, taxes were to be collected, in part, to provide for the general welfare. But supporters of strong states and a weaker central government argued that *provide for the . . . general welfare* was simply another thing that Congress was empowered to do—it was to collect taxes, it was to pay debts, and it was to provide for the general welfare. As evidenced today by ever higher tax bills, the supporters of the first interpretation won. And they do seem to offer the more plausible interpretation of the text. Otherwise, we would expect a comma after *debts* and the repetition of the word *to* in front of *provide*, indicating it is the next distinct item in the series. Further, the sentence is more logical if the first part of it (about collecting taxes) is understood as providing the means to meet the objectives of the second half (about paying debts and providing for the general welfare). We could eliminate the ambiguity by rewriting it thus:

> The Congress shall have power to lay and collect taxes, duties, imposts and excises, *the purpose of which is* to pay the debts and provide for the common defence and general welfare of the United States.

Syntactic and semantic ambiguity sometimes combine their fuzzy forces. The magazine *Free Inquiry* publishes advertisements in its back pages. In one issue, a page of ads includes the following:

> "Free promotional albums" for Barry Publications
>
> "Free brochure and travel directions" for Villa Vegetarian Holistic Retreat
>
> "One free copy" of a booklet called *Biblical Inerrancy*
>
> "Free information" on making homemade booklets
>
> "Free details" on how to be "stronger, smarter, happier, richer, more confident and respected (guaranteed!)"

In their midst, there is a large ad announcing,

> "FREE ATHEIST PRISONERS, Prisoner Atheist League of America. . . ."

When I first saw the ad, I momentarily took *free* as an adjective (as it is in all the other ads) modifying prisoners. Noticing the absurdity—why would they want to send me an atheist prisoner for free?—I shifted to seeing *free* as a verb—an imperative, telling the reader what to do to the prisoners—to set them free. This is syntactic ambiguity, since it has to do with lack of clarity regarding the grammatical construction of the phrase. The expression, however, is semantically ambiguous as well; when *free* is used here as an adjective, it is in the sense of *not requiring any payment*; when used here as a verb it is in the sense of *enjoying personal liberty*. Both ambiguities could be eliminated, of course, with a paraphrase such as this:

Liberate atheist prisoners.

When the apparent success of an argument is due to a shift in the meaning of a syntactically ambiguous expression, the argument commits the ***fallacy of amphiboly.*** You should indicate this in your evaluation of the argument.

Guideline. Eliminate syntactic ambiguity by rewriting the ambiguous sentences in an unambiguous way. If the apparent success of an argument depends on a shift in the meaning of a syntactically ambiguous expression, evaluate the argument as failing due to the fallacy of amphiboly.

Some Fallacies of Ambiguity

1. *The fallacy of equivocation*—due to semantic ambiguity.
2. *The fallacy of amphiboly*—due to syntactic ambiguity.

These can sometimes occur together.

EXERCISES Chapter 5, set (e)

Each passage includes at least one syntactic ambiguity, indicated by italics. Paraphrase so as to eliminate any ambiguity. (If you can't tell which way to disambiguate, state all plausible options.)

Sample exercise. In April, Harvard sold Houston developer Gerald Hines an option to buy the property, for a rumored $20 million. —*Harvard*

Crimson (Note: buying an option is different from buying the property—it is buying dibs on buying the property, should you later decide you want to buy the property.)

Sample answer. Can't tell—either (*i*) In April, Harvard sold Houston developer Gerald Hines an option for a rumored $20 million to buy the property, or (*ii*) In April, Harvard sold Houston developer Gerald Hines an option to buy, for a rumored $20 million, the property.

1. "Forty-six percent of biology graduates and 40 percent of physical sciences graduates at the University have been women since 1985." —University of Richmond *Collegian*
2. Posted on tables at a fast-food restaurant: "If any item in your order is not satisfactory, please return the product to the counter and we will replace it with a smile." —*Reader's Digest*
3. "University of Florida microbiologist Lonni Ingram holds the nation's five millionth patent on how to convert trash to ethanol." —University of Florida *Floridian*
4. "The United States and its allies bombed Iraq and occupied Kuwait for a second day with relentless fury." —Associated Press
5. "Judge: Now, as we begin, I must ask you to banish all present information and prejudice from your minds, if you have any." —*Humor in the Court*, Mary Louise Gilman
6. "Question on employment application in the 1950's: Do you advocate overthrowing the United States government by force or violence?" —*An American Childhood*, Annie Dillard (Dillard's mischievous mother filled in the blank with "force.")
7. Dizzy Dean, responding to a critic who said he didn't know the King's English: "Old Diz knows the King's English. Not only that, I know the Queen is English."

GENERALITY

In everyday language, terms like *ambiguous*, *general*, and *vague* are often used interchangeably to indicate imprecision or lack of specificity. But in this text (to avoid ambiguity, excessive generality, and unnecessary vagueness) we will for the most part use them in quite different and more precise ways.

Generality is present when a term allows for degrees. Suppose you ask your instructor how you are doing in class and she replies, "You're doing just fine." *Fine* in this case is general; for it can cover a range extending from average to superior, and there is nothing in your instructor's reply to suggest precisely where in that range she is placing your performance.

Generality of this sort usually serves some useful everyday purpose. *Bald* and *brown*, for example, can be general in this way. If I am told to meet a bald man in a brown suit on the corner of LeConte and Westwood, I normally don't regret not knowing precisely how many hairs he has on his head, nor the suit's precise shade of brown expressed in the wavelength of the reflected light. Replacing the general terms with more precise ones would make the task of identification harder, not easier. So language is well served by its enormous stock of general terms. Not only is *fine* often general, but generality is often fine.

Generality and the Fallacy of Equivocation

Generality, nevertheless, can sometimes produce problems in reasoning. Consider the statement:

> People who are incompatible should not live together.

Without any context we simply cannot decide whether it is true or false, due to the generality of both *incompatible* and *live together*. How incompatible? Living how intimately together? Slide both of them to one extreme and the statement is obviously true (people who can't stand one another shouldn't try to share their entire lives). But slide them to the other extreme and it is obviously false (people who have different personality types could still live peaceably in the same house).

So generality, as the previous example suggests, can sometimes result in semantic ambiguity. If *fine* can cover a range from *average* to *superior*, then it can be used to mean *average* and it can be used to mean *superior*. Those are two different meanings, and an argument whose apparent success depends on a shift from one to the other commits the fallacy of equivocation.

Generality usually does not result in semantic ambiguity. *You're doing fine* typically just means *You're somewhere in the range of acceptability—I really don't know or care where*. This isn't precise, but it is as precise as it needs to be; there aren't two different meanings here, thus no ambiguity and no lack of clarity. Conversely, semantic ambiguity is usually the result of something other than generality (lexical, referential, or elliptical confusion for example). Suppose you describe a fabric as fine, and I'm not sure whether you mean that its quality is high or that it is closely woven and lightweight. That is semantic ambiguity of the lexical sort. The two meanings are different in kind, not merely in degree, and thus the ambiguity has nothing to do with generality.

When generality does result in semantic ambiguity, it is especially important to eliminate it. Consider Plato's famous argument that all wrongdoing is a result of ignorance—that if we just knew more, we would never do anything wrong. Here is one way of characterizing Plato's argument:[2]

> It is obvious that none of us wants to do evil if we know that it is evil. And, of course, to do wrong is to do evil. So, by the same token, none of us desires to do wrong if we know that it is wrong.

A preliminary clarification of the argument might look something like this.

1. No one who knows that something is evil wants to do it.
2. To do wrong is evil.

∴ *C.* No one who knows that something is wrong wants to do it.

What makes the argument seem to succeed is the generality of the term *wrong*. *Wrong* covers all of the abhorrently wrong offenses that are covered by the term *evil* (thus, while *evil* is itself general, its generality doesn't contribute to the problem here), but it also covers less abhorrently wrong offenses, such as jaywalking and white lies, that are not encompassed by *evil*. We are persuaded by premise two only when we take it to mean the more extreme wrongs, but the conclusion is intended to cover the entire range of wrongs. It is plausible, then, to say that the generality of *wrong* results in semantic ambiguity in both 2 and *C* and leads the argument into the fallacy of

[2]Adapted from a discussion in the 19th century philosopher John Stuart Mill's *System of Logic*. Mill thinks the problem is with the generality of the term *evil*; but, as I indicate in the text, because the term *wrong* is even more general, and encompasses what is encompassed by *evil*, the problem is with the term *wrong*.

equivocation. A much better clarification would eliminate the ambiguity, as follows:

1. No one who knows that something is evil wants to do it.
2. To do an *abhorrent wrong* is evil.

∴ C. No one who knows that something is *in any way wrong* wants to do it.

It is now clear that the premises cannot support the conclusion—that the logic of the argument is unsuccessful.

Usually you should leave generality alone. But on those infrequent occasions when it does present a problem, and when there is information in the context that suggests a more precise way of paraphrasing it, paraphrase it so as to be more specific.

Guideline. Generality is usually unproblematic and even useful. When it does cause confusion, paraphrase with more specific terms.

EXERCISES Chapter 5, set (f)

Each of the following expressions exhibits generality. In each case, describe the range that it covers.

Sample exercise. Unhealthy.

Sample answer. Could range from frequent colds to serious and debilitating diseases.

1. raised in Oklahoma
2. a contemporary of Darwin's
3. a bull market
4. gaining the acceptance of others (two general terms)
5. studied for a test
6. a millionaire

VAGUENESS

Suppose you are still looking for the bald man in the brown suit on the corner of LeConte and Westwood. You finally do spot a man and you wonder whether his hair is thin enough for him to count as bald; you then see that his suit is a sort of khaki color, and you wonder if it counts as brown. You could count each hair (if he would let you); that would eliminate any worry about the generality of the term *bald*—but that wasn't your worry, for you would still be no closer to deciding whether he is bald. And you could measure the wavelengths of the light reflected from his suit (if you had the equipment), but you would be no closer to deciding whether the suit was brown. For the new problem we face with the terms *bald* and *brown* is not their generality, but their ***vagueness***—that is, the lack of a strictly defined boundary between what has the property and what does not. The man is not only on the corner of two streets, but he is also on the border of two vague terms; and, given the way I have described him, the surprising result is that there may be no correct answer to whether he is bald or whether his suit is brown.

Vague terms like *bald* and *brown* can be understood as having *quantitatively* fuzzy borders—their borders are fuzzy because there is no precise number (which specifies either the number of hairs or the length of the light waves) that marks off items that have the property from those that do not. But other vague terms have *qualitatively* fuzzy borders. Terms that have nothing to do with quantities—say, *game* or *religion*—can be vague because there is no fixed set of criteria for their application. Some games have winners and losers (but then there is the "telephone game" of whispering a phrase from one person to the next to see how the phrase changes). Some games have definite rules (but then there is peek-a-boo). Some games are played for fun (but then there is professional football). Some games are social activities (but then there is solitaire). Perhaps the best we can do is list the typical criteria and then call something a game if it satisfies several of them. Games seem to have what the philosopher Wittgenstein called a "family resemblance" to one another, without having a single set of unifying conditions that applies to all games. The result is that the term *game* can be vague; there can be borderline cases—circus tightrope walking, for example—that don't satisfy enough criteria to be definitely in or definitely out of the family of games.

Vagueness, like generality, exists because it can be useful; adopting terminology with more precise borders could make life difficult. First, it could make our concepts more complicated than they need to be. Consider the term *skinny.* The concept is easy to grasp. But what would it take to make the border between *skinny* and *not skinny* more precise? Skinniness has something to do with weight relative to height, so the more precise notion must include the notions of weight, of height, and of some formula that produces a proportional relationship between the two. We would not be able to teach our children the more precise term until they reached junior high school! Second, greater precision could make it more difficult to apply the concept. A quick glance tells you if someone is skinny (unless it is a borderline case); but measuring height and weight and calculating the ratio is hard enough to do to make you wonder whether you really care. And third, greater precision could make our concepts too rigid. A skinny person 100 years ago might not, at exactly the same height and weight, count as a skinny person today. The more precise term would have lost its value to us; but as circumstances change, so can our vague concepts.

Note that even terms that we ordinarily assume to be precise can have beneficially vague uses. A 12 1/8-inch gasket is not a foot long, and if substituted where a foot-long gasket is called for could allow leaks and lead to disaster; but no one would ever object that a 12 1/8-inch hot dog was not a foot long. In short, practicality demands vagueness.

EXERCISES Chapter 5, set (g)

Indicate whether each of the borders below can be vague or not. If it can be vague, describe a borderline case that is undecidable.

Sample exercise. day/night.

Sample answer. Vague; twilight is undecidable.

1. tall/not tall
2. married/not married
3. walking/not walking
4. happy/not happy
5. human/not human
6. pregnant/not pregnant

How to Settle Border Disputes

Vagueness rarely needs to be eliminated when you paraphrase an argument. But it is something you should be aware of in your own reasoning. Sometimes we care very much which side of a vague border something falls on. In such cases, instead of arguing for a more precise border, it is often better to forget the border and ask the following two practical questions: *Why do I care which side of the border it falls on?* and, only then, *What considerations directly bear on what I care about?*

Suppose I am trying to establish the minimal annual income that would constitute the clear borderline for *poverty*. But let's say that what I really care about—my reason for trying to establish the borderline—is whether a family should be eligible for benefits provided by a charitable foundation that I run. I can then focus entirely on the kinds of needs that the foundation wishes to satisfy and the sorts of resources the foundation has. If a fixed threshold for annual income is needed, I can decide it on that basis—say, we want to enhance early childhood education in a certain neighborhood and I conclude that we have enough money to help the families in the neighborhood with an income lower than $15,000 per year. Thus, the distracting question of a borderline for poverty simply drops out. Or suppose I am the basketball coach and am trying to decide whether a particular student trying out for my team is a *good* player; my problem is that he is good in some ways, not so good in others, and I can't decide. Perhaps what I should focus on instead is whether the things he can do are things that my team needs; in that way, I can ignore the distracting question of fixing the borderline for being a good player.

> *Guideline.* If you do need a precise border for a vague term, ask instead why it is you want a precise border and what it is that would address what you want.

The Fallacy of Arguing from the Heap

Vagueness normally causes no trouble unless it is exploited by one of two fallacious styles of argumentation. One of these is the ***fallacy of arguing from the heap,*** which mistakenly concludes that, because fuzzy borders can take longer to pass, they are impassable. Here is a simple example:

> If something is not a heap of sand, then adding one grain of sand will not make it a heap of sand. Therefore, no matter how many grains of sand you add, a layer of sand will not become a heap of sand.

More familiar are claims like *Just one small dessert won't make me fat* and *Just one white lie won't make me a liar.* The premises are true; but the tempting conclusions—*No number of small desserts will make me fat; No number of white lies will make me a liar*—do not follow.

The problem is the small size of the increment—a grain of sand, a small dessert, a white lie—that has been chosen. It is not large enough by itself to bridge the gap between those things that definitely are on one side of the fuzzy border and those that definitely are on the other side. It is nevertheless an increment; if something is not a heap of sand, even though adding one grain of sand may not make it a heap, it does make it more like a heap.

> *Guideline.* If an argument contends that a border cannot be crossed because its vagueness takes it longer to cross the border, evaluate it as committing the fallacy of arguing from the heap.

The Slippery Slope Fallacy

A second fallacy that exploits vagueness is the ***slippery slope fallacy;*** this is the fallacy of mistakenly concluding that because fuzzy borders can be harder to see, they are nonexistent. Such an argument might start with the same premise:

> If something is not a heap of sand, then adding one grain of sand will not make it a heap of sand.

But now the conclusion is this:

> Therefore, there is ultimately no difference between a heap of sand and a layer of sand.

Such arguments have been used to support conclusions such as *There is no difference between amateurs and professionals; There is no difference between plants and animals;* and *There is no difference between sanity and insanity.*

Suppose you are perfectly sane and for no identifiable reason become just a bit more careful about locking the doors and setting the alarms before going to bed at night. That certainly doesn't make you insane. And if you go a step further and begin to glance on the floor of the backseat before getting into your car, there is still no reason to doubt your sanity. A slippery slope argument would conclude that, given that these small increments make no difference in your sanity, there is no difference between a sane and insane person.

The same trick used by the argument from the heap is now being exploited to a different end. An increment is chosen that is too small to bridge the gap between something that definitely has the property (say, sanity) and something that definitely does not—but this time, with the conclusion that this shows there is no difference between having it and not having it. It is, nevertheless, an increment, and it does make a difference.

Guideline. If an argument contends that a border does not exist because its vagueness makes it hard to see the border, evaluate it as committing the slippery slope fallacy.

Some Fallacies of Vagueness

1. *The fallacy of arguing from the heap*—says the border is impassable.
2. *The slippery slope fallacy*—says the border is nonexistent.

EMPTINESS

Robespierre headed the Reign of Terror for a time during the French Revolution and sent thousands of "enemies of the state" to the guillotine. When his political opponents accused him of counting his personal enemies as enemies of the state, Robespierre responded,

> I deny the accusation, and the proof is that you still live.

Dropping the attitude indicator and the argument indicator, a preliminary clarification of his argument might be this:

1. You still live.
∴ *C.* The accusation is false.

The clarified argument is easy to understand in the context of my introductory story. But removed from context and placed alone, the statements are ***empty***—that is, we know how the words in them are defined, but we have no idea to what they refer. (This is a referential problem but is not referential ambiguity, since we do not have too *many* referents to decide among, we have too few—zero.) Who is *you?* What is *the accusation?* We must, without any context, evaluate such an argument as neither sound nor unsound but as undecidable.

The clarified argument is the argument you will evaluate. But, empty as they are, these sentences cannot be evaluated. It is probably more appropriate to call such sentences formulas rather than statements; we would have just as much information if the argument were paraphrased as follows:

1. ___ still lives.
∴ *C.* ___ is false.

A much better paraphrase would be this:

1. Robespierre's personal enemies still live.
∴ *C.* It is not the case that Robespierre counts his personal enemies as enemies of the state.

(For simplicity I have not supplied the obvious implicit premise, namely, *Robespierre does not allow the enemies of the state to live.*)

Whenever possible, give your paraphrased statements enough content so they can be evaluated. If the contextual information is simply not there, the worst that can happen is that you clarify it emptily and evaluate it as undecidable. Be careful not to introduce emptiness yourself when clarifying the argument.

Guideline. Do not include empty sentences in your clarification if you can avoid it. Include in your clarified argument the minimal contextual information that is necessary for evaluation.

EXERCISES Chapter 5, set (h)

Clarify each of these arguments and, if you paraphrase to eliminate an ambiguity, underline the paraphrase. If it commits a fallacy, state the fallacy committed.

Sample exercise. "Mr. Tom McNally, a Lancashire businessman attempting to cross the Atlantic in a yacht only 6 ft. 10 in. long, is apparently refusing to give up his lone voyage after being found, in a search involving three nations without food and water 920 miles off Land's End." —*London Times* (Suppose I argue that, based on this report, something should now be done to help these three hungry and thirsty nations.)

Sample answer.

1. McNally was found without food and water in a search involving three nations.
2. If a nation has no food or water, it should be helped.

∴ *C.* The three nations who found McNally should be helped.
Fallacy of amphiboly.

1. Classified ad: "Now is your chance to have your ears pierced and get an extra pair to take home, too." But I don't need more ears, so I'll pass on the offer.
2. Half of the stores tested illegally sell cigarettes to minors. We should stop the government from doing this illegal testing.
3. I'm locking these exams in a safe, and if any student takes a test, that student will be immediately expelled. But, all students in my course will be required to take a test. So all students in my course who do as required will be immediately expelled.
4. When truckers began to park along a Texas interstate to visit a popular café, the highway department erected "Emergency Parking Only" signs. The eatery quickly changed its name to "Emergency Café." Trucker to police officer: "But I'm parked legally, officer; after all, I'm parking for the Emergency and the signs says it's OK."
5. In Ben Bova's 'Who's There?' psychologist Bruno Bettleheim says, 'There is absolutely no evidence for life in space.' Well, we're alive. We're in space. Aren't we good enough evidence for him?" —letter to the editor, *Psychology Today*

6. "We endeavor to provide financial assistance to all full-time students seeking the J.D. degree from Michigan who would be unable to meet the costs of their law school education if drawing only on their own savings and support from their spouses and families." —University of Michigan's *Pre-Law Handbook* (Suppose I conclude, on the basis of this information, that since I am not from Michigan I am not likely to receive financial assistance.)
7. "All actions, as such, must be motivated. But in that case they all are done, and could only be done, because the agent wants to do them. Since to do always exactly what you want to do is to be utterly selfish, it follows that there is, and could be, no such thing as an unselfish action." —Thomas Hobbes, *Leviathan* (Pay special attention here to the term *wants*—does it mean *selfishly wants* or does it mean *wants, whether selfishly or not?*)

SUMMARY OF CHAPTER FIVE

Ambiguity, generality, vagueness, and emptiness are some ways in which an argument can lack specificity. Although any lack of specificity can potentially interfere with your ability to tell whether premises are true or whether the logic of an argument is good, ambiguity is by far the most problematic and should always be eliminated, when possible, in your paraphrase.

Semantic ambiguity, or equivocation, occurs when it is not clear which of two or more meanings is intended by a term. Some varieties of semantic ambiguity are: lexical ambiguity, when the intended definition of a term is not clear; referential ambiguity, when it is not clear which item a term is intended to pick out; and elliptical ambiguity, when it is not clear which expression has been omitted. When a shift from one such meaning to another accounts for the apparent success of an argument, that argument commits the fallacy of equivocation.

Syntactic ambiguity, or amphiboly, occurs when it is unclear which of two or more grammatical constructions is intended by an expression. When a shift from one grammatical construction to another accounts for the apparent success of an argument, that argument commits the fallacy of amphiboly.

Generality is present when a term allows for degrees. It sometimes results in semantic ambiguity and in such cases should be eliminated in favor of more specific language.

Vagueness exists when there is no strictly defined boundary between what has a property and what does not; when something falls into this fuzzy area, there may be no correct answer to whether the term applies to it. Vagueness can tempt us to think that the border is either impassable (the fallacy of arguing from the heap) or nonexistent (the slippery slope fallacy). Such temptations should be resisted.

Emptiness occurs when there is not enough contextual information to allow for any judgment about whether a claim is true or false. You should be careful not to inadvertently introduce it into an argument's clarification.

GUIDELINES FOR CHAPTER FIVE

- Eliminate lexical ambiguity by replacing or qualifying the ambiguous terms with unambiguous definitions.
- Eliminate referential ambiguity by using conventions such as italics, underlining, or quotation marks and, if necessary, by supplementing the ambiguous terms with names or definite descriptions.
- Eliminate elliptical ambiguity by supplying the omitted expression.
- If the apparent success of an argument depends on a shift in the meaning of a semantically ambiguous term, you should say in your evaluation that the argument commits the fallacy of equivocation. (You will also need to point out that it has either false premises or bad logic.)
- Eliminate syntactic ambiguity by rewriting the ambiguous sentences in an unambiguous way.
- If the apparent success of an argument depends on a shift in the meaning of a syntactically ambiguous expression, you should say in your evaluation that the argument commits the fallacy of amphiboly. (You will also need to point out that it has either false premises or bad logic.)
- Generality is usually unproblematic and even useful. When it does cause confusion, paraphrase with more specific terms.
- If you do need a precise border for a vague term, ask instead why it is you want a precise border and what it is that would address what you want.
- If an argument contends that a border cannot be crossed because its vagueness takes it longer to cross the border, evaluate it as committing the fallacy of arguing from the heap.

- If an argument contends that a border does not exist because its vagueness makes it hard to see the border, evaluate it as committing the fallacy of the slippery slope.
- Do not include empty sentences in your clarification if you can avoid it. Include in your clarified argument the minimal contextual information that is necessary for evaluation.

GLOSSARY FOR CHAPTER FIVE

Ambiguity—occurs when an expression has more than one possible meaning and it is not clear which meaning is intended.

Elliptical ambiguity—semantic ambiguity in which lack of clarity regarding the meaning is due to an expression that has been omitted.

Empty—a statement that in a normal context would have clear referents for all its terms, but is in a context that provides the audience with no idea of what at least one of its terms refers to.

Fallacy of ambiguity—committed by an argument that appears to be successful because of an ambiguous expression that shifts in meaning; the fallacy of equivocation and the fallacy of amphiboly are two varieties.

Fallacy of amphiboly—a fallacy of ambiguity that goes wrong because of syntactic ambiguity.

Fallacy of arguing from the heap—the fallacy of mistakenly concluding that, because fuzzy borders can take longer to pass, they are impassable.

Fallacy of equivocation—a fallacy of ambiguity that goes wrong because of semantic ambiguity.

Generality—possessed by a term that allows for degrees.

Lexical ambiguity—semantic ambiguity in which the competing meanings are due to different definitions of a term (thus *lexical*, indicating that a lexicon, or dictionary, might define the term in more than one way).

Referential ambiguity—semantic ambiguity in which more than one thing might plausibly be picked out, or referred to, by a term.

Semantic ambiguity—a term that has more than one plausible meaning and it is not clear which is intended. Also called *equivocation*, since different things are being called (. . . *vocation*) by the same (*equi* . . .) name.

Slippery slope fallacy—mistakenly concluding that because fuzzy borders can be harder to see, they are nonexistent.

Specifying—paraphrasing in a way that narrows the range of possible things that an expression can mean, so as to increase the clarity of an argument.

Syntactic ambiguity—the sort of ambiguity that occurs when the terms of an expression have more than one plausible grammatical relationship to one another, and when this results in lack of clarity about what the expression means. (Also called *amphiboly*, from a Greek word for a special net that could be cast simultaneously on both sides of the boat, thereby catching twice as many fish—or meanings.)

Use-mention distinction—the difference between the expression of a word to refer to the word itself—in which case the word is, strictly speaking, merely being *mentioned*, not used—and the other more ordinary expressions of the word, when it is being *used*. Confusion about this distinction can cause the sort of semantic ambiguity we have termed *referential ambiguity*.

Vagueness—the lack of a strictly defined boundary between what has a property and what does not have it.

CHAPTER SIX

Structuring

Order and simplification are the first steps toward the mastery of a subject.

—Thomas Mann, *The Magic Mountain*

TOPICS

Variables and Constants
Translating Stylistic Variants
Matching Wording

An argument is not typically offered as a series of independent sentences, but as a structured unit—not as scattered planks, but as a building in which the planks are nailed together according to a design. As you clarify any argument, you should strive from the start to see its underlying design—that is, its logical form.

Identifying the logical form of an argument helps in two important ways. First, it helps in the clarifying process; once you identify the argument's form, you are prepared for the process of ***structuring***—that is, organizing your paraphrase of the argument so as to make its logical form as obvious as possible. Second, it ultimately helps in the evaluating process; for logical form is one of the keys to determining whether an argument is logically successful.

Consider this experiment, described in *Scientific American*, which has to do with the system of flight-enhancing air sacs distributed throughout the bodies of most birds:

> A crucial experiment was performed by the French scientist J. M. Soum, who admitted carbon monoxide into the air sacs of birds. If the air sacs had played any major role in their breathing, the birds would have been rapidly poisoned by the carbon monoxide. But they remained completely unaffected. We can therefore conclude that the air sacs of birds play no direct role in their breathing.

This argument depends on the following simple form:

1. If *P* then *Q*.
2. Not *Q*.

∴ *C.* Not *P.*

The structured paraphrase (which has also been subjected to the guidelines for streamlining and specifying, where appropriate) looks like this:

1. If air sacs of birds play a role in their breathing, then birds are poisoned by carbon monoxide introduced into their air sacs.
2. Birds are not poisoned by carbon monoxide introduced into their air sacs.

∴ *C.* Air sacs of birds do not play a role in their breathing.

Seeing the underlying form enables you to organize the paraphrase much more clearly. And, as a bonus, as soon as you recognize the form of this particular argument you can anticipate your evaluation of the argument's logic—for it turns out that this form is one that is known always to be logically successful.

The vast majority of simple arguments rely on one of only a dozen or so common forms. For all of them, logical success is at least partly a matter of correct form. For many of them (those identified later in the text as *deductive* arguments) logical success is *entirely* a matter of correct form. This chapter uses just a few of these argument forms as examples to illustrate the main guidelines for structuring. For that reason, the chapter is short. The point here is to be clear about the notion of logical form because it plays such an important role in clarifying and evaluating.

VARIABLES AND CONSTANTS

The form of the air sac argument, as noted, is this:

1. If *P* then *Q*.
2. Not *Q*.

∴ *C*. Not *P*.

Not only is this schema far shorter than the argument itself, but also it is uninformative—that is, it is empty; it includes none of the argument's interesting information about birds, air sacs, and carbon monoxide. That is because the content of the argument has been eliminated.

An argument's ***content*** is the part of the argument that can vary without varying the argument's logical form. Thus, in a description of an argument's form, the placeholders such as *P* and *Q* that indicate where the content can *vary* are termed ***variables***. You should be able to intuitively see that the following argument has the same logical form as the air sac argument, but it is about something entirely different—that is, it has different content:

> If you are to make an *A* in this course, you must show that you have a basic understanding of the material. But you have shown no such thing. So you will certainly not make an *A* in this course.

Something about grades and understanding, rather than about air sacs and carbon monoxide, is filling in for the variables *P* and *Q*.

The physical world includes many types of structures. A swimming pool, its form defined by its concrete shell, is one sort of structure. A tent, framed by its poles and pegs, is another. A wide variety of liquids—water, wine, milk, gasoline—can fill out the form of a swimming pool; that is, they can all serve as content for such a structure. (Swimming in some of them might prove to be a memorable experience, but that is a different point.) And a wide variety of fabrics—canvas, nylon, cotton, linen, silk—can serve as content to be structured into the form of a tent. Liquids, however, don't make for good tents and fabrics do not pour very well into swimming pools.

Similarly, in this text we will encounter two sorts of logical forms, each of which requires a certain sort of linguistic material—and only that sort of material—for its content: those forms that require *statements*, and those that require *names and predicates*.

Statements as Content

In the air sac and course grade arguments, only statements can replace the variables *P* and *Q*—one for each occurrence of *P*, another for each occurrence of *Q*. For convenience, in describing an argument's form we will indicate statements by capital letters from *P* to *Z*. In the air sac argument, the variables are filled in by the following statements:

> *P:* Air sacs of birds play a role in their breathing.
> *Q:* Birds are poisoned by carbon monoxide introduced into their air sacs.

But in the course grade argument, these statements would replace the variables:

> *P:* You make an *A* in the course.
> *Q:* You show that you have a basic understanding of the material.

The key point is that in each of these cases, the form of the argument depends solely on relationships among statements.

These sorts of forms are usually described as belonging to ***sentential logic***, since they have to do with logical relationships among entire sentences (and a statement, as we have defined it, is a kind of sentence). This is also sometimes called *propositional logic* (since statements are sometimes also called propositions). Here is an argument with a different logical form that, nevertheless, relies on sentential logic:

> Humans are plants or humans are animals. But they aren't plants, so it follows that they are animals.

Its form is identical to the following argument.

Either the CIA or Oswald killed Kennedy. The CIA didn't do it. Thus, Oswald killed Kennedy.

Again, the content of these two arguments is completely different. But the statements in each of them are arranged in exactly the same way. They share the following logical form:

1. *P* or *Q*.
2. Not *P*.

∴ *C*. *Q*.

For the animals argument, the content can be represented in this way:

P: Humans are plants.
Q: Humans are animals.

For the CIA argument, these are the relevant statements:

P: The CIA killed Kennedy.
Q: Oswald killed Kennedy.

EXERCISES Chapter 6, set (a)

Given the proposed form, identify which statement is represented by each variable.

Sample exercise. It did not rain on our parade. (Not *P*.)
Sample answer. P: It rained on our parade.

1. She could not remember the phone number. (Not *P*.)
2. If you had told me about the exam, then I would have passed the class. (If *P* then *Q*.)
3. The band will sign with either MCA or Geffen Records. (*P* or *Q*.)
4. If you pay me enough, then I will take the job. (If *P* then *Q*.)

Names and Predicates as Content

In many cases, it is not the relationships *between* statements but the relationships *within* statements that matter most from a logical point of view. Take the following familiar argument:

All men are mortal. Socrates is a man. So, Socrates is mortal.

You can intuitively see that it has the same logical form as this one:

All highways are paved. Route 66 is a highway. So, Route 66 is paved.

If we attempted to deal with these two as though they were arguments of sentential logic, then we could only represent their form as three separate statements, as follows:

1. *P.*
2. *Q.*

∴ C. *R.*

This does nothing to display the form that the arguments are depending on for logical success. That form, rather, is this:

1. All *F* are *G*.
2. *A* is *F*.

∴ C. *A* is *G*.

Here, the variable *A* can be filled in by a ***name***—that is, an expression that identifies something that has properties attributed to it. (These do not have to be proper names; for example, the expression *my teacher* in *My teacher is no slave to fashion* can serve as a name for our purposes.) We'll use the letters *A* through *E* as variables for names when describing an argument's form. In the mortality argument, the name fills in for the variable thus:

A: Socrates.

And in the highway argument, it is as follows:

A: Route 66.

The variables *F* and *G*, on the other hand, can each be filled in by a ***predicate***—that is, an expression that identifies a property or attribute that can be ascribed to the thing named. We'll use the letters *F* through *O* as variables for predicates when describing an argument's form. In the mortality argument, the predicates are these:

F: a man.
G: mortal.

And in the highway argument, these are the predicates:

F: a highway.
G: paved.

The branch of logic that deals with relationships among names and predicates is called ***predicate logic*** or, alternatively *quantifier logic* (since these arguments include quantity terms like *all*).

EXERCISES Chapter 6, set (b)

Given the proposed form, identify which statement is represented by each variable.

Sample exercise. Montana is a large state. (*A* is *F.*)
Sample answer. A: Montana. *F:* a large state.

1. All large states have mountains in them. (All *F* are *G.*)
2. My dog is a beagle. (*A* is *F.*)
3. The band will sign with Geffen Records. (*A* is *F.*)
4. Dolphins are mammals. (All *F* are *G.*)

Constants

Regardless of how you vary the fabric of a tent, the pegs and poles determine its form; and no matter which liquid you pour into a swimming pool, the concrete shell fixes its form. The pegs and poles, or the concrete shells, of arguments are called ***logical constants*** (or *connectives*). These are the expressions that cannot vary without varying the form of the argument.

Consider the arguments of sentential logic, in which statements provide the content. The expressions that remain the same—the constants—are terms like *if–then*, *or*, *and*, and *not*. As for the arguments of predicate logic, where names and predicates provide the content, the constants are terms like *is* (which means, roughly, *has the property of . . .*) and *all*. Other constants that might occur in these sorts of arguments are *is not* and other quantities besides *all*, such as *none*, *some*, and *most*.

Be very clear: you will never be asked to display the *mere* form, simply with constants and variables, in your clarified argument. Thinking about the mere form helps you to organize your paraphrase and helps you in evaluating the logic of the argument. But it would normally not help, for example, in evaluating the truth of premises. Is *Not Q* true, or is it false? How can you tell? As it stands, it is empty. You can't think about whether it is true or false until you know what statement is being substituted for *Q*!

Guideline: Identify the logical form of the argument; this will help you in structuring the argument—that is, in organizing your paraphrase of the argument—and eventually in evaluating its logical success.

EXERCISES Chapter 6, set (c)

Given the proposed content, write out the form of the sentence, using only constants and variables.

Sample exercise. Most people who go fishing don't catch a fish.
(*F:* people who go fishing. *G:* catch a fish.)
Sample answer. Most *F* are not *G*.

1. Jeff did not catch a fish. (*P:* Jeff caught a fish.)
2. Jeff did not catch a fish. (*A:* Jeff; *F:* caught a fish.)
3. Jeff either caught a trout or a bass. (*P:* Jeff caught a trout; *Q:* Jeff caught a bass.)
4. If Jeff caught a fish, then it was the first time. (*P:* Jeff caught a fish; *Q:* it was the first time.)

Sentential Logic versus Predicate Logic

	SENTENTIAL LOGIC	PREDICATE LOGIC
LOGICAL CONSTANTS	If–then, and, or, not	Is, is not, all, some, none, most
VARIABLES	*P* through *Z*	*A* through *E*; *F* through *O*
CONTENT OF VARIABLES	Statements	Names; predicates

TRANSLATING STYLISTIC VARIANTS

The point of structuring is to paraphrase the argument in ordinary language so that its logical form is close enough to the surface to be clearly visible. This usually requires both doing something with the constants—namely, translating the stylistic variants—and also doing something with the content—namely, matching the wording.

There are many ways that the same logical constants might be phrased in ordinary English. Consider, for example, the sentence *If you are to make an A in this course, then you must show that you have a basic understanding of the material.* We would ordinarily say that *if–then* is the constant, and that its form is *If P then Q.* But there are many ways of saying the same thing without making any change in the content of *P* and *Q*. Here are only a few examples:

If you are to make an *A* in this course, you must show that you have a basic understanding of the material.
You must show that you have a basic understanding of the material if you are to make an *A* in this course.
Supposing you are to make an *A* in this course, then you must show that you have a basic understanding of the material.
You are to make an *A* in this course only if you show that you have a basic understanding of the material.

If P then Q is the ***standard constant***—the expression that is conventionally thought to be most effective in bringing to the surface an argument's logical form, and thus the one that we will adopt for use in the structuring of the argument. The others are ***stylistic variants*** on the standard constant—that is, they are alternative styles of saying the same thing. Structuring requires that you translate stylistic variants into the standard constant. Each of the preceding four variants must be paraphrased as *If you are to make an A in this course, then you must show that you have a basic understanding of the material.*

Here are some additional examples of stylistic variants and the standard constant into which they should be translated.

STANDARD CONSTANT	STYLISTIC VARIANTS
If *P* then *Q*.	If *P*, *Q*.
	Q if *P*.
	Supposing that *P*, then *Q*.
	Q only if *P*.
	So long as *P*, then *Q*.
P or *Q*.	*P* unless *Q*.
	Q or *P*.
Not *P*.	*P* is false.
	P is not true.
All *F* are *G*.	100% of *F* are *G*.
	Any *F* is *G*.
	Everything that is *F* is *G*.
A is *F*.	One thing that has *F* is *A*.
	A has the property of being *F*.

For every form of argument that is covered in future chapters, there will be a more extensive discussion of the stylistic variants for its standard constants.

Guideline. Translate stylistic variants into the standard constants for the relevant logical form.

EXERCISES Chapter 6, set (d)

For each sentence, translate the stylistic variants into the standard constant for the given logical form. If you get stuck, check the brief list of sample stylistic variants in the preceding section.

Sample exercise. Russia will not perish so long as we shall drink.
—slogan of pro-sobriety campaign in Poland (If *P*, then *Q*.)
Sample answer: If we shall drink, then Russia will not perish.

1. What goes up must come down. (All *F* are *G*.)
2. More voters would come out to the polls if the candidates ran more positive campaigns. (If *P*, then *Q*.)
3. One city with a rich history is Boston. (*A* is *F*.)
4. Unless I'm mistaken, we've met before. (*P* or *Q*.)
5. There is no way that you will catch your plane. (Not *P*.)

MATCHING WORDING

Structuring the argument requires you to standardize not only the argument's logical constants, but also its content. As with logical constants, the same statement, name, or predicate can be expressed in different ways. Socrates, for example, may be referred to as *the teacher of Plato*; instead of *men* (for mankind) you might say *humans*; and for *mortal* you might say *eventually die*. The mortality argument, then, might well be expressed this way in ordinary language:

> All humans are mortal. The teacher of Plato is a man. So, Socrates must eventually die.

When it seems clear that the arguer really means the same thing by the alternative expressions, you should revise them so that they match. As a result, it becomes much clearer that they are the same, and the logical form of the argument comes closer to the surface. When you match wording in this argument, then, your paraphrase might look like this:

1. All men are mortal.
2. Socrates is a man.

∴ *C*. Socrates is mortal.

Of course, the structured paraphrase might just as well look like this:

1. All humans must eventually die.
2. The teacher of Plato is human.

∴ *C.* The teacher of Plato must eventually die.

When faced with such a choice, follow the principles of clarifying as already laid out—pick the wording that is clearest and most loyal to the arguer's intentions or make up your own clearer and more loyal paraphrase. If two choices seem to be on equal footing (such as *mortal* and *must eventually die*), then just pick one, be sure to match the wording throughout the argument, and move ahead.

You might suspect that there is really an implicit inference involved in cases where we match wording. For example, you might think that it's a mistake just to substitute *Socrates is a man* for *The teacher of Plato is a man.* Isn't there actually an implicit premise—namely, *The teacher of Plato is Socrates*—that allows us to connect one to the other? Perhaps there is. But this is a situation where practical common sense should take precedence over excessive logical scrupulosity. Treating every case of matching wording as an implicit subargument would convert many simple arguments into complex arguments with many subconclusions—each subargument with premises and logic of its own that must be evaluated. Usually, the alternative expressions are reasonable; we're not normally giving anything important away, for example, by simply granting that *Socrates* and *the teacher of Plato* can be used interchangeably. If the alternative expressions are reasonable—if allowing them is not likely to weaken the argument in any way—then don't clutter the argument with excessive subconclusions; just match the wording and move ahead.

Guideline. When the same statement, name, or predicate is expressed in more than one way, match the wording in your paraphrase.

Structuring

1. For logical constants—*translate stylistic variants* into standard constants.
2. For content—*match wording* when the same statements, names, or predicates are expressed in different ways.

EXERCISES Chapter 6, set (e)

Structure each argument according to the logical form described in parentheses, paying special attention to translating stylistic variants and matching wording.

Sample exercise. General Halftrack, looking at the overflowing "Complaints" box: "Look at those complaints! It's disgraceful! Either the box is too small or we're not running this camp right."

The General, in reply: "Have a bigger box built." —*Beetle Bailey* (*P* or *Q*. *[Not Q.]* ∴ *P*.)

Sample answer.

1. The complaints box is too small or the general is not running the camp right.
2. It is not the case that the general is not running the camp right.

∴ *C*. The complaints box is too small.

1. Every great university has an excellent library. So Oxford, being one of the best, can be expected to have an outstanding library. (All *F* are *G*. *A is F*. ∴ *A* is *G*.)
2. Epidemiological evidence has consistently indicated that severe alcoholism runs in families, and these findings, the researchers say, lend further support to the idea of a hereditary component to the disorder. If alcoholism were exclusively a social or psychological phenomenon, they point out, all of the alcoholic subjects would be expected to have acquired the same biological abnormality; 20% did not. Further studies of alcoholic and nonalcoholic twins will be necessary to verify the genetic contribution, Rutstein says. —*Science News* (If *P* then *Q*. Not *Q*. ∴ Not *P*.)
3. Certainly most who would go into the death hogan would not be Navajo. White men, yes. So the horse thief was a white.—*The Ghostway*, by Tony Hillerman (Most *F* are *G*. [*A* is *F*.] ∴ *A* is *G*.)
4. "Mankind, he said, . . . have never, as I think, at all understood the power of Love. For if they had understood him they would surely have built noble temples and altars, and offered solemn sacrifices in his honor; but this is not done. . . ." —Plato, *Symposium* (If *P*, then *Q*. Not *Q*. ∴ Not *P*.)
5. It is a common notion that morality simply means conformity to the customs of one's group. But this cannot be the case. If it were, we

could never criticize and improve the morals of our group, at least we would have no moral basis for doing so. However superstitious, or stupid, or cruel the customs of our community are, they would be, by definition, morally right—for us. The unthinking conformist would be the moral man, the moral reformer the immoral man. There would be no moral progress. But no one really believes this. We all constantly criticize the morals of our group. —Durant Drake, *Invitation to Philosophy* (If *P* then *Q*. Not *Q*. ∴ Not *P*.)

6. "The sentence 'I know that I am in pain' makes sense only if 'I doubt that I am in pain' does also. The latter sentence does not make sense. Therefore, the former doesn't either." —Ludwig Wittgenstein, *Philosophical Investigations* (If *P* then *Q*. Not *Q*. ∴ Not *P*.)

SUMMARY OF CHAPTER SIX

Structuring is an important part of clarifying an argument, since it organizes the paraphrase in such a way that the argument's logical form is close enough to the surface to be clearly visible. Logical form is always relevant to the logical success of an argument; thus, structuring contributes to the overall goal of all argument clarification—it makes it easier to evaluate the argument.

An argument's form is determined by certain logical constants (like *all* and *or*) and by certain content (like statements, names, and predicates) that is linked together by the constants. Structuring requires that when you determine an argument's logical form, you do something to both the constants and the content. With respect to the constants, translate stylistic variants (like *every*) into the standard constant (like, *all*). With respect to the content, match the wording of statements, names, or predicates when they occur more than once and the meaning is clearly the same (such as paraphrasing *must eventually die* to *is mortal* when both expressions are used).

GUIDELINES FOR CHAPTER SIX

- Identify the logical form of the argument; this will help you in structuring the argument—that is, in organizing your paraphrase of the argument—and eventually in evaluating its logical success.

- Translate stylistic variants into the standard constants for the relevant logical form.
- When the same statement, name, or predicate is expressed in more than one way, match the wording in your paraphrase.

GLOSSARY FOR CHAPTER SIX

Content—the part of the argument that can vary without varying the argument's logical form. It can be made up of statements, names, or predicates. In a description of an argument's form, the placeholders—such as *P* and *Q*—that indicate where the content can *vary* are termed *variables.*

Logical constants—the expressions that provide an argument with its logical form. These cannot vary without varying the form of the argument. Also called *connectives.*

Name—an expression that identifies something to which, typically, properties are attributed. Names do not have to be proper names; for example, the expression *my teacher* in *My teacher is no slave to fashion* can serve as a name for our purposes. We are using the letters *A* through *E* as variables for names when describing logical form.

Predicate—an expression that identifies a property or attribute that can be ascribed to the thing named. We are using the letters *F* through *O* as variables for predicates when describing an argument's form.

Predicate logic—the branch of logic that deals with logical relationships among names and predicates. This is also sometimes called *quantifier logic*, because their arguments include quantity terms like *all.*

Sentential logic—the branch of logic that deals with logical relationships among entire statements (which are a kind of sentence). This is also sometimes called *propositional logic* because statements are sometimes called *propositions.* We are using the letters *P* through *Z* as variables for statements when describing the form of an argument of sentential logic.

Standard constants—when there are various ways of expressing the same constant, the one expression that we are adopting for use in the structuring of the argument. The alternative expressions are termed *stylistic variants* and are to be translated into the standard constants. For example, *if–then* is the standard constant, *assuming–then* is a stylistic variant of it.

Structuring—organizing your paraphrase of the argument so as to make its logical form as obvious as possible. This typically requires two procedures: translating stylistic variants into their standard constants, and matching the wording of statements, names, or predicates when they are expressed more than once in different language.

Stylistic variants—when there are various ways of expressing the same constant, the expressions that are to be translated into the standard constants. For example, *if–then* is the standard constant, *assuming–then* is a stylistic variant of it.

Variables—placeholders such as *P* and *Q* that indicate where the content can vary. These appear only in a description of an argument's form, not in its clarification.

PART THREE

EVALUATING ARGUMENTS

CHAPTER SEVEN

A Framework for Evaluating

The main aim of education is practical and reflective judgment, a mind trained to be critical everywhere in the use of evidence.

—Brand Blanshard, *Four Reasonable Men*

TOPICS

Standard Evaluating Format
Complex Arguments
A Reasonable Objector over Your Shoulder

We now arrive at the portion of the book that is most important for good reasoning, the portion that Parts One and Two have been pointing toward: the evaluation of arguments.

In Part One we saw that good reasoning is ultimately a matter of cultivating the intellectual virtues, including the virtues of critical reflection, empirical inquiry, and intellectual honesty. This requires close attention to arguments, since cultivating each of these virtues is greatly enhanced by skill in clarifying and evaluating arguments. And *close attention to arguments* is shorthand, really, for *close attention to whether arguments have the four merits of clarity, true premises, good logic, and conversational relevance.*

In Part Two we saw that clarity is the starting point. This starting point is not only a matter of asking whether an argument is clear, but is also a matter of enhancing the argument's clarity through the clarifying process. This process includes two general procedures: outlining the argument in standard clarifying format, and, at the same time, paraphrasing the argument for greater clarity. Paraphrasing should accomplish three things: streamlining, specifying, and structuring. And it should be governed by two general principles. The principle of loyalty tells you to imagine that the arguer is looking over your shoulder, checking to be sure that the paraphrased argument reflects the arguer's intentions. The principle of charity applies if the context does not indicate the arguer's intentions; it tells you to paraphrase in a way that makes the arguer as reasonable as possible—to paraphrase according to what you probably would have meant had you expressed the same words under similar circumstances.

The whole point of clarifying is to make it simpler to determine whether arguments have the other three merits. The remainder of the book has to do with asking these three questions of clarified arguments: *Are the premises true? Is the logic good?* And, to a lesser extent, *Is the argument conversationally relevant?*

STANDARD EVALUATING FORMAT

Just as there is a standard clarifying format, so is there a standard evaluating format. It systematically links your evaluation to the clarified argument and provides a framework for considering the questions about truth, logic, and conversational relevance. Let's start with the clarified argument from *Scientific American* about the air sacs that are spread throughout the bodies of most birds:

1. If air sacs of birds play a role in their breathing, then birds are poisoned by carbon monoxide introduced into their air sacs.
2. Birds are not poisoned by carbon monoxide introduced into their air sacs.

∴ *C*. Air sacs of birds do not play a role in their breathing.

Standard evaluating format provides a simple system for discussing the truth of each premise, the logic of the argument, and (where appropriate) the conversational relevance of the argument. Begin with the main heading EVALUATION, and under it provide at least three subheadings: TRUTH, LOGIC, and SOUNDNESS. (In some cases you will need a fourth subheading, CONVERSATIONAL RELEVANCE.)

Under TRUTH, provide an entry for each premise, and for each premise do two things: state whether you judge the premise to be true, and provide your defense of that evaluation. For the air sac argument, this part of the evaluation would look something like this:

EVALUATION

TRUTH

Premise 1. This premise is probably true, assuming large enough quantities of carbon monoxide are involved, since carbon monoxide is known to be poisonous to any animal when breathed in sufficient quantities.

Premise 2. This premise is probably true, since this is reported in *Scientific American*, known to be a highly reliable publication on topics of this sort, and there is no reason to doubt this particular report.

Under the next subheading, LOGIC, do the same things: state whether you think the logic of the simple argument is good, and provide a defense of that evaluation. The evaluation would continue roughly as follows:

LOGIC

The argument is valid, since it has the form denying the consequent.

It isn't important at this point in the text that you understand the exact technical meaning of expressions like *valid* or *denying the consequent.* For now you only need to know what is intuitively obvious—that expressions like *valid, very strong,* and *fairly strong* are ways of saying that the logic is good, while expressions like *invalid, fairly weak,* and *very weak* are ways of saying that it is bad.

After this, under the heading SOUNDNESS, provide your summary judgment—*sound* or *unsound*—based on the two preceding sections of the evaluation. If you judge that the argument is not sound, state whether this is owing to a problem either with a premise or with the argument's logic. But if you judge that it is sound, there is no need for further explanation since saying it is sound is the same as saying the premises are true and the logic is good. In our sample air sac case, it would look like this:

> SOUNDNESS
>
> The argument is probably sound.

Notice the argument is judged *probably* sound. Your judgment of the argument's soundness cannot be any better than the poorest thing said under TRUTH and LOGIC. While under the heading of LOGIC the logic of the air sac argument is judged to be good, under the heading of TRUTH each of the premises is judged merely *probably* true. Thus, the argument cannot be evaluated as any better than *probably* sound.

We have not yet provided a place in the format for conversational relevance. This can be an extremely important question, but it will turn out that the majority of the arguments you evaluate will not appear to be defective in this way. My suggestion—which we will follow in this text—is that a fourth subheading, CONVERSATIONAL RELEVANCE, be optional. Include it when an argument is conversationally flawed, and under the heading explain how the argument is thus flawed. But otherwise omit it, simply for the practical reason that it will save you extra writing.

The air sac argument is, so far as I can tell, conversationally relevant. Without any context, there is no good reason to think that it begs the question or misses the point. We could imagine, however, contexts in which it would be conversationally flawed. Suppose, for example, that the same argument had been put forward by a laboratory assistant who was asked by the laboratory director to look into whether air sacs in birds played any role in their *breeding*. We would in that case add a fourth subheading, as follows:

> CONVERSATIONAL RELEVANCE
>
> Even though it is sound, the argument commits the fallacy of missing the point, since the point is to show whether the air sacs play any role in breeding, but the argument only addresses whether they play a role in breathing.

By following this format, you can develop the habit of systematically asking all the right evaluative questions of an argument, and you will always have a straightforward way of presenting your judgments.

Guideline. Evaluate the clarified argument in standard evaluating format.

Guideline. Your evaluation of the argument's soundness should be no better than the poorest evaluation you have provided of its logic and of the truth of its premises.

Standard Evaluating Format

Heading: EVALUATION

Subheading: TRUTH. For each premise, state whether you judge it to be true and provide your defense of that judgment.

Subheading: LOGIC. State whether you judge the logic to be successful and provide your defense of that judgment.

Subheading: SOUNDNESS. State whether you judge the argument to be sound; then, if it is not sound, state whether this is owing to a problem with a premise or with the logic.

Subheading (optional): CONVERSATIONAL RELEVANCE. If and only if the argument is flawed in this way, state whether it commits the fallacy of begging the question or missing the point, and explain how.

EXERCISES Chapter 7, set (a)

Given the brief evaluations provided for truth and logic, provide, in standard form, the correct evaluation of the argument's soundness.

Sample exercise (1).

TRUTH. Premise 1 is probably true. I can't decide about premise 2. LOGIC. The argument is valid.

Sample answer (1).

SOUNDNESS. I can't decide whether the argument is sound, since I can't decide about the truth of one of the premises.

Sample exercise (2).
TRUTH. Premise 1 is certainly true. *LOGIC.* The argument is fairly weak logically.
Sample answer (2).
SOUNDNESS. The argument is fairly unsound, since the logic is fairly weak.

1. TRUTH. Premise 1 is probably false. I can't decide about premise 2. LOGIC. The argument is invalid.
2. TRUTH. Premise 1 is probably false. LOGIC. The argument is extremely weak.
3. TRUTH. Premise 1 is certainly false. I can't decide about premise 2. LOGIC. The argument is valid.
4. TRUTH. Premise 1 is certainly true. LOGIC. The argument is valid.
5. TRUTH. Premise 1 is probably true. I can't decide about premise 2. Premise 3 is certainly true. LOGIC. The argument is fairly strong.
6. TRUTH. Premise 1 is probably true. Premise 2 is probably true. Premise 3 is certainly true. LOGIC. The argument is very strong.

The Conclusion

You may have noticed there is no place in this format for evaluating whether the main conclusion of any argument is itself true. This may initially strike you as a serious oversight. But it is not. What we are evaluating here is not the truth of the conclusion, but the quality of the reasoning for the conclusion. Suppose you decided that an argument was utterly unsound, yet at the same time suspected that the conclusion was true. That would be no problem. Recall that for any true statement, it is possible to offer a bad argument in the attempt to support the statement. (If it then turned out that you were especially interested in such a conclusion, it would be up to you to see if you could come up with a better argument for it.) On the other hand, suppose you had a strong hunch that a conclusion was false, even though the argument itself appeared to be sound. This would give you good reason to check more carefully for a flaw in the argument, one that may have initially escaped your notice. Or you could end up changing your mind and accepting the initially implausible conclusion.

Guideline. If you have judged an argument to be sound, but you find that you still have doubts about the truth of the conclusion, carefully examine the argument again. You may initially have overlooked a flaw.

COMPLEX ARGUMENTS

There is no important difference between evaluating a simple argument and a complex one. If the argument is complex—that is, if it is a series of linked simple arguments—then, after the clarification of the complex argument, evaluate separately each simple argument that makes up the complex argument. Instead of the heading EVALUATION, use the heading EVALUATION OF ARGUMENT TO N, where *n* identifies the relevant subconclusion or conclusion. To illustrate, suppose other air sac experiments by Professor Soum, reported in the same *Scientific American* story, had independently narrowed down the role of air sacs in birds to either flight-enhancement or breathing-enhancement. Suppose further that the air sac argument had been the first part of a larger argument that was designed to settle this issue, concluding thus:

> Therefore, since air sacs in birds are known to play a role in either flight or breathing, we can conclude that they play a role in flight.

The complex argument would be clarified thus (adding premise 4 and a new conclusion):

1. If air sacs of birds play a role in their breathing, then birds are poisoned by carbon monoxide introduced into their air sacs.
2. Birds are not poisoned by carbon monoxide introduced into their air sacs.

∴ 3. Air sacs of birds do not play a role in their breathing.

4. Air sacs of birds play a role in their breathing or air sacs in birds play a role in their flight.

∴ *C.* Air sacs of birds play a role in their flight.

The evaluation, framed in standard evaluation format, would then look like this:

EVALUATION OF ARGUMENT TO 3

TRUTH

Premise 1. This premise is probably true, assuming large enough quantities of carbon monoxide are involved, since carbon monoxide is known to be poisonous to any animal when breathed in sufficient quantities.

Premise 2. This premise is probably true, since this is reported in *Scientific American*, known to be a highly reliable publication on topics of this sort, and there is no special reason to doubt this particular report.

LOGIC

The argument is valid, since it has the form of denying the consequent.

SOUNDNESS

The argument is probably sound.

EVALUATION OF ARGUMENT TO C

TRUTH

Premise 3 is probably true, since it is supported by an argument that we have seen is probably sound (see evaluation of argument to 3).

Premise 4 is probably true, since (according to my hypothetical addition to the actual story, for the sake of this illustration) the experiments are reported in *Scientific American*, known to be a highly reliable publication on topics of this sort, and there is no reason to doubt this particular report.

LOGIC

The argument is valid, since it has the form of the process of elimination.

SOUNDNESS

The argument is probably sound.

The evaluation of the first simple argument remains exactly the same, except for expanding the heading to say EVALUATION OF THE ARGUMENT TO 3. And we add to it the evaluation of the second simple argument—the evaluation of the argument to *C*. Premise 3 is the subconclusion of the complex argument—so it is both the conclusion of the argument to 3 and a premise in the argument to *C*. When evaluating its truth (under the heading EVALUATION OF THE ARGUMENT TO C) it is good to point out that the premise is supported by an argument that you have just evaluated as probably sound.

Guideline. Evaluate separately each simple argument that serves as a component of a complex argument.

When a Simple Argument within the Complex Argument Is Unsound

In a complex argument, when one simple argument is sound it has an important effect on your entire evaluation. When you evaluate the subconclusion as a premise in the next simple argument, the soundness of the preceding simple argument serves as a good defense for judging its subconclusion to be true.

But this ripple effect does not naturally occur if the simple argument is *unsound.* Obviously, its unsoundness would not be something to appeal to in defense of the truth of the subconclusion. But—note this carefully—neither would it be something to appeal to in defense of the falsity of the subconclusion. Any statement, whether true or false, can have an unsound argument offered for it.

This presents an interesting problem: in a complex argument, you can evaluate a simple argument as unsound without its affecting your evaluation of the next simple argument. Thus, in a complex argument, you may evaluate as perfectly sound the argument to the main conclusion, even though the previous simple arguments have been unsound. This is as it should be. But at the same time, since the arguer has presented the complex argument as a whole, there should be some way of indicating earlier problems when you evaluate later simple arguments.

The solution is this: in a complex argument, when one simple argument is unsound and the next one is sound, qualify your evaluation of it as ***sound but not shown.*** In this way, you indicate that even though the simple argument is, in your judgment, sound, the arguer has failed to carry out the job of *showing* it to be sound by the previous simple arguments.

Here is an easy-to-understand example:

> You have to be extremely good-looking to get hired as a lifeguard. Not many people are that good-looking, so it's very tough to land such a job. For that reason, even though it would be great to work on the beach, most people should probably try to find some other sort of summer job.

This argument can be clarified as follows:

1. If someone qualifies for a job as a lifeguard, then that person is extremely good-looking.
2. Not many people are extremely good-looking.

∴ 3. Not many people qualify for a job as a lifeguard.

4. If not many people qualify for a particular job, then most people should try for some other sort of job.

∴ *C.* Most people should try for some other summer job than that of a lifeguard.

The subconclusion—*Not many people qualify for a job as a lifeguard*—seems clearly to be true. And even though the simple argument offered in its support is a bad one (premise 1, despite "Baywatch," is surely false), the simple argument from premises 3 and 4 to the main conclusion is a pretty good one. A very brief evaluation might take this rough form:

EVALUATION OF ARGUMENT TO 3

TRUTH

Premise 1. This premise is certainly false; it isn't looks, but experience and ability, which qualify you for a job as a lifeguard.

Premise 2. This premise is very probably true. My observations are that most people are average-looking (it may even be that *average-looking* just means *the way most people look*).

LOGIC

The argument is valid, since it has the form of singular denying the consequent.

SOUNDNESS

The argument is unsound, due to the falsity of premise 1.

EVALUATION OF ARGUMENT TO C

TRUTH

Premise 3 is certainly true. Most people *need* a lifeguard just because they aren't qualified to be one. Qualifying to be a lifeguard requires that you be in excellent physical shape, that you be able to swim well, and that you have extensive training. (Before completing the evaluation, note that even though the argument to 3 has just been evaluated as *unsound*, I have nevertheless defended here the truth of 3—but for entirely different reasons than those offered in the argument to 3.)

Premise 4 is probably true. Under most circumstances, it doesn't make good practical sense for people to apply for a job if their chances of getting it are extremely low.

LOGIC

The argument is valid, since it has the form of singular affirming the antecedent.

SOUNDNESS

The argument is probably sound, but is not shown to be so by the rest of the argument.

Note that the argument to C is judged as *probably sound* (since the poorest thing said about it under TRUTH and LOGIC is that its premises are *probably true*). But, to reflect the unsoundness of the simple argument used to lead into it, it is noted that it was *not shown* to be sound by the preceding simple argument.

> *Guideline.* In a complex argument, if one simple argument is unsound and a later one is sound, qualify your evaluation of the sound one by saying that it is *sound but not shown.* This applies only to complex arguments.

EXERCISES Chapter 7, set (b)

Briefly describe the general conditions under which each of the following evaluations would apply.

1. Briefly describe the general conditions under which each of the following evaluations would apply:
   a. Sound.
   b. Probably sound.
   c. Unsound.
   d. Sound but not shown.
   e. Can't decide whether it is sound.
2. Briefly explain why each of these evaluations would not make sense, given the framework for evaluation defined here:
   a. Unsound but not shown.
   b. True but not shown.
   c. Logically successful but not shown.
   d. Logically successful because the preceding simple argument has been evaluated as sound.

A REASONABLE OBJECTOR OVER YOUR SHOULDER

Whenever you write anything, it is crucially important that you know who your audience is. You may be writing for introductory students, your professor, your parents, a customer, a friend, your professional colleagues, or the general public. Different writing is designed for different audiences. And this applies to argument evaluations. Often they are directed at the arguer, whom you may hope to prove wrong. When doing the exercises in this text, you will be aiming them to your professor, who will grade your paper. When you do them on your job, you may be aiming them to a potential customer, whom you may hope to convince of the flaws in your competitor's product.

But in the background, your primary audience should always be you. You should be aiming to arrive at the best evaluation you can *for your own sake*—the evaluation that is most likely to result in *your arriving at knowledge* and the one most likely to cultivate the habits that would continue to be conducive to your arriving at knowledge. In short, always evaluate arguments with a view to being the most honest, critically reflective, and inquisitive thinker you can be.

It may not always be easy to think in this way when evaluating an argument. It can be much easier to think in terms of an opponent who must be won over. And this can be turned to your advantage. Recall that an important guideline for *clarifying* is to imagine the arguer looking over your shoulder, checking your paraphrase for loyalty to the arguer's intentions. I now recommend that you be similarly accompanied while *evaluating* the argument. In evaluating, though, imagine that looking over your shoulder is a reasonable person who disagrees with your evaluation. This ***reasonable objector*** has roughly the same evidence that you have and possesses the intellectual virtues of honesty, critical reflection, and inquiry. What reasons are most likely to persuade this person to accept your evaluation? What objection is this person most likely to raise? Be sure to express your defense in a way that defeats—or ultimately agrees with—the objections of this hypothetical adversary. In this way, you are more likely to exemplify the intellectual virtues yourself.

Guideline. While writing your evaluation, imagine that there is a reasonable objector looking over your shoulder, one whom you must persuade.

SUMMARY OF CHAPTER SEVEN

Frame your evaluation of every argument in the standard evaluation format, thereby ensuring that you appropriately present and defend your evaluation of the truth of every premise, the success of the argument's logic, and, when necessary, the conversational relevance of the argument. The key judgment in every case is whether the argument is sound—that is, whether it is successful with respect to both truth and logic. Failure in either respect makes the argument unsound; and the poorest judgment in either respect should be reflected in your evaluation of the argument's soundness. (Thus, for example, an argument that is logically successful and with a premise you have judged to be probably true can, at best, be probably sound.)

When the argument is complex, separately evaluate each component simple argument. If one of the simple arguments other than the argument to the main conclusion is unsound, and if a later simple argument is sound, be sure the earlier failure is reflected by noting that even the sound argument has not been shown to be sound in the preceding portion of the complex argument.

While thinking about and writing your evaluation, imagine that a reasonable objector—an intellectually virtuous person who has roughly the same evidence you have but disagrees with you—is watching over your shoulder and must be persuaded by your evaluation.

GUIDELINES FOR CHAPTER SEVEN

- Evaluate the clarified argument in standard evaluating format.
- Your evaluation of the argument's soundness should be no better than the poorest evaluation you have provided of its logic and of the truth of its premises.
- If you have judged an argument to be sound, but you find that you still have doubts about the truth of the conclusion, carefully examine the argument again. You may initially have overlooked a flaw.
- Evaluate separately each simple argument that serves as a component of a complex argument.
- In a complex argument, if one simple argument is unsound and a later one is sound, qualify your evaluation of the sound one by saying that it is *sound but not shown.* This applies only to complex arguments.
- While writing your evaluation, imagine there is a reasonable objector looking over your shoulder, one whom you must persuade.

GLOSSARY FOR CHAPTER SEVEN

Reasonable objector—someone who has approximately the same information you have, who exhibits the virtues of honesty, critical reflection, and inquiry, yet who disagrees with your evaluation. Imagine that this is your audience for every evaluation you write.

Sound but not shown—evaluation to use under the SOUNDNESS subheading in a complex argument when one simple argument is sound but a preceding simple argument, on which it depends, is unsound. Using this terminology reflects the fact that even though this simple argument happens to be sound, the arguer has failed to show it to be so, by virtue of having supported it with an unsound argument.

CHAPTER EIGHT

Fallacies

Some people are beautiful thanks to their beauty, while others merely seem to be so, due to their efforts to embellish themselves. In the same way both reasoning and refutation are sometimes genuine, sometimes not. Inexperienced people look at these things, as it were, from a distance; so to them the embellishments often seem genuine.

—Aristotle, *Sophistical Refutations*

If we think of a fallacy as a deception, we are too likely to take it for granted that we need to be cautious in looking out for fallacies only when other people are arguing with us.

—L. Susan Stebbing, *Thinking to Some Purpose*

TOPICS

Argument-Based Fallacies
Motive-Based Fallacies
How to Think about Fallacies

Fallacies, as we will define them, are the easiest-to-make sorts of intellectual mistakes. These mistakes are so easy to make that even the most skillful and well-intentioned reasoners sometimes fall into them. Over the centuries they have acquired special names of their own. Some of these names will be familiar to you; for example, you may have heard of *ad hominem* arguments, even if you're not quite sure what the term means. Others will be unfamiliar, though in most cases you will recognize them as mistakes you have encountered in everyday arguments.

Learning to identify fallacies can help you in evaluating arguments and in becoming a better reasoner. Naming the easy-to-make mistakes makes the mistakes more vivid—recall the vividness shortcut as described in Chapter 1—and thus makes them easier to identify and to avoid. So, before we launch into the detailed discussions of evaluating truth and logic that make up the rest of this book, it should prove useful to survey the easiest-to-make errors.

In this book we will be concerned with two broad categories of fallacies: those that are argument-based, and those that are motive-based. ***Argument-based fallacies*** are specific flaws in one of the four merits of an argument: its clarity, the truth of its premises, its logic, or its conversational relevance. ***Motive-based fallacies*** typically result in a flaw in at least one of these four areas, but the location of the flaw in the argument may vary. These fallacies are flaws in the motives that this sort of argument tends to promote.

Two Broad Categories of Fallacies

1. *Argument-based fallacies*—indicate a specific flaw in the argument itself.
2. *Motive-based fallacies*—indicate a flaw in the motives the argument tends to promote.

ARGUMENT-BASED FALLACIES

We need to look only briefly at argument-based fallacies. This book has substantial sections on clarity (Chapters 3 through 6), truth (Chapter 9), and logic (Chapters 10 through 16); the fallacies associated with each of these three merits are discussed in those sections. Regarding clarity, recall, we covered two fallacies that have to do with ambiguity—the fallacy of equivocation and the fallacy of amphiboly—and two that have to do with vagueness—the slippery slope fallacy and the fallacy of arguing from the heap. Regarding truth, as we will see, fallacies—though they exist—are ordinarily not the appropriate sort of thing to look for when evaluating. And regarding logic, we will discuss a wide variety of fallacies, ranging from the fallacy of denying the antecedent to the fallacy of hasty generalization.

Argument-Based Fallacies

1. Those bearing on clarity (see Chapters 3–6).
2. Those bearing on truth (see Chapter 9).
3. Those bearing on logic (see Chapters 10–16).
4. Those bearing on conversational relevance (see below).

Fallacies and Conversational Relevance

Because this book has no separate section on the simplest of the four merits—conversational relevance—we will cover the fallacies of conversational relevance here in a bit more detail.

We are using the term *conversation* in its broadest sense; it can refer to interaction between two people, between author and audience, or even between arguer and imaginary adversary. In principle, the conversation can be spoken, written, or merely thought through as you pursue an issue on your own. Conversations of all these sorts generate questions, and arguments usually arise as the attempt to answer such questions. An argument that is conversationally relevant is an argument that does two things: it addresses the question that is asked, and it does so without presupposing the answer. To say that an argument is relevant is not to say that it answers the question well; conversational relevance has nothing to do with soundness. An unsound argument can still address the question asked and can do so in a way that does not presuppose the answer. And a sound argument can go wrong by answering the wrong question or by presupposing the answer.

The Fallacy of Missing the Point

An argument that answers the wrong question commits the ***fallacy of missing the point,*** also known as the *fallacy of ignoratio elenchi.* (This was explained in Chapter 3, where the straw man fallacy was introduced as a variety of the fallacy of missing the point.)

There are embarrassingly obvious ways of missing the point; recall, for example, the Chapter 1 argument that concluded with my explanation of why you had hives—even though the question, which I had simply misunderstood in the noisy restaurant, was why you had chives. But a more common, and more difficult to detect, way of making this mistake is when the argument's conclusion has some indirect bearing on the question and purports to answer the question but clearly falls short of directly addressing it.

Suppose, for example, your argument concludes *The order that we see in the universe is the result of intelligent design.* If this is offered as your sole answer to the question *Does an all-powerful, all-knowing, and all-good God exist?* then your argument—even if it is perfectly sound—falls far short of answering it. Intelligent design could be the work of a committee of designers, an evil designer, or even a designer who produced the design and promptly committed suicide. To say there is intelligent design is one thing; to say there is an all-powerful, all-knowing, all-good God is another. In short, your argument commits the fallacy of missing the point; and the evaluation of it should say so, under the subheading CONVERSATIONAL RELEVANCE, and should provide an explanation such as the one just given.

Don't be overeager, however, in finding this fallacy everywhere you look. There is nothing fallacious about such an argument, for instance, if you qualify it by saying, "I don't pretend to fully answer the question with this argument, but it might at least advance the conversation and ultimately help us in answering the question." The conversational defect in the argument occurs only when the impression is created that the question has been directly addressed—and, thus, if the argument is a sound one, that the question has been settled.

Note that the fallacy is not necessarily committed if the conclusion merely uses wording that differs from the way the background question has been previously worded. Such a conclusion may, nevertheless, capture what is most important about the question and thus may address the question. Suppose you seek my advice regarding whether you should travel to Europe this summer, and I give you an argument that concludes *You'll never have the same wonderful opportunity again.* Even though I haven't directly said you should go, you are unlikely to think that I have missed your point. By my arguing that the opportunity is wonderful and unique, I may have addressed the only things that matter with respect to whether you should go.

Guideline. If you know the question that is at issue in the conversation, then ask whether the conclusion addresses it. If it does not, then, even if the argument is sound, evaluate the argument as committing the fallacy of missing the point.

EXERCISES Chapter 8, set (a)

For each situation described below, state whether my argument commits the fallacy of missing the point and explain.

Sample exercise. In question: whether Southerners were immoral to own slaves in the antebellum South. My argument concludes: Thomas Jefferson owned slaves.

Sample answer. Fallacy of missing the point. The mere fact that Thomas Jefferson owned slaves doesn't seem to count in either direction, since many quite moral (otherwise) Southerners owned slaves.

1. In question: whether your city's baseball team is better than mine. My argument concludes: my team has a better overall record, a better record when the two teams meet, and better players at every position.
2. In question: whether smoking causes lung cancer. My argument concludes: the pleasures of smoking offset any risks it presents.
3. In question: whether democracy is a better form of government than communism. My argument concludes: ancient Athens was a democracy.
4. In question: whether you should go to graduate school. My argument concludes: your talents and interests are such that you're most likely to be successful in life as an entrepreneur.
5. John Cleese, formerly of "Monty Python's Flying Circus" and now preparing to make a movie called *Fierce Creatures* with dozens of animals, when asked by the *Los Angeles Times* why he would fly in the face of the famous advice of W.C. Fields never to work with children or animals:

   "Let's put all this in context, shall we?" he says, a touch imperiously. "I think you'll find the full saying is "Never work with children, animals, *or Stewart Granger.*" He nods complacently, like a man who has answered a tricky question really well.

The Fallacy of Begging the Question

Another requirement of conversational relevance is that the argument does not presuppose what is in question in the conversation. If an argument violates this requirement, it commits the ***fallacy of begging the question,*** sometimes more formally termed the *fallacy of petitio principii.* (*Petitio* comes from a word meaning *appeal to*, or *beg*, as in the English word *petition. Principii* is closely related to the English word *principle.* So, *petitio principii* is the fallacy of appealing to a principle that is in question—as though it were already settled.) Rather than putting in an honorable day's work, we might say, such an argument stoops to begging to get its conclusion.

You can look for several things as clues to the presence of this fallacy. The clearest clue would be a premise that is a carbon copy of the conclusion. *Why do I believe that Mozart is the greatest Austrian composer of all time? Because Mozart is the greatest Austrian composer of all time!* Here is a plausible way of clarifying and evaluating such an argument:

1. Mozart is the greatest Austrian composer of all time.

∴ *C.* Mozart is the greatest Austrian composer of all time.

EVALUATION

TRUTH

Premise 1 is almost certainly true. Many experts would assert something stronger—that he is the greatest composer of all time, regardless of national origin—given the amazing variety, quantity, and quality of his output. And every expert would put him *among* the greatest, regardless of national origin. None of the composers typically mentioned as competitors for the plaudit of greatest—Bach or Beethoven—is a fellow Austrian.

LOGIC

The argument is logically valid, by repetition.

SOUNDNESS

The argument is almost certainly sound.

CONVERSATIONAL RELEVANCE

Even though it is sound, the argument almost certainly commits the fallacy of begging the question, since the premise just is the conclusion.

Notice that in the evaluation of the argument's conversational relevance, I slightly hedge my critique by saying that it *almost certainly* begs the question. This is because I have evaluated this argument without any knowledge of its conversational context. To be fully confident that this is a fallacy, I must know the context.

But how could it possibly not beg the question, given that the premise just is the conclusion? Imagine the following conversational context. Last night, you and I had a scintillating conversation in which we decided on the greatest Austrians of all time in a wide variety of categories. Among other things, we settled on the greatest Austrian philosopher, the greatest Austrian novelist, the greatest Austrian scientist, and the greatest Austrian soccer player. And, after some discussion, we settled on Mozart as the greatest Austrian composer.

Tonight we find ourselves in a different, though equally riveting, conversation about the greatest composer from each of a variety of countries. We settle on Ives for America, Handel for England, Villa-Lobos for Brazil, and our tour finally arrives at Austria. We scratch our heads for a moment, and then you suddenly remember last night's conversation. "Hey!" you say. "Remember? Mozart is the greatest Austrian *composer* of all time. So, obviously, he's the greatest *Austrian* composer of all time." By stressing the word *composer* in your premise you remind me of last night's conversation in which we selected him in the composer category; and by stressing the word *Austrian* in the conclusion you return to tonight's conversation, reminding me that this qualifies him for the Austrian category. The premise refers to the answer to last night's question, which, in the broader context, was different from the current question; last night it was a question about categories of Austrians, not a question about categories of composers. And for that reason, insofar as I understand your point, I find your argument relevant and helpful. The argument does not beg the question.

The value of this example is not that it is typical—it is not. Its value is that it illustrates that even in what seems to be the most obvious sort of begging the question, whether it *is* a fallacy must be determined by the conversational context. In most normal contexts, of course, if a premise just is the conclusion, the fallacy has been committed.

A second, harder-to-detect, thing to look for is the case in which the arguer chooses language for a premise that sneaks in the answer to what is in question. In the most extreme sort of case, the premise just is the conclusion, but is phrased in slightly different words. "All of us cannot be famous, because all of us cannot be well known," contends Jesse Jackson in a *New Yorker* profile. And a 19th century logic textbook provides the following classic example:

> To allow every man unbounded freedom of speech must always be, on the whole, advantageous to the state; for it is highly conducive to the interests of the community that each individual should enjoy a liberty perfectly unlimited of expressing his sentiments.

In most conversational contexts—where the question at issue is whether free speech is good for the state—this argument would be guilty of the fallacy of begging the question. Look at the passage carefully; if you follow the structuring guidelines of Chapter 6 and match wording where the content is roughly the same, the premise and conclusion will match.

But in other cases the paraphrasing might be less blatant. Suppose the conversation is concerned with the question *Should assisted suicide be legal?* and you argue as follows:

> To assist in a suicide is no different from murder, which is always illegal; so of course assisted suicide should be illegal.

In most conversational contexts, those who are asking whether assisted suicide should be legal are asking the question because they wonder whether it is in any important way different from murder. To simply assert that it is no different from murder, then, would in those conversational contexts beg the question. Without any knowledge of the context, it is still safe to evaluate such an argument as *probably* committing the fallacy of begging the question.

Third, and even trickier, are cases in which the question-begging premise is implicit. The magazine *Decision*, aiming to persuade readers that the Bible is a reliable document, presents the following argument:

> Christians believe—and rightly so—that the Bible is without error. When we study the Bible carefully, we find that it consistently claims to be the directly revealed Word of God. God would not lie to us. So the Bible, His Word, must be trusted completely.

Clarifying just the explicit premises, we get the following clarification:

1. The Bible claims to be direct revelation from God.
2. God would be reliable.

∴ *C*. The Bible is reliable.

Notice, however, that there is a big gap between premises 1 and 2. Premise 1, clearly, is intended to establish that the Bible is revelation from God. Adding that implicit subconclusion, we get this revised clarification (with revisions highlighted):

1. The Bible claims to be direct revelation from God.

∴ **[2. The Bible is direct revelation from God.]**

3. God would be reliable.

∴ *C*. The Bible is reliable.

But this still does not capture everything of substance that is intended by the original argument. Why would the arguer think that premise 1 provides any support for subconclusion 2? Because the arguer is assuming that if the Bible claims something about itself, it should be believed—that is, the arguer must be assuming that the Bible is reliable. The full clarification then, would look like this:

1. The Bible claims to be direct revelation from God.

[2. The Bible is reliable.]

∴ [3. The Bible is direct revelation from God.]

4. God would be reliable.

∴ *C*. The Bible is reliable.

In short, the most plausible way to use the Bible's own claims in support of the conclusion that the Bible is reliable is by assuming, at the outset, that the Bible is reliable. And this begs the question. (It does not necessarily follow from this critique that the Bible is unreliable—only that this argument is.)

In this complex argument, the fallacy is committed in the simple argument to 3. Thus, under the heading EVALUATION OF ARGUMENT TO 3 you should include the subheading CONVERSATIONAL RELEVANCE and note the fallacy there. At the same time, its presence in the simple argument to 3 infects the remainder of the argument. To the extent that the remainder of the complex argument depends on a component that begs the question, the remainder of the complex argument also begs the question. So, the following should appear under the heading EVALUATION OF ARGUMENT TO C:

CONVERSATIONAL RELEVANCE

Begs the question, since the preceding argument to 3 begs the question.

Thus, the ripple effect of this particular fallacy continues to be reflected in your evaluation.

> *Guideline.* If you know the question that is at issue in the conversation, then ask whether the argument presupposes an answer to it. If it does, then, even if the argument is sound, evaluate the argument as committing the fallacy of begging the question.

> *Guideline.* If you do not know the question that is at issue in the conversation, but if a premise seems to merely repeat the conclusion, evaluate the argument as probably committing the fallacy of begging the question.

EXERCISES Chapter 8, set (b)

Compose in each case a brief argument that commits the fallacy of begging the question and does so by means of either a close paraphrase of the answer or an implicit premise that presupposes the answer (and that does not do so merely by blatantly repeating the conclusion as a premise).

Sample exercise. In question: whether birds are descended from dinosaurs.

Sample answer. Since dinosaurs are the ancestors of birds, birds are descended from dinosaurs.

1. In question: whether Fords are better than Chevys.
2. In question: whether the Vietnam War was a just war.
3. In question: whether the stock market will keep going up.
4. In question: whether it is morally OK to cheat on your taxes.

Fallacies of Conversational Relevance

1. The fallacy of missing the point.
2. The fallacy of begging the question.

MOTIVE-BASED FALLACIES

Another broad category of fallacies has not so much to do with the merits of arguments as with the merits of the motives that certain arguments tend to promote; thus, we will call them motive-based fallacies. These fallacies are tendencies in certain sorts of arguments to distract the arguer or the audience from the proper goal of good reasoning—that is, from the goal of knowing the truth about the question at hand—and, thereby, the tendency to foster intellectual dishonesty. They do not reflect some particular defect in the clarity, soundness, or relevance of an argument (although, in the end, these arguments can almost always be found to have some such defect). They are not exclusively limited to arguments; a mere assertion that appeals to improper motives can also be guilty of one of these motive-based fallacies.

The Ad Hominem *Fallacy*

One well-known motive-based fallacy is the ***ad hominem fallacy,*** more formally referred to as the fallacy of *argumentum ad hominem* and once known as the fallacy of *argumentum ad personam.*[1] This is the mistake of rejecting a view by irrelevantly drawing attention to an undesirable person (*ad hominem* meaning, literally, *to the human*) who holds it, rather than drawing attention to the merits of the view itself. It is motive-based because it takes advantage of our natural desire to distance ourselves from undesirables; one easy and unthinking way of doing this is to distance ourselves from their beliefs.

The fallacy is not frequently found in print, since the flaw often becomes too glaringly obvious by the time the argument gets written down. But it is often heard. For example, in casual conversation, you might hear, "The

[1]Three hundred years ago the term *argumentum ad hominem* was used in a very different way; it referred to an argument showing that the logical consequences of someone's *views* were inconsistent or otherwise unacceptable.

Republicans can't be right about school vouchers. After all, my *parents* are Republicans."

The *ad hominem* fallacy is a special case of a broader sort of mistake called the ***genetic fallacy.*** This fallacy is committed when a belief is evaluated on the basis of its source (that is, on the basis of its genesis—thus, the term *genetic*) when the source of the belief is irrelevant. "This theory comes from the 19th century," someone might fallaciously argue, "so it must be false."

It can be a powerful tool in the hands of an unscrupulous orator. If I am short on evidence, then I can always say good things about those who agree with me and nasty things about those who agree with you. In *The Art of Controversy*, philosopher Arthur Schopenhauer provides the following tongue-in-cheek advice to debaters:

> A last trick is to become personal . . . when you perceive that your opponent has the upper hand. . . . It consists in passing from the subject of dispute, as from a lost game, to the disputant himself. . . . This is a very popular trick, because every one is able to carry it into effect.

If I can do this without being too obvious about it, then less careful reasoners are likely to find themselves leaning my way.

But be careful not to dismiss unthinkingly every argument that appeals to a belief's source. Sometimes the source is directly relevant to the merits of the belief. Suppose, for example, that your testimony is the only reason I have for holding a belief. If I later decide that you are a liar, then that can be a very good reason for me to give up the belief. I am drawing attention to something undesirable about a person who holds the view, but not irrelevantly so. In such a case it draws attention to the merits of the view itself.

Note this *Wall Street Journal* account of the woman who first offered testimony against Ray Buckey; Buckey was a worker in a day-care school in which all the employees were charged with—and eventually acquitted of—sensational crimes against children.

> Ray Buckey is a man whose life has already been effectively destroyed. The first charge of child abuse against this teacher at the McMartin day-care school in Manhattan Beach, California, was laid against him in the summer of 1983. The allegations against him had been extorted from her two-year-old by a mother—now dead—with a history of mental illness who also claimed that an AWOL Marine had sodomized her dog.

If I now argued that her charge of child abuse was false because of this very unattractive information about her, it would not be an *ad hominem* fallacy. For her credibility is undermined by the claim that she coerced the information from her two-year-old, that she had a history of mental illness, and that she had a history of making preposterous accusations. Insofar as the charge against Buckey depends on her credibility, anything that undermines her credibility is relevant.

It is not always clear whether an *ad hominem* attack is an argument or a diversionary tactic. Consider the note passed by one defense attorney to the other as their case opened: "No case. Abuse the plaintiff's attorney." On the one hand, we could take this as a fallacious argument with the premise "The plaintiff's attorney is worthy of abuse" and the implicit conclusion: "Therefore the defendant is not guilty." On the other hand—and more plausibly—we might assume that the abuse is planned simply as a diversionary tactic, with no actual argument anywhere in sight. But it hardly matters, since either way we take it, intellectual honesty is being undermined by irrelevancy, and the *ad hominem* fallacy is being committed.

Guideline. Ask whether the negative appeal to the person undermines the credibility of an important witness or is otherwise relevant to the conclusion. If not, the *ad hominem* attack is probably fallacious.

EXERCISES Chapter 8, set (c)

Consider in each of the following cases whether the appeal to the person is legitimate or an *ad hominem* fallacy. Explain your reasoning.

Sample exercise. Woman arrested for shoplifting, to police officer: "I can't respect laws made by men."

Sample answer. Ad hominem fallacy. Even if the shoplifting laws were made by men, that has nothing to do with whether they are worthy of respect.

1. It's doubtful that scientists can achieve nuclear fusion in an inexpensive tabletop apparatus. Fleischman and Pons, the physicists at Utah who claimed to have done so, were not very careful and suffered from more than a little wishful thinking.

2. It's doubtful that scientists can achieve nuclear fusion in an inexpensive tabletop apparatus. Fleischman and Pons, the physicists at Utah who claimed to have done so, were Mormons.
3. Politician to assembled crowd: "You can be sure that this proposed law will not benefit you; my opponent—who drives a better car than any of you can ever hope to drive—dreamed it up!"
4. Politician to assembled crowd: "You can be sure that this proposed law will not benefit you; my opponent—who has no expertise in this area whatsoever—dreamed it up."

The Fallacy of Appealing to Authority

Another motive-based fallacy is the ***fallacy of appealing to authority.*** This is the mistake of encouraging deference to someone else's view when, in fact, those listening to or reading the argument are at least as competent to reason it through as is the presumed authority. The more formal name for this error is the fallacy of *argumentum ad verecundiam*, which translates into *appealing to modesty*—apt since the arguer is calling for modesty in the presence of authority. This is another variety of the genetic fallacy, with an important difference from *ad hominem:* the source of the belief is illegitimately counted in favor of the belief, not against it.

This fallacy is motive-based since it tends to promote intellectual timidity where courage is called for; like the natural inclination to distance ourselves from undesirables, we should be careful not to allow timidity to undermine the ultimate goal of knowing the truth. Consider, for example, the Vietnam-era *New Yorker* cartoon that shows five military officers seated behind a long table with a younger military officer standing before them; the younger officer has obviously expressed moral reservations about the war. Says one of the older officers:

> Aren't you being a little arrogant, son? Here's Lt. Col. Farrington, Major Stark, Capt. Truelove, Lt. Castle, and myself, all older and more experienced than you, and we think the war is very moral.

Perhaps he would be right to defer to them as experts in matters of military strategy, but there is every reason to think that he should think through matters of morality for himself. Thus, their reasoning is fallacious appeal to authority.

Often, we have much to be modest about; and when we do, there is nothing fallacious about appealing to authority. Vast numbers of our beliefs rightly depend on appeals to various sorts of authorities—parents, teachers, scientists, and journalists, to name a few—who have information or expertise that far exceeds our own. In these cases, we may appeal to authorities because they give us a better chance of gaining knowledge, not because of an inclination toward timidity. So, like *ad hominem* attacks, some appeals to authority are legitimate.

Guideline. Ask whether the appeal to authority is a case in which the audience for the argument should think it through for themselves and not be tempted to timidity; if so, it probably commits the fallacy of appealing to authority.

EXERCISES Chapter 8, set (d)

Consider in each of the following cases whether the appeal to authority is legitimate or fallacious. Explain your reasoning.

Sample exercise. All the history books say that Lincoln was assassinated in 1865. So 1865 it is.

Sample answer. There is nothing fallacious about this appeal to authority. We have no better way of reasoning out this sort of conclusion than checking out the history books.

1. An environmental activist, working for stringent new regulations on the oil shipping industry, quotes Jacques Cousteau (the well-known oceanographer) on the long-term hazards of oil spills.
2. A beloved celebrity with no known expertise in health care endorses a pain reliever, saying, "This product is the best; take my word for it."
3. Mayor's press secretary to reporter: "The mayor says that all the city's expenditures have been carefully monitored and are entirely in order. There's no need for you to pursue this allegation of improper spending."
4. Our founding fathers believed in the right to bear arms—even built it into the Bill of Rights. Gun control would go against them—you wouldn't want to do that, would you?

Two Genetic Fallacies

1. *Ad hominem* fallacy.
2. Fallacy of appealing to authority.

The Fallacy of Appealing to Sympathy

The ***fallacy of appealing to sympathy,*** which translates the more formal and old-fashioned expression fallacy of *argumentum ad misericordiam,* occurs when there is an irrelevant appeal to pity, sympathy, or compassion in support of a conclusion, rather than an appeal to considerations that directly bear on the conclusion. This fallacy is committed, for example, by the student who says, "But, Professor, I stayed up all night studying for your exam (or, I'm only .001 away from a 3.0 GPA, or, I've never made a grade this low before, or my father will cut off my funding)—surely it deserves a better grade than this." The professor may feel sorry for the student and may even be moved to read the exam one more time, but feeling sorry for the student does not make the exam a better exam.

As with the other motive-based fallacies, the fallacy often takes the form of a diversionary tactic rather than a real argument. Note the following *Los Angeles Times* account of one of the judge's decisions in the O. J. Simpson double murder trial:

> The gruesome autopsy photos that had badly shaken several panelists Thursday were placed much farther away from the jury box Friday, and most of the panel was able to get through the half-day of testimony without showing emotion. Still, prosecutors and defense attorneys recognized the power of the autopsy photographs. At the defense's request, Superior Court Judge Lance Ito opened the session Friday morning by reminding jurors that "mere sentiment, conjecture, sympathy, passion, prejudice, public opinion or public feeling" should not sway their verdict.

The prosecution does not actually present the following argument: "The victims deserve our sympathy, so Simpson is guilty of murder." Nevertheless, all seem to recognize that strong sympathy for the victims could tend to distract the jury from evidence really bearing on the question of Simpson's guilt—and, thus, that use of the photos could amount to a fallacious appeal to sympathy.

There are many cases in which feelings of sympathy can be relevant to a conclusion. You may arrive at the conclusion, for example, that a career in medicine is the right path for you, in part because your heart goes out to the sick. Or you may come to believe that you should leave part of your estate to Amnesty International because you feel so sorry for those who are falsely imprisoned. Note that both these arguments have to do with beliefs about what you should do, not beliefs about the way the world is. And your feelings can be pertinent to decisions about what to do. These arguments would not be fallacious.

Guideline. Ask whether the appeal to sympathy is relevant to the conclusion; if not, the argument probably commits the fallacy of appealing to sympathy.

EXERCISES Chapter 8, set (e)

Consider in each of the following cases whether the appeal to sympathy is legitimate or fallacious. Explain your reasoning.

Sample exercise. The down-and-out salesman tells you of how he has been cheated out of his bonus for five months due to unscrupulous colleagues and asks you to believe him when he says he will not cash your check until you notify him that your husband has approved of the purchase.

Sample answer. Fallacy of appealing to sympathy. This information gives you no reason whatsoever to expect him to be trustworthy—rather, it simply clouds your judgment.

1. The commercials lead you to feel sorry for starving children you see on TV, then urge you to send money to a charitable agency that helps them.
2. A homeless person tells you about his sad life, then assures you that you should disbelieve those who told you that he is the one who stole your money.
3. Because you feel sorry for a hitchhiker, you decide you should give him a ride.

4. The hitchhiker encourages your sympathy for all his bad luck, then asserts that he was named in Howard Hughes's will but has been cut out of the inheritance.

The Fallacy of Appealing to Consequences

The ***fallacy of appealing to consequences***—what we commonly call wishful thinking—occurs when the practical advantages of a belief are cited as reasons for adopting it. Suppose I say to you, "You should believe that you are going to win the lottery; if you do believe it, that's a good way to snap out of your depression." Or I might advise you, "You should remember your childhood fondly, because people who had a happy childhood are usually happy adults." In making these arguments, I am pointing to practical benefits you will enjoy if you adopt the belief. I am not pointing to anything that makes it likely that you will win the lottery or that you did have a happy childhood. This is motive-based, since it tempts you to reason with a concern for your own self-interest rather than with a concern for knowing the truth.

A variety of this fallacy is sometimes called the ***fallacy of appealing to force***, or, more formally, the fallacy of *argumentum ad baculum* (*baculum* is a word for *rod*, our closest English word being *bacteria*, which are rod-shaped). Ambrose Bierce refers to one sort of appeal to force in his *Devil's Dictionary* when he defines the rack, a medieval torture device, thus:

> An argumentative implement formerly much used in persuading devotees of a false faith to embrace the living truth . . . now held in light popular esteem.

Appealing to consequences is exactly like appealing to sympathy in one important way—both are not only relevant but extremely important when we reason about how we should *act*. I do not suggest that you reject the mugger's threat of force as fallacious, as you reflect on whether to hand over your wallet. It is in conclusions about the nature of the world, not about how to act, that practical consequences tend to be irrelevant, and thus that appealing to them is usually fallacious.

The most famous example of the fallacy of appealing to consequences comes from 17th century philosopher and mathematician Blaise Pascal. The smart money, he says, is on God. Believe that God exists, since that belief is a good bet. If it turns out that you get it right, you win eternal happiness; if not, your existence will be short anyway, and a devout and short existence is no worse than a depraved but short one. But if you don't believe that God exists and you get it wrong, you suffer eternal punishment. (This, as you can see, is where Pascal appeals to the rod.) Focusing as he does on the practical consequences of belief, Pascal illegitimately distracts our attention from considerations that bear on whether God actually exists.

Guideline. Ask whether the appeal to consequences is offered in support of a belief about what you should *do* or about the way the world is; if it is about the way the world is, then it probably commits the fallacy of appealing to consequences.

EXERCISES Chapter 8, set (f)

Consider in each of the following cases whether the appeal to consequences is legitimate or fallacious. Explain your reasoning.

Sample exercise. Prison guard to prisoner: "You might as well learn to get along here, because cooperative prisoners get the best treatment."

Sample answer. Not fallacious, since it recommends a certain sort of behavior on the basis of consequences.

1. Scientist to colleague: "I firmly believe that my hypothesis is true. I have to—I've already put so much money and time into it, that if I'm wrong it will be a huge embarrassment."
2. Scientist to colleague: "I firmly believe it's a good idea to pursue my hypothesis further. I really have to—I've already put so much money and time into it, that if I throw in the towel now it will be a huge embarrassment."
3. Father to daughter: "Consider carefully what will happen if you marry this guy. Ten years from now you'll be the only one supporting the family, while he still sits in the garage strumming his guitar and trying to write a hit. Face it—he's not the one for you."

4. I continue to believe that the President has not engaged in illegal or unsavory behavior. It's just too hard to live with the idea that the leader of the free world is no better than the rest of us.

Some Motive-Based Fallacies

1. *Ad hominem*—takes advantage of inclination to distance ourselves from undesirables.
2. *Appealing to authority*—takes advantage of inclination toward timidity.
3. *Appealing to sympathy*—takes advantage of sympathetic feelings.
4. *Appealing to consequences*—takes advantage of self-interested inclinations.

EXERCISES Chapter 8, set (g)

Each of these arguments can, under some circumstances, be seen as committing a motive-based fallacy. State the likely fallacy and explain.

1. Mother to child: "You'd better start believing in Santa Claus or he won't bring you any presents."
2. "Mr. Martin assigns his students several of my articles on the current debate about African influence on ancient Greece in conjunction with his new book. . . . In this book, Mr. Martin seeks to dismiss the arguments of anyone who has criticized his work . . . on the grounds that his critics have overtly racist motives. He dismisses my discussion of the Afrocentric claim that Aristotle stole his philosophy from the Library of Alexandria (which was not built until after Aristotle's death) as 'an eloquent testimonial to the power of white Jewish skin privilege.'" —Mary Lefkowitz, *Chronicle of Higher Education*
3. "Part of Clarence Darrow's argument in defense of Thomas Kidd, a union official on trial for criminal conspiracy: I appeal to you not for Thomas Kidd, but I appeal to you for the long line—the long, long line reaching back through the ages and forward to the years to come—the long line of despoiled and downtrodden people of the

earth. I appeal to you for those men who rise in the morning before daylight comes and who go home at night when the light has faded from the sky and give their life, their strength, their toil to make others rich and great. I appeal to you in the name of those women who are offering up their lives to this modern god of gold, and I appeal to you in the name of those little children, the living and the unborn." —Irving Stone, *Clarence Darrow for the Defense*

4. "In 1932 Germany, millions of Germans sat quietly by while Hjalmar Schacht, Hitler's Finance Minister, imposed "fiscal austerity" policies to cool down inflation. By 1940, millions of Jews and others were gassed to death to feed the Nazi war machine. Others avoided death by siding with the fascists, donning Nazi uniforms and gassing their fellow Jews. Milton Friedman is the latter kind of Jew. He publicly admitted on a radio program that he models his economics on Hjalmar Schacht. Milton Friedman is committed to imposing fascism on the United States. He poses the greatest threat to American democracy since Hitler. If you want to stop fascism in the U.S., you must stop Friedman and the Schachtian program he is implementing. You must support Lyndon Larouche for President—the only candidate who can stop the Nazi austerity policies being imposed on our people by the Friedman fascists." —from a poster on a college campus saying, "Authorized by Citizens for Lyndon Larouche"

5. "MR. PANSCOPE. I have heard, with the most profound attention, everything which the gentleman on the other side of the table has thought proper to advance on the subject of human deterioration; and I must take the liberty to remark, that it augurs a very considerable degree of presumption in any individual to set himself up against the authority of so many great men, as may be marshalled in metaphysical phalanx under the opposite banners of the controversy; such as Aristotle, Plato, the scholiast on Aristophanes, St. Chrysostom, St. Jerome, St. Athanasius, Orpheus, Pindar, Simonides, Gronovius, Hemsterhusius, Longinus, Sir Isaac Newton, Thomas Paine, Doctor Paley, the King of Prussia, the King of Poland, Cicero, Monsieur Gautier, Hippocrates, Machiavelli, Milton, Colley Cibber, Bojardo, Gregory Nazianzenus, Locke, D'Alembert, Boccaccio, Daniel Defoe, Erasmus, Doctor Smollett, Zimmerman, Solomon, Confucius, Zoroaster, and Thomas-a-Kempis.

   "MR. ESCOT. I presume, sir, you are one of those who value an *authority* more than a reason.

"MR. PANSCOPE. The *authority*, sir, of all these great men, whose works, as well as the whole of the Encyclopedia Britannica, the entire series of the Monthly Review, and the complete set of the Variorum Classics, and the Memoirs of the Academy of Inscriptions, I have read through from beginning to end, deposes, with irrefragable refutation, against your ratiocinative speculations. . . ." —Christopher Peacock, *Headlong Hall*

HOW TO THINK ABOUT FALLACIES

Learning about fallacies can be valuable. As the easiest-to-make sorts of mistakes, they can be especially insidious. Greater familiarity can make you more aware—and thus more wary—of them. Two warning labels should go on this package of fallacies, however—one of them about fallacies in general, the other about motive-based fallacies in particular.

Warning about Fallacies in General

As may now be apparent, there is nothing especially systematic about any list of named fallacies. However they are organized, such lists are little more than casseroles made up of folk wisdom that has accumulated over the centuries. No *theory* of fallacies is likely to be any more promising than, say, a general theory of automobile accidents. There are different causes in different cases. And as helpful as it may be to master a list of famous fallacies, that would not by itself provide the key to good reasoning—no more so than memorizing the most common causes of automobile accidents would by itself provide the key to good driving.

One reason for this limitation is that names for fallacies are often misleading. They can describe more than one sort of mistake or even reasoning that under some circumstances is not fallacious. This may be initially surprising; after all, many of them have impressive Latin names that give the same impression of scientific precision as imparted by the Linnaean system of biological classification. But a logical term like *argumentum ad hominem* is not nearly so precise as a biological term like *homo sapiens.*

Another reason for the limitation is that lists of fallacies provide an accounting only of how to miss the target, not how to hit it; they do little to help you understand what makes a good argument good.

A final reason for this limitation is that any "taxonomy" of the named fallacies is not comprehensive; there are many important sorts of mistakes that it would not include. *Most unsound arguments are defective not because they commit a named fallacy, but because of subtler sorts of problems in their construction.* Investigation of these subtler problems takes up a good portion of this book.

Warning about Motive-Based Fallacies

Notice that there is no place in the standard evaluating format for identifying the motive-based fallacies—no fifth subheading called, say, ARGUER'S MOTIVES under which you can say "commits the *ad hominem* fallacy" or, more generally, "shows intellectual dishonesty." There is an important reason for this omission: your focus should always be on evaluating the merits of the argument itself, not on the motives that may be behind the argument. *The moment you reject an argument solely because it commits a motive-based fallacy, you are making the very sort of mistake you are criticizing.*

Motive-based fallacies are fallacies because they direct attention away from the merits of whatever argument might be legitimately offered for a particular belief. To reject an argument solely because it makes this sort of mistake represents a failure on *your* part to look at that argument on its own merits—you ignore its own clarity, soundness, and conversational relevance. (It can sometimes be appropriate to reject someone's assertion of authority about a subject because of doubts about the person's motives—but that is rejection of an assertion, not of an argument.) When it comes to any argument that commits a motive-based fallacy, it is far better to reject it because of a false premise, bad logic, or conversational irrelevance. These features are for the most part publicly visible, and your critique can provide the opportunity for constructive conversation so that all involved have a better opportunity to arrive at knowledge. Motives—other than your own—are largely hidden from your view; and a focus on invisible motives rather than the visible argument is likely to generate more heat than light.

The real value of learning about motive-based fallacies is that you will be less likely to commit them yourself and, thus, be better able to cultivate the virtue of intellectual honesty. Consistent with this, the chief reason for stressing the virtue of intellectual honesty in Chapter 1 was so you would be better able to cultivate it in yourself, not so you could point the finger at others for their dishonesty. If you are to help others to become more intellectually honest, let it be because of the example you set in focusing strictly on clarifying and evaluating arguments on their merits alone.

Guideline. Reject an argument only because it lacks one of the merits of arguments, not because it commits a motive-based fallacy. Otherwise, you too are guilty of shifting focus away from the merits of the argument itself.

SUMMARY OF CHAPTER EIGHT

Fallacies are the easiest-to-make intellectual mistakes. The fallacies we will be concerned with can be divided into two categories. First, there are argument-based fallacies, which point to specific flaws in one of the four merits of an argument. The fallacies that have specifically to do with three of these merits—clarity, truth, and logic—are treated elsewhere in the book. As for the fourth merit, conversational relevance, there are two fallacies. The first, the fallacy of missing the point, is committed when an argument does not address the question that is asked. The second, the fallacy of begging the question, is committed when an argument presupposes an answer to what is in question in the conversation.

Second, there are motive-based fallacies. These fallacies tend to promote the sort of motives that undermine intellectual honesty; they do not have to do with specific flaws among the four merits of arguments, but do generally result in a flaw somewhere in the argument itself. The *ad hominem* fallacy rejects a view by irrelevantly drawing attention to something undesirable about a person who holds it, rather than drawing attention to the merits of the view itself. The fallacy of appealing to authority encourages deference to someone else's view when, in fact, the argument's audience is at least as competent to reason it through as is the presumed authority. (Both the *ad hominem* fallacy and the fallacy of appealing to authority are genetic fallacies—that is, fallacies that draw attention to the source of a view rather than the merits of the view.) The fallacy of appealing to sympathy encourages reliance on feelings of compassion rather than qualities of argument. And the fallacy of appealing to consequences draws attention to practical consequences rather than evidence. (Both sympathy and practical consequences can often be relevant to how we should act, but are rarely relevant to beliefs about the way the world is.)

Learning about motive-based fallacies is valuable not because it enables you to point the finger at others, but because it helps you cultivate proper motives in your own reasoning. Critiquing arguments solely on the basis of motive-related features is itself a mistake because it distracts from focusing on the actual merits of the argument. Always focus your evaluation on the clarity, soundness, and conversational relevance of arguments.

GUIDELINES FOR CHAPTER EIGHT

- If you know the question that is at issue in the conversation, then ask whether the conclusion addresses it. If it does not, then, even if the argument is sound, evaluate the argument as committing the fallacy of missing the point.
- If you know the question that is at issue in the conversation, then ask whether the argument presupposes an answer to it. If it does, then, even if the argument is sound, evaluate the argument as committing the fallacy of begging the question.
- If you do not know the question that is at issue in the conversation, but if a premise seems to merely repeat the conclusion, evaluate the argument as probably committing the fallacy of begging the question.
- Ask whether the negative appeal to the person undermines the credibility of an important witness or is otherwise relevant to the conclusion. If not, the *ad hominem* attack is probably fallacious.
- Ask whether the appeal to authority is a case in which the audience for the argument should think it through for themselves and not be tempted to timidity; if so, it probably commits the fallacy of appealing to authority.
- Ask whether the appeal to sympathy is relevant to the conclusion; if not, the argument probably commits the fallacy of appealing to sympathy.
- Ask whether the appeal to consequences is offered in support of a belief about what you should *do* or about the way the world is; if it is about the way the world is, then it probably commits the fallacy of appealing to consequences.
- Reject an argument only because it lacks one of the merits of arguments, not because it commits a motive-based fallacy. Otherwise, you too are guilty of shifting focus away from the merits of the argument itself.

GLOSSARY FOR CHAPTER EIGHT

***Ad hominem* fallacy**—motive-based fallacy that rejects a view by irrelevantly drawing attention to something undesirable about a person who holds it, rather than drawing attention to the merits of the view itself. It takes advantage of our desire to distance ourselves from undesirables; often a diversionary tactic rather than an argument.

Argument-based fallacies—fallacies that reflect a specific flaw in one of the four merits of an argument: its clarity, the truth of its premises, its logic, or its conversational relevance.

Fallacy—the easiest-to-make; type of intellectual mistake.

Fallacy of appealing to authority—motive-based fallacy that encourages deference to someone else's view when, in fact, those listening to or reading the argument are at least as competent to reason it through as is the presumed authority. Takes advantage of tendency to intellectual timidity. Also known as the *fallacy of argumentum ad verecundiam*, which literally means *appealing to modesty*.

Fallacy of appealing to consequences—motive-based fallacy that directs attention to the practical advantages of a belief rather than the evidence for it. Commonly called *wishful thinking*.

Fallacy of appealing to force—an example of the fallacy of appealing to consequences in which the avoidance of force is the practical advantage of a belief. Also known as the fallacy of *argumentum ad baculum*. *Baculum* translates to our word *rod* (our closest English word being *bacteria*, which are rod-shaped).

Fallacy of appealing to sympathy—motive-based fallacy that irrelevantly appeals to pity, sympathy, or compassion in support of a conclusion, rather than to considerations that directly bear on the conclusion. Also known as the fallacy of *argumentum ad misericordiam*.

Fallacy of begging the question—conversational fallacy that errs by presupposing the answer to what is in question in the conversation. Also known as the fallacy of *petitio principii*. *Petitio* comes from a word meaning *appeal to*, or *beg*, as in the English word *petition*. *Principii* is closely related to the English word *principle*. *Petitio principii* is the fallacy of appealing to a principle that is in question—as though it were already settled.

Fallacy of missing the point—conversational fallacy that errs by answering the wrong question. Also known as the fallacy of *ignoratio elenchi*. *Elenchi* is from a Greek term for *cross-examination;* this might be said to be the fallacy of ignoring (*ignoratio*) the question that is being asked (the *elenchi*).

Genetic fallacy—fallacy that evaluates a belief according to its source (that is, its genesis—thus, *genetic*) rather than according to the relevant evidence. The *ad hominem* fallacy and the fallacy of appealing to authority are examples.

Motive-based fallacy—fallacy that reflects a flaw in the motives that an argument tends to promote. Typically such a fallacy does result in a flaw in at least one of the four merits of an argument, but the location of the flaw in the argument itself may vary.

PART FOUR

EVALUATING THE TRUTH OF THE PREMISES

CHAPTER NINE

How to Think About Truth

For to say of what is that it is not, or of what is not that it is, is false. And to say of what is that it is, and of what is not that it is not, is true.

—Aristotle, *Metaphysics*

TRUTH, n. An ingenious compound of desirability and appearance.

—Ambrose Bierce, *The Devil's Dictionary*

TOPICS

Objectivity and Truth
Probability, Evidence, and Truth
Self-Evidence
Experiential Evidence
Strategies for Evaluating Premises

This chapter provides an introduction to one of the central merits of arguments: the truth of premises. In a way, the entire book is about truth, since it aims to offer guidance, by way of good reasoning, for anyone who wishes to know the truth. But the point of this chapter is more specific: it aims to provide detailed practical directions for thinking about whether premises are true.

Remember—it takes only one false premise to render any argument unsound.[1] A false premise doesn't guarantee that the conclusion is false, since anyone can concoct a bad argument for a true conclusion. But if the unsound argument is the best reason you have for that conclusion, then it does guarantee that you have no good reason to *accept* the conclusion as true.

OBJECTIVITY AND TRUTH

Two Laws of Truth

There are two venerable so-called laws of truth which serve us well for practical purposes. One of them, the ***law of noncontradiction,*** says that no statement is both true and false. It follows from this that truth is objective and absolute—there cannot be any statement, for example, that is true for you but false for me. Its flip side is the ***law of the excluded middle,*** which says that every statement is either true or false. It follows from this that there is no middle ground between the true and the false. ***Truth-values*** are evaluations—like *true* and *false*—that can be given of how well a statement fits with the world. (In the same way, moral values include evaluations—like *good* and *evil*—that can be given of, say, actions; and aesthetic values include evaluations—like *beautiful* and *ugly*—that can be given of, say, paintings). Another way of stating the law of the excluded middle is to say there are exactly two truth-values—namely, *true* and *false*—with nothing in the middle.

Why, then, is it so commonly asserted that truth is relative, that "what is true for you may be false for me"—a remark that seems to violate the law of noncontradiction? According to a recent poll, 62 percent of American

[1]There is one exception. Some arguments have "throwaway premises" that should not be included in the clarification because they make no logical contribution to the argument. If one of these is false, it is not in the clarification so it doesn't make the argument unsound (so, excluding it is an application of the principle of charity). Suppose someone argues as follows: All men are mortal; Socrates is a man; Socrates is fat; and thus Socrates is mortal. You would not include *Socrates is fat* in your clarification, so it doesn't matter whether it is true or false.

adults believe that "there is no such thing as absolute truth." The proportion rises to 74 percent for those ranging in age from 18 to 25.[2]

Should this be interpreted as flagrant disregard for the law of noncontradiction? Probably not. The survey response provides a good opportunity to apply the principle of charity; these apparent denials of absolute truth are often used as a convenient shorthand for a variety of other related and reasonable expressions, including these:

What you believe to be true I may believe to be false.
What works in your life may not work in mine.
The way you see things may not be the way I see things.
The evidence available to you may not be available to me.
What is reasonable for you may not be reasonable for me.
Neither one of us is in the position to decide the truth for everyone everywhere always.

These paraphrases not only are fully harmonious with the law of noncontradiction, but also are absolutely true.

As Aristotle says, a true statement is one that says of what is that it is and of what is not that it is not. *What is* may appear to you to be different from the way it appears to me. And you may desire it to be different from the way I desire it to be. But this can't make *what is* be two different ways at the same time; it can be only the way it is. When Ambrose Bierce writes satirically of "an ingenious compound of desirability and appearance" it is not really *truth* that he refers to (and he knows it) but *what is often believed to be the truth.*

Guideline. For practical purposes, assume that no statement is both true and false and that every statement is either true or false.

Two Practical Laws of Truth

1. *Law of noncontradiction*—no statement is both true and false.
2. *Law of excluded middle*—every statement is either true or false.

---

[2]Poll conducted by the Barna Research Group in 1992. It does not say whether those polled believed it to be absolutely true that there is no absolute truth.

Ambiguity Rather than Relative Truth

Some statements *appear* to violate these laws even though, on closer inspection, they do not. Consider the following:

Today is July 9.
My name is Dave Wilson.
A train station is one mile from here.
Chocolate ice cream tastes bad.

When I express these words here and now the statements are true. But when you express them at a different place and time, the statements are probably false. Does this mean they are both true and false or, perhaps, that they are neither?

No. In each case there are two different statements, one true, the other false. We are tempted to think otherwise only because the statements can be referentially ambiguous (to make use of terminology from Chapter 5). When I say *today* on July 9, it refers to July 9—thus, it can be disambiguated with the true statement *Today, July 9, is July 9.* But when you say it on November 18, it refers to November 18, and would be properly disambiguated by the false statement *Today, November 18 is July 9. My name is Dave Wilson* and *A train station is one mile from here* are similar. The referents of *my* and *here* would change with a change of speaker and location; when disambiguated, it would become clear that the statement with a different referent is a different statement.

Chocolate ice cream tastes bad is a trickier case. When I say it now it is true, but I probably mean to allow that it *could* be false when you say it or even when I say it next month. (If I mean instead that it tastes bad always and for everyone—and that you're just mistaken if you *think* it tastes good—then I may have a strange view, but there is no apparent lack of objectivity to explain away.) But the statement includes no expression that changes its referent when expressed by a different person or at a different time or in a different place. This is because such an expression is implicit; what I am really saying is *Chocolate ice cream tastes bad to me now*, which can be made even clearer as *Chocolate ice cream tastes bad to Dave Wilson on July 9.* So when you say it, or when I say it next month, it really is a different statement with potentially a different truth-value. The same thing is usually true of any other sentence including a subjective verb such as *tastes*, *looks*, *smells*, *feels*, or *sounds*.

Guideline. If it looks as though the truth-value of a statement will be different depending on who expresses it, it is usually because the statement is referentially ambiguous. Look for the ambiguous term, which may be implicit, and eliminate the ambiguity before evaluating its truth.

EXERCISES Chapter 9, set (a)

Paraphrase each statement to eliminate the appearance that its truth is relative. (You do not need to make the statement true; simply eliminate any possibility of referential ambiguity.)

Sample exercise. My state is one of the biggest in America.
Sample answer. California is one of the biggest states in America.

1. Harleys are the best-sounding bikes on the road.
2. My brother is shorter than I am.
3. Last year our country enjoyed a boom in the stock market.
4. The home team is enjoying a winning season.

Some Cases in Which You Can't Decide

I have described the two laws of truth as "useful for practical purposes"—not as necessary, inviolate, and unbending. This is because language is not always law-abiding. The ordinary folks who constantly use language in new and serviceable ways seldom get a note from their logician first. The result is that there are some interesting and puzzling cases in which it is at least conceivable that a statement is both true and false, or that it is neither true nor false. And in each case, there is not any simple and uncontroversial way of settling the matter (though in none of these cases is there any worry about whether truth is objective).

- *Robert is bald.* (Imagine that Robert is exactly in the border area between bald and not bald.)
- *Hans is a Kraut.* (Imagine that it is true that Hans is German, but false that Hans is deserving of disparagement on that count.)
- *This sentence is false.* (Just think about it!)

- *Hercules cleaned the Augean stables.* (It isn't clearly true, since Hercules didn't even exist, but it also seems mistaken to say it is false, since it is certainly truer than, say, *Hercules cleaned the Augean stables using power tools.*)

Sometimes there is a well-defined fictional world that a character such as Hercules inhabits; in those cases, the best strategy is to evaluate premises like *Hercules cleaned the Augean stables* according to whether they are true or false *in their fictional world.* Otherwise, in the fairly unusual instances when statements like these four appear as premises, it is best to evaluate them as *can't decide*, with an explanation.

Generally, as we will see, when you evaluate a premise as *can't decide* it will be because the evidence you have is more or less evenly balanced; if you were able to collect more evidence, you would be able eventually to settle the question. But it is at least conceivable in these four cases that the reason for evaluating a premise as *can't decide* is that there is no fact of the matter—perhaps the statement is neither true nor false, or both true and false, and thus there is no choice to be made regardless of how much evidence you go on to collect. (On this option, *indeterminate* could actually be a third truth-value, between *truth* and *falsity*.) Fortunately, given our practical aims in this text, we don't need to decide *why* we can't decide in these sorts of cases.

> *Guideline.* The rare statements that appear to violate the two laws of truth, yet do not merely suffer from a referential ambiguity, should be evaluated as *can't decide*, with an explanation.

PROBABILITY, EVIDENCE, AND TRUTH

What makes a statement true is the way the world is; and it is always possible for me to make a mistake about the way the world is. This is because the world is one thing, while my judgment about the world is something else—and as the ancient proverb says, there is many a slip 'twixt the cup and the lip. Many things can go wrong in that gap between the world and my judgment about it, no matter how tiny the gap might be. I may have poor evidence. I may be subject to wishful thinking. I may be inattentive. I may be fooled. Thus, it is ordinarily better to avoid evaluating premises with the unmodified adjectives *true* and *false* and to prefer expressions such as *probably true* and *probably false* (or even, in the strongest cases, *certainly* true and *certainly* false, assuming that by this we mean extremes in probability).

Probability as a Measure of Evidence

But what exactly is meant here by *probably*? There are at least three different and legitimate notions of probability. The one that we are most concerned with in this text is ***epistemic probability***, which is the likelihood that a statement is true, given the total evidence available to you—that is, given all of your background beliefs and experiences. (***Epistemic*** means *having to do with knowledge*.) This is the notion of probability that should be used in your evaluation of premises. To say in your evaluation that a premise is *probably true* is just to say that you have fairly good evidence for its truth.

Unlike truth, epistemic probability always comes in degrees. It ranges along a continuum that can be expressed either colloquially (ranging from *certainly true* to *certainly false*) or quantitatively (ranging from 1 to 0, respectively). Here are some examples:

Degrees of Epistemic Probability

COLLOQUIAL	QUANTITATIVE
Certainly true	Probability of about .99 or 1
Probably true	Probability of about .75
Can't decide	Probability of about .5
Probably false	Probability of about .25
Certainly false	Probability of about .01 or 0

Although it can sometimes be useful to express these probabilities quantitatively, doing so is likely to convey a false sense of precision. I might be able to tell the difference between beliefs with epistemic probabilities of .6 and .9 (that is, those that are somewhat probable and those that are very probable), but I doubt that I could discriminate between a .84 and a .85 belief. So I will rely chiefly on the less precise—but less misleading—colloquial expressions.

Epistemic probability, again unlike truth, has a very definite relative component. It is relative to you. It is *your* evidence—*your* background beliefs and experiences—that determine whether a statement is epistemically probable for *you*. There is widespread agreement about epistemic probabilities among many people regarding many statements. This is because we share such a wide range of background beliefs and experiences. Anyone with a rudimentary understanding of U.S. geography, for example, would assign a very high epistemic probability to this statement:

Alaska is larger than Rhode Island.

But consider this statement:

Minnesota is larger than Oregon.

I would have to say that I can't decide (or that it has an epistemic probability of about .5). My meager evidence does not point clearly in either direction. But there are others (the current governors of the two states, for example, or those who are interested enough to check reliable references works) who have evidence for its truth or falsity which is every bit as strong as the evidence most of us share regarding the statement about Alaska and Rhode Island. For them, it is either almost certainly true or almost certainly false (that is, it has an epistemic probability either close to 1 or close to 0).

It is important to add that epistemic probability has an objective component as well. Given the evidence that you have, there is nothing relative about how probable it makes the premise. There is a fact of the matter about how probable it is—regardless of whether you assess its probability correctly or not. In this way, epistemic probability is like the strike zone in baseball. A pitched ball is in the strike zone if it is over home plate and between the knees and arms of the batter. The strike zone is relative to the batter because a shorter batter or a batter who crouches will have a smaller strike zone. But it also has an objective component. Given the size and stance of the individual batter, there is an objective fact about whether the ball is in the zone—regardless of whether the batter assesses it correctly or not.

Guideline. Evaluate premises according to their epistemic probability —that is, according to how strong your evidence is for their truth or falsity—using expressions such as *probably true* and *probably false.*

EXERCISES Chapter 9, set (b)

Provide two statements to which most people would assign the following measure of epistemic probability.

Sample exercise. Certainly false.
Sample answer. Two and two are five.
The United States has 100 states.

1. Certainly true.
2. Probably true.
3. Can't decide.
4. Probably false.
5. Certainly false.

Probability as a Measure of Confidence

There is a second notion of probability, one that is not necessarily connected to evidence. Suppose you say, "I'm probably going to win the lottery, even though I realize that everything points against it." You are acknowledging that the evidence is bad and thus that the epistemic probability of your winning is low. In this case, to say that you will probably win is to say merely that you have confidence you will win. You are not describing the strength of your evidence but the strength of your confidence, that is, the strength of your belief.

This is sometimes termed ***subjective probability*** and may be roughly defined as the amount of confidence you have that a given statement is true. Like epistemic probability, it is a matter of degrees and can also be expressed in colloquial terms ranging from *certainly true* to *certainly false* or in quantitative terms ranging from 1 to 0. But, unlike epistemic probability, it is relative to you; there is no fact over and above your level of confidence.

If we are intellectually honest—if our aim is to know the truth regarding the questions we care about—then we will endeavor to match subjective probability to epistemic probability. That is to say, we will aim to have the amount of confidence in a statement's truth that is warranted by the total available evidence. When we succeed, our evaluations of probability will at the same time indicate both epistemic and subjective probability. This frequently does not happen. Even when my evidence for a belief remains the same from today to tomorrow, my mood about it may change. In Chapter 1 much was said about cases in which we adopt and support beliefs with little regard for the evidence—sometimes because of our innocent misuse of shortcuts in reasoning, sometimes because of bad motives. The problem in those cases can now be stated in another way—as the problem of mismatch between the subjective and epistemic probabilities.

The importance of matching subjective with epistemic probability, however, should not tempt you to make certain mistakes. Note, for example, that if I find that my confidence outstrips my apparent evidence—if, for example, I have a hunch that you are a decent human being despite my inability to say exactly why—this is not *necessarily* an indicator of bad reasoning or dishonesty on my part. It may mean there is some good reason submerged within my total evidence that I have not yet been able to put my finger on—I sense a reason is there, but it isn't vivid enough for my thinking to have quickly turned it up. Hunches can go in either direction, however—they may be caused by still-subconscious evidence, or they may be caused by wishful thinking. There is no formula for telling the difference; continued cultivation of the intellectual virtues is the only way to get better at doing so.

Another mistake to avoid is the assumption that I must *act* with tentativeness if my belief is tentative—that is, if my belief is only slightly probable (whether epistemically or subjectively). Consider the statement *My child is at the bottom of the pool.* If both my evidence and my confidence are only slightly greater than .5 that this is true, it surely does not follow that I should be tentative as I dive in to rescue what may be my child. In short, when it comes to beliefs about the way the world is, confidence about how the belief translates into action must be distinguished from confidence in the belief itself.[3]

> *Guideline.* Aim to match your subjective and epistemic probabilities —that is, to have the amount of confidence that is warranted by the evidence.

[3]Some theorists have tried to make subjective probability more scientific—to move it from the vague and hidden realm of inner moods to the measurable realm of external behavior—by spelling it out in terms of betting behavior. Consider these two statements:

Sitting Pretty will win the third race.
Harvest Moon will win the third race.

The subjective probability of the first statement would be higher than the second if and only if I were willing either to bet more money or to take longer odds on Sitting Pretty. The same principle would apply to any belief (say, *It is wrong to tell a lie*). This approach ultimately does not completely work, for there are many reasons that my betting behavior might *not* reflect my actual confidence level. For example, if I strongly believed it was wrong to bet, then I would probably not bet any money on the statement *It is wrong to bet,* even though it would have a high subjective probability! But is does nicely illustrate how it is that our subjective probability has much more influence on behavior than does epistemic probability—and, thus, the importance of matching them.

EXERCISES Chapter 9, set (c)

For each of these statements, describe a way in which your own epistemic and subjective probabilities might differ.

Sample exercise. The Yankees will win the World Series this year.

Sample answer. The epistemic probability might be in the area of "somewhat probable that this is false," since the evidence suggests that they are one of the best teams, but only one of the teams will get through every round of the playoffs and end up on top. But the subjective probability might be very high—I may strongly believe it strictly because I am a lifelong Yankee fan.

1. The proposed law eliminating a state sales tax will pass.
2. Napoleon was the greatest military leader of all time.
3. The professor was biased against me when he graded my paper.
4. It won't rain today.
5. Even though I'm only three months pregnant, I can just tell this baby is going to be a boy.
6. My nephew is the best candidate for the position I'm now hiring for.
7. My car can go a long way after the gas gauge is on empty.
8. I don't have a cold, just allergies.

Probability as a Measure of Frequency

There is a third notion of probability—one that occurs often in science, and that differs from the others in that it is entirely objective. Suppose I say, "50 percent of all fair coin tosses come up heads, so there is a .5 probability that this coin toss will come up heads." I am talking about ***frequency probability,*** which may be roughly defined as the likelihood that a specific thing has a property, based on the frequency with which all things of that sort have the property. The probability statement in the example (*There is a .5 probability that this coin toss will come up heads*) is based on a frequency statement about how frequently fair coin tosses do come up heads (*50 percent of all fair coin tosses come up heads*).[4] This is why it is called frequency probability. And

[4]Frequency statements used for this purpose are sometimes called *base rates.*

because these frequencies are said to occur in the world, independently of our beliefs about them, frequency probability is entirely objective.

Determining the objective facts does involve us subjectively; I try to establish the epistemic probability of a certain frequency probability—that is, I rely on evidence that a certain sort of thing occurs in the world with a certain frequency. But the *truth* of a typical statement about frequency has nothing to do with whether anyone believes it, has evidence for it, or makes any judgment about it; so this is an entirely objective notion. (Frequency probability is introduced here solely to contrast it with subjective and epistemic probability. We will not need to otherwise refer to it until Chapter 13, when we cover frequency syllogisms.)

Types of Probability

	RELATIVE TO BELIEVER?	OBJECTIVE?
1. *Epistemic*	Yes	Yes
2. *Subjective*	Yes	No
3. *Frequency*	No	Yes

SELF-EVIDENCE

Because your evaluations must be expressed in language, you will typically support your beliefs by referring to other beliefs of yours. Recall sample evaluations we have already done. Why do I think, for example, that the sentence *Not many people are qualified to work as lifeguards* is probably true? Because of another belief of mine—*Lifeguards must be in excellent physical shape, must be able to swim well, and must have extensive training.* And why do I believe that the sentence *If air sacs in birds play a role in their breathing, then carbon monoxide introduced into the air sacs will kill them* is probably true? Because of another belief of mine—*Carbon monoxide interferes with the ability of blood to carry life-sustaining oxygen.*

You are making use of ***inferential evidence*** when you support a belief by another belief, since you are saying that you infer one from the other. But you have more than inferential evidence available to you when you consider your evidence. If you had only inferential evidence, then ultimately all of your beliefs would be supported only by one another—and they would together be as well supported as a castle in the clouds. You also have ***noninferential evidence***—that is, you can appeal to something other than your beliefs in support of your beliefs. Noninferential evidence may be divided into two categories: self-evidence and experiential evidence. (Of course, you will be able to express even your non-inferential evidence only as beliefs; but since they are beliefs *about* self-evidence and experiential evidence, that is enough to bring the castle down out of the clouds and put it on firm ground.)

Self-Evidence and Definition

Suppose you have the easy task of evaluating the following premise:

> All bachelors are unmarried.

In most contexts, you do not have to think very hard about why you believe that a premise like this is true. There seems to be no need, for example, to think about what other beliefs lead you to believe this or to look for experiential evidence—to interview bachelors, for example, to find out whether they are married. You can see that it is simply true by definition. Suppose, alternatively, the premise had been this:

> Some married men are bachelors.

You might, for similar reasons, say that you can see that it is false by definition.

The evidence we have in these cases is ***self-evidence,*** since within the statement *itself* is found the most important evidence bearing on its truth or falsity—namely, the evidence of the meanings of the words themselves.[5] A statement that can be seen to be true or false by definition may be described as *self-evidently true or false.* In self-evidently true or false statements, if you understand what the words mean you ordinarily need no other evidence to make a reasonable decision about truth or falsity.

Shakespeare illustrates this when he has Hamlet tell his friends that he brings "wonderful news," namely that "there's ne'er a villain dwelling in all Denmark, but he's an arrant knave." Horatio answers, "There needs no ghost, my Lord, come from the grave to tell us this." In other words, to say that all villains are knaves is self-evidently true to all those who understand the words *villain* and *knave.* Self-evidence, however, like all other evidence, is relative to the person; if *villain* and *knave* are not included in your vocabulary, Hamlet's statement will nevertheless be true, but its truth will not be evident to you.

[5]Philosophers sometimes refer to such statements as *analytic a priori.*

There is much to keep in mind, however, before blithely judging premises to be self-evidently true or false. The term *self-evident* easily lends itself to abuse; Ambrose Bierce defined it as "evident to one's self and to no one else." The point is to avoid using it as another way of saying "it is obvious to me." Even if something is obvious to you, the purpose of your evaluation is to provide the reasons why it is obvious to you. And only one such reason may be that it is self-evident.

The most famous use of the expression is in the Declaration of Independence: "We hold these truths to be self-evident, that all men are created equal. . . ." But Thomas Jefferson's use here—while entirely appropriate for that context—is broader than the use recommended for your evaluations. Jefferson might be described as appealing not to definitional but to *conversational* self-evidence (that is, he appeals to what is evident *to ourselves*). Jefferson's conviction that all men are created equal was not based on his understanding of the meanings of terms such as *men*, *created*, and *equal*. His point was that it was evident to all participants in the conversation—to the writers and to the intended audience—that all men are created equal; given this agreement, for the purposes of the conversation there was no need to provide any supporting reasons. This is a perfectly good way to use the expression, but we will use it more narrowly.

Likewise, exercise caution before you judge a premise to be self-evidently *false*. Consider again the preceding simple example:

> Some married men are bachelors.

It would be extremely unusual for someone to make such an obvious mistake. Thus, it provides an especially important opportunity to apply the principle of charity. Is there some clue in the context to suggest, for example, that the arguer is using *bachelor* or *married* metaphorically or as shorthand for something else? Maybe the context suggests that the arguer simply means that some married men *behave like* bachelors. If that proved to be the case, then rather than calling the premise self-evidently false, it would be preferable to paraphrase it charitably and grant that it is almost certainly true—based, perhaps, on your own experience of the behavior of some married men.

This doesn't mean you will find no self-evidently false statements. The great actor John Barrymore once received a call from the secretary of one of Hollywood's most important producers. "I am speaking for Mr. Laskin, who wants you to attend an important party he is giving tomorrow," said the other voice imperiously. "And I," said Barrymore, "am speaking for John Barrymore, who has a previous engagement which he will make as soon as you have hung up." There is no problem in understanding Barrymore's reply to be self-evidently false. The context shows that he meant it to be so, since he clearly meant to return Mr. Laskin's insult.[6]

Guideline. If a premise can charitably be seen to be almost certainly true or false solely on the basis of your understanding of the meanings of the words within it, evaluate it as self-evidently true or false.

EXERCISES Chapter 9, set (d)

For each premise, state whether it is self-evidently true, self-evidently false, or neither.

Sample exercise. Abraham Lincoln was president of the United States.
Sample answer. Neither.

1. Squares have four sides.
2. Mammals are larger than insects.
3. Milk is white.
4. The future lies before us.
5. My mother is one of my parents.
6. Instruction at the beginning of a Robert Schumann composition: "To be played as fast as possible." Instruction a few measures later: "Faster." Consider the statement: The second instruction can be followed.
7. NBA star Charles Barkley published an autobiography titled *Outrageous.* Asked about a particular remark he made in it, he replied, "I was misquoted."
8. In *Tom Sawyer Abroad,* Mark Twain has Huck Finn report: "They was all Moslems, Tom said, and when I asked him what Moslems was, he said it was a person that wasn't a Presbyterian. So there is plenty of them in Missouri, though I didn't know it before." Suppose the premise is this: Moslems are, by definition, any persons who are not Presbyterians.

---

[6]It is also possible to have a self-evidently false *pair* of premises. If two premises are contradictory, you know that at least one of them is false even if you don't know which.

Stipulative Definitions

When we say that a statement is seen to be true by definition, or that it is self-evidently true, we are normally assuming that the words in the statement are being used in a standard way. On some occasions, however, an arguer will decree a nonstandard definition for a term; in such a case, the arguer is using a ***stipulative definition.***

Stipulative definitions can be quite useful. They are sometimes used to add precision to a discussion; in an argument about poverty, the arguer might say, "By *poor* I mean a family of four that earns less than $12,000 per year." On other occasions, new words are introduced and defined by stipulation, usually for picking out a notion for which we have no handy term; "By *blik*," the philosopher R. M. Hare has said, "I refer to the theoretical framework one uses to interpret the world."

Premises that stipulate a definition are certainly entitled to be evaluated as self-evidently true, since they are, by stipulation, true by definition. But they do present opportunities for committing the fallacy of equivocation. Suppose after stipulating the preceding definition for *poor*, I say, "So quit claiming to be poor; you earn almost $13,000 a year for your family." The conclusion has to do with someone's real-world concern about being poor; as such, it uses *poor* in its normal sense, which involves not only yearly earnings but also how many people are supported by the earnings, the other financial resources the family has, and the necessary expenses of the family. But the premise uses it in the more precise, stipulated sense. So the meaning of the term *poor* has shifted between premise and conclusion, and this means the argument commits the fallacy of equivocation. As described in Chapter 5, the ambiguity should be eliminated in the clarifying process.

A newspaper story seeking to determine the greatest athletes of all time includes the following argument:

> Defining athletic greatness as the ability to prove it in at least two highly competitive areas, Babe Ruth was number one. As a pitcher he was a World Series winner, and as a hitter he revolutionized the game. He was the greatest of them all.

One premise of this argument is found in the first sentence, which might be paraphrased as follows:

1. Athletic greatness is to be defined as the ability to prove it in at least two highly competitive areas.

But (skipping the remainder of the argument) the conclusion is this:

∴ *C.* Babe Ruth was the greatest athlete.

Since 1 is a stipulated definition, C is supported only if "greatest athlete" is used there in the same stipulated, nonstandard way as in 1. To avoid equivocation, it should be disambiguated something like this:

∴ *C.* Babe Ruth did more than anyone else to prove his athletic ability in at least two highly competitive areas.

Once paraphrased, the question whether he was the greatest athlete (in the standard, non-stipulative sense of the term) remains unanswered by the argument. The argument may now be seen to commit a second argument-based fallacy—the fallacy of missing the point.

> *Guideline.* Stipulative definitions, in which the arguer offers a revised or new definition for a term, may be considered self-evidently true. But be sure that arguments with such definitions do not commit the fallacy of equivocation.

EXERCISES Chapter 9, set (e)

Create an argument that commits the fallacy of equivocation due to a stipulative definition.

Sample exercise. Term: *fish.* Argue that you did not exceed the limit on fish.

Sample answer. Trout are too wonderful to be considered mere fish. I do not include trout in the definition of fish. So, Mr. Ranger, you can't cite me for exceeding the limit of 12 fish, since I have 4 bass and 11 trout.

1. Term: *gift.* Argue that you did not forget to give your friend a birthday gift since you did leave a voice mail.
2. Term: *music.* Argue that your friend's "Chopsticks" rendition on the piano is not music.
3. Term: *steal.* Argue that by shoplifting a bar of candy you were not stealing.

4. Term: *dependent.* Argue that you can claim four dependents on your federal tax return since you have a cat and three still-uncaught mice.

EXPERIENTIAL EVIDENCE

So far we have covered two broad categories of evidence that you will find relevant in putting together the evaluation of a premise. First, there is inferential evidence—that is, other beliefs of yours from which you can infer your evaluation. Second, there is noninferential evidence of a sort that we have termed self-evidence; this is the evidence found in the meanings of terms themselves. But there is another important category that is also noninferential in nature. It is ***experiential evidence,*** the evidence provided by sense experience.

What You Have Directly Observed

The most obvious experiential evidence is that which you have observed—what you have seen, heard, smelled, tasted, or touched. Suppose an arguer uses the following premise:

1. All swans are white.

In your evaluation of this premise you might be fully entitled, on the basis of your observations—that is, your sense experience—to say this:

> Premise 1 is almost certainly false because I personally saw a black swan at the local zoo.

These sorts of appeals to observation are natural, intuitive, and legitimate. There are, however, three important questions that you should ask when you make such appeals to observation.

The first question is *How reliable was your observation, given the circumstances?* Perhaps you are not particularly skilled at identifying swans. Or perhaps the lighting was bad, you had a poor viewing angle, you had left your glasses in the car, or the swan had just emerged from the mud. Any of these circumstances would make your observation less than reliable, and if you were aware of the undermining circumstances you should have had less confidence in the observation and, on that basis, should have adjusted the probability in your evaluation.

The second question is *How reliable is your memory of the observation?* Observations that you appeal to as evidence are ordinarily observations that you remember, not observations that are occurring at that moment. If you just a moment ago made the observation, your memory is probably highly reliable. But you depend on many observations that you made days, weeks, and years ago. Time presents opportunities for memories to fade and to be unconsciously revised—all the more likely if wishful thinking or someone else's suggestion is prompting you to remember one way rather than another. We are all familiar with this phenomenon, and scientific research has confirmed it. As for the black swan, chances are that your memory is serving you well. But you may have reason to consider it less reliable if I said to you, "After all, it was a couple of years ago. And haven't you conveniently forgotten that you argued heatedly with me at the time, since I was insisting that it was just an odd-shaped piece of wood protruding from the water?"

The third question is *How probable would your belief be had you not made the observation?* A slightly more technical way of putting exactly the same thing is to ask what the ***prior probability*** of the belief is. (In this case, *prior* simply means *independent of the observation*; and it is epistemic probability that is referred to.) The higher the prior probability of the observation, the more reliable it is. Thus, the more likely it is that there is a black swan at the zoo, independent of your having observed it, the more you can trust your observation of it to be reliable. Suppose you read a feature story in the local newspaper that comments on the pride the zoo takes in its collection of five white swans, the only swans it has ever had for the last 10 years. This would significantly reduce the prior probability that there is a black swan and would render your observation somewhat less reliable. It would not mean that you *didn't* see one—the news account could have been mistaken, or a black swan may have stopped over for a visit on the day you were there. But it would mean that a single observation has only limited evidential weight.

If someone tells you that a car is coming down the road, you accept it with no question. If someone tells you that several frogs flying on lily pads are coming down the road, you may suggest they take another look. Consider the observations, contained in the following *Los Angeles Times* account, that some have made on the Willcox Playa, a remote and eerie expanse of desert in southern Arizona:

> Most stunning are the Playa's endless mirages. Everyone sees them. Everyone swears by them—buildings rising from the shimmering horizon, trucks speeding along upside down, groups of people dancing. Pete Cowgill, former outdoor writer for the *Arizona Daily Star,* once saw a Southern Pacific train chugging across the Playa. As

> he watched, the engine disappeared into the earth. The next car followed it, then the next, and the next. "One by one, about a hundred cars flat disappeared," says Cowgill. "It was the most fascinating non-sight I ever saw."

On the desert and far from any railroad tracks, the prior probability that a train will pass by—and disappear into the earth—is virtually nil. Seeing it was not reason enough for Cowgill to believe it and should not have been. In short, the more preposterous the belief—that is, the lower its prior probability—the stronger the evidence needed to support it. As Sherlock Holmes says in *The Valley of Fear:*

> I ought to know by this time that when a fact appears opposed to a long train of deductions, it invariably proves to be capable of bearing some other interpretation.

And this applies even if what is opposed to the long train of deductions is a long train of Southern Pacific rail cars.

> *Guideline.* Observations made by any of your five senses can provide powerful evidence in evaluating your beliefs. Be on the alert, however, for circumstances that can weaken them.

Three Questions to Ask of Any Observation

1. How reliable was your observation, given the circumstances?
2. How reliable is your memory of the observation?
3. How probable would your belief be had you not made the observation?

EXERCISES Chapter 9, set (f)

Propose a way in which the described observation might be unreliable, and explain why.

Sample exercise. You recall that your older brother was at your 10th birthday party.

Sample answer. Your parents and brother all remember that he was away at camp that year. This means that there is a very low prior probability that he was there.

1. You hear someone blowing a whistle.
2. You remember hearing someone blowing a whistle.
3. You see your mother at the bus station.
4. You see the president of the United States at the bus station.
5. You remember your professor saying that there would be no final exam.
6. You remember your professor saying there would be a final exam.
7. You feel a spider on your neck.

What Authorities Have Reported

Reports from authorities make up one important part of your experience. (They are part of your experience because the reports are themselves something that you see or hear.) An ***authority*** is simply someone who is presumed to be in a better position than you to know the truth about the premise in question. This superiority may be due to either special ability or special access. A scientist or expert may have special ability to evaluate certain information; an eyewitness or a journalist may have special access to certain information.

As noted in Chapter 8, appealing to authority should be scrupulously avoided in circumstances where you are just as capable as anyone else of thinking through a view. In such cases, appealing to authority merely promotes intellectual timidity and can undermine the virtue of intellectual honesty. But we are quite right to rely on the authoritative reports of others for vast numbers of our beliefs, including most of our beliefs about science, history, and current affairs. There are two questions that you should ask to be sure that your use of authority is appropriate.

The first question is, *How reliable is the authority's report, given the circumstances?*

A variety of circumstances can undermine the reliability of an authority's report. A witness's memory can be subject to "creative" forces of which the witness is unaware. Or an expert might be an expert—but on a different topic. But perhaps the most important undermining circumstance is conflict of interest. It would ordinarily be in the best interest of most authorities to be reliable. But that interest can be overridden by other competing interests. This can be a problem for journalists, for example. One media critic, David Shaw of the *Los Angeles Times*, identifies what he calls several "basic flaws in the way the contemporary news organizations function." They include the following: "Pack journalism. Laziness. Superficiality. Cozy relationships with prosecutors. A competitive zeal that sends reporters off in a frantic search to be first with the latest shocking allegation, responsible journalism be damned. A tradition that often discourages reporters from raising key questions. . . ."

Like journalists, trained experts can also be rendered less than reliable due to overriding interests. Note, for example, this brief item from the *Chronicle of Higher Education*:

> The spring sale catalog from LSU Press includes ads for a collection of essays by Cleanth Brooks and one by Louis Rubin. The blurb for the Brooks collection calls him "our best critic" and continues, "These essays are vintage Brooks." The blurb for Rubin's book calls him "one of the very best of our literary critics" and goes on to affirm that "these essays are vintage Rubin." Curiously, the commendation for Brooks comes from the pen of Rubin, whose commendation comes from—you guessed it—Brooks.

This provides no reason to think that either Brooks or Rubin is deceiving us; but they *do* apparently have a conflict of interest, and thus we should have more to go on than their reports if we are to confidently believe that either of them is "among our best critics."

The second question is, *How probable would the statement be if you had no report from the authority?* As in the last section, a more technical way of putting this is to ask what the prior probability of the statement is, where *prior* simply means *supposing you had no report from the authority*. If a normally reliable witness reports seeing green men come out of a spaceship or Elvis come out of a deli on Broadway, that should not be enough to persuade us. If a normally reliable scientist reports success in building a perpetual motion machine or in achieving cold fusion in a tabletop apparatus, we should reserve judgment until additional evidence is amassed. Improbable things often do turn out to be true. But the more improbable it is, the less ready we should be to accept it solely on the report of an authority.

Sometimes a report will reach you after passing through a chain of authorities. Your friend may tell you that she heard on the news that a scientist has made a certain new discovery. Every link in the chain—your friend, the newscaster, and the scientist—must be reliable; and the more improbable the discovery, the more reliable each must be. And note that there are probably other links that you do now know about—the individuals or services, for example, who got the information from the scientist and passed it on to the newscaster. Those links must also be reliable.

Guideline. Reports of authorities can provide powerful evidence in evaluating beliefs. Be on the alert, however, for circumstances that can weaken them.

Two Questions to Ask of Any Presumed Authority

1. How reliable is the authority, given the circumstances?
2. How probable would the statement be if you had no report from the authority?

EXERCISES Chapter 9, set (g)

Identify the authority and the claim supported by the authority in each of the passages below. State what makes the authority less than perfectly reliable.

Sample exercise. Philadelphia lawyer Jay Lambert recalls a tough medical malpractice case against his client, a neurosurgeon, eight years ago. Lambert was fretting over a damaging report filed by an opposing "expert." On the eve of trial, Lambert called a contact in the expert's hometown and hit pay dirt. It seems the expert wrote the report but was in a federal penitentiary—where he was doing time for falsifying medical reports. —*Forbes*

Sample answer. The medical expert filed a report showing that Lambert's client might well be guilty. But his reliability as a medical expert is questionable, given that he has been convicted of falsifying medical reports.

1. A network news program advertises that their exclusive interview with the president will definitively settle the latest White House scandal.
2. A large corporation announces that, overall, employees have benefited from the latest round of downsizing.
3. The National Golf Foundation (which in part exists in order to promote golf) has projections which show that the country's golf boom will require more than 300 new courses a year for the next several years.
4. A young doctor listened intently to a panel of distinguished physicians discuss advances in hypertension treatment at the annual meeting of the American Academy of Family Physicians. By the end of the three-hour presentation, he was thinking seriously about switching some of his hypertensive patients to a drug called a calcium channel blocker, which was much discussed at the presentation. The pharmaceutical company G.D. Searle sponsored the seminar, as the young physician knew. But he didn't realize that Searle—which was then running a promotional campaign for Calan, one of several calcium channel blockers—had carefully picked speakers who were well-known advocates for this class of drugs. —*Consumer Reports*
5. An unemployed Texas salesman on Monday claimed that his father was one of three people who killed John F. Kennedy. Ricky Don White contends that his father joined the Dallas police department in September 1963 to carry out the assassination. He said his father, Roscoe White, was one of three CIA operatives who fired the shots. He said that his father also killed Dallas police officer J. D. Tippet about an hour after the assassination. Tippet's killing has long been blamed on Oswald. White said that his father served in the Marines with Oswald. He made his claims during a news conference at the JFK Assassination Information Center, a privately run group that researches various assassination theories. White acknowledged that he has tried to sell a book or movie on his theory. —Associated Press

Two Kinds of Evidence

1. Inferential evidence
2. Noninferential evidence

a. Self-evidence

b. Experiential evidence

STRATEGIES FOR EVALUATING PREMISES

To evaluate the truth of a premise is to consider its epistemic probability—that is, to consider the quality of your evidence for it. How should you describe this evidence in the relevant portion of your evaluation of the argument?

The Reasonable Objector over Your Shoulder

In evaluating premises, try not to focus on what others—say, your peers or professors—expect you to believe or what beliefs they might find impressive. A much better place to start is by asking yourself what you actually do believe, more or less instinctively, about the premise, and what your actual evidence seems to be for that belief. And be sure that what you settle on is a real reason and not merely a restatement of the premise in slightly different words (nor a restatement of the denial of the premise, if you take it to be false).

As you think about the premise, remember the strategy of writing your evaluation as though there is a reasonable objector looking over your shoulder. Thus, you must satisfy someone who has roughly the same evidence that you have and who possesses the intellectual virtues of honesty, critical reflection, and inquiry. This may help you to keep the intellectual virtues in the forefront of your mind, in ways such as this:

- Exhibit critical reflection by asking what your evidence is, whether it supports your belief, and whether either your evidence or your belief can be improved.
- Exhibit inquisitiveness by seeking more evidence if it is meager (and withhold judgment if there is no opportunity to seek further evidence).
- Exhibit intellectual honesty by insuring that your chief objective in evaluating this premise is to know whether it is true or false regardless of your prejudices. Try to identify your own biases and habitual modes of thinking, and watch for them as you evaluate your evidence.

In your evaluation of every premise, you will provide your judgment and your defense of that judgment. Given that you will be doing this with a reasonable objector over your shoulder, you should also be prepared to provide, where necessary, a brief response to reasonable objections that might be raised. To the premise *All swans are white*, for example, we've already seen the following sample evaluation:

> Premise 1 is almost certainly false, since I personally saw a black swan at the local zoo.

But black swans are rare; since the prior probability of your sighting is quite low, a reasonable objector is likely to object that it is best to remain unpersuaded until stronger evidence comes along. Your evaluation is much stronger if you anticipate that objection and deal with it in advance; here is one way you might do that:

> Premise 1 is almost certainly false, since I personally saw a black swan at the local zoo. I realize, of course, that they are quite rare; so I made a special effort to be sure that I got a good look and wasn't being misled in any way. I checked with others around me and they agreed that they also saw a black swan.

At this point, the objector would probably have to be unreasonable to continue to object.

Or consider the premise *If air sacs in birds play a role in their breathing, then carbon monoxide introduced into the air sacs will kill them.* Our sample evaluation goes something like this:

> Premise 1 is probably true, since carbon monoxide interferes with the ability of blood to carry life-sustaining oxygen.

How might a reasonable objector find fault with this? One sensible objection might be that nothing has been said here about how much carbon monoxide it takes to have this effect, nor how much is being administered to the birds. It might be better to say *can't decide*, due to the limited information. You have two choices at this point: concede that the objector has a good point (as always, since by definition the objector is reasonable!) and revise your judgment to *can't decide*, or revise your defense slightly, as follows:

> Premise 1 is probably true, since carbon monoxide interferes with the ability of blood to carry life-sustaining oxygen. This, of course, is based

> on the assumption that the scientist who is conducting the experiment is competent enough to know how much carbon monoxide is required and to introduce at least that much into the air sacs.

This seems to be a reasonable assumption and should satisfy the objector.

Let's look at one more example, the premise *Not many people are qualified to work as lifeguards.* The sample evaluation is this:

> Premise 1 is almost certainly true, since lifeguards must be in excellent physical shape, must be able to swim well, and must have extensive training—qualifications that are rare.

I can't think of a reasonable objection to this defense and thus would leave the evaluation as it is.

These guidelines apply to any judgment you have about the premise—even if it is *can't decide.* When you cannot decide, explain *why* you cannot decide. Chances are it will be because the evidence—whether there is a lot or a little—is balanced. In these cases, state the best reason you can come up with on each side. Don't feel that you must force a decision, but don't use *cannot decide* as an excuse for not thinking. When you do use it, be sure to show that you have thought carefully about it.

> *Guideline.* For each premise, state your judgment, your defense of the judgment, and, where relevant, a brief response to any objections that might be posed by a "reasonable objector over your shoulder."

EXERCISES Chapter 9, set (h)

For each of the evaluations of a premise below, augment it by providing a response to an objection that might be posed by a reasonable objector over your shoulder. (In your augmentation, continue to agree with the evaluation already presented.)

Sample exercise. Premise: All triangles have 180 degrees. Evaluation: The premise is almost certainly true, since it is self-evident. This is just what we mean by the word *triangle.*

Sample answer. Add the following: It might be objected that in real life, we grant that triangles do exist even though perfect triangles don't exist; the fact that a man-made or natural object is off imperceptibly doesn't mean that it isn't a triangle. This is a reasonable objection, and means I must add that the premise is only true on the charitable, and thus reasonable, assumption that it is talking about geometry and not real life.

1. Premise: Taxes will continue to rise during our lifetime. Evaluation: This is probably false, since there is a rising tide of opinion that government is growing too big, taking too much of our income, and not using it responsibly. The politicians will get the message.
2. Premise: James Cameron's *Titanic* is one of the best movies ever made. Evaluation: This is almost certainly false. A good script is necessary for a good movie, and just about everyone agrees that the script for this movie is extremely weak.
3. Premise. Large cities provide a higher quality of life than small towns. Evaluation: This is probably true. Cultural opportunities make a huge contribution to quality of life, and large cities far outweigh small towns in this regard.
4. Premise: Most of the wealth created in America in the last decade has been from high technology. Evaluation: This is probably false. Lists of the wealthiest people in America are full of people who made their money in the stock market (like Warren Buffet), in retailing (like the Waltons), and in entertainment (like Sumner Redstone).

Thinking Backward and Thinking Ahead

As you consider your evidence, one natural strategy is to think backward—to look for what seems to have led you to believe or disbelieve the premise. Almost all of the examples provided so far have been of this sort. Why do I believe that all triangles have 180 degrees? I think back and recall that I learned it as a definition in high school geometry. Why do I not believe that all swans are white? Because I think back to my sighting of a black swan at the zoo. Other examples are easy to come by. Suppose you clarify an argument that has the following premise:

1. For any liquid, its freezing and melting temperature is the same.

Plausible though this may be, you realize that it is probably false on thinking back and recalling a magazine article you once read. You might then evaluate it in this preliminary way:

> Premise 1 is probably false. *Science News*, which is normally a very reliable publication on matters of science, recently carried a story about the discovery of fish that live in very cold waters; their blood has a very low freezing temperature, even though, once frozen, the melting temperature is far higher.

In this way, by thinking backward you are able to appeal to a reliable authority.

But another useful strategy is to think ahead. This second strategy can take one of two forms. One way of doing this is to *assume that the premise is true* and see if anything obviously false *follows* from it; if so, that would show the premise to be false. Suppose, for example, the premise is this:

1. The meaning of any word is the thing that it picks out in the world.

This might seem superficially plausible. But you might arrive at the following evaluation:

> Premise 1 is very probably false. It entails, for example, that the word *unicorn* has no meaning; for there are no unicorns, and thus the word picks out nothing in the world. But this is absurd—it is self-evidently false. The word *unicorn* is obviously meaningful, otherwise we wouldn't know how to check and see whether there were any unicorns.

In this example, by thinking ahead you have run into a consequence that is self-evidently false; for by understanding the very meaning of the term, you understand that the word *unicorn* is meaningful.

Another way of doing this is to *assume that the premise is false* and see if anything obviously false follows from *that*; if so, then that would show the premise to be *true*. Suppose, for example, there is a premise such as this:

4. It is sometimes morally acceptable to break the law.

Your preliminary evaluation might be as follows:

> Premise 4 is very probably true. Assume it is false. This would mean that it is never morally acceptable to break the law. But this would mean that you would be morally obligated to obey the speed limit even if driving faster would save someone's life. But this is absurd. Since this absurdity results from assuming that the premise is false, the premise is very likely not false.

These two forward-thinking strategies search for implications that are absurd, concluding that the assumption that led to the absurdity must be rejected. Because they attack the assumption indirectly, via its implications, they are known as ***indirect arguments.*** They are also known as *reductio ad absurdum* arguments, since they aim to reduce the assumption to absurdity.

Such arguments can be effective but should be used with care. It is always possible that the absurd implication is produced not by the falsity of your assumption about the premise, but by some other false assumption that you are implicitly making. In the first case, for example, someone might argue that the mistake doesn't lie in the premise *The meaning of any word is the thing that it picks out in the world*, but in this additional assumption: *The word "unicorn" picks out nothing.* Perhaps there really are unicorns (and thus the word picks out unicorns). Or, safely assuming that there are no unicorns, perhaps it picks out the *idea* of unicorns; in that case it does pick out *something*, so it is meaningful. This sort of mistake—failing to blame a false secondary or implicit premise—is common enough that it long ago earned a name of its own: the ***fallacy of non causa pro causa*** (i.e., the absurdity is *not caused by the cause that is set forth*).

Note that the practice of assuming there is a reasonable objector over your shoulder applies to indirect arguments as well. And you should be prepared for the possibility that your reasonable objector will accuse you of committing the fallacy of *non causa pro causa.* Return to the premise *The meaning of any word is the thing that it picks out in the world.* The evaluation, as it now stands, is as follows:

> Premise 1 is very probably false. It entails, for example, that the word *unicorn* has no meaning because there are no unicorns, and thus the word picks out nothing in the world. But this is absurd—in fact, it is self-evidently false. The word *unicorn* is obviously meaningful, otherwise we wouldn't know how to check and see whether there were any unicorns.

But it is stronger if you append the following sentences to it:

> It might reasonably be objected, however, that the word *unicorn* does pick out something—namely the *idea* of unicorns (and thus, the fault would lie in the assumption that it does not pick out anything; the fault would not lie in Premise 1). But this objection cannot be right, because the objector would then have to admit that there are indeed unicorns in the world—since the objector says that *unicorn* means *idea of unicorn*, and the idea indeed exists even though unicorns do not.

Again, in this way you identify what is probably the weakest part of your defense and convince yourself (by convincing the reasonable objector over your shoulder) that your indirect argument is successful after all.

> *Guideline.* Ask yourself what you really think about the premise and your evidence for or against it. You might do this by thinking backward about how you arrived at your belief or by thinking ahead to see whether you can produce an indirect argument (though you should avoid the fallacy of *non causa pro causa* in doing so). As you do so, keep in mind the reasonable objector over your shoulder.

Indirect Arguments

("Thinking ahead")

1. Assume the premise is true and show that this leads to an absurd consequence. This shows the premise is false.
2. Assume the premise is false and show that this leads to an absurd consequence. This shows the premise is true.

EXERCISES Chapter 9, set (i)

For each premise, provide an evaluation that uses an indirect argument. Where relevant, respond to the reasonable objector over your shoulder.

Sample exercise. No one who has broken the law should be allowed to serve on a jury.

Sample answer. This is certainly false. Assume it's true. It would follow that juries would no longer exist, since virtually everyone has broken the law at some time (even if only by speeding or jaywalking.) It might be reasonably objected that, in practice, this wouldn't happen, since there would have to be a way of establishing that someone broke the law before you could exclude the person from a jury. This turns out to be a weak objection, however, since one way of establishing it would be to ask them. Most people would probably admit to it if it meant getting out of jury duty.

1. Some males are unmarried. (Assume it is false.)
2. People can do whatever they decide they want to do. (Assume it is true.)
3. To become a millionaire requires more than just intelligence. (Assume it is false.)
4. The only painting that should be counted as art is painting that literally represents the world, such as portraits and landscapes. (Assume it is true.)

Fallacies and Truth

Sometimes false beliefs are branded as fallacies. In *Aristotle to Zoos*, for example, P. B. and J. S. Medawar write,

> It is a popular fallacy that chewing gum regains its flavor if removed from the mouth and parked, say, under a chair. What is regained is not the flavor but the ability to taste the flavor as sensory adaptation wears off.

This is not a misuse of the term; a fallacy, recall, is an easy-to-make intellectual mistake, and there are many mistakes about truth (such as believing that chewing gum regains its flavor overnight) that are easy to make.

But although this is not a misuse of the term, it is not helpful in evaluating the premise. To say the premise *Chewing gum regains its flavor overnight* commits the fallacy of believing that chewing gum regains its flavor overnight is simply to say that the premise is false (note that the terms *fallacy* and *false* are closely related) and that a lot of people think it is true. It does not tell us anything about why people make the mistake, which is what it must do if it is to be useful in an evaluation. The other uses of the term *fallacy* that we look at in this text are generic. They tell us something about why an argument has gone wrong, regardless of the subject matter of the argument. The fallacy of equivocation, for example, can occur in any argument where the meaning of a word might shift—which is to say, in any argument. It can occur in an argument about *gum* (which might shift from *chewing gum* to *the flesh under the teeth*); and—to simply reverse the word—it can occur in an argument about a *mug* (which might shift from a *cup* to a *face*—reaffirming the many slips 'twixt cup and lip). When we identify such a fallacy we are saying that the argument has gone wrong, in part, because of such a shift.

Since the point of your evaluation of each premise is to defend your judgment in a way that would satisfy the reasonable objector over your shoulder, it is best to skip the unhelpful step of accusing a premise of committing a fallacy. Instead, go straight to the explanation of why you believe it to be false. No need to bother saying, for example, that the belief commits the fallacy of believing that chewing gum regains its flavor overnight. Better simply to say that the premise is almost certainly false, and that the reasonable objection that our experiences support the premise—since the gum always does taste better the next morning—is explained by a change that occurs in our sense of taste (due to sensory adaptation) and not by any change in the gum.[7]

> *Guideline.* Instead of accusing any premise of committing a fallacy, focus on explaining why you believe the premise to be false.

SUMMARY OF CHAPTER NINE

Although people often reasonably disagree about the truth of a premise, that does not mean that what is true for one person may be false for another. Truth has to do with whether a belief fits with the world. It is not relative to the believer. This is consistent with the law of noncontradiction, which says that a statement cannot be both true and false, and with the closely related law of the excluded middle, which says that it must be either true or false. These two laws are valuable practical guidelines in thinking about truth.

Evidence, however, is relative to the believer; so evaluations of premises must be made in shades of gray. The best you can hope for is to evaluate a premise's epistemic probability—that is, how strong your evidence is for its truth or falsity—using expressions such as *probably true* and *probably false.* One alternative notion of probability, subjective probability, is simply a measure of how much confidence you have in the truth of a belief; you should attempt to match your subjective with your epistemic probability.

[7]Philosophers have not been reluctant to brand certain beliefs as fallacies. G. E. Moore, to cite a famous example, coined the term *naturalistic fallacy* to describe the belief that moral properties (such as *goodness*) are ultimately nothing more than certain natural properties of the world (such as the amount of pleasure the "good" thing provides). But, as you might expect, other philosophers think this is no mistake at all, and thus no fallacy. As in other cases, it would be more helpful to focus on why he thinks the belief is false rather than to be told that it is a fallacy.

Some of your evidence will be found in other beliefs of yours—that is, it will be inferential. But some of it—self-evidence and experiential evidence —will be noninferential. Self-evidence is what you have when the premise itself, by virtue of the very meanings of the words, provides you with all the evidence you need to make a reasonable judgment. Experiential evidence is what is provided by the observations that you make with any of your five senses. One important category of experiential evidence is reports that you hear or read from authorities who have special access to information or special abilities to evaluate it.

For any experiential evidence, it is important to be aware of circumstances that might undermine its reliability. It is also important that you require more evidence whenever the prior probability of your belief is extremely low.

In preparing your evaluation, ask yourself what you really think, both about the premise and about your evidence for or against it. You might do this by thinking backward about how you arrived at your belief or by thinking ahead to see whether you can produce an indirect argument. As you do so, keep in mind the intellectual virtues of honesty, critical reflection, and empirical inquiry. Then present your evaluation for each premise by stating your belief, your evidence for that belief, and, if there is a reasonable objection, a brief response to it as though there is a reasonable objector over your shoulder.

GUIDELINES FOR CHAPTER NINE

- For practical purposes, assume that no statement is both true and false and that every statement is either true or false.
- If it looks as though the truth-value of a statement will be different depending on who expresses it, it is usually because the statement is referentially ambiguous. Look for the ambiguous term, which may be implicit, and eliminate the ambiguity before evaluating its truth.
- The rare statements that appear to violate the two laws of truth, yet do not merely suffer from a referential ambiguity, should be evaluated as *can't decide*, with an explanation.
- Evaluate premises according to their epistemic probability—that is, according to how strong your evidence is for their truth or falsity—using expressions such as *probably true* and *probably false*.
- Aim to match your subjective and epistemic probabilities—that is, to have the amount of confidence that is warranted by the evidence.
- If a premise can charitably be seen to be almost certainly true or false solely on the basis of your understanding of the meanings of the words within it, evaluate it as self-evidently true or false.

- Stipulative definitions, in which the arguer offers a revised or new definition for a term, may be considered self-evidently true. But be sure that arguments with such definitions do not commit the fallacy of equivocation.
- Observations made by any of your five senses can provide powerful evidence in evaluating your beliefs. Be on the alert, however, for circumstances that can weaken them.
- Reports of authorities can provide powerful evidence in evaluating beliefs. Be on the alert, however, for circumstances that can weaken them.
- For each premise, state your judgment, your defense of the judgment, and, where relevant, a brief response to any objections that might be posed by a "reasonable objector over your shoulder."
- Ask yourself what you really think about the premise and your evidence for or against it. You might do this by thinking backward about how you arrived at your belief or by thinking ahead to see whether you can produce an indirect argument (though you should avoid the fallacy of *non causa pro causa* in doing so). As you do so, keep in mind the reasonable objector over your shoulder.
- Instead of accusing any premise of committing a fallacy, focus on explaining why you believe the premise to be false.

GLOSSARY FOR CHAPTER NINE

Authority—someone who is presumed to be in a better position than you to know the truth about a statement. This superiority may be due to either special ability (as with a scientist or expert) or special access (as with an eyewitness or a journalist).

Epistemic—having to do with knowledge.

Epistemic probability—the likelihood that a statement is true, given the total evidence available to you—that is, given all of your background beliefs and experiences. This is the notion of probability that should be used in your evaluation of premises. To say that a premise is *probably true* is, then, just to say that you have fairly good evidence for its truth.

Experiential evidence—evidence provided by sense experience—that is, that which is seen, heard, touched, smelled, or tasted. It is one kind of noninferential evidence.

Fallacy of *non causa pro causa*—the mistake in an indirect argument of relying on a secondary assumption—often implicit—that is false, so that it is really the secondary assumption that should be blamed, not the assumption blamed by the arguer. (It literally means that the absurdity is *not caused by the cause that is set forth.*)

Frequency probability—the likelihood that a specific thing has a property, based strictly on the frequency with which all things of that sort have the property.

Indirect argument—an argument that shows a statement is false by showing that it leads to an absurd consequence. This is sometimes, alternatively, used to show that the negation of the statement is true (which amounts to the same thing as showing that the belief itself is false). Sometimes also called a *reductio ad absurdum* argument or, for short, *reductio.*

Inferential evidence—beliefs that are appealed to in support of another belief (which is *inferred* from them).

Law of the excluded middle—every statement is either true or false. It follows from this that there is no middle ground between the true and the false.

Law of noncontradiction—no statement is both true and false. It follows from this that truth is objective and absolute—there cannot be any statement, for example, that is true for you but false for me.

Noninferential evidence—things other than beliefs that are appealed to in support of a belief. This includes self-evidence and experiential evidence.

Prior probability—the epistemic probability of a belief independent of (i.e., prior to) a specified piece of evidence. When considering, for example, the prior probability of something you heard, its prior probability is simply how probable it would be if you had not heard it.

Self-evidence—evidence that comes from understanding the very meanings of the words themselves in a statement. Statements that are self-evidently true or false can be seen to be true or false largely by virtue of understanding the words of the statement. Philosophers sometimes refer to these statements as *analytic a priori* statements; they are also sometimes described as statements that are seen to be true or false by definition.

Stipulative definition—a nonstandard definition for a term, decreed by a speaker or writer for some specific use.

Subjective probability—the degree of confidence you have that a given statement is true. It is entirely relative to the believer; there is no fact of the matter over and above the believer's level of confidence.

Truth-values—evaluations, like *true* and *false*, which can be given of how well a statement fits with the world.

PART FIVE

EVALUATING DEDUCTIVE LOGIC

CHAPTER TEN

How to Think About Deductive Logic

Logical consequences are the . . . beacons of wise men.

—T. H. Huxley, *Science and Culture*

Insanity is often the logic of an accurate mind overtasked.

—Oliver Wendell Holmes, *The Autocrat of the Breakfast Table*

TOPICS

Deduction and Induction
Deductive Validity
Validity Counterexamples
Some Valid Deductive Forms
Evaluating the Truth of Premises with Not *or* And

The ***logic*** of an argument is the reasonableness conferred on the argument's conclusion by its premises. In an argument that is logically successful the conclusion *follows from* the premises—or, to put it differently, the premises *support* the conclusion.

Although we often use the term *logical* as a synonym for *reasonable*, we are clearly using it in a narrower way in this text, since good reasoning requires more than a certain kind of relationship between premises and conclusion. What does logic have to do with reasoning? Recall that reasoning is the thinking we do to answer questions that interest us; it is modeled by arguments—good reasoning by good arguments, bad reasoning by bad ones. Good logic is one of the merits of arguments; and good logic is important, since we need to understand how it is that beliefs of ours are supported by others that we judge to be true. But logic is only part of the story. We must also judge whether the premises are true; further, we must judge whether the argument is relevant to the conversation that gave rise to it. And the argument must be clear enough for us to be able to tell. An argument is a model of *good* reasoning only when it exhibits all four of these merits—not merely good logic.

When used properly, as Huxley notes, logic can serve as a beacon for the wise. But when we rely on it to the exclusion of the other merits of arguments, then, as Oliver Wendell Holmes suggests, at its very worst it can tidily sever our connection to reality.

DEDUCTION AND INDUCTION

For any argument, the best way to think about its logic is to ask this question: *If the premises were true, would that make it reasonable to believe the conclusion?* This is roughly the same thing as asking any of these questions:

Is the argument's logic good?
Does the conclusion follow from the premises?
Do the premises support the conclusion?

Logic is traditionally divided into two broad categories according to the level of support the argument aims to provide the conclusion. In ***deductive arguments***, the premises are intended to guarantee, or make certain, the conclusion. To determine whether the logic of a deductive argument is successful, a good rule of thumb is to ask questions such as these:

Do the premises guarantee the conclusion?
If the premises were true, would that make the conclusion certain?

For example, in the deductive argument *All men are mortal, Socrates is a man, so Socrates is mortal,* it is easy to see that the truth of the premises would make certain the conclusion, and thus that it is logically successful.

In ***inductive arguments,*** however, the premises are intended merely to count toward, or make probable, the conclusion. To determine whether the logic of an inductive argument is successful, a good rule of thumb is to ask these questions:

Do the premises count toward the conclusion?
If the premises were true, would that make the conclusion probable?

Take, for example, the inductive argument *All the men that have filled out my survey are mortal; therefore, all men are mortal.* The premise certainly seems to count toward the conclusion—although it is hard to say how much. It is easy to say, however, that despite its counting toward the conclusion, it cannot make the conclusion certain.

There is no need for now to be concerned with telling the difference in particular cases between deductive and inductive arguments. Chapters 10 through 12 will introduce the most common deductive forms, and Chapters 13 through 16 will introduce the most common inductive forms. As you become familiar with the forms, it will be easy to keep them straight.

If you read more broadly on this topic, you will find that a few authors adopt different terminology. Deductive logic is sometimes referred to as *demonstrative* or *apodictic* logic (*apodictic* is from a Greek word for *demonstrative*) while inductive logic is sometimes referred to as *nondemonstrative* or *ampliative* logic (*ampliative* because the conclusion *amplifies*, or adds to, the premises). Furthermore, the boundaries are sometimes drawn in different ways. The terms *deductive* and *inductive* are, for example, sometimes strictly reserved for arguments in which the logic succeeds. We will use the terms more broadly, however, allowing for deductions and inductions that fail as well as for those that succeed.[1] Finally, there is the common but mistaken definition of deduction as "reasoning from the general to the particular" and of induction as "reasoning

[1] Some authors have identified a third category of logic, namely, *abduction*. This, however, is the same as our *explanatory* arguments; in this text, then, it is encompassed by induction.

from the particular to the general." Some deductive arguments do move from the general to the particular (our familiar *All men are mortal, Socrates is a man, so Socrates is mortal,* for example), but here is a simple deductive argument that moves from the particular to the general:

> This marble is red. That one is also red. And that one is too. These are all the marbles. Therefore, all the marbles are red.

And many others go from the general to the general or the particular to the particular. The mark of deduction is simply the aim for a conclusion guaranteed by the premises.

Likewise, some inductive arguments do move from the particular to the general (the preceding argument, for example that *All the men that have filled out my survey are mortal, therefore all men are mortal*). But here is a simple one that moves from the general to the particular:

> Most men are mortal. Socrates is a man. So, Socrates is mortal.

All that is required for induction is simply the aim for a conclusion merely made probable by the premises.

You should be aware of this lack of unanimity so that you are not puzzled if you find variant accounts when you read other sources. The account in this text aims to provide the best mix of accuracy, practicability, and common usage.

Deduction versus Induction

1. *Deductive arguments*—premises are intended to guarantee the conclusion.
2. *Inductive arguments*—premises are intended merely to make probable the conclusion.

DEDUCTIVE VALIDITY

Since a deductive argument is one in which the premises are intended to guarantee the conclusion, a logically successful deductive argument is one in which this guarantee is achieved. In looking at a particular argument, does it seem as though the argument's conclusion would be made certain if the premises were assumed to be true? Then, chances are, you are looking at a deductive argument that is logically successful. That is the case with this argument:

1. All men are mortal.
2. Socrates is a man.

∴ *C.* Socrates is mortal.

A logically successful deductive argument such as this is valid. We will call an argument ***valid*** if and only if it is impossible for an argument with such a form to have true premises and a false conclusion. Conversely, it is ***invalid*** if and only if it is possible for an argument with such a form to have true premises and a false conclusion. Validity, therefore, is a perfect preserver of truth. If you want to be sure of true conclusions then find a valid form, feed in true premises (setting aside how to be sure that the premises are true!), and out will come a true conclusion.

There are two mistakes, however, that you should avoid. First, resist the temptation to think that validity also perfectly preserves falsity. It does not. A valid argument with false premises can still have a true conclusion. Note the following argument:

1. All presidents of the United States have been women.
2. David Letterman has been president of the United States.

∴ *C.* David Letterman is a woman.

This is indeed a valid argument with false premises (assuming that he has not been elected since this book was written) and a false conclusion. But with one small adjustment we get the following argument:

1. All presidents of the United States have been women.
2. Madonna has been president of the United States.

∴ *C.* Madonna is a woman.

The argument is still valid and still has false premises (making a similar assumption about Madonna); but now the conclusion is true. Validity does not perfectly preserve falsity.

Second, don't jump to the conclusion that every argument with true premises and a true conclusion is valid. Suppose I more or less indiscriminately take four sentences that everyone would agree are true:

1. George Washington was the first president of the United States.
2. Triangles have three sides.
3. Three plus one equals four.
4. Dogs normally have four legs.

All it takes to have an argument (recalling Chapter 2) is for at least one statement to be offered as reason to believe another statement. The reason does not have to be a good one. All I need to do is argue as follows:

> You wonder how many legs dogs usually have? Well, surely you know that George Washington was president number one. Combine that with the fact that triangles have three sides. Since one plus three is four, it follows that dogs have four legs.

Silly (though I've seen equally silly arguments offered by believers in numerology), but it is an argument. Furthermore, the premises and the conclusion are all true. But it clearly is not valid.

The lesson is this: in an invalid argument, you can find any combination of truth-values in the premises and conclusion. And in a valid argument you can likewise find any combination of truth-values in the premises and conclusion—*but with one major exception.* A valid argument—by definition—cannot have true premises and a false conclusion.

> *Guideline.* An argument with true premises and a false conclusion should be judged invalid. Every other combination of truth-values in the premises and conclusion can occur in either a valid or invalid argument.

EXERCISES Chapter 10, set (a)

Suppose all that you know about an argument are the truth-values of the premises and conclusion that are provided. What can you conclude about the validity of the argument?

Sample exercise. 1. True. 2. False. 3. True. ∴ *C.* False.
Sample answer. Can't say.

1. 1. False. 2. False. ∴ *C.* False.
2. 1. True. 2. True. ∴ *C.* True.
3. 1. True. 2. True. 3. True. ∴ *C.* False.
4. 1. True. 2. True. ∴ *C.* False.
5. 1. False. 2. False. 3. False. ∴ *C.* True.

VALIDITY COUNTEREXAMPLES

If you know, then, that an argument has true premises but a false conclusion, you know that the argument is invalid. Similarly, if you know that the materials in a building are good but the building collapses anyway, you know the problem must be in the way the materials were put together.

But it is seldom so easy. More often than not you must decide about validity when the conclusion is true, or when a premise is false, or when you are unsure about whether they are true or false. In many cases you will recognize the form as one that has been introduced and named in this text; if so, provide the name of the valid or invalid form as part of your defense of your judgment. But for any deductive argument that is invalid, even if you can provide the name of the invalid form, you should also provide a ***validity counterexample.*** This is a simple two-step method for checking any argument for validity. The first step is to extract the form that the argument is depending on for logical success (using the principles described in Chapter 6). The second is to attempt to construct a new argument by appropriately substituting new sentences, predicates, or names in a way that produces obviously true premises and an obviously false conclusion. If you can thus use the argument's form to create a new argument with true premises and a false conclusion, then you have shown that it *is* possible for an argument with this form to have true premises and false conclusion. You in this way show the argument to be invalid. But if you cannot do this, you have a case for the argument's validity.

Let us return to Socrates:

1. All men are mortal.
2. Socrates is a man.

∴ *C.* Socrates is mortal.

The first step in constructing a validity counterexample, extracting its form, yields this:

1. All *F* are *G*.
2. *A* is *F*.

∴ *C.* *A* is *G*.

The second step is to produce obviously true premises and an obviously false conclusion by substituting a new property for *F*, a new property for *G*, and a different name for *A*. Alas, it cannot be done. This is a good reason to conclude that the original argument is deductively valid. But try the same thing on this variation:

1. All men are mortal.
2. Socrates is mortal.

∴ *C.* Socrates is a man.

The first step yields this:

1. All *F* are *G*.
2. *A* is *G*.

∴ *C.* *A* is *F*.

In this case, the second step is easy. Try these assignments for the variables:

F: ponds
G: bodies of water
A: Atlantic Ocean

This yields the following argument:

1. All ponds are bodies of water.
2. The Atlantic Ocean is a body of water.

∴ *C.* The Atlantic Ocean is a pond.

Since this argument uses the form depended on by the original argument, yet has obviously true premises and an obviously false conclusion, it shows that it is possible for the form to have true premises and a false conclusion. Thus, it shows the original argument to be invalid.

Consider an argument from the philosopher Descartes; the question is whether your mind is nothing more than a part of your body:

> If mind and body are one and the same, then mind (like body) is divisible. However, the mind cannot be divided into parts. Consequently, mind and body are not the same.

If we attempt to provide a validity counterexample, we first extract the form that it seems to depend on, namely, this:

1. If *P*, then *Q*.
2. Not *Q*.

∴ *C*. Not *P*.

We then look for sentences to substitute for *P* and *Q* that will produce obviously true premises and an obviously false conclusion. It cannot be done, for the argument is valid.

For the sake of example, suppose that Descartes had been concerned with a different question, and had argued thus:

> If mind and body are one and the same, then mind (like body) is divisible. But mind and body are not the same thing. Consequently, mind cannot be divided into parts.

Is this new argument valid? The answer is not immediately apparent. Let's try to produce a validity counterexample. First, the form it seems to depend on is this:

1. If *P*, then *Q*.
2. Not *P*.

∴ *C*. Not *Q*.

Can we substitute for *P* and *Q* in a way that produces obviously true premises and an obviously false conclusion? Easily. Consider the following argument:

1. If cars run on coal, then cars cause air pollution.
2. Cars do not run on coal.

∴ *C.* Cars do not cause air pollution.

The premises are clearly true, the conclusion clearly false. The argument in question is shown to be invalid, since it has been shown that it is possible for an argument with its form to have true premises and a false conclusion.[2]

Guideline. Demonstrate invalidity by creating a validity counterexample, which illustrates that it is possible for an argument with such a form to have true premises and a false conclusion.

Two Steps in a Validity Counterexample

1. *Extract the form* that the argument depends on for logical success.
2. *Attempt to construct a new argument* by appropriately substituting new sentences, predicates, or names in a way that produces obviously true premises and an obviously false conclusion.

[2] There is an alternative method of providing validity counterexamples that is much easier, but that is seldom possible. Sometimes you can leave the argument as it is and simply describe some possible change that could be made in the world that would make the premises true and the conclusion false. This, too, shows that it is possible for an argument with this form (namely, the very argument) to have true premises and a false conclusion. Suppose this is the argument you started with:

1. If Dave Wilson lives in Phoenix, then Dave Wilson lives in Arizona.
2. Dave Wilson does not live in Phoenix.

∴ *C.* Dave Wilson does not live in Arizona.

As it stands, every statement in the argument is true. But, here's the validity counterexample: *Suppose Dave Wilson lives in Tucson.* Clearly, it's possible. And premises would be true, conclusion false. The argument, thus, is invalid.

EXERCISES Chapter 10, set (b)

Below are various invalid forms that arguments might depend on. They are already presented abstractly, which is the first step of the counterexample method. For this exercise do step two, providing substitutions (different from those already suggested by the text or in class) for the variables such that the premises are obviously true and the conclusion obviously false. (See the *If cars run on coal, then cars cause air pollution* argument, above, for a sample exercise.)

1.
   1. *P*
   ∴ C. *Q*

2.
   1. All *F* are *G*.
   2. *A* is *G*.
   ∴ C. *A* is *F*.

3.
   1. If *P* then *Q*.
   2. Not *P*.
   ∴ C. Not *Q*.

4.
   1. Most *F* are *G*.
   2. *A* is *F*.
   ∴ C. *A* is *G*.

5.
   1. *P* or *Q*
   2. *P*
   ∴ C. *Q*

The Value and the Limitations of Validity Counterexamples

Validity counterexamples can be a powerful tool. In this book you will be introduced only to the most common deductive forms. With this tool in hand, you will not only be able to see vividly the invalidity of the invalid ones in the book, but you will also be in the position to evaluate the logic of any deductive argument not included in the book.

Here, for example, is one such argument. There is an interesting passage in Descartes' *Meditations* in which he points out that our senses sometimes deceive us; note, for example, mirages and hallucinations.[3] Therefore, he says, it just could be that our senses *always* deceive us. Here is one attempt to clarify that argument.

1. Some sense experiences are deceptive.

∴ *C.* It is possible that all sense experiences are deceptive (that is, all sense experiences for all time).

The argument appears to be deductive—it looks as though the premise is offered as a guarantee of the conclusion—but it is an uncommon sort of argument and surely does not depend on any deductive form that is covered in this book. To test it by the method of validity counterexample, let us first extract what seems to be the logical form the argument is depending on:

1. Some *F* are *G*.

∴ *C.* It is possible that all *F* are *G*.[4]

It is possible that seems here to roughly mean, *there is a way of imagining the world so that.*

Having taken the first step, we now see if we can take the second. The first few things we try may fail. Try, for example, *trees* for *F* and *evergreen* for *G*. The premise *Some trees are evergreen* would be true. But it seems that the conclusion, *It is possible that all trees are evergreen,* would also be true. (They aren't all evergreen, but there is a way of imagining the world such that they are.) But let's try *paintings* for *F* and *forgeries* for *G*. That gives us the following argument.

1. Some paintings are forgeries.

∴ *C.* It is possible that all paintings are forgeries (that is, all paintings for all time).

The premise is clearly true; and the conclusion is false, since there cannot be a forgery unless there is at some time an original to be forged.

[3] This example is adapted from Jay Rosenberg's *The Practice of Philosophy* (Englewood Cliffs, NJ: Prentice-Hall, 1983).

[4] Rather than discard "it is possible" as a hedge, I have left it in as a logical constant. To discard it would be extremely uncharitable; no smart person would suppose we could argue to "all *F* and *G*" from "some *F* and *G*." Nor should it be a variable; it is the very possibility (not the probability, not the necessity) of "all *F* and *G*" that seems to be supported by "some *F* and *G*"; thus, it remains as a logical constant.

This is by no means the last word on Descartes' argument—we may, for example, be somehow misunderstanding the form that Descartes is depending on, or he may not intend it to be a deductive argument. But the forgery argument provides good reason to think that if it is deductive, it is invalid. Note that even though I have provided a validity counterexample, I am not counting it as absolutely conclusive, for showing that the argument is invalid. All we really show by a counterexample is that the form we have extracted from the argument is an invalid form. The possibility may remain that we have extracted the wrong form—that there is some other form, as yet undetected, that the argument is really depending on for its logical success. Take yet again our Socrates argument:

1. All men are mortal.
2. Socrates is a man.

∴ *C.* Socrates is mortal.

It is correct to say that this argument takes the following form:

1. *P*
2. *Q*

∴ *C. R*

That is, it is true that the argument is made up of three different sentences. But anyone can easily produce a counterexample to that form, substituting for *P* and *Q* any two obviously true sentences and for *R* any obviously false sentence.

The problem is that the form I have identified is not the form that the argument depends on for its logical success. For it is not the relationship among its complete sentences that the argument depends on for logical success, but the relationship among its various predicates and names. That is to say, referring back to Chapter 6, it does not depend on sentential logic but on predicate logic.

Just as in the case of truth, you are stuck with epistemic probabilities when it comes to your judgments about logic. It may be that the best anyone can do is to judge arguments as *almost certainly* valid or invalid. Although this is worth keeping in mind, since it is always worth being reminded that we might be making a mistake, there is ordinarily no need to hedge your judgments about logic in this way. Once you become comfortable with making judgments about validity, the level of probability will ordinarily be so high that it will make good practical sense to express your judgments simply as *valid* or *invalid.*

Note, on the other hand, that if you cannot find a counterexample, then that is good reason to judge an argument valid. But it is, at most, a good reason; it is not an absolutely conclusive reason, since your inability to find one may be better explained by your lack of imagination in thinking up ways to produce true premises and a false conclusion.

Guideline. Although the method of validity counterexample is very useful, it isn't perfect. Failure to come up with a counterexample could be due to lack of imagination. Success in coming up with a counterexample could be due to overlooking the actual form depended on by the argument.

SOME VALID DEDUCTIVE FORMS

A handful of deductive forms are so obviously valid that they almost never occur in ordinary arguments. They tend to be taken for granted. On the rare occasions that they are explicitly invoked, it is either for rhetorical purposes or because there is a special need for care in spelling out an argument.

One such form is ***repetition***, in which the structure is this:

1. *P*

∴ C. *P*

This occurs when a premise is simply repeated—perhaps disguised in different terminology—as the conclusion of an argument, as in the following:

Walking is healthy since it is good for you.

It is the most obvious case of validity we can find, since, for an argument with this form to have a true premise and false conclusion, it would have to violate the law of noncontradiction. Such arguments are typically bad ones—not because of any logical problem but because they usually commit the fallacy of begging the question.

Two obviously valid forms are found in ***both–and arguments.*** These are arguments that include a premise of the form *P and Q*, which we will term a ***both–and statement*** (sometimes known as a *conjunction*, though we will reserve that term for a valid form of argument). The statements that fit into the variables *P* and *Q* we will simply refer to as the both–and statement's ***parts.*** (They are more formally called *conjuncts.*) Simplification and conjunction are valid both–and forms that are closely allied to repetition. ***Simplification*** takes this form:

1. *P* and *Q*

∴ C. *P*

The both–and premise asserts the truth of its two parts; the argument concludes that one of the two parts is true. Once clarified, a remark such as the following might be seen as taking this form:

> It's going to be rainy and cold tomorrow, so of course it's going to be rainy.

Conjunction goes in the other direction. Its form is this:

1. *P*
2. *Q*

∴ C. *P* and *Q*

As you can see, it *conjoins* two statements. An argument such as the following, once clarified, might be seen as depending on this form:

> He's 6'4". His hair is black. So, there you have it—he's tall and dark.

In each case, it should be obvious that true premises would make a false conclusion impossible.

Bear in mind that common stylistic variants for *and* may need to be translated, according to the guidelines of Chapter 6, into the standard constant for purposes of clarification. These include the following:

Stylistic Variants for *P and Q*

Q and *P*
P also *Q*
P as well as *Q*
P likewise *Q*
P in addition to *Q*
P but *Q*

Translating the stylistic variant does not necessarily preserve *all* the meaning of the translated expression; it merely translates what matters from a strictly logical point of view. Suppose the conclusion above had been *He's tall but dark*, expressed that way because I know you are looking for someone who is tall and blond. Translating *but* into *and* makes more vivid its logical role of conjoining *He is tall* with *He is dark;* but it loses the conversational role of signaling your likely disappointment.

Finally, there is ***double negation.*** To say *it is not the case that the statement is false*—where *it is not the case* is one negation and *false* doubles it—is ordinarily a complicated way of saying *the statement is true.* Suppose I assert, "It is false that exercise is good for you," to which you may reply, "It is *not* false that exercise is good for you." You might just as well have replied, "Exercise *is* good for you," but you have communicated the same thing by doubly negating it. This can go in either direction:

1. *P*

∴ *C.* Not not *P*

1. Not not *P*

∴ *C.* *P*

Neither case lends itself to a validity counterexample; if the premise is true, so is the conclusion.

As already mentioned, these forms are so obvious that they seldom occur explicitly. And if they do occur, they are seldom interesting enough to warrant the trouble it takes to clarify them separately. So, although they are worth knowing about, it will usually make the best practical sense to eliminate them in the streamlining phase of the clarification process.

Guideline. The most obviously valid forms of deductive logic—such as repetition, simplification, conjunction, and double negation—can normally simply be paraphrased away when clarifying an argument.

Some Valid Deductive Forms

1. Repetition
2. Simplification
3. Conjunction
4. Double negation

EXERCISES Chapter 10, set (c)

Clarify and write the LOGIC portion of the evaluation for each of these arguments. (Each uses an obviously valid deductive form.)

Sample exercise. Reading this author makes me nauseated. I'm also thoroughly bored with reading him. In short, I'm sick and tired of reading this stuff.

Sample answer.

1. I am sick of reading this.
2. I am tired of reading this.

∴ *C.* I am sick of reading this and I am tired of reading this.

The argument is valid, by conjunction.

1. It is not the case that there is no God—so, surely, God does exist.
2. As you say, she studied history at Ohio State, so it does follow that she went to Ohio State.
3. Being married is highly desirable, since having a spouse is a good thing.
4. You are wrong. A flat tax is certainly not a mistake. So a flat tax is a good thing.
5. America is a country. And it is free. So it's a free country.

The Fallacies of Composition and of Division.

Two famous fallacies that date back to antiquity[5] can typically best be seen as misguided applications of the valid forms of conjunction and simplification.

The ***fallacy of composition*** is the mistake of concluding that a property applies to the whole of something because it applies to all of its parts. *My team is the best team because it has the best players* might at first look like a good argument, although *My book is a good book because it is made up of good words* does not. But both commit the fallacy of composition. The words, regardless of how good they are, obviously have to work together in the right way to make the book a good one; so, likewise, must the players to make the best

[5]They now, however, mean something different from what Aristotle had in mind when he first named them.

team. This is reminiscent of conjunction, but importantly different. A valid conjunction would go something like this:

> Player A is the best shooting guard, player B is the best point guard, player C is the best center, player D is the best power forward, and player E is the best small forward, therefore Players A, B, C, D, and E are each the best.

It differs from the fallacy because there is no shifting of the property *best* from the players to the team; it applies only to players throughout the argument.

Economists, trying to avoid a similar trap in their field, have formulated this maxim:

> The sum of all locally optimal decisions is not always globally optimal.

That is to say, even if each person is making decisions that are in that person's best interest (they are "locally optimal"), it doesn't add up to what is best for society (what is "globally optimal"). We must sometimes sacrifice our own best interest if we are to serve the larger interest. Those who miss this point commit the fallacy of composition.

The ***fallacy of division*** is the reverse—it is the mistake of concluding that a property applies to one or more of the parts because it applies to the whole. *My team is the best so my center is the best* is an example. It does seem a great deal like simplification. But the closest valid simplification might look like this: *Each of my players is the best so my center is the best.* In the valid version the property *best* does not shift from team to player; it is applied to the same thing in both premise and conclusion.

> *Guideline.* Beware of the fallacies of composition and of division, which are patterned closely after the valid forms of conjunction and simplification. They are invalid because the property shifts in application from the part to the whole (in composition) or from the whole to the part (in division).

Fallacies of Both–And Arguments

1. Fallacy of composition
2. Fallacy of division

EXERCISE Chapter 10, set (d)

Which is the fallacy and which is the valid form? Provide the name of each.

Sample exercise. (a) This cake contains the best ingredients; therefore, it is the best cake. (b) This cake contains the best eggs. This cake contains the best flour. Therefore, this cake contains the best eggs and the best flour.

Sample answer. (a) fallacy of composition (b) valid, conjunction

1. (a) Professor Smith and Professor Jones are reputable. So, Professor Smith is reputable. (b) My university is reputable; so Professor Smith of my university is reputable.
2. (a) All the parts in my computer work, so my computer works. (b) My hard disk works. My monitor works. Therefore, my hard disk and monitor work.

EVALUATING THE TRUTH OF PREMISES WITH *NOT* OR *AND*

We have covered two logical constants in this chapter: *not* and *and.* We will briefly consider whether there is anything special to think about when evaluating the truth of premises that include them.

Negative Premises

Negative premises and both–and premises are, for the most part, uncomplicated. Negation is typically a simple on-off switch. Add *it is not the case* to the front of a statement and its truth-value is reversed. *Dolphins are mammals* is true. So, *It is not the case that dolphins are mammals* is false.

There are traps, however, that you should avoid. You may, for reasons of style, choose to put *not* somewhere inside the sentence rather than tacking *It is not the case* to the front of it. *Attitude contexts,* which report someone's attitude—what someone believes, feels, or wants—present one such trap. *It is not the case that she believes you are guilty* means one thing, while *She believes that it is not the case that you are guilty* means something else. The second version does not allow for the possibility that she has no view on the question of your guilt. *Modal contexts,* which state modes such as probability, possibility, and necessity, provide another opportunity for caution. *It is not possible that you are guilty* means one thing, while *It is possible that you are not guilty* has quite a different meaning.

Guideline. Negating a statement reverses its truth-value; but be careful about placing the negation inside the statement, especially in attitude and modal contexts.

Both–and Premises

Both–and statements are also usually straightforward. If you are almost certain of each part that it is true, then you should judge the both–and statement as almost certainly true. If even one part is almost certainly false, then the both–and statement is almost certainly false.

It is not so straightforward, however, when you can say of the parts merely that they are *probably* true or false. Usually you can arrive at the probability of the both–and statement by applying this simple rule: *multiply the probabilities of the parts.* Suppose your plans for tomorrow depend on two things: good weather and your ability to get off work. You are interested in whether the following both–and statement is true:

> Tomorrow's weather will be good and I can get off work tomorrow.

You believe that each part is probably true; the TV forecaster said there was roughly a 35 percent chance of showers, and your boss lets people off approximately 3 out of every 4 times they ask. This means there is about a .65 probability for *Tomorrow's weather will be good* and about a .75 probability for *I can get off work tomorrow.* Multiplying the probabilities of the two parts, you find that the probability of the both–and statement is in the neighborhood of a mere .49. This is in the same neighborhood as .50, so you can't decide whether the both–and statement is true. Take special note of this: even if you judge the parts to be fairly probable, you might find that the probability of the both–and statement is .50 or below.

The simple rule of multiplying the probabilities of the parts, however, doesn't work when the truth of one part would affect the probability of the other part.[6] Suppose you work for a company that lays cement. There is more work when the weather is good. So even though the boss generally lets people off about 3 in every 4 times, the chances of getting a day off in good weather drop to about 1 in 2. There is a broader rule that applies here (and it encom-

[6]Statisticians refer to this as *correlation*.

Strategies for Evaluating the Truth of Both–And Statements

WHAT YOU KNOW ABOUT THE PARTS	*HOW TO EVALUATE THE BOTH–AND STATEMENT*
Both parts are almost certainly true.	Almost certainly true.
At least one part is almost certainly false.	Almost certainly false.
Parts are merely probable and the truth of *P* would not affect the probability of *Q*.	Multiply the probabilities of *P* and *Q*
Parts are merely probable and the truth of *P* would affect the probability of *Q*.	Multiply the probability of *P* times the probability that *Q* would have if *P* were.

passes the simpler situation as well): when you multiply the probabilities of the parts, *for the affected part, use the probability that the part would have if the other part were true.* So, in this case, multiply .65 (the probability for *Tomorrow's weather will be good*) by .50 (the 1-in-2 probability for *I will be able to get off tomorrow* when I assume that tomorrow's weather will be good). It may be time to start thinking about changing your plans.

You will usually have to make an educated guess about probability assignments. You might not have specific information about the frequency probabilities of the parts or, even if you do, you might have additional information that bears on the probabilities of the parts. It can still be helpful to convert these judgments temporarily into numbers so that you can be guided by the rules of probability. Suppose that after you heard the weather forecast you saw some clouds rolling in, making it less probable than the predicted .65 that tomorrow's weather will be good. The most you can now say is that you can't decide; but tentatively call it .50. And suppose you know the boss is in a bad mood this week, meaning that his general practice of letting people off about 1 in every 2 times in good weather is overoptimistic. You're not sure how overoptimistic, but tentatively call it a .30 probability that he will let you off on the assumption that the weather is indeed good. Multiplying these two numbers produces a .15 probability for the both–and statement. This is misleadingly precise; but it does vividly show that you have strong grounds for saying that the both–and statement is *very probably false*.

Guideline. When the two parts of a both–and statement are merely probable, tentatively assign them a probability (even if the result is misleadingly precise) so that you can apply the rules of probability. Convert the numbers back into everyday language for your final evaluation.

Exercises Chapter 10, set (e)

Explain your calculations and then state your evaluation of the truth of the statement based on the information provided.

Sample exercise. After the next national election the Republicans will have the majority of the House and after the next national election the president will be a Democrat. (The form is *P and Q*. P is .60; Q is .55; if P were true, Q would be .50, since strong voter sentiment for Republican representatives might be accompanied with similar sentiment for a Republican president.)

Sample answer. .60 times .50 is .30, so the premise is probably false.

1. I made an *A* is psychology and I made a *B* in English. (The form is *P and Q*. P is .80; Q is .70; if P were true, Q would still be .70 since the two grades have nothing to do with one another.)
2. It is not the case that after the next national election the Republicans will have a majority in the House. (The form is *Not P.* P is .60.)
3. You will pay the rent on time and your check will not bounce. (Form is *P and Q*. P is .90; Q is .90; if P were true, Q would be .80, since when you pay on time it's more likely you don't yet have the money on hand.)
4. This rock is granite and this one is agate. (Form is *P and Q*. P is .99; Q is .90; if P were true, Q would still be .90 since, in this case, there is no special relationship that I know of between granite and agate.)

SUMMARY OF CHAPTER TEN

Good logic, which is one of several criteria for good reasoning, is present when an argument's premises (whether true or not) support its conclusions, or, alternatively, when its conclusion follows from its premises. Deductive logic has to do with those arguments that aim to make certain, or guarantee, their conclusions; inductive logic has to do with those arguments that aim merely to make probable, or count toward, their conclusions. Later chapters will introduce various forms of each sort, making it easy to keep them straight.

A successful deductive argument is valid, meaning that it depends on a form such that it is impossible for an argument with that form to have true premises and a false conclusion. A validity counterexample can provide a useful—though not perfect—test for validity. It first extracts the form the argument depends on and, second, makes substitutions for all variables in a way that produces an argument with obviously true premises and an obviously false conclusion. When you evaluate an argument in this text, you should provide a validity counterexample for every deductive argument that is invalid. Also, if there is a name for the invalid form, you should state the name.

The most obviously valid deductive forms—which clearly do not lend themselves to attack by validity counterexample—include repetition, double negation, simplification, and conjunction. Their logic is simple, but evaluating the truth of their premises—especially in the case of both–and statements—can be helped by special rules regarding the epistemic probabilities of the parts.

GUIDELINES FOR CHAPTER TEN

- An argument with true premises and a false conclusion should be judged invalid. Every other combination of truth-values in the premises and conclusion can occur in either a valid or invalid argument.
- Demonstrate invalidity by creating a validity counterexample, which illustrates that it is possible for an argument with such a form to have true premises and a false conclusion.
- Although the method of validity counterexample is very useful, it isn't perfect. Failure to come up with a counterexample could be due to lack of imagination. Success in coming up with a counterexample could be due to overlooking the actual form depended on by the argument.
- The most obviously valid forms of deductive logic—such as repetition, simplification, conjunction, and double negation—can normally simply be paraphrased away when clarifying an argument.
- Beware of the fallacies of composition and of division, which are patterned closely after the valid forms of conjunction and simplification. They are invalid, because the property shifts in application from the part to the whole (in composition) or from the whole to the part (in division).

- Negating a statement reverses its truth-value; be very careful, however, about placing the negation inside the statement, especially in attitude and modal contexts.
- When the two parts of a both–and statement are merely probable, tentatively assign them a probability (even if the result is misleadingly precise) so that you can apply the rules of probability. Convert the numbers back into everyday language for your final evaluation.

GLOSSARY FOR CHAPTER TEN

Both–and argument—one of a loosely defined group of deductive arguments that have a both–and statement as a premise.

Both–and statement—a statement of the form *P and Q*. Also called a *conjunction,* though we are reserving this term for a valid deductive form.

Conjunction—valid deductive form, as follows:

1. *P.*
2. *Q*

∴ C. *P* and *Q*

The term is also sometimes used for a both–and statement.

Deductive argument—an argument in which the premises are intended to guarantee, or make certain, the conclusion. To determine whether the logic of a deductive argument is successful, a good rule of thumb is to ask questions such as these:

Do the premises guarantee the conclusion?
If the premises were true, would that make the conclusion certain?
Alternatively toward *apodictic* or *demonstrative* argument.

Double negation—valid deductive form, as follows:

	1. *P*		1. Not not *P.*
∴	*C.* Not not P	∴	*C.* *P*

Fallacy of composition—the mistake of concluding that a property applies to the whole of something because it applies to each of its parts.

Fallacy of division—the mistake of concluding that a property applies to one or more of the parts because it applies to the whole.

Inductive argument—an argument in which the premises are intended merely to count toward, or make probable, the conclusion. To determine whether the logic of an inductive argument is successful, a good rule of thumb is to ask these questions:

Do the premises count toward the conclusion?
If the premises were true, would that make the conclusion probable?
Alternatively termed *probabilistic, nondemonstrative*, or *ampliative* argument.

Invalid—a deductive argument that is not logically successful. An argument is invalid if and only if it is possible for an argument with such a form to have true premises and a false conclusion.

Logic—the reasonableness conferred on an argument's conclusion by its premises. In an argument that is logically successful the conclusion *follows from* the premises—or, to put it differently, the premises *support* the conclusion. In deductive arguments, this is strictly a matter of the fit of the conclusion to the premises. In inductive arguments, it is also a matter of the fit of the conclusion to the total available evidence.

Part—a statement connected to another by *and.* Also known as *conjunct.*

Repetition—valid deductive form, as follows:

1. *P*
∴ *C. P*

Simplification—valid deductive form, as follows:

1. *P* and *Q*
∴ *C. P*

Valid—a logically successful deductive argument. An argument is valid if and only if it is impossible for an argument with such a form to have true premises and a false conclusion.

Validity counterexample—a two-step method for checking any argument for validity. The first step is to extract the form that the argument is depending on for logical success. The second step is to attempt to construct a new argument by appropriately substituting new sentences, predicates, or names in a way that produces obviously true premises and an obviously false conclusion.

CHAPTER ELEVEN

If–Then Arguments

"Contrariwise," continued Tweedledee, "if it was so, it might be; and if it were so, it would be: but as it isn't, it ain't. That's logic."

—Lewis Carroll, *Through the Looking-Glass*

TOPICS

Forms of If–Then Arguments
Evaluating the Truth of If–Then Premises
If–Then Arguments with Implicit Statements
Bringing It All Together

If–then arguments, also known as *conditional arguments* or *hypothetical syllogisms*, are the workhorses of deductive logic. They make up a loosely defined family of deductive arguments that have an ***if–then statement***—that is, a *conditional*—as a premise. The conditional has the standard form *If P* *then Q*. The *if* portion, since it typically comes first, is called the ***antecedent***; the *then* portion is called the ***consequent.***

These arguments—often with implicit premises or conclusions—are pressed into service again and again in everyday communication. In *The De-Valuing of America*, for example, William Bennett gives this brief if–then argument:

> If we believe that good art, good music, and good books will elevate taste and improve the sensibilities of the young—which they certainly do—then we must also believe that bad music, bad art, and bad books will degrade.

The if–then premise—lightly paraphrased—is this:

> If good art, good music, and good books elevate taste and improve the sensibilities of the young, then bad music, bad art, and bad books degrade taste and degrade the sensibilities of the young.

The second premise—set off in the original by dashes—is:

> Good art, good music, and good books elevate taste and improve the sensibilities of the young.

And the implicit conclusion is this:

> Bad music, bad art, and bad books degrade taste and degrade the sensibilities of the young.

Whether the argument is sound depends on whether the logic of the argument is successful and whether the premises are true. We now look at each of these two categories of evaluation.

FORMS OF IF–THEN ARGUMENTS

The arguments of this chapter are deductive, so the success of their logic is entirely a matter of form. The form of Bennett's argument in the preceding paragraph is the most common and the most obviously valid. It is normally termed ***affirming the antecedent***; a common Latin term for this form is *modus ponens*, which means "the method (or mode, from *modus*) of affirming (or propounding, from *ponens*)."

1. If *P* then *Q*.
2. *P*

∴ *C*. *Q*

Almost as common is the valid form ***denying the consequent***; the Latin term for this is *modus tollens*, which means "the method of denying."

1. If *P* then *Q*.
2. Not *Q*.

∴ *C*. Not *P*.

This is the form of my argument if I say to you, "If you like working with the Boy Scouts, then you've gotta like camping out. But, you know how much you hate camping out. So Boy Scouts isn't for you."

Each of these two valid forms may be contrasted with an *invalid* form that unsuccessfully mimics it. The invalid form that is tempting due to its similarity to affirming the antecedent is the ***fallacy of affirming the consequent***; its structure is this:

1. If *P* then *Q*.
2. *Q*

∴ *C*. *P*

I've committed this fallacy if I argue, "If you like working with the Boy Scouts, then you've gotta like camping out. And you know how much you like camping out. So you'll go for the Boy Scouts." After all, you may love camping out but hate people; the conclusion surely does not follow.

And deceptively similar to denying the consequent is the ***fallacy of denying the antecedent***; this invalid form is as follows:

1. If *P* then *Q*.
2. Not *P*.

∴ *C*. Not *Q*.

I made this mistake in the following argument: "If you like working with the Boy Scouts, then you've gotta like camping out. But you've always hated the

Boy Scouts. So, I conclude you're not fond of camping either." Perhaps you just think the uniforms are ugly, but nevertheless love camping. Again, the conclusion does not follow.

Recall that when you find these fallacious forms, there is normally no need to apply the principle of charity in your paraphrase. The ease with which such mistakes are made (thus earning each fallacy a name of its own) is usually reason to think that the arguer might have been truly mistaken in his or her thinking, and thus is reason to clarify the argument in the invalid form.[1]

Another form of argument, a valid one, that belongs to the if–then family is often termed ***transitivity of implication.*** This form of argument links if–then statements into a chain, as follows:

1. If *P* then *Q*.
2. If *Q* then *R*.

∴ *C*. If *P* then *R*.

I've given an argument of this form if I contend, "If you like working with the Boy Scouts, then you've gotta like camping out. If you like camping out,

[1]Note, incidentally, that *If P then Q* and *If not Q then not P*, which are called the *contrapositives* of one another, are logically equivalent; each is true—or false—under exactly the same circumstances. Consider, for example, these contrapositives:

If construction begins before July 4, then the building will be ready to be occupied before snow falls.

If the building is not ready to be occupied before snow falls, then construction did not begin before July 4.

This equivalence produces an interesting implication for the four if–then forms that have just been introduced. There is always a logically equivalent affirming the antecedent argument for every denying the consequent argument (and vice versa). Likewise for each fallacy of denying the antecedent/affirming the consequent. Consider, for example, the following denying the consequent argument.

1. If construction begins before July 4, then the building will be ready to be occupied before snow falls.
2. The building will not be ready to be occupied before snow falls.

∴ *C*. Construction did not begin before July 4.

This is equivalent to the following affirming the antecedent argument—note that the only change is to substitute for premise 1 its contrapositive:

1. If the building is not ready to be occupied before snow falls, then construction did not begin before July 4.
2. The building will not be ready to be occupied before snow falls.

∴ *C*. Construction did not begin before July 4.

you don't mind bugs. So, if you like working with the Boy Scouts, you don't mind bugs." There is no limit to the number of if–then links that this chain could contain and still be valid.[2]

Incidentally, Lewis Carroll's argument at the chapter's opening presents some interesting evaluative possibilities. Here is one reasonable paraphrase:

1. If it is, then it is.
2. It is not.

∴ *C.* It is not.

On the one hand, it has the form of the fallacy of denying the antecedent, which is invalid; on the other hand, it has the form of denying the consequent, which is valid. Further, it also has the form of repetition—looking only at 2 and *C*—which is also valid. The solution to the puzzle is that it is valid—not because the two valid forms outnumber the one invalid one, but because we should charitably suppose that the valid form is the one that was intended. Charity, unfortunately, cannot prevent us from noting that whatever the form, this argument probably commits the fallacy of begging the question.

If–Then Arguments

VALID	INVALID
Affirming the antecedent	Affirming the consequent
Denying the consequent	Denying the antecedent
Transitivity of implication	

[2]It would also be valid transitivity of implication if the argument took the following negative form:

1. If *P* then *Q*.
2. If *Q* then *R*.

∴ *C.* If not *R* then not *P*.

The term *transitivity of implication*, then, is a more generic sort of name than is affirming the antecedent or denying the consequent.

EXERCISES Chapter 11, set (a)

Create a brief argument that takes the specified form.

Sample exercise. Transitivity of implication.

Sample answer: If I run out of gas I'll be late. And if I'm late I'll get fired. So, if I run out of gas I'll get fired.

1. Affirming the antecedent
2. Affirming the consequent
3. Denying the consequent
4. Denying the antecedent
5. Transitivity of implication

Stylistic Variants for If–Then

If–then arguments, as we have seen, make crucial use of statements of the form *If P then Q* as premises. Using the terminology of Chapter 6, the expression *if–then* is the logical constant of such statements, while *P* and *Q* are the variables—*sentential* variables, you will recall—replaceable by declarative sentences as the content of the argument.

These constants are anything but constant in ordinary language; a wide variety of everyday English expressions are used to express *if–then.* In the structuring phase of the clarifying process, it is important that you translate them into standard constants. This helps bring the structure of the argument close to the surface and makes it much easier to tell whether the argument is logically successful.

All of the expressions listed below—and many more—can be used as stylistic variants for *if–then.* More precisely, each of the expressions can be translated, for logical purposes, into *If P then Q.*

Stylistic Variants for *if P then Q*

Q if *P.*
P only if *Q.*
Only if *Q*, *P.*

Assuming *P*, *Q*.
Q assuming *P*.
Supposing *P*, *Q*.
Q supposing *P*.
Given *P*, *Q*.
Q given *P*.
That *P* is a sufficient condition for that *Q*.
That *Q* is a necessary condition for that *P*.

This list includes some of the most obvious variants, but it is not comprehensive. Unexpected variants for if–then statements show up with regularity. A politician says, for example, "Vote for my bill *and* I'll vote for yours." This can be taken as a stylistic variant for, "If you vote for my bill, then I'll vote for yours." A story about new television shows says, "*With* good summer ratings, the series will end up on the fall schedule of NBC." This translates into, "If the series gets good summer ratings, then it will end up on the fall schedule of NBC." And language watcher Thomas Middleton, complaining in the *Los Angeles Times* about a tendency he has noticed among teens to use expressions like "and then my friend *goes* so-and-so" instead of "and then my friend *said* so-and-so," presses his point thus:

> The ability to say things . . . is consummately precious, and *to* describe "saying" as "going" *is to* debase this glorious gift. *It is to* treat speech as though it were no more than, as Random House says, making a certain sound—like a cat's purr.

This passage, it seems, translates into something like the following:

> If someone describes "saying" as "going," then that person debases the gift of speech and treats it as though it were no more than making a sound.

Be very careful, however, with words like *with*, *and*, and *to*; they are rarely stylistic variants for *if–then*. It is only when they are used in these distinctive kinds of contexts that they should be taken this way.

> *Guideline.* Translate the stylistic variants for the if–then premise into the standard constant.

EXERCISES Chapter 11, set (b)

Translate the stylistic variant in each of the following if–then statements.

Sample exercise. As long as history textbooks make white racism invisible in the 19th century, students will never be able to analyze racism intelligently in the present.—James Loewen, *Lies My Teacher Told Me*

Sample answer. If history textbooks make white racism invisible in the 19th century, then students will never be able to analyze racism intelligently in the present.

1. Oxygen is necessary for combustion.
2. The governor agreed Tuesday to a legislative compromise for ending the community colleges' financial troubles—but only if lawmakers can find another $121 million.
3. The teacher should assign the passage and require the student to summarize it in his own words. Do that consistently, and he will not only learn to write a lot better, he will also learn to analyze, evaluate, sort out, and synthesize information.
4. "The man who is not willing to give to every other the same intellectual rights he claims for himself is dishonest, selfish, and brutal." —Robert Ingersoll, *Ingersoll: The Immortal Infidel*
5. "To address kids in masses, you have to be an entertainer, which I'm not," Dr. Seuss said, sounding a little like the Grinch.—*Los Angeles Times*
6. "Strip a woman's body of its breasts and hips, of all of its nurturing curves, and replace it with enough stringy, sinewy muscle, and a lot of people will simply not know what to make of what you have left." —*Pumping Iron II: The Women*

EXERCISES Chapter 11, set (c)

Clarify each of the if–then arguments. Then state whether the argument is valid and provide the name of the valid or invalid form.

Sample exercise. "I submit that the author is thoroughly wrong to criticize analogical argumentation, that if argument by analogy were really as weak as he allows we would not use it as extensively as we do."—book review in *Teaching Philosophy*

Sample answer.

1. If argument by analogy is as weak as the author allows, then we do not use argument by analogy as extensively as we do.

[2. We do use argument by analogy as extensively as we do.]

∴ *C.* Argument by analogy is not as weak as the author allows.
Valid, denying the consequent.

1. Universal mandatory screening for AIDS can be justified on the basis of beneficence when a therapeutic intervention is available or when an infectious state puts others at risk merely by casual contact. However, neither is the case with AIDS. Thus, there is no demonstrable public health benefit that justifies universal mandatory screening.—N. F. McKenzie, ed., *The AIDS Reader* (Even though an extremely charitable reading of this argument might suggest otherwise, go ahead and clarify it as a fallacy.)
2. "The prolonged study of ethics does not by itself make you a better person. If it did, philosophy professors would in general be better people than average. But they aren't."—William Bennett, *The De-Valuing of America*
3. "If the North Koreans are smart—and we know they are smart—they will move in the direction of reform."—Daryl Plank, Korea expert and visiting fellow at Washington's Heritage Foundation
4. "If, instead of offering the occasional high-profile prize of $35 million, New York awarded 350 prizes of $100,000, making not one multimillionaire, but a great number of $100,000 winners, it would create an environment where far more people would know, or know of, large prize winners. More people will buy tickets if they know large prize winners. So experimenting with such a format should reverse the current negative trend." —letter to the editor, *New York Times*
5. "Ladies and Gentlemen, I'll be brief. The issue here is not whether we broke a few rules or took a few liberties with our female party guests. We did. But you can't hold a whole fraternity responsible for the behavior of a few sick perverted individuals. For if you do, then shouldn't we blame the whole fraternity system? And if the whole fraternity system is guilty, then isn't this an indictment of our educational insti-

tutions in general? I put it to you, Greg: Isn't this an indictment of our entire American society? Well, you can do what you want to us, but we're not going to sit here and listen to you badmouth the entire United States of America."—Eric "Otter" Stratton, in the film *Animal House* (This is a complex argument with the subconclusion *If the fraternity is guilty, then the entire American society is guilty.*)

6. "And if, for example, antiabortionism required the perverting of natural reason and normal sensibilities by a system of superstitions, then the liberal could discredit it—but it doesn't, so he can't."—Roger Wertheimer, *Philosophy and Public Affairs*

Singular Inferences

One common variation on the preceding forms is worth our attention. Note the remark made by former heavyweight boxing champ Joe Frazier to a more recent winner of the title, Jimmy Ellis:

> You ain't no champ. You won't fight anybody. A champ's got to fight everybody.

This provides several opportunities for following the rules of paraphrasing arguments—a stylistic variant for *if–then*, the need to follow the principle of charity (because of the rather extreme words *everybody*, *anybody*, and even what Frazier means by being a champ), wording to be matched, and emptiness to be avoided (because of the word *you*). The result of clarifying it is something like this:

1. If any person deserves to be the heavyweight boxing champion, then that person will fight all worthy contenders.
2. Jimmy Ellis will not fight all worthy contenders.

∴ *C.* Jimmy Ellis does not deserve to be the heavyweight boxing champion.

This looks very much like denying the consequent—that is, it seems to depend on this form:

1. If *P* then *Q*.
2. Not *Q*.

∴ *C.* Not *P*.

But the *Q* of premise 1 and the *Q* of premise 2 do not really match, nor do the *P* of premise 1 and the *P* of *C*. For there is no mention of Jimmy Ellis anywhere in premise 1, yet Jimmy Ellis is the subject of premise 2 and of the conclusion. This certainly does not harm the argument's logic, however, since Jimmy Ellis is included—as a single person—among those encompassed by the term *any person* in the first premise. So, for practical purposes, we can continue to call this form denying the consequent, but with a slight difference. It will be identified as ***singular denying the consequent.***

The same modification is permitted for every form of sentential logic that we cover, assuming two things hold. First, there must be a ***universal statement*** as a premise—that is, a premise with a term like *all, none, anything,* or *nothing,* to mention a few examples. *If any person deserves to be the heavyweight boxing champion, then that person will fight all worthy contenders* is universal, since it applies to any person. Second, there must be a conclusion in which a single instance is specified that is encompassed by the universal term. *Jimmy Ellis will not fight all worthy contenders* provides an example, since *Jimmy Ellis* is encompassed by *any person.* All the if–then forms mentioned above can be modified in this way. ***Singular affirming the antecedent*** and ***singular transitivity of implication*** are also valid forms, while the ***fallacy of singular affirming the consequent*** and the ***fallacy of singular denying the antecedent*** are invalid ones.

Guideline. When an argument has *both* a universal premise *and* a conclusion about a single thing that is encompassed by the universal premise, consider whether it is the *singular* version of a sentential logical form.

Singular If–Then Arguments

VALID	INVALID
Singular affirming the antecedent	Singular affirming the consequent
Singular denying the consequent	Singular denying the antecedent
Singular transitivity of implication	

EXERCISES Chapter 11, set (d)

Clarify the following arguments as examples of singular if–then arguments. Then state whether the argument is valid and provide the name of the valid or invalid form.

Sample exercise. "*Q*: You mentioned that Bundy was mentally ill? *A*: Sane people do not go round killing dozens of women, and the person that the state of Florida strapped in the electric chair was a man who was severely mentally ill."—I. Gray and M. Stanley, eds., *A Punishment in Search of a Crime: Americans Speak Out Against the Death Penalty*

Sample answer:

1. If anyone is sane, that person does not kill dozens of women.

[2. Bundy killed dozens of women.]

∴ *C*. Bundy was not sane.

Valid, singular denying the consequent.

1. If someone is in Birmingham, then that person is in Alabama. And if someone is in Alabama, then that person is in America. So, if I am in Birmingham, then I am in America.
2. I conceded that speeding is sufficient reason for getting pulled over by a police officer. But I wasn't speeding. So I should not have been pulled over.
3. One argument for the immorality of adultery might go something like this: it involves the breaking of a promise, and it is immoral to break a promise.—from a lecture by philosopher Richard Wasserstrom
4. I refer you to the verdict in the English Court sustaining Whistler's contention that a man did not wholly own a picture by simply buying it. So, although I may have sold my painting to him, I have a right to protect my picture from the vandalism of his cleaning it.—from American artist Albert Pinkham Ryder

EVALUATING THE TRUTH OF IF–THEN PREMISES

If–then statements usually propose a special connection between the if-clause and then-clause. Identifying the specific nature of the connection is usually the key to judging the truth of such a statement and to successfully defending that judgment.[3]

Sometimes the proposed connection is *causal*, as in the case of the statement *If you turn the key in the ignition, then the car will start.* Turning the key would *cause* the car to start. But in other cases the proposed connection is broadly *logical*; the if-clause does not *cause* the then-clause but is offered as counting toward or even guaranteeing its truth.[4] Consider the statement that became a book and movie title—*If it's Tuesday, this must be Belgium.* It's being Tuesday cannot cause this to be Belgium, but could presumably (combined with other statements about the itinerary) count in favor of the belief that this is Belgium. Or consider the statement *If there is intelligent life on other planets, then we are not alone in the universe.* That there is intelligent life elsewhere in the universe is just what we mean by not being alone in the universe. So the connection here is also a logical one—and in this case it is such a tight connection that we can safely call it self-evidently true.

Whether the proposed connection is causal or logical, it is helpful to think of the if-clause as not being offered as *alone* sufficient for the then-clause. When we use if–then statements we are typically allowing for other relevant factors as well. We have simply picked out the if-clause for special mention because it is the one factor that happens to be most important in the context. These implicit assumptions about other relevant factors are termed ***secondary assumptions*** (or auxiliary hypotheses).

Return to the if–then statement *If you turn the key in the ignition, then the car will start.* Behind such a statement there usually are implicit secondary assumptions about many other factors that contribute to the starting of the car—but that are presumed to be already in place, and thus do not merit mention. They may include assumptions about the specific situation, such as these:

[3]If you have studied formal logic, you have learned that you only need to know the truth-values of the antecedent and the consequent to know the truth-value of the if–then statement; you may have memorized truth tables in support of this. But this applies only to a specialized form of the if–then statement called the *material*, or *truth-functional*, conditional. This sort of if–then statement is not used in ordinary language.

[4]For practical purposes, it may be helpful to think of both sorts of connections as ultimately epistemic—that is, as providing in the antecedent a reason for believing the consequent to be true, on the strictly hypothetical assumption that the antecedent is true.

There is a functioning engine in the car.
There is gas in the tank.
The battery is not dead.
The ignition system is not defective.

They may also include more general assumptions about the relation between the if-clause and then-clause, such as this:

Ignition systems are designed to start properly functioning cars.

And they may include even broader principles that guide much of our reasoning, such as this:

The laws of nature will not suddenly change.

When you judge an if–then statement to be true, a good way to defend your judgment is to identify the secondary assumptions that are most likely to be in question, given the circumstances, and to point out their truth. You might say, for example,

I judge this premise to be very probably true because this is what ignition systems are designed to do, and there is no reason to think that this car is out of gas, has a dead battery, or has a defective ignition system.

Thus a connection between if-clause and then- 288clause is affirmed.

Alternatively, if you judge the if–then statement to be false, a good defense is to point out that a secondary assumption is false; for example,

This premise is probably false, since the headlights were left on all day and the battery is dead by now.

Thus you have denied one of the secondary assumptions and shown that the connection between if-clause and then-clause is severed.

The same strategy works well for if–then statements in which the connection is broadly logical rather than causal. Consider *If you are reading this book, then you understand English.* One important secondary assumption is *This book is written in English.* Another is *Reading something just means that you understand it.* (You might wonder whether this, or the earlier life on other planets example, should count as a *secondary* assumption, since it is part of the very meaning of the terms used—what we have in preceding chapters called self-evidently true. It will nevertheless make good practical sense in this text for us to count it so.) So here is an exemplary defense of the statement:

> This premise is certainly true, since the book is written in English, and part of what it means to read something is to understand it.

Again, its truth is defended by pointing out the cords that connect if-clause to then-clause.

Consider, finally, *If New York City were in Quebec, then it would still be in the United States.* There is, unfortunately, no way of knowing what secondary assumptions are supposed to connect this if-clause and then-clause. Is New York City to be located further north, or Quebec further south? And, on either scenario, what historical events would have caused such a difference—and would they, perhaps, have resulted in Quebec's being included within the United States? There is simply not enough information to decide. The best evaluation of this premise, then, would be something like this:

> I can't decide whether this premise is true or false. There is no way of knowing whether New York City is to be located further north, Quebec further south, or what relevant historical events might have led to it.

The daughter of Rudolf Carnap, one of the great philosophers and logicians of the 20th century, tells of asking her father, when she was a young child, "If you were offered a million dollars, would you be willing to have your right arm amputated?" "I don't know," he replied. "Would I be given an anesthetic?" Lack of information about relevant secondary assumptions can sometimes make it impossible for any of us, even Carnap, to say any more than "can't decide" in evaluating if–then statements.

> *Guideline.* Defend your judgment that an if–then statement is true by affirming the truth of the most questionable secondary assumptions. Defend your judgment that it is false by showing that a secondary assumption is false.

EXERCISES Chapter 11, set (e)

For each of the following if–then statements, list the most plausible and relevant secondary assumptions (or explain why you cannot do so). Then provide a judgment of the premise's truth by reference to your list. (They are not provided with any context, so you will have to use your imagination.)

Sample exercise. If the auto industry manufactured more electric cars, then air pollution would decrease.

Sample answer. Secondary assumptions: Consumers will buy more electric cars if they become available. Electric cars produce less pollution than conventional cars.

Probably false, at least currently, since electric cars do not currently compete well with conventional cars in price or performance; so having more available does not mean that more will be purchased by consumers.

1. If there were more classical music on the radio, then there would be more appreciation of classical music among the public.
2. If George Bush was the 43rd president, then Bill Clinton was the 44th.
3. If it rains tomorrow, then you should take your umbrella to work.
4. If people recycled more, the environment would be in better shape.
5. If I were two feet taller, I would have played in the NBA.
6. If it's Tuesday, this must be Belgium.
7. If the stock market rises next year, then Microsoft stock will rise in value.
8. If all private ownership of guns were made illegal, then violence in our country would drop dramatically.
9. If you can do 20 pushups, then you are in good shape.
10. If you are planning to go to medical school, then you can expect to take several science courses.

The Retranslation Mistake

Consider the statement *If New York City is in the state of New York, then it is in the United States.* It is certainly true, but it is tempting to defend that judgment by more or less repeating the if–then statement in slightly different words, as follows:

> My view is that the premise is certainly true, since New York City has to be in the United States, given that it is in the state of New York.

You have said nothing that goes beyond the premise itself, thus nothing that would be enlightening to the reasonable objector over your shoulder. You have merely retranslated the *if–then* constant back into one of its stylistic variants! Be careful to avoid this sort of defense. (I'll leave it as an exercise for you to identify the simple secondary assumption that provides the crucial connection for this if–then statement.)

> *Guideline.* Do not defend your judgment of an if–then statement by simply rewording the statement (or, if false, by rewording the denial of the statement).

Truth Counterexamples

It can be especially tempting to ignore mention of secondary assumptions when the if-clause is clearly true and the then-clause is clearly false. These are the most straightforward cases, for if you know that the if-clause is true and the then-clause is false, you know that the if–then statement is false. The if–then statement has vividly failed to deliver on its promise.

But even here it is better, if possible, to show the severed connection between the two by identifying the false secondary assumption. Take, for example, *If New York City is in the state of New York, then it is in Canada.* You might defend your judgment as follows:

> I consider the premise to be certainly false since, based on my experience in my own travels and based on the testimony of every authority I've ever encountered, New York City is in the state of New York and it is not in Canada (but in the United States).

But this makes no mention of any connection between the if-clause and then-clause. If there is supposed to be one, it is the assumption that the state of New York is itself in Canada. And your defense is stronger if you include the rejection of this assumption, as follows:

Further, the state of New York is wholly located within the United States, not Canada.

There can be, however, exceptions to this rule. One exception applies when it is a universal if–then statement that is false. Universal if–then statements, recall, are if–then statements with a universal term like *anything*, *anyone*, *nothing*, or *nobody* in the if-clause. An example we have already seen is *If any person deserves to be the heavyweight boxing champion, then that person will fight all worthy contenders.* A property—such as *deserving to be champ*—is applied universally—to *any person*—rather than to a single instance. When such statements are false, the method of ***truth counterexample*** can be a simple and effective way of defending that judgment. This method identifies a single instance in which the if-clause is obviously true and the then-clause is obviously false.

A newspaper story on the homeless, for example, contains the line, "No one is poor by choice." This is a stylistic variant of the universal if–then statement, "If anyone is poor, then it is not by choice." Yet the same newspaper, on the facing page, has a story about Mother Theresa's religious order, stating, "These nuns have voluntarily taken an oath of poverty." Here we have a ready-made truth counterexample. The nuns are instances of the if-clause's truth—they are poor—and at the same time are instances of the then-clause's falsity—their poverty is by choice. Thus armed, your defense of your judgment of the universal if–then statement can be stated simply as follows: "The premise is certainly false, since certain orders of nuns are poor by choice."

Guideline. When a universal if–then statement is false, try to defend that judgment by providing a truth counterexample.

EXERCISES Chapter 11, set (f)

Provide a truth counterexample for each of these false universal if–then statements. If necessary, first translate stylistic variants into the standard constant.

Sample exercise. Only animals that can fly are endowed with wings.

Sample answer. If any animal has wings, then it can fly. Certainly false; the ostrich has wings but cannot fly.

1. No major-party presidential or vice presidential candidate has been a female.
2. If any substance is made of metal, then it is attracted to a magnet.
3. Everything reported in the newspaper is true.
4. Nice guys finish last.
5. What goes up must come down.

The Educated Ignorance Defense

Another occasion for ignoring secondary assumptions—also occurring under the true if-clause/false then-clause scenario—is when the evidence for the truth of the if-clause and the evidence for the falsity of the then-clause are each stronger than the evidence for the truth of the if–then statement. In these cases, even though you may not know which secondary assumption is at fault, it can be reasonable to say that the premise is false "because some secondary assumption—not yet identified—is mistaken." This we will term the ***educated ignorance defense.*** ("Ignorance" because you admit ignorance regarding which secondary assumption is faulty; "educated" because you nevertheless have good evidence that the if-clause is true and the then-clause is false.)

Return, for example, to our car-starting example. Imagine that when you pick up your car after extensive repairs your mechanic says to you, "If you turn the key in the ignition, then the car will start." He has extremely good reasons to believe this is true. He has checked out the ignition, the battery, the fuel system—in short, his experience and expert judgment support the truth of any secondary assumption that might be reasonably questioned. You turn the key in the ignition. But the car does not start.

Something has to give. There are three statements for which you apparently have very good evidence:

If you turn the key in the ignition, then the car will start.
You turn the key in the ignition. (The if-clause is true.)
The car will not start. (The then-clause is false.)

They cannot all be true at the same time. *You* will probably quickly give up on the truth of the if–then statement, not knowing what went wrong but knowing quite well that you turned the key and the car didn't start. But the mechanic, who has especially good reasons to believe the if–then statement—he did the work, and he has his reputation to think about—will probably start off by doubting the if-clause, asking you suspiciously, "Are you sure you turned the key in the ignition?" "I'm sure," you reply, anxiously turning it again and again. "Let me see," he says with a hint of disdain and gets in to turn the key himself. Only when it does not start for him does he say, "Well, OK, I was mistaken, but I just can't figure out what's wrong with it."

The mechanic's initial reluctance to give up the truth of the if–then statement is because he cannot imagine which secondary assumption is mistaken. And he only concedes that the if–then statement is false when he sees that evidence in favor of the if-clause—that the key has been turned—is conclusive. (The evidence that the then-clause is false—that the car did not start—is already conclusive.) He is still ignorant of which secondary assumption to blame, but now that he is duly educated—about the truth of the if-clause and falsity of the then-clause— he can reasonably resort to the educated ignorance defense. Eventually something better than educated ignorance will be required if the car is to be driven away.

Science provides many examples of this defense. In the 18th century, for example, astronomers used the new Newtonian mechanics to accurately predict the orbits of many of the planets in our solar system. The following if–then statement describes the general shape of these predictions:

> If Newtonian mechanics is true, then the orbit of planet *A* will be observed to be *F*.

(In this case, *A* is the name of the planet and *F* is a mathematical description of the predicted observed orbit of the planet around Earth.) After many successes, the astronomers did their work on the orbit of Uranus and discovered, to everyone's surprise, that the predicted orbit did *not* accord with their observations. They thus found themselves with good evidence for the following three statements, not all of which could be true:

> If Newtonian mechanics is true, then the orbit of Uranus will be observed to be *F*.
> Newtonian mechanics is true. (The if-clause is true.)
> It is not the case that the orbit of Uranus is observed to be *F*. (The then-clause is false).

They checked and rechecked their equipment to be sure of their evidence that the then-clause was false, but they found their surprising observations to be accurate. They reminded themselves of the mountains of other evidence in favor of the if-clause. And they checked and rechecked their calculations, in the futile hope of finding some faulty secondary assumption that would falsify the if–then statement. In the end, the only reasonable thing to do was to reject the if–then statement with a defense something like this:

> This premise is probably false; the support for Newtonian theory is so strong, and the quality of this observation so good, that it is most likely that some not-yet-identified faulty secondary assumption lies behind its falsity.

Incidentally, that is where things stood until the 19th century, when the Englishman John Adams and the Frenchman Urbain Leverier, working independently, realized that the mistake had been in assuming *Uranus is the outermost planet.* Due to this secondary assumption, the earlier Newtonians had not factored into their calculations any gravitational pull from the other side of Uranus. They each reworked the calculations and predicted where they should be able to observe an outer planet exercising gravitational attraction on Uranus. In 1846 they independently observed this planet, later named Neptune, in the predicted location. (Pluto, which is beyond Neptune, was not found until 1930.)

The strategy of saying, "There is some unidentified secondary assumption that is mistaken" should be employed with great care. Again, it works only when there is *independent strong evidence in favor of the truth of the if-clause and against the truth of the then-clause.* These lines are from the final letter written to his wife by one of the doomed soldiers of the German Sixth Army outside Stalingrad:

> "If there is a God," you wrote me in your last letter, "then he will bring you back to me soon and healthy." But, dearest, if your words are weighed now you will have to make a difficult and great decision.

Her own words, quoted by her husband, committed her to the statement *If God exists, then the soldier will return to his wife soon and healthy.* The report of his death that she later received supported this statement: *The soldier will not return to his wife soon and healthy.* But by a valid denying the consequent argument, these two premises entail *God does not exist.* This, then, presented his wife with the difficult and great decision that the soldier foretold—she must stop believing in God, or she must go back on her own words.

Let's set this up in the same way as we did with the auto mechanic and the Newtonians. There are three statements before her, at least one of which must be false:

If God exists, then the soldier will return to his wife soon and healthy.
God exists. (The if-clause is true.)
The soldier will not return to his wife soon and healthy. (The then-clause is false.)

Let's suppose that instead of giving up her belief in God, she chose the option of going back on her words and rejecting her if–then statement. Her most reasonable defense, as we have seen, would be for her to sever the connection between the if-clause and the then-clause by identifying and rejecting the false secondary assumption. Candidates might include:

God cares about human suffering.
God cares about the suffering of this particular soldier and his wife.
God is able to prevent this suffering.
God knows about this suffering.

But let's further suppose that she insisted on continuing to embrace all these secondary assumptions, on the grounds that to do otherwise would be to unsuitably diminish God. Instead, she took the step that many believers in God take—the step of saying, "God's ways are beyond the understanding of man. When I get to heaven he will reveal to me his reasons. Until then, I will continue to believe in him." This is an attempt to use the educated ignorance defense. We give up on the if–then statement in the expectation that we will eventually discover the car's mechanical defect, the flaw in our astronomical calculations, or the hidden mysteries of God.

Whether this is a reasonable move for the soldier's wife depends on one condition: it is *educated* ignorance—and thus a reasonable defense—only if the wife has independent strong evidence that God exists (evidence for the if-clause). If she does not—if she accepts by faith alone not only God's mysterious ways but also his very existence—then she cannot reasonably defend her rejection of the if–then statement unless she identifies and rejects the false secondary assumption.

Guideline. It is reasonable to judge an if–then premise false "because some secondary assumption must be mistaken, though I don't know which one" only if there is very powerful evidence both that the if-clause is true and that the then-clause is false.

EXERCISES Chapter 11, set (g)

In each problem there are three statements, at least one of which must be false. Provide an "educated ignorance" defense for the claim that the if–then statement is false; you'll need to state evidence for the if-clause and against the then-clause in your defense.

Sample exercise.

If the instructor is fair, then he will not give higher grades to males than to females.

The instructor is fair.

The instructor gave higher grades to males than females.

Sample answer. The if–then statement is probably false, although I can't say exactly what the mistaken assumption is. Even though the record shows that in this class the males did much better than the females, he has a widespread reputation for bending over backward to treat everyone fairly. It seems likely that his reputation is deserved and that in this case there is an explanation that will eventually emerge.

1. If you patch that hole, then the roof will stop leaking. You patch the hole. The roof does not stop leaking.
2. If your boyfriend loves you, then he will be on time tonight. Your boyfriend loves you. He is not on time tonight.
3. If you are the most talented, then you will win the talent show. You are the most talented. You do not win the talent show.
4. If it is impossible to move physical objects by only thinking about it, then when Uri Geller concentrates on bending the spoon it will not bend. It is impossible to move physical objects by only thinking about it. When Uri Geller concentrates on bending the spoon it does bend.

Strategies for Evaluating the Truth of If–Then Statements

WHAT YOU KNOW	HOW TO EVALUATE THE IF–THEN STATEMENT
1. *You can identify secondary assumptions.*	
a. You can show a secondary assumption is probably false.	Probably false.
b. You can show the most questionable secondary assumptions are probably true.	Probably true.
c. Otherwise.	Can't decide.
2. *You cannot identify secondary assumptions.*	
a. You can provide a truth counterexample.	Almost certainly false.
b. You can provide the educated ignorance defense.	Probably false.
c. Otherwise.	Can't decide.

Secondary Assumptions and Indirect Arguments

Secondary assumptions can also play an important role in the evaluation of indirect arguments (which we have also called *reductios*). Introduced in Chapter 10, such arguments, in their simplest form, exhibit the structure of denying the consequent. They begin with a statement that may seem quite innocuous and attempt to show that it is false by pointing out, in what amounts to an if–then premise, an absurd consequence that it forces on you. You accept the absurdity of the consequence by accepting a premise that says the then-clause is false. You must then conclude, by the valid form of denying the consequent, that the seemingly innocuous if-clause must be rejected.[5] An example is found in these remarks by David Wilson (no known relation to the author), adapted from a newspaper report:

> Melina Mercouri, Greece's minister of culture, swept into the staid old British Museum to examine what she called the soul of the Greek people—the Elgin Marbles. Lord Elgin took them from the Parthenon in Athens in the early 19th century. Mercouri is expected

[5]In formal logic, this sort of argument must produce a logical contradiction. In common usage, however, it only needs to produce something preposterous.

> to make a formal request soon for the marbles' return. But Dr. David Wilson, director of the British Museum, opposes the idea. "If we start dismantling our collection," Wilson said, "it will be the beginning of the end of the museum as an international cultural institution. The logical conclusion of the forced return of the Elgin Marbles would be the utter stripping of the great museums of the world."

Wilson's argument can be clarified thus:

1. If it is acceptable to force the British to return the Elgin Marbles to Greece, then it is acceptable to strip the great museums of the world.

[2. It is not acceptable to strip the great museums of the world.]

∴ *C.* It is not acceptable to force the British to return the Elgin Marbles to Greece.

Melina Mercouri must avoid the conclusion without rejecting premise 2, so her only recourse is to reject the if–then premise. But when she does reject it, she is no position to respond with the educated ignorance defense; the evidence for the if-clause is exactly what is in question, so for her to simply say the if-clause is obviously true would be to beg the question. In short, her only reasonable strategy is to reject the if–then premise by identifying a faulty secondary assumption that it depends on. Here is a strong candidate for the role of faulty secondary assumption:

> The only principle for returning the Elgin Marbles would be that *any* item, great or small, removed from its original culture, whether by consent or by force, must be returned to that culture.

This secondary assumption is clearly false. So Mercouri might defend her rejection of premise 1 as follows:

> Premise 1 is almost certainly false, since it assumes that *all* items must be returned to their original culture; but the return of the Elgin Marbles only depends on a principle calling for the return of great national treasures that have been forcibly removed.

What Mercouri would be doing is accusing Wilson of committing the fallacy of *non causa pro causa* (introduced in Chapter 10). This is the fallacy of blaming the absurd consequence (*It is acceptable to strip the great museums of the world*) on what is set forth as its cause (*It is acceptable to force the British to return the Elgin Marbles to Greece*) instead of blaming the unnoticed assumption that is the real cause of the absurdity (*All items must be returned to their original culture*).

Because indirect arguments are typically offered in support of controversial conclusions, only rarely can the educated ignorance approach be used in evaluating them without begging the question. Be especially watchful for faulty secondary assumptions behind the if–then premise of indirect arguments; when there is such an assumption, the indirect argument can be criticized for committing the fallacy of *non causa pro causa.*

Guideline. In indirect arguments, be alert for faulty secondary assumptions behind the if–then premise.

EXERCISES Chapter 11, set (h)

Clarify each of these simple indirect arguments; then evaluate only the if–then premise, on the grounds that it commits the fallacy of *non causa pro causa.* (Use the Elgin Marbles case as your sample.)

1. If you are right in your claim that income taxes should be eliminated, then you must accept the consequence that the government will be left with no money to do even its most important business. But we would all agree that government cannot be done away with. So income taxes must remain.
2. If children who misbehave are not immediately and severely punished, they will grow up with the belief that misbehavior has no negative consequences. We all agree, of course, that our children cannot be allowed to grow up with that belief. So don't spare the rod with your children.

EXERCISES Chapter 11, set (i)

Each of the passages below indicates what could be seen as a misuse of secondary assumptions. In the Kelvin case, clarify the denying the consequent argument and identify the secondary assumption that, perhaps, Kelvin should have questioned. In the Azande case, clarify the affirming the antecedent argument that the Azande are trying to avoid, and identify the secondary assumption that they, perhaps, too readily reject to show that the if–then premise is false.

1. Lord Kelvin, the leading British physicist of his day, dismissed Darwin's work on the ground that it violated the principles of thermodynamics. The sun could be no more than 100 million years old; evolution demanded a much longer period in which to operate; therefore evolution must be rejected. Kelvin wasted no time pursuing the minutiae of the geological and palaeontological evidence on which evolution was based. Physics in the guise of thermodynamics had spoken clearly and whatever failed to fit into its scheme had to be rejected. Kelvin's thermodynamics were later shown to be wrong. Unaware of radioactivity, he had inevitably failed to allow for its effect in his calculations.—Derek Gjertsen, *Science and Philosophy*
2. According to the Azande, witchcraft is inherited unilinearly, from father to son, and mother to daughter. How, therefore, can I accept that my brother is a witch and yet deny that I am also infected? To prevent this absurdity arising, the Azande adopt further "elaborations of belief." They argue, for example, that if a man is proven a witch beyond all doubt, his kin, to establish their innocence, deny that he is a member of their clan. They say he was a bastard, for among Azande a man is always of the clan of his genitor [natural father] and not of his pater [mother's legal husband]. In this and other ways, Evans-Pritchard concluded, the Azande freed themselves from "the logical consequences of belief in biological transmission of witchcraft."—Derek Gjertsen, *Science and Philosophy*

IF–THEN ARGUMENTS WITH IMPLICIT STATEMENTS

If–then arguments, like any other sort of arguments, frequently have implicit premises or conclusions. To use a term from earlier in the book, they are frequently enthymemes. In extreme cases, only the if–then premise is explicit. Suppose, for example, that you've complained for the 10th time that the party across the hall is too loud, and I say to you, "Hey, if you can't beat 'em, join 'em." What I've actually given is an affirming the antecedent argument. I've explicitly provided the if–then premise; the implicit premise, obviously, is *You can't beat them;* and the implicit conclusion is *You should join them.*

Consider the following, more sophisticated example, from a *New York Review of Books* review of a book of film criticism by Stanley Cavell:

> When Katharine Hepburn in *The Philadelphia Story* brightly says, "I think men are wonderful," Cavell hears an "allusion" to *The Tempest* that amounts "almost to an echo" of Miranda's saying, "How beauteous mankind is!" If this is an echo, then Irene Dunne's saying of her marriage, "It was pretty swell while it lasted" is a reminiscence of Gibbon's *Decline and Fall.*

This argument is an example of denying the consequent. But only one statement of the argument is explicit. The full clarification proceeds thus:

1. If Hepburn's remark "I think men are wonderful" in *The Philadelphia Story* is an echo of Miranda's "How beauteous mankind is" in *The Tempest,* then Irene Dunne's saying of her marriage, "It was pretty swell while it lasted" is a reminiscence of Gibbon's *Decline and Fall.*

[2. Irene Dunne's saying of her marriage, "It was pretty swell while it lasted" is not a reminiscence of Gibbon's *Decline and Fall.*]

∴ [C. Hepburn's remark "I think men are wonderful" in *The Philadelphia Story* is not an echo of Miranda's "How beauteous mankind is" in *The Tempest.*]

This is the reviewer's sideways—but effective—way of saying that perhaps Cavell takes himself a bit too seriously.

If–Then Bridges

In the preceding examples, only the if–then premise was explicit. But in other cases, only the if–then premise is *implicit.* Note, for example, this episode recorded by Jean Piaget in his book, *The Child's Conception of the World*:

> A little girl of nine asked: "Daddy, is there really God?" The father answered that it wasn't very certain, to which the child retorted: "There must be really, because he has a name!"

This does not look, on the face of it, like an if–then argument. But there must be an implicit premise connecting the two parts of her retort. A good clarification, it seems, is this:

> [1. If any name exists, then the thing it names exists.]
> 2. God has a name.
> ∴ *C*. God exists.

Premise 1 serves as a universal if–then bridge. It is a universal if–then statement (note the term *any*) and serves as a bridge of sorts between 2 and *C*. We might have proposed a more specific sort of bridge, as follows:

> [1*. If God has a name, then God exists.]

Either bridge produces a valid argument—the first one by singular affirming the antecedent, the second one by affirming the antecedent. But the second doesn't produce an argument that will convince us—after all, you can add a premise to any argument that says, "If the premises are true, then the conclusion is true," and thereby say something that the arguer surely intended, without saying anything illuminating. (There is a specialized term for such an if–then statement, namely, the *corresponding conditional* of an argument.) When the conditional is expressed in its universal form, on the other hand, we get some idea of the general principle being assumed by the arguer.

> *Guideline.* Consider providing a universal if–then bridge when an explicit link between premise and conclusion has not been provided by the arguer.

EXERCISES Chapter 11, set (j)

Clarify each of these arguments, proposing for each a universal if–then bridge.

Sample exercise. "An idealist is one who, on noticing that a rose smells better than a cabbage, concludes that it will also make better soup."—H. L. Mencken

Sample answer:

[1. If anything smells better than another thing, then it also tastes better.]

2. A rose smells better than a cabbage.

∴ *C*. A rose tastes better than a cabbage.

1. The Internet, as another high-tech innovation, will inevitably fragment community rather than enhance it.
2. "Spirituality turns out to be central to cognitive psychology, and therefore to artificial intelligence, and therefore to computer science, and therefore to the whole history of science and technology."—David Gelernter, *The Muse in the Machine*
3. Most striking of their claims is that among the 7,000 people executed in this century, at least 23 people, and possibly many more, have been innocent. This alone is reason, the authors conclude, that the death penalty should be abolished.—review of Hugo Bedau and Michael Radelet, *In Spite of Innocence*
4. "There will always be newspapers and magazines. You can take them to the lavatory and you still cannot do that with television."—Robert Maxwell
5. "Although these textbooks purport to be a universal guide to learning of great worth and importance, there is a single clue that points to another direction. In the six years I taught in city and country schools, no one ever stole a textbook."—W. Ron Jones, *Changing Education*

BRINGING IT ALL TOGETHER

After learning a wide array of distinct skills, you now have the opportunity to use all of them together. If–then arguments provide us with our first of six groupings of arguments that can be substantial and interesting. And you are now equipped to fully clarify and evaluate them.

There is nothing new to be said, but a few things bear repeating. In your evaluation, separately evaluate the truth of the premises (considering each premise individually), the logic of the argument (naming the form if it has a name, and providing a validity counterexample if it is invalid), the soundness of the argument (which depends entirely on truth and logic), and, if necessary, the conversational relevance of the argument. Always provide a defense of your judgment, and do so as if there were a reasonable objector over your shoulder whom you were trying to persuade.

I'll provide a sample clarification and evaluation of this brief argument found in Gilbert Harman's *The Nature of Morality*:

> Total pacifism might be a good principle if everyone were to follow it. But not everyone is, so it isn't.

CLARIFICATION

1. If everyone followed total pacifism, then total pacifism would be a good principle.
2. Not everyone follows total pacifism.

∴ *C.* Total pacifism is not a good principle.

EVALUATION

TRUTH

Premise 1 is probably true, since the main objection to total pacifism is that it leaves you with no defense against those who are not pacifists. But if everyone were a pacifist, that would be no problem. (This seems to be the main secondary assumption of the premise.)

Premise 2 is certainly true. We all have firsthand experience with violent people, not to mention the experience of them that we have via the media.

LOGIC

Invalid, fallacy of denying the antecedent. Here is a validity counterexample:

1. If anything is a chihuahua, then it is a dog.
2. Beethoven (of movie fame) is a dog.

∴ *C.* Beethoven is a chihuahua.

SOUNDNESS

Unsound, due to invalidity.

EXERCISES Chapter 11, set (k)

Clarify and evaluate. Where appropriate, provide implicit statements in the clarification (including universal if–then bridges) and original validity counterexamples in the evaluations.

1. "With the layout of the San Francisco-Oakland area, a rail line there had a better chance than most," said rail critic Peter Gordon, a re-

gional planner at USC. "If it doesn't work there, and I assert it doesn't, there is no way rail transit will work in a place like Los Angeles." —*Los Angeles Times*

2. "But if evolution proceeded as a lockstep, then the fossil record should display a pattern of gradual and sequential advance in organization. It does not, and I regard this failure as the most telling argument against an evolutionary ratchet."—Stephen Gould, *Panda's Thumb* (It might help you to know that Gould is a noted professor of paleontology at Harvard. By a "ratchet" and a "lockstep" he means a "gradual, uniform progression.")
3. "If each man had a definite set of rules of conduct by which he regulated his life he would be no better than a machine. But there are no such rules, so men cannot be machines."—A. M. Turing, *Mind* (Turing is an expert in artificial intelligence, i.e., what it would take to make a machine think.)
4. "*Q*: Even so, don't you think that the use of computers reinforces a child's problem-solving ability? *A:* If that were true, then computer professionals would lead better lives than the rest of the population. We know very well that isn't the case."—interview with computer expert Joseph Weizenbaum, *Le Nouvel Observateur* (The argument is in the answer.)
5. Pjeter Ivezaj, a U.S. citizen, was sentenced Wednesday to seven years in prison by a panel of judges in Yugoslavia for participating in peaceful anti-Yugoslav activities in this country. Said his brother Frano, 28, "I intend to take this matter to the court of world opinion. If U.S. citizenship has any value, which I believe it does, now is the time for the U.S. government to make a move."—*Detroit Free Press*
6. Scientists believe that the most likely location of our country's next severe earthquake is a fault zone that centers on New Madrid, MO. But residents here, where the quake probably will be centered, are unimpressed. "I'm just a non-believer," said L. H. Rector, publisher of the *New Madrid Weekly Record*, whose motto is "The only paper in the world that cares about New Madrid." "It hasn't been proved that we're going to have one," Rector said. "Now, out in California, they can see the fault. It's been proved. But no one here in New Madrid has seen one fault."—*Los Angeles Times* (Provide Rector's argument with a universal if–then bridge.)
7. "The church never wanted disease to be under the control of man. Timothy Dwight, president of Yale College, preached a sermon

against vaccination. His idea was that if God had decreed from all eternity that a certain man should die with the smallpox, it was a frightful sin to avoid and annul that decree by the trick of vaccination. Smallpox being regarded as one of the heaviest guns in the arsenal of heaven, to spike it was the height of presumption."—Robert Ingersoll, *Ingersoll, The Immortal Infidel*

8. The key premise is that a human fetus is a full-fledged, actualized human life. Supposing human embryos are human beings, their innocence is beyond question. So nothing could justify our destroying them except, perhaps, the necessity of saving some other innocent human life.—Roger Wertheimer, "Understanding the Abortion Argument" (Clarify as a complex argument with an if–then bridge in the second inference.)
9. "If there be righteousness in the heart, there will be beauty in the character. If there be beauty in the character, there will be harmony in the home. If there be harmony in the home, there will be order in the nation. If there be order in the nation, there will be peace in the world."—Confucius (Suppose that this is a transitivity of implication argument with an implicit conclusion.)
10. "If a man could not have done otherwise than he in fact did, then he is not responsible for his action. But if determinism is true, it is true of every action that the agent could not have done otherwise. Therefore, if determinism is true, no one is ever responsible for what he does."—Winston Nesbitt and Stewart Candlish, *Mind*
11. Their children, they soon saw, were being presented by EPIC, an organization to help children learn to think about values, with hypothetical situations that called for the students to make choices and decisions. On a spaceship survival trip, an EPIC question asks, "Determine what to take with you. Pretend the ship develops trouble and the load must be lightened. What could you discard?" There was, to a number of parents, something very troubling about these types of questions. The questions seemed to carry with them the presumption that the children were free to reason through to their own answers. If they could do that, it meant that there were no moral absolutes, and nothing was clearly right or wrong, good or bad. This was not the worldview of fundamentalists who believe in the literal word of the Bible. "Once you tell a child that he has to decide upon his own values system, that's like saying that values are not real, and you can just make them up as you go along," said Marjorie McNabb,

a former Episcopalian who now attends a Baptist church. "Children would be better raised by a street gang than EPIC. At least, they'd learn two values, courage and loyalty. That's better than no values."—*Los Angeles Times* (Look for the actual argument to begin in about the middle, with the words "If they could do that. . . .")

12. In spite of the popularity of the finite-world picture, however, it is open to a devastating objection. In being finite the world must have a limiting boundary, such as Aristotle's outermost sphere. That is impossible. This objection was put forward by the Greeks, reappeared in the scientific skepticism of the early Renaissance and probably occurs to any schoolchild who thinks about it today. On the basis of the objection, one must conclude that the universe is infinite.—J. J. Callahan, *Scientific American* (The stylistic variant for the if–then statement is unusual—it is "in being . . . must have . . .")

13. "There is one insuperable obstacle to a belief in ghosts. A ghost never comes naked: he appears either in a winding-sheet or 'in his habit as he lived.' To believe in him, then, is to believe that not only have the dead the power to make themselves visible after there is nothing left of them, but that the same power inheres in textile fabrics. Supposing the products of the loom to have this ability, what object would they have in exercising it? And why does not the apparition of a suit of clothes sometimes walk abroad without a ghost in it? These be riddles of significance. They reach away down and get a convulsive grasp on the very taproot of this flourishing faith."—Ambrose Bierce, *Devil's Dictionary* (Treat this as an indirect argument in which the only explicit premise is really the one starting "To believe in him . . .")

14. There was little doubt, then, that if the earth moved through an immovable sea of ether, there would be an ether wind, and if there were an ether wind, the Michelson-Morley apparatus would detect it. In fact, both scientists were confident that they would not only find such a wind, but that they could also determine (by rotating the slab until there was a maximum difference in the time it took light to make the two journeys) the exact direction, at any given moment, of the earth's path through the ether. Michelson was astounded and disappointed. This time the astonishment was felt by physicists all over the world. Regardless of how Michelson and Morley turned their apparatus, they found no sign of an ether wind! Michelson never dreamed that this 'failure' would make the experiment one of the most successful, revolutionary experiments in the history of science.

The reason Michelson and Morley were unable to detect an ether wind, Einstein said, is simple: there is no ether wind.—Martin Gardner, *Relativity for the Million*

SUMMARY OF CHAPTER ELEVEN

There are three common valid forms of if–then arguments: affirming the antecedent, denying the consequent, and transitivity of implication. There are two common invalid forms: the fallacy of affirming the consequent and the fallacy of denying the antecedent. When an argument takes one of these forms but has both a universal if–then premise and a conclusion about a single instance to which the universal applies, describe it in the same terms but for the addition of the phrase *singular. . . .*

When paraphrasing, translate variants such as *P only if Q* and *Q assuming P* into the standard constant *If P then Q*.

When judging the truth of if–then premises, concentrate chiefly on the proposed connection—whether causal or broadly logical—between the if-clause and the then-clause. Typically the if-clause is not alone presumed to be sufficient for the then-clause, but to be sufficient only in combination with secondary assumptions that are themselves *not* in question. The if-clause is the only one mentioned because it is presumed, in this particular context, to be the only factor in doubt. In defending your judgment that an if-then premise is true, point out the truth of the most doubtful secondary assumptions. In defending your judgment that the if–then premise is false, point out the falsity of a secondary assumption. In this way you either reinforce or sever the connection between if-clause and then-clause.

When the if-clause is clearly true and the then-clause is clearly false, you may have the opportunity to effectively show the falsity of the if–then premise without reference to secondary assumptions in two different ways. First, you may provide a truth counterexample, assuming the if–then premise is universal. And second, you may provide an "educated ignorance" defense, which requires that the evidence for the truth of the if-clause and the falsity of the then-clause is strong—much stronger than the evidence for the if–then premise itself.

If–then arguments are frequently enthymematic. When the if–then premise is the implicit statement, be especially attuned to the likely need for a universal if–then bridge.

GUIDELINES FOR CHAPTER ELEVEN

- Translate the stylistic variants for the if–then premise into the standard constant.
- When an argument has *both* a universal premise *and* a conclusion about a single thing that is encompassed by the universal premise, consider whether it is the *singular* version of a sentential logical form.
- Defend your judgment that an if–then statement is true by affirming the truth of the most questionable secondary assumptions. Defend your judgment that it is false by showing that a secondary assumption is false.
- Do not defend your judgment of an if–then statement by simply rewording the statement (or, if false, by rewording the denial of the statement).
- When a universal if–then statement is false, try to defend that judgment by providing a truth counterexample.
- It is reasonable to judge an if–then premise false "because some secondary assumption must be mistaken, though I don't know which one" only if there is very powerful evidence both that the if-clause is true and that the then-clause is false.
- In indirect arguments, be alert for faulty secondary assumptions behind the if–then premise.
- Consider providing a universal if–then bridge when an explicit link between premise and conclusion has not been provided by the arguer.

GLOSSARY FOR CHAPTER ELEVEN

Affirming the antecedent—valid deductive form, as follows:

1. If *P* then *Q*.
2. *P*

∴ C. *Q*

Also known as *modus ponens*, which is Latin for "the method (or mode, from *modus*) of affirming (or propounding, from *ponens*)."

Antecedent—the if-clause of an if–then statement.

Consequent—the then-clause of an if–then statement.

Denying the consequent—valid deductive form, as follows:

1. If *P* then *Q*.
2. Not *Q*.

∴ *C*. Not *P*.

Also known as *modus tollens,* which is Latin for "the method of denying."

Educated ignorance defense—defense of your judgment that an if–then premise is false even though you cannot tell which secondary assumption is at fault (thus, it reflects ignorance); it can be a reasonable defense only if your evidence for the truth of the if-clause and for the falsity of the then-clause is especially strong (thus, the defense is educated).

Fallacy of affirming the consequent—invalid deductive form, as follows:

1. If *P* then *Q*.
2. *Q*

∴ *C*. *P*

Fallacy of denying the antecedent—invalid deductive form, as follows:

1. If *P* then *Q*.
2. Not *P*.

∴ *C*. Not *Q*.

Fallacy of singular affirming the consequent—invalid affirming the consequent in which the if–then premise is universal and the conclusion is about a single instance that is encompassed by the universal term.

Fallacy of singular denying the antecedent—invalid denying the antecedent in which the if–then premise is universal and the conclusion is about a single instance that is encompassed by the universal term.

If–then argument—one of a loosely defined group of deductive arguments that have an if–then statement as a premise. Also known as a *conditional argument* or *hypothetical–syllogism.*

If–then statement—a statement in the form of *If P then Q*. Also known as a *conditional.*

Secondary assumption—when an if–then statement is asserted, this is an assumption made, often implicit because it is not in doubt, about another factor besides the if-clause that contributes to the truth of the then-clause. Also known as *auxiliary hypothesis.*

Singular affirming the antecedent—valid affirming the antecedent in which the if–then premise is universal and the conclusion is about a single instance that is encompassed by the universal term.

Singular denying the consequent—valid denying the consequent in which the if–then premise is universal and the conclusion is about a single instance that is encompassed by the universal term.

Singular transitivity of implication—valid transitivity of implication in which the if–then premises are universal and the conclusion is about a single instance that is encompassed by the universal term.

Transitivity of implication—valid deductive form, as follows:

1. If *P* then *Q*.
2. If *Q* then *R*.

∴ *C.* If *P* then *R*.

It can have any number of if–then premises. It can also have a negative conclusion, as follows:

∴ *C.* If not *R*, then not *P*.

Truth counterexample—strategy for defending your judgment that a universal if–then premise is false, by identifying a single instance in which the if-clause is obviously true and the then-clause is obviously false.

Universal statement—a premise with a term like *all*, *none*, *anything*, or *nothing*.

CHAPTER TWELVE

Either–Or Arguments and More

Chrysippus considers the actions of the dog, who comes to a path that leads three ways in search of his master, whom he has lost, and sniffs first one way and then another. Having assured himself of two, because he does not find his master's track, without more ado the dog furiously follows the third path. Such a dog, Chrysippus says, must necessarily discourse thus with himself: "I have followed my master's scent this far, he must of necessity pass by one of these three ways; it is neither this nor that, then consequently he is gone this other." And by this conclusion of discourse assuring himself, coming to the third path, the dog sniffs no more, but by the power of reason suffers himself to be carried violently through it.

Michel de Montaigne, *Essays*

TOPICS

Either–Or Arguments
Evaluating the Truth of Either–Or Premises
Dilemmas
Categorical Arguments

EITHER–OR ARGUMENTS

Either–or arguments, sometimes more formally called *disjunctive syllogisms,* are so common and intuitive that—if Chrysippus, cited above, is right—even our pets are capable of using them. Either–or arguments prominently feature a statement of the form *P or Q,* which is called an ***either–or statement*** (sometimes known as a *disjunction,* though we will reserve that term for a valid form of argument). *P* and *Q* are the ***alternatives,*** known by logicians as *disjuncts.*

Here is a valid either–or argument form:

1. *P* or *Q*.
2. Not *P*.

∴ C. *Q*

You are following this form, for example, if you argue, "He's either lying or he's crazy. He's not lying. He must be crazy."

Another valid form is:

1. *P* or *Q*.
2. Not *Q*.

∴ C. *P*

For example: "He's either lying or he's crazy. He's not crazy. He must be lying."

Valid either–or arguments can include more than one alternative, as in this case:

1. *P* or *Q* or *R*.
2. Not *P*.

∴ C. *Q* or *R*.

For example: "He's either lying or he's crazy or, well, I'm crazy. I don't think he's lying. So one of us must be crazy."

And, finally, here's another example of a valid either–or form with more than two alternatives:

1. *P* or *Q* or *R*.
2. Not *P*.
3. Not *Q*.

∴ C. *R*

For example: "He's either lying or he's crazy or, well, I'm crazy. I can't see how he would be lying. And he's the sanest person I know. So I must be crazy."

An ordinary English term covers all of these valid forms: the ***process of elimination.*** There is also a more formal Latin term, *modus tollendo ponens,* which means "the method of denying in order to affirm."[1] In principle, there is no limit to the number of alternatives in the either–or premise. All that matters, to ensure that it is a valid process of elimination argument, is that the conclusion includes all the alternatives that have not been eliminated by a premise.

When clarifying either–or arguments that eliminate more than one alternative, eliminate each alternative in a separate premise. Don't, for example, represent *He is neither lying nor crazy* as a single premise; rather, separate it into two premises, *He is not lying* and *He is not crazy.* This puts you in the position to evaluate the truth of each claim independently.

Chrysippus's cerebral dog seems to be using the fourth valid form of the process of elimination. A clarification of the argument might look like this:

1. The master took the first path or the master took the second path or the master took the third path.
2. The master did not take the first path.
3. The master did not take the second path.

∴ *C.* The master took the third path.

As always, be prepared to translate stylistic variants for *or* into the standard constant. Some of the expressions that can be variants for *or* are in the following list.

Stylistic Variants for *P* or *Q*

Q or *P.*
Either *P* or *Q.*
P unless *Q.*
P or else *Q.*
If not *P,* then *Q.*

[1]Some logicians reserve the term *disjunctive syllogism* for these valid forms alone.

Also, when clarifying be alert for implicit statements. Often the either–or premise will be the implicit one. Suppose I said, "He's not crazy. And he's not lying. So I must be crazy." It is evident that I'm relying on the implicit premise *He's lying or he's crazy or I'm crazy.*

Guideline. Translate stylistic variants for the either–or premise into the standard constant. Also, be alert for implicit statements, including the either–or premise.

EXERCISES Chapter 12, set (a)

Paraphrase the either–or statement in each of these passages, translating the stylistic variant into the standard constant.

Sample exercise. "One could not be a successful scientist *without* realizing that, in contrast to the popular conception supported by newspapers and mothers of scientists, a goodly number of scientists are not only narrow-minded and dull, but also just stupid." —James Watson, co-discoverer of the structure of DNA, in his memoir *The Double Helix*

Sample answer. One is not a successful scientist or one realizes that many scientists are stupid.

1. Either Mondale or Rockefeller would have been a good president.
2. Unless you have salami today, I'll have the tuna sandwich.
3. Mr. Duesberg charges that the HIV virus is incapable of causing AIDS. He contends that a virus that later immobilizes the immune system cannot exist in a person's body for several years unless it causes serious ill effects. —*Chronicle of Higher Education*
4. I wasn't drunk. I wasn't impulsive. I damned well wanted a tattoo. Unless you're convinced you want it, you shouldn't do it. —John McPhee, *Looking for a Ship*

EXERCISES Chapter 12, set (b)

Clarify each of the either–or arguments below.

Sample exercise. "His 'Nothing' doesn't suggest the debates of existentialism these days so much as it does the plight of the homeless, bedding down on the sidewalk for another night. Today we know what Beckett is talking about; he has become a realist. And yet he didn't change one inch over the last 30 years. It must have been us." —obituary for writer Samuel Beckett

Sample answer.

[1. Beckett changed over the last 30 years of his career or Beckett's audience changed over the last 30 years of his career.]
2. Beckett didn't change over the last 30 years of his career.
∴ *C.* Beckett's audience changed over the last 30 years of his career.

1. In a departmental meeting, one professor commented, "Either this is the best bunch of graduate students we have produced or I've lost my mind." He paused, then concluded, "This bunch is the best."
2. The Atlanta Braves accused the Dodgers of ratting on them to the National League office for allowing players to work out ahead of the date agreed to with the players' association. "The league told us the complaint came from Vero Beach," said a Braves official in the Braves' camp at West Palm Beach. "That means it either came from the Dodgers or the New Orleans Saints (who train at Dodgertown in July)." "And we've eliminated the Saints," said another Braves official. "It's just a petty thing to do, but that's the Dodgers for you." —from a February newspaper story
3. (A priest is apparently unconscious on the floor of a bar.) Man 1: "He got bushwhacked." Man 2: "There ain't but two reasons why a man gets bushwhacked: love or money." (We hear the sound of the two men going through the unconscious priest's pockets and then the jingling of small coins.) Man 2: "Well it ain't money. Musta been love." —*Powder River Policy*, a play by E. Jack Newman
4. "It goes without saying that my work couldn't be bogus or I wouldn't be doing it." (Second premise and conclusion are implicit.) —*Chronicle of Higher Education*, quoting response by Professor John Bockris of Texas A&M to criticisms of his attempts to convert mercury to gold
5. "But the power of Marxism cannot be explained solely by his theories; for these were at least partially limited by his nineteenth-century experience, and they have been superseded by the considerable devel-

opment of the social science. The power of Marxism must therefore be located to a considerable degree in its religious impulse and its moral protest."—Paul Kurtz, *Free Inquiry*

Other Related Forms

A handful of other valid forms use either–or statements. A fairly rare yet very simple form is called ***disjunction***, as follows:

1. *P*
∴ *C*. *P* or *Q*.

It is rare because (like the forms repetition, simplification, and conjunction from Chapter 10) there is seldom any reason to use it. Perhaps I might argue in this way: "Why do I agree with you that the assignment for tomorrow was either postponed or even canceled? Because—I happen to know—the fact is, it was canceled." Not a very illuminating argument, but a valid one all the same. There is a commonsense way of thinking about this form: if one of the alternatives is true, then *either that alternative or something else* is true.

Two other related forms that are occasionally useful are together referred to as ***DeMorgan's laws*** (after the logician who formulated them). They combine either–or statements with negative statements and both–and statements, as follows:

1. Not (*P* or *Q*).
∴ *C*. Not *P* and not *Q*.

1. Not (*P* and *Q*)
∴ *C*. Not *P* or not *Q*.

There is likewise a commonsense way of thinking about these. In the case of the first law, the argument says that if an either–or statement is false, then neither of the alternatives is true. From *It is false that either Mondale or Rockefeller would've been a good president*, it follows validly that *Mondale would not have been a good president, and Rockefeller would not have been a good president.*

The second law tells us that if a conjunction is false, then at least one of the conjuncts is false. So, from *It is false that Mondale and Rockefeller would both have been good presidents*, it follows validly that *Either Mondale would not have been a good president, or Rockefeller would not have been a good president.*

EXERCISES Chapter 12, set (c)

State, in standard form, a conclusion that validly follows from each premise according to the specified rule. (We are concerned here only with logical validity, so it does not matter whether the premise is true.)

Sample exercise. By the applicable DeMorgan's law. Neither the rain nor the snow kept the mail carrier from delivering the mail.

Sample answer. The rain did not keep the mail carrier from delivering the mail and the snow did not keep the mail carrier from delivering the mail.

1. By disjunction. George Strait will perform in town in April.
2. By the applicable DeMorgan's law. To say that her work is both good and original is profoundly misleading.
3. By the process of elimination. You guaranteed that we would either hit the jackpot or lose everything. Let's put it this way—we didn't hit the jackpot.
4. By the applicable DeMorgan's law. I expected the championship to be won by either the Bulls or the Lakers. I was wrong.
5. By the process of elimination. As I expected, the championship was won by either the Bulls or the Lakers. And it wasn't the Bulls.
6. By disjunction. Abraham Lincoln was the first president of the United States.

The Exclusivity Premise

So far, we have been concerned with either–or statements that communicate the core idea that *at least one of these alternatives is true.*[2] But there are also exclusive either–or statements, which are used to communicate, in addition to the core idea, the idea that *only one of these alternatives is true*. This

[2]When only this core idea is intended, the *or* is called the *non-exclusive or.* (It is sometimes, alternatively, misleadingly called the *inclusive or.*)

addition of exclusivity—of the truth of *only* one of the alternatives—can have implications for the evaluations of both truth and logic.

Sometimes the alternatives happen to be exclusive, but the exclusivity is not important to the argument. Suppose you and I agree that the greatest American writer is either Mark Twain or Herman Melville. They cannot both be *the* greatest, so the either–or statement is exclusive. You then state that you do not think highly of Melville, and thus you consider Twain to be the greatest. You have offered a valid process of elimination argument that does not depend on the exclusivity of the two alternatives; it depends solely on the core idea that at least one of the alternatives is true, and it should be evaluated solely on that basis.

But suppose the discussion had taken a different turn; suppose after we agreed that the greatest was either Twain or Melville, you instead had remarked, "Surely Twain is the greatest, so Melville is not." It would be tempting, though highly uncharitable, to paraphrase this argument according to the following form:

1. *P* or *Q*.
2. *P*

∴ *C*. Not *Q*.

This form is in fact invalid; the name of the invalid form is the ***fallacy of affirming an alternative.*** Its invalidity can easily be demonstrated by a validity counterexample. Suppose a student who is having a hard time in class comes to me for advice, and I discover that, out of nothing but sheer laziness, he seldom attends and that he never does the exercises. So I say to him, "Well, you can come to class more often or you can do the exercises." Someone might then reason thus:

1. The student can come to class more often or the student can do the exercises.
2. The student can come to class more often.

∴ *C*. The student cannot do the exercises.

The premises are obviously true and conclusion obviously false, according to my story. The form, then, is invalid.

A more charitable paraphrase of the Twain-or-Melville argument would revise premise 1 so that it conveys not only the core idea of the either–or statement, but also the additional idea of exclusivity. Called the ***exclusivity***

premise, it has the following form: *P or Q and only one.*[3] The overall argument, then, would take this form:

1. *P* or *Q* and only one.
2. *P*

∴ *C.* Not *Q.*

You will not be able to find a counterexample for this form. It is valid, and we will call it ***affirming an exclusive alternative.*** There was a time when this form was known as *modus ponendo tollens*—that is, the method of affirming in order to deny. This Latin term, however, has fallen out of use, and you should probably avoid it even if you love Latin. Those who do not know quite as much as you do will suspect that you have doubly erred: that you have not only misidentified the argument as *modus tollendo ponens* (the formal Latin term, still in use, for the process of elimination), but also that you have garbled the term.

Some Arguments with Either–Or Premises

VALID	INVALID
Process of elimination	Fallacy of affirming an alternative
Disjunction	
DeMorgan's laws	
Affirming an exclusive alternative	

Guidelines. When the context and the logic of the argument call for it, paraphrase exclusive alternatives by including *and only one* as part of the standard constant.

[3]Some writers use the premise *P or Q and not both*. This does not serve the purpose as well as a generic form; if there are three exclusive alternatives, it would miss the point to say *P or Q or K and not all three*. That would still allow two to be true, which is not exclusive.

EXERCISES Chapter 12, set (d)

Clarify each of these either–or arguments, then evaluate its logic. (Some of them require an exclusivity premise, others do not.)

Sample exercise. You're right that either Tom Hanks or Robert De Niro won the Oscar for best actor last year. In fact, it was Tom Hanks—I remember his speech well. So it wouldn't have been De Niro.

Sample answer.

1. Tom Hanks won the best actor Oscar last year or Robert De Niro won the best actor Oscar last year, and only one.
2. Tom Hanks won the best actor Oscar last year.

∴ *C.* Robert De Niro did not win the best actor Oscar last year.
Valid, affirming an exclusive alternative.

1. You should major in something useful, like business, unless you're really committed to studying ideas for the sake of studying ideas. But I don't get the impression that you're an idea person. So stick with business.
2. Sure, I've been to Abilene before. Wait a minute—it was either Abilene or Amarillo. Oh, yeah, now I remember, that was Amarillo. So, no, I guess I haven't been to Abilene.
3. The department says that either Smith or Jones will be teaching the course. But I talked to Smith—he's going to be out of the country. So apparently it's going to be Jones.
4. Her letters of reference say that she's qualified to work as either a manager or a sales representative. I can see from the interview that she's qualified as a sales rep. So we can conclude, based on the letters, that she's not qualified as a manager.

EVALUATING THE TRUTH OF EITHER–OR PREMISES

There is an obvious—but not always very helpful—thing to be said about evaluating the truth of either–or statements. All it takes to judge an either–or statement to be certainly true is to find that one of the alternatives is certainly true. And to find the either–or statement to be certainly false, both alternatives must be certainly false. This, for example, would be the simple basis for judging it certainly true that *Either two plus two equals four or the moon is made of green cheese*, and certainly false that *Either two plus two equals five or the moon is made of green cheese.*

This strategy serves us well in cases where we have overwhelming evidence for the truth or falsity of the alternatives. But there are many cases in which there is less certainty—cases in which we might be able to make a judgment about the probability of each alternative but are not sure what to say about the either–or statement. Here is a simple, two-step rule that can guide you in such cases: *first, add the individual probabilities for each of the alternatives; and second, subtract the probability that both alternatives are true.*

Suppose I want to offer a research job to a student using funding that can be used only to support an upperclassman. I do not know what class she is in, and I need to evaluate the truth of this statement:

She is a junior or she is a senior.

Until I have the chance to ask her or to check her file, all I have to go on is my knowledge that enrollments drop by 2 percent with each class. This would mean that it has 28 percent freshmen, 26 percent sophomores, 24 percent juniors, and 22 percent seniors. I would thus assign a .24 probability to the alternative *She is a junior* and a .22 probability to the alternative *She is a senior.* Step one, adding the probabilities, yields a probability of .46. Since there is no probability that she is *both* a junior and a senior, step two requires me to subtract nothing. Based on the limited frequency information I have, the probability of the either–or statement is .46—that is, there is a very slight probability that the statement is false, and that she is ineligible.

Suppose, however, I have a different source of funding, one that can be spent only on graduates of California high schools, whatever their class, or on seniors, whatever state they are from. Now I must judge the following either–or statement:

She is a senior or she is a California high school graduate.

Again, assume that I haven't had the chance to collect information specifically about her, but only have information about frequencies. I again assign a .22 probability to the first alternative and, knowing that 90 percent of the undergraduates are graduates of California high schools, I assign a .90 probability to the second alternative. After taking the first step of adding them together, I have a 1.11 probability. But it would be a glaring mistake to stop here. Saying that the probability of a statement's truth is greater than 1.00 is as incongruous as an athlete's saying, "I always give 110 percent." By definition, 100 percent is everything that the athlete can give and 1.00 is as high as a probability can be.

The problem is that students who are both seniors and California high school graduates are being counted twice—once in each category. Using the Chapter 10 guidelines for both–and statements,[4] I conclude that 20 percent of the students are both seniors and California high school graduates. I subtract this .20 probability from the 1.11 of the first step (that is, I subtract the students that were counted twice), and I conclude that there is a .91 probability that the either–or statement is true. Based on the very limited information that I now have, it is highly probable that the statement is true, and that she is eligible for the funding.

As we saw in the discussion of both–and sentences in Chapter 10, we often don't have such tidy information about frequency probabilities at our fingertips. Further, even when we do, we usually have other relevant evidence as well—suppose the student asked me to write her a letter of reference to law school, and that I've heard her talk about missing snow in the wintertime. This evidence must be considered in evaluating the overall epistemic probability of the either–or statement. In light of this additional information, I may now think that *She is a senior* is somewhat probable, but may now be undecided about *She is a graduate of a California high school.*

Strategies for Evaluating the Truth of Either–Or Statements

WHAT YOU KNOW ABOUT THE ALTERNATIVES	HOW TO EVALUATE THE EITHER–OR STATEMENT
Both alternatives are almost certainly false.	Almost certainly false.
At least one alternative is almost certainly true.	Almost certainly true.
Alternatives are merely probable.	Add the probabilities of the alternatives, then subtract the probability that both are true.

[4] I multiply .22 times .9, with no need to subtract anything since the truth of neither part would affect the probability of the other part.

Despite the vagueness of our probability judgments, it can be helpful to assign tentative numbers to the alternatives so that arithmetic can provide a helping hand. Let's take "somewhat probable" to be .60 and "can't decide" to be .50; these add up to 1.10. I now have to subtract the probability that she is both, which is .30; this yields a .80 probability for the either–or statement. Although this number is misleadingly precise, it is clear that the new information still allows me to judge the either–or statement as probably true—though somewhat less probable than it was.[5]

Guideline. When the alternatives of an either–or statement are merely probable, tentatively assign them a probability (even if the result is misleadingly precise) so that you can apply the rules of probability. Convert the numbers back into everyday language for your final evaluation.

EXERCISES Chapter 12, set (e)

Explain your calculations and then state your evaluation of the truth of the statement based on the information provided.

Sample exercise. The Republican candidate for president will be elected or the Democratic candidate for president will be elected. (The form is *P or Q*. *P* is .55; *Q* is .43; the probability of both is zero, since there can't be two presidents—or, to put it in the terminology of Chapter 10, if we assumed the Republican candidate were president, then the probability of the Democratic candidate's also being president would be zero; and .55 times zero is still zero.)

Sample answer. Add .55 and .43, then subtract 0, for .98. It is almost certainly true.

1. His father will buy a Lexus next year, or his father will buy a Cadillac next year. (*P* is .30; *Q* is .05; probability of both is .01.)

[5]For an exclusive either–or statement, there is an extra step in judging its truth. It takes the form *P or Q and only one. Only one* is short for *Only one of the alternatives is true.* This is itself a statement—call it *R*—that must be evaluated. For our purposes, the form to be evaluated is *(P or Q) and R*. Evaluate *P or Q* first. Then, using the rule for the probability of both–and sentences, evaluate *(P or Q) and R*. Suppose you conclude that the probability of *P or Q* is .70 and that the probability that only one of them is true (that is, the probability of *R*) is .99. The probability of the exclusive either–or statement, then, is just under .70—that is, it is somewhat probable.

2. My heart was beating last year, or I was breathing last year. (*P* is 1.00; *Q* is 1.00; both is 1.00)
3. My new love will either break my heart or make me the happiest person alive. (Assign plausible probabilities yourself.)
4. My library book was due today, or it was due yesterday. (*P* is .5; *Q* is .4; both is zero.)

DILEMMAS

In everyday life, a dilemma is a problem. Not so in logic, where a ***dilemma*** points out the consequences, whether good or bad, of two inevitable alternatives. (The word comes from the Greek words *di*, for *two*, and *lemma*, for *proposition*.) They come in two varieties: either–or dilemmas and, less common, if–then dilemmas.

Either–Or Dilemmas

Either–or dilemmas usually take one of these four forms:

First,

1. *P* or *Q*.
2. If *P* then *R*.
3. If *Q* then *R*.

∴ C. *R*

For example: "I'm definitely going to take either Psychology 101 or Biology 101. If I take Psychology 101, I'll satisfy a requirement for my major. If I take Biology 101, I'll satisfy a requirement for my major. So either way I'll satisfy a requirement for my major."

Second,

1. *P* or *Q*.
2. If *P* then *R*.
3. If *Q* then *S*.

∴ C. *R* or *S*.

For example: "I'm definitely going to take either Psychology 101 or Biology 101. If I take Psychology 101, then I'll have to get up at 6 A.M. If I take Biology 101, I'll have to park on the other end of campus. So I'll either have to get up at 6 A.M. or park on the other end of campus."

Third,

1. *P* or *Q*.
2. If *R* then not *P*.
3. If *R* then not *Q*.

∴ *C*. Not *R*.

For example: "I'm definitely going to take either Psychology 101 or Biology 101. Now, if I also take Sociology 101, then I won't be able to take Psychology 101. Furthermore, if I take Sociology 101, I won't be able to take Biology 101. So, there's no way I'll take Sociology 101."

Fourth,

1. *P* or *Q*.
2. If *R* then not *P*.
3. If *S* then not *Q*.

∴ *C*. Not *R* or not *S*.

For example: "I'm definitely going to take either Psychology 101 or Biology 101. If I take Sociology 101, then I won't be able to take Psychology 101. And if I take Philosophy 101, then I won't be able to take Biology 101. So, I'll have to do without either Sociology 101 or Philosophy 101."

The first two are by far the most common. As you can see, they are modeled after the valid form of affirming the antecedent; in effect, they say, "You must affirm the antecedent of either the first or the second if–then statement." The next two, similarly, are modeled after denying the consequent. There are no widely accepted names for these forms; so, when evaluating a valid dilemma, identify it simply as *correct form for a dilemma*.

In popular jargon—which presumes that dilemmas are problems—the two alternatives expressed in the first premise are often referred to as the *horns* of the dilemma. Showing that the either–or premise is false is termed *escaping between the horns of the dilemma*, since it provides a way out of the forced choice. And showing that one of the if–then premises is false is termed *attacking a horn of the dilemma*, since this renders the choice harmless by removing the threat of the purported consequence.

Dilemmas are usually enthymematic. Sometimes both the either–or premise and the conclusion are implicit; sometimes both of the if–then premises are implicit. As an example for both clarifying and evaluating, here is a dilemma expressed in a political cartoon from the early 1970s, shortly after Republican operatives were caught breaking into the Democratic Party offices in the Watergate office complex:

> President Nixon to his press secretary, Ronald Zeigler: "OK, Mr. Press Secretary, give me some answers! If I knew about the Watergate Caper, what am I doing in the White House? And if I *didn't* know anything about the affair what am I doing in the White House?"

CLARIFICATION

[1. Nixon knew about Watergate or Nixon didn't know about Watergate.]
2. If Nixon knew about Watergate, then Nixon did not deserve to be president.
3. If Nixon did not know about Watergate, then Nixon did not deserve to be president.
∴ [*C*. Nixon did not deserve to be president.]

EVALUATION

(The anti-Nixon view, for illustration's sake.)

TRUTH

Premise 1. Certainly true, since the form *P or not P* is the law of the excluded middle.

Premise 2. Probably true; if he knew about it then he lied repeatedly about it, and we should hold our presidents to higher moral standards than this. An objector might protest that we have come to expect presidents to lie to us whenever it is politically expedient, even that they need to do so due to the peculiar demands of the office. But political leadership is strongest when it incorporates moral leadership, and only the strongest political leaders deserve to be president.

Premise 3. Probably true; a president should have enough influence over his inferiors either to insure that they are in line with his policies or to be quickly informed when they are seriously out of line. An objector might argue that a president surely cannot be expected to be fully informed about every unauthorized activity of his associates. This is true, but the Watergate break-in involved people at a high enough level that this does not excuse him.

LOGIC

The argument is valid, since it has the correct form for an either–or dilemma.

SOUNDNESS

Probably deductively sound.

Note that dilemmas don't require us to learn much that is new. Evaluating the logic is simple, and evaluating the truth of the premises—given that they combine if–then and either–or premises—is already a familiar process.

EXERCISES Chapter 12, set (f)

Clarify and evaluate (to the extent that context allows) each of these dilemmas.

1. "If one worries a lot, one is obviously unhappy, since worry itself is one of the most painful things in life. If one fails to worry enough, then (at least so I have been told) one may be even worse off because one may fail to take the precautions necessary to ward off even greater catastrophes than worry."—Raymond Smullyan, *This Book Needs No Title*
2. "The strapping rodeo bull rider grabbed Jerry Jeff Walker's arm in a viselike grip and stared angrily at the singer, who bore a beatific, far-away expression on his face. "Didn't you hear me, boy?" he growled. "I told you to play that song about red-necks. Now play it. Fast." Stoned and drunk and uncertain if he was in a honky-tonk in Austin or in Oklahoma City, Walker struggled to concentrate on his dilemma. If he played the song, which he knew the cowboy hated, he would probably be beaten up. If he refused the request, he would also be beaten up. Finally, he began to play. The cowboy hit him three times, smashed his guitar, and left him bloody."—*Newsweek*
3. " 'There's so much pressure,' Tarkanian says. 'But what else would I do? I have no other skills. Two years ago I was losing and I was going nuts, and I was thinking of getting out. I have a very good friend who said, "What would you do if you quit? You'd go nuts." ' It's refreshing to meet a man who knows where he's going."—Scott Ostler, *Los Angeles Times,* on basketball coach Jerry Tarkanian
4. "At this point an annoying, though obvious, question intrudes. If Skinner's thesis is false, then there is no point in his having written the book or in our reading it. But if his thesis is true, then there is also no point in his having written the book or our reading it."—Noam Chomsky, "The Case Against B.F. Skinner," in the *New York Review of Books,* criticizing Skinner's view that humans have no free will, but act only in ways that are wholly determined by the physical world
5. I described to him an impudent fellow from Scotland, who maintained that there was no distinction between virtue and vice. Johnson: "Why,

Sir, if the fellow does not think as he speaks, he is lying; and I see not what honor he can propose to himself from having the character of a liar. But if he does really think that there is no distinction between virtue and vice, why, Sir, when he leaves our houses let us count our spoons." —James Boswell, *Life of Samuel Johnson*, referring to philosopher David Hume

6. Either God cannot eliminate the evil that is in the world, or he does not want to eliminate it. If he cannot eliminate evil, then he is not omnipotent. And if he does not want to eliminate it, he is not perfectly good. Therefore, either God is not omnipotent or he is not perfectly good.—classical form of the argument from evil against the existence of God

---

If–Then Dilemmas

If–then dilemmas are like either–or dilemmas, but for one exception. Whether you take one of the alternatives presented in the either–or premise depends on something else; whether you are stuck with the outcome in the conclusion hangs on the same condition. For any either–or dilemma, prefix *If T, then* . . . to the either–or premise and to the conclusion (and leave alone the two if–then premises); that makes it an if–then dilemma. Below is the scheme for the first, most common, form of if–then dilemma:

1. If *T*, then *P* or *Q*.
2. If *P* then *R*.
3. If *Q* then *R*.

∴ *C*. If T, then R.

For example: "If I decide on psychobiology as my major, then I'm definitely going to take either Psychology 101 or Biology 101 next term. If I take Psychology 101, I'll satisfy a requirement for my major. If I take Biology 101, I'll satisfy a requirement for my major. So, if I decide on psychobiology as my major, then I'll satisfy a requirement for my major next term."

The other forms of if–then dilemmas follow the same pattern.

Types of Valid Dilemmas

1. Either–or dilemmas
2. If–then dilemmas

EXERCISES Chapter 12, set (g)

Clarify and evaluate (to the extent that context allows) each of these dilemmas. If–then and either–or dilemmas are mixed together.

Sample exercise. From the old "Sanford and Son" TV series: Fred to Lamont, afraid he has shot his neighbor, "If I go and find him dead, I'll have a heart attack. If I go and find him alive, I'll jump around for joy and have a heart attack. So, either way, if I go, I'll go."

Sample answer.

CLARIFICATION

[1. If Fred visits next door, then Fred finds his neighbor alive or Fred finds his neighbor dead.]
2. If Fred finds his neighbor dead, then Fred will have a heart attack.
3. If Fred finds his neighbor alive, then Fred will have a heart attack.
∴ [*C.* If Fred visits next door, then Fred will have a heart attack.]

EVALUATION

TRUTH

Premise 1 is probably true (in the fictional world). It assumes that the neighbor is there and that Fred will find the neighbor if he is there. Those assumptions are, I suppose, likely; and if they turn out to be true, there's no doubt that he'll be either dead or alive.

Premises 2 and 3 are probably false (in the fictional world); I don't know much about Fred's health in the fictional world of "Sanford and Son," but this seems to assume that Fred's health is extremely fragile, and also that in a situation comedy they would allow a leading character to have a heart attack. These assumptions seem unlikely to me—probably the premises are exaggerated for the humor.

LOGIC

This argument is valid—it has correct form for an if–then dilemma.

SOUNDNESS

Probably unsound, due to probably false premises 2 and 3.

1. If I get a job next summer, then I'll either get a better car or move into a nicer apartment. If I get a better car, the money I earn will be gone. If I move into a nicer apartment, then the money I earn will be gone. So, if I get a job next summer, the money I earn will be gone. (Evaluate this on the assumption that it applies to you.)

2. In AD 642, as legend has it, the Caliph Omar commanded that all the books in the Great Library of Alexandria be burned as fuel to heat the city. The city fathers begged him to spare what was one of the Seven Wonders of the World. With diabolical logic, Omar refused. "The Koran is the source of all wisdom," said the Caliph. "So if these books all agree with the Koran, they are redundant and thus can be burned. If they disagree, then they are heretical and thus should be burned."
3. Suppose you wish to get "enlightened" and a person asks you: "Why do you wish to get enlightened?" Now, the amazing thing is that however you answer, you will find yourself trapped! Suppose you answer, "For my sake." Then people will descend upon you with the fury of hell and say: "You selfish egotist! How will that help the problems of the world? It is purely a selfish enterprise!" On the other hand, suppose you answer, "I primarily wish to help others, but I must first get enlightened myself before I can spread enlightenment to others." Well, if you give that answer, people will descend upon you with the fury of hell and say: "You arrogant, conceited egotist! So it is up to you to enlighten others, eh? You have to be in the limelight. This whole 'enlightenment' business is just to feed people's vanities!" —Raymond Smullyan, *This Book Needs No Title*
4. "Either my piece is a work of the highest rank, or it is not a work of the highest rank. In the latter (and more probable) case I myself am in favour of it not being printed. And in the former case it's a matter of indifference whether it's printed twenty or a hundred years sooner or later. After all, who asks whether the *Critique of Pure Reason*, for example, was written in 17x or y." —letter to Bertrand Russell from Ludwig Wittgenstein regarding his troubles finding a publisher for the *Tractatus*

CATEGORICAL ARGUMENTS

Categorical Syllogisms

Until the last century or so, the study of logic was the study of the categorical syllogism. We will not, however, need to cover this style of argument in any detail. An important goal of this book is to equip you with the tools for handling arguments that you are likely to encounter in your own experience, but you will probably never meet a categorical syllogism anywhere outside of a textbook. This section is included primarily for the historical context it provides and for the opportunity to introduce a common argument form that is related to the categorical syllogism.

The categorical syllogism, as codified by Aristotle in the fourth century BC, is made up of two premises and a conclusion, each of which takes one of these four forms:

A: All *F* are *G*.
I: Some *F* are *G*.
E: No *F* are *G*.
O: Some *F* are not *G*.

The statements identified as *A* and *I*, which are affirmative, are named for the first two vowels of the Latin *affirmo; E* and *O*, the negative statements, are named for the first two vowels of the Latin *nego*.

Since these statements have to do entirely with whether things that are in one category also belong to some other category (whether things that are *F* are also *G*), they are ***categorical statements.*** And an argument, or syllogism, made up entirely of categorical statements is a ***categorical syllogism.*** (Recall from Chapter 6 that the variables here are *predicates*, not sentences; so categorical syllogisms fall under the heading of predicate logic rather than sentential logic.)

Early Methods of Evaluating Logic

Logic students in the Middle Ages were asked to evaluate categorical syllogisms like this one:

1. All prophets are men.
2. Some prophets are not mortal.

∴ *C.* Some men are not mortal.

They would have determined that the argument was valid based on the following verse—made up of personal names of the era—which identifies all valid categorical syllogisms:

Barbara, Celerant, Darii, Ferioque, *prioris;*
Cesare, Camestres, Festino, Baroco, *secundai;*

Tertia, Darapti, Disami, Datisi, Felapton,
Bocardo, Ferison habet. *Quarta* insuper addit
Bramantip, Camenes, Dimaris, Gesapo, Fresison.

The first three vowels of each name pick out which three categorical statements make up the syllogism. Our argument is *AOO*, so it matches the name Baroco. Does the verse deem it valid? Yes. There are four different ways in which the *Fs* and *Gs* can be arranged in any categorical syllogism. The terms *prioris*, *secundai*, *tertia*, and *quarta* in the doggerel indicate whether the *Fs* and *Gs* are in the first, second, third, or fourth arrangement. Our argument is in the second arrangement, and Bacoro is indeed grouped with the names labeled *secundai.* The student thus ascertains that the argument is valid by solving this puzzle.

This system, unfortunately, did little to inspire a deep understanding of logic within those who memorized it. A better approach was to have students memorize a series of rules followed by any valid categorical syllogism. Our sample argument, for example, conforms to rules such as these:

There must be exactly three terms. (Our example has *prophet*, *mortal*, and *men.*)
At least one premise must be of the *all* or *none* variety. (Premise 1 is.)
It cannot have two negative premises. (Ours has only one, premise 2.)
If the conclusion is particular (*I* or *O*), it cannot have two universal premises (*A* or *E*). (Ours, appropriately, does not.)
If one premise is negative, then the conclusion must be negative. (Ours is.)

Because it follows these rules, it can be evaluated as valid.

The Venn Diagram Method

The best system—because it is simple and because it promotes understanding of the underlying logic of any categorical syllogism—was introduced by mathematician John Venn in the 19th century. Alas, he made this contribution when Aristotelian logic was about to be eclipsed by the vastly superior system of logic founded by Gottlob Frege.

Venn's system, as it is normally implemented, requires the drawing of three overlapping circles, one circle representing each of the three categories. (See the accompanying figure.) For our sample argument, we can represent the first premise by shading the entire area of the *prophet* circle that does not overlap with the *man* circle (showing that there is no such thing as a prophet that is not a man, that is, *All prophets are men*). We then represent the second premise by putting an *x* in the part of the *prophet* circle that does not overlap the *mortal* circle (showing that there do exist some prophets that are outside the category of mortality, that is, *Some prophets are not mortal*); we avoid the shaded area, of course, since premise 1 has precluded our putting anything there. We can then see that the argument is valid, since it can be read off the diagram; we find an *x* in the *man* circle that is outside the *mortal* circle, that is, *Some men are not mortal.*

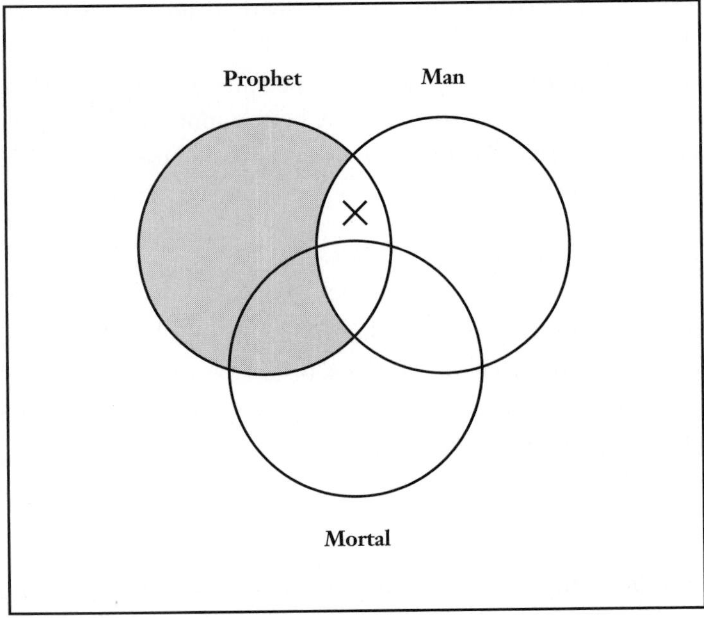

Singular Categorical Arguments

There is, however, one near relative of the categorical syllogism that does occur with some frequency and thus does merit a more careful look. Recall this familiar example:

1. All men are mortal.
2. Socrates is a man.

∴ *C.* Socrates is mortal.

Strictly speaking, this does not count as a categorical syllogism because neither the second premise nor the conclusion are in the form of *A, E, I,* or *O.*[6] The insertion of Socrates into the second premise and conclusion moves the argument from the universal to the particular. Following the pattern of the preceding chapter, we might term this form a ***singular categorical argument.*** Not all singular categorical arguments are valid. The preceding argument is valid and can be defended on the grounds that it has *correct form for a singular categorical argument.* The following argument, however, would not be valid:

1. All men are mortal.
2. Socrates is mortal.

∴ *C.* Socrates is a man.

The evaluation of the logic of this argument should say that it has *incorrect form for a singular categorical syllogism* and should provide a validity counterexample.

For the sake of simplicity, however, I suggest that such arguments ordinarily be paraphrased so that they become examples of singular if–then arguments. As noted in Chapter 11, *All F are G* can be a stylistic variant for *If anything (or anyone or anytime) is an F, then it is a G.* The example above, then, is the exact logical equivalent of this:

1. If anything is a man, then it is mortal.
2. Socrates is a man.

∴ *C.* Socrates is mortal.

And it is valid by singular affirming the antecedent.

If the first premise had been *No men are mortal,* it would have validly followed that Socrates was immortal; the clarification would have looked like this:

1. If anything is a man, then it is not mortal.
2. Socrates is a man.

∴ *C.* Socrates is not mortal.

There are a few easy-to-spot variants of categorical statements that also can be translated into if–then statements. *Only G is F,* for example, is logically

[6]Aristotelian logic does have its awkward techniques for converting such arguments to categorical syllogisms.

equivalent to *All F are G* and can typically be paraphrased as *If anything is F, then it is G*. Here is an example from ordinary English:

> Now they know that she was a real princess, since she had felt the pea that was lying on the bedstead through twenty mattresses and twenty eiderdown quilts. Only a real princess could be so sensitive.
> —Hans Christian Andersen, "The Princess and the Pea"

The clarification would look like this:

1. If anyone is sensitive enough to feel a pea through 20 mattresses and 20 quilts, then she is a princess.
2. She is sensitive enough to feel a pea through 20 mattresses and 20 quilts.

∴ *C*. She is a princess.

It is valid by singular affirming the antecedent.

There are some rare cases in which it is better to leave a categorical statement as it is rather than paraphrase it as an if–then statement. Standard format requires, in certain cases, that you represent a conclusion in the form *All F are G*. In Chapter 14, for example, we will look at arguments like this: "All computer programs I ever used have had bugs in them. I conclude, then, that all computer programs have bugs." As we will see, clarifying the argument in standard format gives us this:

1. All sampled computer programs have bugs in them.

∴ *C*. All computer programs have bugs in them.

What makes these arguments distinctive is that they move from a sample to the general population; this move is made clear when the conclusion looks exactly like the premise but for the omission of the word *sampled*. This clarity of structure would be lost if we paraphrased the conclusion's categorical statement as an if–then statement, as you can see:

1. All sampled computer programs have bugs in them.

∴ *C*. If anything is a computer program, then it has bugs in it.

Keep the categorical statement in such cases. This means that you will still have the occasional singular categorical argument to evaluate. Suppose, for example, I further argued, "So, the word processing program I'm using right now has a bug in it." The clarified complex argument would look like this:

1. All sampled computer programs have bugs in them.

∴ 2. All computer programs have bugs in them.

[3. This word processing program is a computer program.]

∴ *C.* This word processing program has a bug in it.

The inference from 1 to 2 will be dealt with in Chapter 14; the inference from 2 and 3 to *C* is valid on the grounds that it has correct form for a singular categorical argument.

Guideline. Convert categorical statements, in most cases, into if–then statements. Retain the categorical statement, however, when standard format for the argument calls for it, as with the conclusion in some inductive generalizations.

EXERCISES Chapter 12, set (h)

Clarify the following arguments, treating the categorical statements as stylistic variants for if–then statements. Then evaluate the logic. (Not all are valid.)

Sample exercise. Only those with incomes above $100,000 per year are eligible. I know what you make. No need to apply.

Sample answer.

1. If any person is eligible, then the person's income is above $100,000.

[2. Your income is not above $100,000.]

∴ *C.* You are not eligible.

Valid, singular denying the consequent.

1. Nobody with an income below $100,000 per year is eligible. I know what you make. No need to apply.
2. Only the lonely come to this nightclub. I was lonely. So, of course, I had to come.

3. Everything he cooks is delectable. He's the chef tonight. So, as you might expect, it will be delectable.
4 Only those actions that can be demonstrated by empirical evidence to warrant criminal sanctions should be punished. On this basis, prostitution should not be punishable in our legal system.
5. Yon Cassius has a lean and hungry look; such men are dangerous. — Shakespeare, *Julius Caeser*

SUMMARY OF CHAPTER TWELVE

Two valid forms of either–or arguments are the process of elimination and disjunction. An invalid form is the fallacy of affirming an alternative; if, however, an argument with this form has an exclusive either–or premise (which can be paraphrased as *P or Q and only one*) it is a valid example of affirming an exclusive alternative.

Several other valid forms use either–or premises in combination with both–and premises (DeMorgan's laws) or if–then premises (dilemmas).

All either–or statements express the core idea that at least one of the alternatives is true. Thus, if all alternatives are false then the either–or statement is false; otherwise, it is true. When thinking in terms of probabilities, a helpful guideline is to add the probabilities of both alternatives (but then to subtract the probability that both are true) to arrive at the probability for the entire either–or statement.

Some arguments require an either–or statement that, in addition to the core idea, expresses the idea that only one of the alternatives is true—that is, that the alternatives are exclusive. In such cases, paraphrase as *P or Q and only one.*

Historically, logic has mainly been concerned with categorical syllogisms. These arguments occur rarely in ordinary language, and logicians in the last century have abandoned the study of the categorical syllogism for much more sophisticated approaches that are taught in formal logic courses. But the singular categorical argument is related to the categorical syllogism and does occur in ordinary language from time to time. It is usually best, however, to treat categorical statements like *All F are G* and *No F is G* as stylistic variants of if–then statements and to paraphrase—and evaluate—them accordingly.

GUIDELINES FOR CHAPTER TWELVE

- Translate stylistic variants for the either–or premise into the standard constant. Also, be alert for implicit statements, including the either–or premise.
- When the context and the logic of the argument call for it, paraphrase exclusive alternatives by including *and only one* as part of the standard constant.
- When the alternatives of an either–or statement are merely probable, tentatively assign them a probability (even if the result is misleadingly precise) so that you can apply the rules of probability. Convert the numbers back into everyday language for your final evaluation.
- Convert categorical statements, in most cases, into if–then statements. Retain the categorical statement, however, when standard format for the argument calls for it, as with the conclusion in some inductive generalizations.

GLOSSARY FOR CHAPTER TWELVE

Affirming an exclusive alternative—valid argument form, as follows:

1. *P* or *Q* and only one.
2. *P*

∴ *C*. Not *Q*.

Historically known as *modus ponendo tollens*, Latin for "the method of affirming in order to deny."

Alternative—a statement connected to another by *or*. Also known as *disjunct*.

Categorical statement—statement of the form *All F are G*, *No F are G*, *Some F are G*, or *Some F are not G*.

Categorical syllogism—one of a family of deductive arguments, some valid and others invalid, each with three categorical statements—two as premises, one as conclusion.

DeMorgan's laws—valid deductive forms, as follows:

1. Not (*P* or *Q*).

∴ *C*. Not *P* and not *Q*.

1. Not (*P* and *Q*).

∴ *C.* Not *P* or not *Q*.

Dilemma—a valid argument form that points out the consequences, whether good or bad, of two inevitable alternatives. The word comes from the Greek words *di*, for *two*, and *lemma*, for *proposition*. Dilemmas come in two varieties: either–or dilemmas and if–then dilemmas.

Disjunction—valid deductive form, as follows:

1. *P*

∴ *C.* *P* or *Q*.

The term is sometimes also used for an either–or statement.

Either–or argument—one of a loosely defined group of arguments that has an either–or premise. Also called *disjunctive syllogism.*

Either–or dilemma—a valid dilemma that begins with an either–or premise. The most common forms are these:

1. *P* or *Q*.
2. If *P* then *R*.
3. If *Q* then *R*.

∴ *C.* *R*

1. *P* or *Q*.
2. If *P* then *R*.
3. If *Q* then *S*.

∴ *C.* *R* or *S*.

1. *P* or *Q*.
2. If *R* then not *P*.
3. If *R* then not *Q*.

∴ *C.* Not *R*.

1. *P* or *Q*.
2. If *R* then not *P*.
3. If *S* then not *Q*.

∴ *C.* Not *R* or not *S*.

Either–or statement—statement of the form *P* or *Q*. Also sometimes called a *disjunction.*

Exclusivity premise—either–or premise that includes the notion that only one of the alternatives is true; it has the form *P or Q and only one.*

Fallacy of affirming an alternative—an invalid argument form, as follows:

1. *P* or *Q*.
2. *P*

∴ *C.* Not *Q*.

If–then dilemmas—valid dilemmas that are constructed like any either–or dilemmas, except for an if–clause prefixed both to the either–or premise and to the conclusion. The most common form is as follows:

1. If *T*, then *P* or *Q*.
2. If *P* then *R*.
3. If *Q* then *R*.

∴ *C.* If *T*, then *R*.

Process of elimination—a valid form of either–or argument in which premises eliminate alternatives, while the conclusion includes all the alternatives that have not been eliminated by a premise. Examples include:

1. *P* or *Q*.
2. Not *P*.

∴ *C. Q*

1. *P* or *Q*.
2. Not *Q*.

∴ *C. P*

1. *P* or *Q* or *R*.
2. Not *P*.

∴ *C. Q* or *R*.

1. *P* or *Q* or *R*.
2. Not *P*.
3. Not *Q*.

∴ *C. R*

Also called *modus tollendo ponens*, Latin for "the method of denying in order to affirm."

Singular categorical argument—a deductive argument, either valid or invalid, with a universal categorical statement as a premise, but with a conclusion about a single instance that is included in the universal category. For example, a valid form is:

1. All *F* are *G*.
2. *A* is *F*.

∴ C. *A* is *G*.

PART SIX

EVALUATING INDUCTIVE LOGIC

CHAPTER THIRTEEN

How to Think About Inductive Logic

The known is finite, the unknown infinite; intellectually we stand on an islet in the midst of an illimitable ocean of explicability. Our business in every generation is to reclaim a little more land, to add something to the extent and solidity of our possessions.

—T. H. Huxley

Our instincts certainly cause us to believe that the sun will rise tomorrow, but we may be in no better a position than the chicken which unexpectedly has its neck wrung.

—Bertrand Russell, *The Problems of Philosophy*

TOPICS

Inductive Arguments
Frequency Arguments

INDUCTIVE ARGUMENTS

Deductive logic, even at its best, can help us to see no more than truths that are already built into an argument's premises. To use Huxley's metaphor—it can help us to better understand the small island of knowledge that we find ourselves standing on, but only that island. It is by inductive logic that we can go beyond our premises, that we can expand the size of our island of knowledge by reclaiming land from the surrounding ocean of the unknown. In these chapters, we will cover the most common varieties of inductive arguments.

Most of our arguments have conclusions that go well beyond their premises. Consider these examples:

- Based on my experience of sunrises in the past, I believe that the sun will rise tomorrow—but even if I am right about my experience of the past, it is at least possible that I am wrong about what tomorrow will bring.
- Public opinion organizations interview only a thousand people, yet they draw conclusions about how millions of voters—not just the thousand interviewed—are likely to cast their votes. Even if their data are correct about the opinions of the thousand that were interviewed, they could be mistaken about the millions.
- A detective finds fingerprints, a motive, and an opportunity and concludes that the butler did it. But even if there is nothing wrong with her evidence, it is still possible that she is wrong about the butler.

These arguments are not deductive. Deductive arguments are those in which the premises are intended to make the conclusions certain. Rather, they are ***inductive arguments***, which we define as arguments in which the premises are intended to make their conclusions merely probable. The aim for an inductive argument is not validity but ***inductive strength***, meaning that the premises of the successful argument make the conclusion probable. And, while deductive arguments are either valid or invalid with no middle ground, inductive arguments may be judged as having various degrees of strength—ranging from *no support* to *very weak* to *fairly strong* to *very strong*.

The difference between induction and deduction has to do with standards for logical success. Put simply, the logical standards for inductive arguments are *lower*, but there are *more of them*. They are lower, since inductive arguments aim only for probability, not for certainty. But there are more of them, since in inductive arguments, like deductive arguments, the conclusion must fit the premises; but, unlike deductive arguments, the conclusion must also fit the total available evidence.

Inductive Arguments Aim for Probability, Not for Certainty

Suppose you get on the freeway only to realize that you're going south when you meant to go north. You see an off-ramp ahead and wonder whether there is an on-ramp that would allow you to return to the freeway in the opposite direction. You reason as follows:

1. Almost all freeway off-ramps are paired with on-ramps in the opposite direction
2. The Firestone Boulevard exit is a freeway off-ramp.

∴ *C*. The Firestone Boulevard exit is paired with an on-ramp in the opposite direction.

It turns out that you are right, and your trip continues successfully. But, even assuming the truth of your premises, your argument does no better than make probable your conclusion. It surely doesn't guarantee there will be an on-ramp, for it is possible that this off-ramp is among those not covered by the "almost all" of the first premise.

Another way of saying that the premises do not guarantee the conclusion is to say that the argument is invalid—that it is possible for an argument of this form to have true premises and a false conclusion. We can show this by using the now-familiar two step procedure for producing validity counterexamples. The first step, recall, is to extract the form that the argument apparently relies on; the off-ramp argument is apparently relying on this form:

1. Almost all *F* are *G*.
2. *A* is *F*.

∴ *C*. *A* is *G*.

The second step is to substitute for the variables to produce clearly true premises and a clearly false conclusion. That can readily be done, as follows:

1. Almost all species of birds can fly.
2. Penguins are a species of birds.

∴ *C*. Penguins can fly.

Both premises are clearly true. But the conclusion is clearly false. So the argument is shown to be invalid. It cannot provide certainty.

Validity counterexamples can be given for nearly any inductive argument, no matter how logically strong it is. But inductive arguments can no more be faulted for invalidity than can tenor Luciano Pavarotti be faulted for failure to be enshrined in the Country Music Hall of Fame. Inductive arguments aim to make their conclusions probable, and that is the standard against which they should be judged.

Recall the question posed in Chapter 10 as the best way to think about the logic of any argument: *If the premises were true, would that make it reasonable to believe the conclusion*? With deductive arguments, it is *certainty* that makes it reasonable to believe the conclusion; but with inductive arguments, it is *probability*. It would be nice if we could always reason with certainty. But we have to reason with what we have. The off-ramp argument would have been valid if I had used the premise *All freeway off-ramps are paired with on-ramps in the opposite direction*, but it would also have been unsound, since the new premise would have certainly been false.

> *Guideline.* When asking whether an inductive argument is logically successful, ask the same general question you ask of deductive arguments: *If the premises were true, would that make it reasonable to believe the conclusion?* In this case, however expect only probability, not certainty.

Inductive Arguments Must Fit with the Total Available Evidence

The standards for logical success in inductive arguments are lower. But, at the same time, there are more of them—there are twice as many. Deductive arguments must satisfy only one condition to be logical; they must exemplify some correct form—that is, they must satisfy the ***correct form condition***. For deductive arguments, it must be a deductive form such as affirming the antecedent or the process of elimination. Inductive arguments must also satisfy the correct form condition—that is, they must exemplify some correct *inductive* form. In this chapter and in the following three, we will cover the four most common forms of inductive arguments:

- Frequency arguments
- Inductive generalizations
- Arguments from analogy
- Explanatory arguments

Once you become familiar with each of these forms, you will find it fairly simple to determine whether you have an inductive or a deductive argument and, when inductive, to determine whether the correct form condition is satisfied (it usually is). As we will see, inductive arguments that make formal mistakes, like deductive arguments that make formal mistakes, typically provide *no support* to their conclusions.

An inductive argument, however, can satisfy the correct form condition but at the same time be logically defective. This is because inductive arguments must also satisfy a second condition, the ***total evidence condition***. For each inductive form we will cover a customized way of stating this condition. To express it, for now, in general terms, the condition requires that the conclusion fit appropriately with the ***total available evidence***—that is, with all of the beliefs and experiences (i.e., the *total evidence*) that you personally have (i.e., that are *available* to you). Do not confuse this condition with the requirement of true premises. The total evidence condition bears on logic and is evaluated on the assumption that the premises are true; that is, this condition is to be considered as part of the process of answering the question, "If the premises were true, would they make it reasonable for me to believe the conclusion?"

Inductive Arguments: Two Conditions for Logical Success

1. *Correct form condition*—conclusion must fit the premises.
2. *Total evidence condition*—conclusion must also fit the total available evidence.

These vary with each form of induction.

Consider again the off-ramp argument:

1. Almost all freeway off-ramps are paired with on-ramps in the opposite direction
2. The Firestone Boulevard exit is a freeway off-ramp.

∴ C. The Firestone Boulevard exit is paired with an on-ramp in the opposite direction.

Suppose this argument has occurred to you when you suddenly think, "Wait a minute—I made the same mistake last week, and when I took the

Firestone exit then I was stranded—no way back onto the freeway in either direction." You still believe that each of the two premises is true, but they clearly no longer make the conclusion probable. Why not? Because there is evidence available to you—your background belief about what you experienced last week—that undermines the conclusion. Even though the argument satisfies the correct form condition, it fails the total evidence condition and is thus, from a logical point of view, extremely weak.

Guideline. Inductive arguments must satisfy not only the correct form condition, but also the total evidence condition (that is, the conclusion must fit not only the premises, but also the total available evidence). This means that even if an inductive argument is formally correct, you can judge it to be a logical argument only if it also fits appropriately with your background beliefs and experiences.

Standard Evaluating Format

The same format should be used for evaluating inductive arguments as for deductive ones. By way of review, this is the format:

Standard Evaluating Format

Heading: EVALUATION

Subheading: TRUTH. For each premise, state whether you judge it to be true and provide your defense of that judgment.

Subheading: LOGIC. State whether you judge the logic to be successful and provide your defense of that judgment.

Subheading: SOUNDNESS. State whether you judge the argument to be sound; then, if and only if it is not sound, state whether this is owing to a problem with a premise or with the logic.

Subheading (optional): CONVERSATIONAL RELEVANCE. If and only if the argument is flawed in this way, state whether it commits the fallacy of begging the question or missing the point, and explain how.

As always, direct your evaluation to the reasonable objector over your shoulder. The only new wrinkle is this: under the subheading LOGIC, in your defense of the evaluation always consider whether it satisfies the total evidence condition, and always include a clear defense of that evaluation.

> *Guideline.* When evaluating inductive arguments, continue to follow the standard format for argument evaluation, but be sure to include in the LOGIC section a discussion of the total evidence condition.

FREQUENCY ARGUMENTS

Correct Form for Frequency Arguments

The off-ramp argument is a ***frequency argument,***[1] the simplest and most intuitive form of inductive argument. Such arguments attempt to show that a specific item has a property because that sort of thing usually does have the property—or that it does not have a property because that sort of thing usually does not. Because the form (like repetition, simplification, conjunction, and disjunction, as we have seen in preceding chapters) is so simple and intuitive, it is not often explicitly offered. But it does provide a useful starting place for introducing inductive arguments. A frequency argument typically takes either a positive or negative form. The positive form is this:

    1. n of F are G (where n is a frequency $>.5$ and <1, i.e., more than half but less than all).
    2. A is F.
∴   C. A is G.

This is the form of the off-ramp argument.

The negative form is this:

    1. n of F are G (where n is a frequency $<.5$ and >0, i.e., less than half but more than none).
    2. A is F.
∴   C. A is not G.

[1] There is no generally accepted term for these arguments. They are also called *proportional syllogisms, probabilistic syllogisms, myriokranic* (i.e., thousand-headed) *syllogisms*, and *direct singular inferences.*

This would be the form of my argument if I had said, "Almost no off-ramps leave you without a way to get back onto the freeway. The Firestone Boulevard exit is an off-ramp, so it's reasonable to think that it won't leave me without a way to get back onto the freeway."

The premise *Almost all freeway off-ramps are paired with on-ramps in the opposite direction* is a ***frequency statement***[2] of the sort that is used in the Chapter 10 discussion of frequency probability. These statements take the form *n of F are G*. The variable *n* stands for some frequency, or proportion; it may be stated in ordinary language—as with "almost all" in this premise—or as a decimal, a fraction, or a percentage. (We will use the lowercase letters *m* and *n* as variables standing for frequencies.) *F* and *G*, as always, are predicate letters. In inductive arguments, the predicate in the *F* position is usually termed the *population*, while the predicate in the *G* position is usually termed the *property*. A frequency statement states that with a certain frequency (*n*), a certain population (*F*) has a certain property (*G*). Here are a few frequency statements:

> Almost all early Woody Allen movies are comedies.
> Thirty-seven percent of adult American men smoke cigarettes.
> Half of all adult women are employed.
> In 1999, 53 percent of all graduating high school seniors had tried marijuana.

Note that *none* of the following qualifies as a frequency statement:

> Many early Woody Allen movies are comedies.
> Millions of adult American men smoke cigarettes.
> 57,897,332 adult women are employed.
> In 1999, graduating high school seniors had frequently tried marijuana.

The quantities expressed in the last four cases are not proportional; they provide no estimate of how the quantity relates to the total population.

Frequency arguments use a form that is very close to that of a familiar deductive argument—namely, the singular categorical argument of which the Socrates argument is our stock example. Universal categorical statements are frequency statements in which the frequency is either *all* or *none*, so *All men are mortal* does qualify as a frequency statement. But *All men are mortal*,

[2]Sometimes termed a *simple statistical hypothesis*.

Socrates is a man, so Socrates is mortal is deductive, not inductive, so we will not categorize it as a frequency argument. The frequency statement in a frequency argument, as noted in the two forms above, cannot express a proportion of 1 or 0 (i.e., of all or none), since we are defining frequency arguments as inductive, and universal statements would make them deductive.[3]

Note also that the frequency statement in a frequency argument (shown as the first premise in each of the preceding two typical forms) cannot be exactly .5. If it were .5, it would mean that exactly half of the things that are *F* are also *G*—but that the other half are *not G*, making it exactly as probable as not that *A* is *G* and thus giving no reason to believe one over the other. An argument with such a premise may still be categorized as a frequency argument, but as one that fails the correct form condition—and thus, that is logically unsuccessful.

There are other ways that frequency arguments can fail the correct form condition. Charlie Hough, a major league pitcher for many years who was steady but never dominant, was quoted in the sports pages as saying, "They say most good managers were mediocre players. I should be a helluva manager." His argument seems to be best clarified as follows:

1. Most good managers were mediocre players.
[2. Charlie Hough was a mediocre player.]
∴ C. Charlie Hough will be a good manager.

Its form is this:

1. Most *F* are *G*.
2. *A* is *G*.
∴ C. *A* is *F*.

The *F* and *G* of premise 2 and the conclusion are reversed, creating a problem that is analogous to Chapter 11's fallacy of singular affirming the consequent. This argument provides no support for the conclusion.

Inductive strength and deductive validity have this in common: if either sort of argument fails the correct form condition, it normally provides no support for its conclusion. But after this they part ways. For even if an inductive argument satisfies the correct form condition, how strong it is remains an

[3]This is a boundary drawn solely for practical convenience, enabling us to say without qualification that frequency arguments are inductive arguments and that singular categorical arguments are deductive ones.

open question. How that question is to be closed is determined by how well the argument satisfies the total evidence condition—to which we now turn.

Guideline. Structure frequency arguments, when it would be loyal to do so, as follows: the first premise is a frequency statement about a property found in a population; the second premise identifies a member of the population; and the conclusion says whether this member has the property.

EXERCISES Chapter 13, set (a)

Clarify each of the passages below as a frequency argument; state whether it satisfies the correct form condition and, if not, explain.

Sample exercise. I'm counting on good weather tomorrow; after all, it was rainy today, and at least half the time around here, clear days follow rainy ones.

Sample answer.

1. .50 of days after rainy days are clear.
2. Tomorrow is a rainy day after a clear day.

∴ *C.* Tomorrow will be clear.

Not correct form for frequency argument; frequency must be greater than .5 if it is to provide any support for the conclusion.

1. Mechanic to car owner: I would advise you to get some new radiator hoses on your car. Nine times out of ten, when steam is coming out of an engine like that it's because of old hoses.
2. Many professional wrestling matches are staged; I wouldn't believe that wrestler was really hurt, if I were you.
3. One fisherman to another: Oops—your tackle is snagged on the bottom of the lake. When that happens, it comes loose less than half the time. You might as well just cut your line and be done with it.

4. Professor to class: Students remember about 80 percent of what they both see and hear. I am providing a handout to go with today's lecture; therefore, I will expect you to remember this material.
5. Most French painters late in the 19th century were impressionists. Seurat is an impressionist, so chances are he was a late 19th century French painter.

Correct Form for Frequency Arguments

POSITIVE FORM

1. *n* of *F* are *G* (*n* is a frequency >.5 and <1).
2. *A* is *F*.

∴ C. *A* is *G*.

NEGATIVE FORM

1. *n* of *F* are *G* (*n* is a frequency <.5 and >0).
2. *A* is *F*.

∴ C. *A* is not *G*.

The Total Evidence Condition (1): How High the Frequency Is

For frequency arguments, there are typically two simple components to the total evidence condition: first, the closer the frequency is to 1 or 0, the stronger the argument can be; and second, there must not be strong background evidence against the conclusion.

Total Evidence Condition for Frequency Arguments

1. The closer the frequency is to 1 or 0, the stronger the argument can be.
2. There must not be strong undermining evidence.

First, you should consider how high the frequency is. For the positive form of the argument the closer the frequency is to 1, the stronger the argument can be. This establishes a ceiling for the argument's logical strength. The argument's logic, for example, can never be judged as stronger than *extremely weak* if the frequency is a mere .51. It can ultimately be judged as weaker than that, however, since failure to satisfy the second part of the total evidence condition would offset anything gained by this first part. The negative form of frequency argument is the mirror image of the positive. The weakest arguments are just under .5, and the closer to 0 the stronger they can be.

You should be especially careful when evaluating colloquial terms on this criterion. *Most*, for example, is quite vague—ranging from just over half to practically all. If you are stuck with such a term, it is usually best not to assume that it moves you any more than halfway from .5 to 1—that is, that it represents anything greater than a .75 frequency. So a frequency argument with *most* cannot usually be judged as any better than "moderately strong."

Guideline. In a frequency argument, the frequency establishes a ceiling for the argument's logical strength. It cannot be higher, but it can be lower.

EXERCISES Chapter 13, set (b)

For each argument, give a preliminary judgment of each argument's strength based solely on the first part of the total evidence condition. (These are the same as set (a), except for some small revisions to ensure that all of them satisfy the correct form condition.)

Sample exercise. I'm counting on good weather tomorrow; after all, it was rainy today, and a little more than half the time around here, clear days follow rainy ones.

Sample answer. Very weak.

1. Mechanic to car owner: I would advise you to get some new radiator hoses on your car. Nine times out of ten, when steam is coming out of an engine like that it's because of old hoses.
2. The vast majority of professional wrestling matches are staged; I wouldn't believe that wrestler was really hurt, if I were you.

3. One fisherman to another: Oops—your tackle is snagged on the bottom of the lake. When that happens, it comes loose less than half the time. You might as well just cut your line and be done with it.
4. Professor to class: Students remember about 80 percent of what they both see and hear. I am providing a handout to go with today's lecture; therefore, I will expect you to remember this material.
5. Most French painters late in the 19th century were impressionists. Seurat is a late 19th century French painter, so chances are he was an impressionist.

The Total Evidence Condition (2): No Strong Undermining Evidence

In addition, there must not be strong undermining evidence—that is, strong background evidence against the conclusion. You must carefully consider whether you know anything else about *A* that would undermine the argument. This is exactly what happened in our revised version of the off-ramp argument. You reflected on your total evidence, remembered that you had already discovered that this exit was an exception—that is, that it allowed no way of getting back onto the freeway—and so you discounted the initial argument without further ado.

There is a more careful way of stating this part of the total evidence condition for frequency arguments. It is slightly more complicated, but is worth introducing because it will in some cases be helpful. You should consider whether there are *other populations to which A belongs* that weaken the initial support provided by the argument. Return once again to the off-ramp argument; the Firestone exit, according to the second premise, belongs to the population of *freeway off-ramps.* But when you reflect on your total evidence, you realize it also belongs to the population of *things that you vividly remember as not having an opposing on-ramp.* When expressed in this way, it may at first look as though you are in an evaluative logjam. On the one hand, *almost all* freeway on-ramps do provide an opposing return to the freeway; on the other hand, *almost all* things that you vividly remember are true. The frequency is about the same in each of the statements, yet one of them points to the truth of the conclusion while the other points to its falsity. It is intuitively clear that the second frequency statement wins—that is, that you are right to trust your memory. Why?

A simple, general procedure provides the solution. When you recognize the undermining evidence, you should consider yet another population, namely, the population that is made up of items belonging to *both* of the populations in question, and ask with what frequency this new population has the property in question. In the current case, the new, combined population is *freeway off-ramps* (original population) *that you vividly remember as not being paired with opposing on-ramps* (undermining population). With what frequency are members of this population likely to still have the property of *being paired with an on-ramp in the opposite direction*? Almost never. The argument does not satisfy the second part of total evidence condition. The logic portion of your evaluation would look something like this:

> The logic of the argument is extremely weak. The argument does satisfy the correct form condition for a frequency argument, but does not satisfy the total evidence condition. Although the frequency ("almost all") is high enough, I remember that there is no opposing on-ramp for this off-ramp, and my memories of this sort of thing are almost always accurate.

One more example may prove useful. Suppose you are looking for a friend to join you for a skiing trip, and you want to be sure that you do not end up with a partner who will spend the whole time on the bunny slopes. You consider your Irish friend, Joseph Vaughan, but then reason as follows:

1. Less than 1 percent of the residents of Ireland are experienced downhill skiers.
2. Joseph Vaughan is a resident of Ireland.

∴ *C.* Joseph Vaughan is not an experienced downhill skier.

This is a frequency argument of the second, negative form. The form is correct and the frequency is extremely low, so, at first glance, you might expect to evaluate it as inductively strong. But then you must ask whether there is any undermining evidence that you know of—that is, whether Vaughan belongs to any populations in which the frequency of experienced downhill skiers is *high*. To make it easy, suppose you know that he is a former member of an Olympic downhill skiing team. With what frequency are members of *both* populations—residents of Ireland who have been Olympic downhill skiers—experienced skiers? Always. Your evaluation of the logic of the argument would look something like this:

> The logic is extremely weak. The argument does satisfy the correct form condition for a frequency argument, but does not satisfy the total evidence condition. Though the frequency (under 1 percent) is low enough,

Vaughan is a former Olympic skier, and no Olympic skier, even if from Ireland, is inexperienced at skiing.

Guideline. When assessing the logic of a frequency argument, one way of considering whether there is undermining evidence is to ask whether *A* is a member of another population in which the frequency of those that do *not* have the property in question is high, and then to ask about the frequency of the property in the population of those who are members of *both* the first and the second population.

EXERCISES Chapter 13, set (c)

Evaluate the logic of each of these frequency arguments, considering the background evidence in parentheses.

Sample exercise. I'm counting on good weather tomorrow; after all, it was rainy today, and a little more than half the time around here, clear days follow rainy ones. (You just saw a newscast that reported that the hurricane brewing over the Atlantic will hit your coastal town during the night.)

Sample answer. The logic of this argument is no good—the premises provide no support for the conclusion. It does satisfy the correct form condition, but the meager "more than half" frequency is more than offset by the likelihood that the newscaster was reliably reporting a very high probability of disastrous weather.

1. Mechanic to car owner: I would advise you to get some new radiator hoses on your car. Nine times out of ten, when steam is coming out of an engine like that it's because of old hoses. (Suppose you are the car owner and you recall that you just replaced all the hoses last week.)
2. The vast majority of professional wrestling matches are staged; I wouldn't believe that wrestler was really hurt, if I were you. (Suppose you don't have any other relevant background beliefs or experiences.)
3. One fisherman to another: Oops—your tackle is snagged on the bottom of the lake. When that happens, it comes loose less than half the time. You might as well just cut your line and be done with it.

(Suppose you know that you are using super-lightweight line and you can see that you've gotten the tackle caught under a big rock.)

4. Professor to class: Students remember about 80 percent of what they both see and hear. I am providing a handout to go with today's lecture; therefore, I will expect you to remember this material. (Suppose the professor is exceptionally boring and the handout is confusing.)
5. Most French painters late in the 19th century were impressionists. Seurat was a late 19th century French painter, so chances are he was an impressionist. (Suppose you've recently been to an exhibit of his work and you know that he was an impressionist.)

Arguments that Appeal to Authority

Arguments that appeal to authority can often best be understood as frequency arguments. In a text called *Thinking Better*, by David Lewis and James Greene, we are told this:

> Ulrich Neisser, one of the world's foremost specialists in the field of mental functioning, sets the record straight when he explains: "Human cognitive activity would be more usefully conceived of as a collection of acquired skills than as the operation of a single, fixed mechanism." In other words, "intelligence" is something we acquire from experience rather than an inborn ability.

The authors are telling us, apparently, that because an expert such as Neisser supports their conclusion, we should accept it. This can be clarified as an argument in which the claim that Neisser is an expert on the relevant subject is charitably paraphrased as a frequency statement.

1. Most of what Ulrich Neisser says about mental functioning is true.
2. That intelligence is not innate is something that Ulrich Neisser says about mental functioning.

∴ *C*. That intelligence is not innate is true.

It is particularly important that you be careful when you specify the population in these sorts of arguments. It is most charitable to suppose that the argument is not depending on the implicit supposition that most of *what Neisser says* is true, but that most of *what Neisser says about mental functioning* is true. It is most charitable because a premise that declared Neisser to be an expert in everything would be almost certainly false, while a premise that declared him to be an expert in this particular arena would likely be true.

What can be said about the logic of the argument? It does have correct form for a frequency argument. As for the total evidence condition, the argument is prevented from being any more than moderately strong since the frequency is expressed merely as "most." But is there undermining evidence? Yes, because even the experts disagree sharply on this question. Some, such as Neisser, believe that intelligence is not innate; many others, however, are persuaded that it is largely innate. If this information is all you have to go on, the next thing to determine is the frequency with which any statement is true when the experts disagree about its truth. (That is, the next thing to determine is the frequency with which a statement is true when it belongs to the population that includes *both* the things that one set of experts says are true and the things that another set of experts says are false). This frequency is half the time. So it turns out that the argument is logically impotent. The premises, if true, provide no more reason to believe the conclusion than to disbelieve it, given the total evidence condition. (When evaluating appeals to authority that are represented as frequency arguments, it can be very useful to review the discussion of appeals to authority in Chapter 9.)

Guideline. When it is consistent with the principles of loyalty and charity, present arguments that appeal to authority as frequency arguments in which the frequency statement declares that most of what the authority says about a particular subject is true.

EXERCISES Chapter 13, set (d)

Clarify and evaluate each of these appeals to authority as frequency arguments.

Sample exercise. "An author of this book remarked after walking about the principality of Monaco, 'Just think—only eight square miles!' 'I don't see how you even get eight out of it,' his brother replied. Yet the *Encyclopaedia Britannica*, the *World Almanac*, Scott's stamp album, various American atlases, and the gazetteers in the dictionaries had agreed on eight square miles." —Quine and Ullian, *The Web of Belief* (The book then provides the following additional information that can be useful background for evaluating the quality of the argument from authority above. On further investigation, the author found that the 11th edition of the *Encyclopaedia Britannica*, from the early 20th century, had made a mistake in arithmetic, stating: "Area about 8 square miles, the length being 2 miles and the width varying from 500 to 1,800 yards." Apparently all of the reference works, which were later, had simply copied the *Britannica's* mistaken "8 square miles.")

Sample answer.

[1. Almost all of the statements about geography found in the *Britannica*, the *World Almanac*, Scott's stamp album, various American atlases, and the gazetteers in the dictionaries are true.]

2. That Monaco is eight square miles is a statement about geography found in all of these sources.

∴ *C*. That Monaco is eight square miles is true.

EVALUATION

TRUTH

Premise 1 is probably true; theses sources depend on extensive careful research and are, in general, abundantly confirmed by the experience of their users.

Premise 2 is probably true; there is no reason to doubt the reliability of Quine and Ullian; the statements are not so improbable that I would not be willing to take their word for it; and I checked some of the older sources just to make sure, and they do make this claim.

LOGIC

Extremely weak, given the background information provided above. It is in the correct form for frequency argument, and the frequency is high enough for it to be strong. But the doubts of the passage's author, combined with his success in tracking down the source of the mistake in a mathematical error committed by the *Britannica*, leave the argument failing to fit the total evidence condition.

SOUNDNESS

The argument is unsound, because the argument is logically weak.

1. I should think that Peter Jennings knows what he's talking about if he reports on the evening news that America has struck at terrorist bases in the Middle East. So, yes, I do have good reason to believe we are fighting back against terrorism.

2. The fire in the abandoned oil well got so bad that city officials consulted with Red Adair, the legendary fireman of the oil fields. "You're not going to kill that fire with conventional methods," said Adair. "The first thing I would try is explosives." (Suppose a city official argues that Adair should be trusted, due to his expertise in this area.)
3. "A scholar meeting a person, said to him, 'I heard you were dead.' To which the other answered, 'You see I am alive.' The scholar replied, 'Perhaps so, but he who told me was a man of much more credit than you.'" —Robert O. Foote, "Who Was Joe Miller?" (Clarify and evaluate the scholar's argument, again as an appeal to authority that can be taken as a frequency argument.)
4. "The street ran adjacent to a highway in San Diego and seemed like a good shortcut to the busy truck route. But to the dismay of all the big-rig drivers who spotted the side street on their Thomas Bros. map, the road came to a dead end. Turning around on a homeowner's lawn was the only way out. In the process, one trucker drove through a resident's fence, destroying it. The truckers responded to their misfortune with a chorus of astonishment. Thomas Bros., they protested, just couldn't be wrong. As it turned out, they were right. Thomas Bros. had accurately identified the street as a dead end; the truckers had simply misread the map. The truckers' reaction is a good illustration of how California truck drivers have come to equate the name of Thomas Bros. with virtual infallibility in map making." —Herbert Vida, *Los Angeles Times* (Clarify and evaluate the argument the truckers are relying on *before* they take the apparent shortcut, again treating it as a frequency argument. Note that the problem with their argument is not necessarily with its logic.)
5. "Seven years of largely unrecognized and unrewarded effort have led a mathematician to solve one of the most famous problems in mathematics. Until Louis de Branges of Purdue University recently proved that it was true, this problem, known as the Bierbach conjecture, had challenged mathematicians for almost 70 years. Last March, de Branges sent out his proof, as part of a 350-page manuscript for a book on power series, to about a dozen mathematicians so that the proof could be verified. 'Every one of them wrote back and said that they would not be able to read it at the time,' says de Branges. Explains U. of Mich. mathematician Peter Duren, one of the recipients of the manuscript, 'We were frankly skeptical that he had done it. De

Branges had a history of announcing proof of important theorems that turned out to be wrong. It has certainly shaken up the field.'"—*Science News* (Clarify Duren's initial argument for thinking that de Branges was wrong. It provides an interesting twist on the ordinary appeals to authority. To simplify your evaluation, suppose you don't have the information in the first part of the passage stating that the proof was successful.)

SUMMARY OF CHAPTER THIRTEEN

Inductive arguments differ from deductive ones in their standards for logical success. In both cases we ask whether true premises would make it reasonable for us to believe the conclusion. But, first, the standards for induction are *lower.* The aim of an inductive argument is for the premises to make the conclusion probable, while the aim of a deductive argument is for the premises to make the conclusion certain. Second, there are *more* standards for induction. Like deductive arguments, inductive ones must satisfy the correct form condition. But, unlike deductive arguments, they must also satisfy the total evidence condition. (The conclusion must not only fit the premises, but it must also fit the total available evidence.) There is a different version of this condition for each form of induction, and each will be introduced in the text in subsequent chapters. For now, you need only know that this condition requires that the conclusion accord with the total available evidence—that is, with all of the beliefs and experiences that you personally have.

Logical inductive arguments are not termed *valid* (they are in fact not valid, nor do they aspire to be so); rather, they are termed *strong*. And their success is a matter of degree, ranging from *no support at all* to *very weak* to *fairly strong* to *very strong*.

The simplest and most intuitive inductive form is the frequency argument. It always includes a frequency statement, which states that a specified population (say, dogs) has a certain property (say, being flea-ridden) with a certain frequency (say, 40 percent of the time). There are two parts to the total evidence condition for frequency arguments. First, the higher the frequency, the stronger the logic can be. (If the argument takes the form of denying that something has a property because the frequency in the population is so low, then the reverse holds and the lower the frequency, the stronger the argument.) And, second, you must not have any substantial undermining evidence among your background beliefs and experiences.

Appeals to authority are often aptly interpreted as frequency arguments, since they typically include an implicit premise to the effect that *Most of what this expert says about this topic is true.*

GUIDELINES FOR CHAPTER THIRTEEN

- When asking whether an inductive argument is logically successful, ask the same general question you ask of deductive arguments: *If the premises were true, would that make it reasonable to believe the conclusion?* In this case, however, expect only probability, not certainty.
- Inductive arguments must satisfy not only the correct form condition, but also the total evidence condition (that is, the conclusion must fit not only the premises, but also the total available evidence). This means that even if an inductive argument is formally correct, you can judge it to be a logical argument only if it also fits appropriately with your background beliefs and experiences.
- When evaluating inductive arguments, continue to follow the standard format for argument evaluation, but be sure to include in the LOGIC section a discussion of the total evidence condition.
- Structure frequency arguments, when it would be loyal to do so, as follows: the first premise is a frequency statement about a property found in a population; the second premise identifies a member of the population; and the conclusion says whether this member has the property.
- In a frequency argument, the frequency establishes a ceiling for the argument's logical strength. It cannot be higher, but it can be lower.
- When assessing the logic of a frequency argument, one way of considering whether there is undermining evidence is to ask whether *A* is a member of another population in which the frequency of those that do *not* have the property in question is high, and then to ask about the frequency of the property in the population of those who are members of *both* the first and the second population.
- When it is consistent with the principles of loyalty and charity, present arguments that appeal to authority as frequency arguments in which the

frequency statement declares that most of what the authority says about a particular subject is true.

GLOSSARY FOR CHAPTER THIRTEEN

Correct form condition—the logical requirement on any argument that it exemplify some correct form (that its conclusion fit with its premises). Correct deductive form is sufficient for deductive validity. But correct inductive form is sufficient for inductive strength if and only if it is paired with satisfaction of the total evidence condition.

Frequency argument—an inductive argument that takes one of these two forms:

1. *n* of *F* are *G* (where *n* is a frequency >.5 and <1, i.e., more than half but less than all).
2. *A* is *F.*

∴ C. *A* is *G*.

1. *n* of *F* are *G*. (where *n* is a frequency <.5 and >0, i.e., less than half but more than none)
2. *A* is *F.*

∴ C. *A* is not *G*.

These are also called *statistical syllogisms*, *probabilistic syllogisms*, *myriokranic* (that is, thousand-headed) *syllogisms*, and *direct singular inferences*.

Frequency statement—a statement of the following form: *n* of *F* are *G*. The variable *n* stands for some frequency, or proportion, stated in ordinary language (as with *almost all*) or as a decimal, a fraction, or a percentage. The predicate in the *F* position is usually termed the *population*, while the predicate in the *G* position is usually termed the *property*. A frequency statement states that with a certain frequency (*n*), a certain population (*F*) has a certain property (*G*). Also called a *simple statistical hypothesis.*

Inductive argument—an argument in which the premises are intended to make the conclusion probable. Alternatively termed a *probabilistic*, *ampliative*, or *nondemonstrative argument.*

Inductive strength—the measure of an inductive argument's logical success (contrast with deductive validity) based on how probable the premises make the conclusion. To be logically strong an inductive argument must satisfy both the correct form condition and the total evidence condition. There is a continuum of logical strength, ranging from *no support at all* to *very weak* to *fairly strong* to *very strong*.

Total available evidence—all of the beliefs and experiences (i.e., the *total evidence*) that you as the evaluator personally have (i.e., that are *available* to you).

Total evidence condition—the logical requirement upon any inductive argument that its conclusion fit appropriately with the total available evidence. Do not confuse this condition with the requirement of true premises. The total evidence condition bears on logic and is evaluated on the assumption that the premises are true; that is, this condition is to be evaluated as part of answering the question *If the premises were true, would they make it reasonable for me to believe the conclusion*?

CHAPTER FOURTEEN

Inductive Generalization

There is nothing in which an untrained mind shows itself more hopelessly incapable, than in drawing the proper conclusions from its own experience.

—John Stuart Mill, *Inaugural Address at St. Andrews*

There's nothing like instances to grow hair on a bald-headed argument.

—Mark Twain

TOPICS

Correct Form for Inductive Generalization
The Total Evidence Condition (1): Sample Size
The Total Evidence Condition (2): Random Selection
Evaluating the Truth of Premises about Sampling
Complex Arguments

A certain raja, according to a story told by the Buddha, took all the blind men of Savatthi to show them an elephant. As each one felt the elephant, the raja said, "Tell me, what sort of thing is an elephant?" Those who had been presented with the head answered, "Sire, an elephant is like a pot." Those who had felt the ear replied, "An elephant is like a winnowing basket." Those who had been presented with a tusk said it was a plowshare. Those who knew only the trunk said it was a plow; others said the body was a granary; the foot, a pillar; the back, a mortar; the tail, a pestle; the tuft of the tail, a brush. Then they began to quarrel, shouting, "Yes it is!" "No, it is not!" "An elephant is not that!" "Yes, it's like that!" and so on, until they came to blows over the matter.

In one important way we are all like the blind men examining the elephant: there is much that we wish to understand but do not directly experience. Whether we are tasting a spoonful of soup to see if the pot has enough salt or reading about the polling of registered voters to learn who the electorate prefers for president, we habitually draw general conclusions from a few observations—that is, we habitually reason by ***inductive generalization.***

Many writers actually mean inductive generalization when they write about induction—which helps explain why some have dubiously defined induction itself as inference that moves from the particular to the general. This particular-to-general feature highlights the most fundamental difference between inductive generalization and frequency arguments; frequency arguments, recall, move from the general to the particular.

CORRECT FORM FOR INDUCTIVE GENERALIZATION

If an inductive generalization is to be logically successful, it—like all other inductive arguments—must satisfy both the correct form condition and the total evidence condition. This is typically the correct form for inductive generalizations:[1]

1. n of sampled F are G (where n is any frequency, including 0 and 1).

∴ C. n (+ or − m) of F are G.

[1]This is not the only form, just the most common. There are also, for example, *comparative inductive generalizations*; which may be clarified as follows:

1. Sampled F has H n more (or less) than sampled G.

∴ C. F has H n (+/−m) more (or less) than G.

Both the premise and the conclusion are frequency statements of the sort described in the preceding chapter. Note that in this form of argument, the premise and conclusion differ in only two ways—*sampled* is in the premise but not in the conclusion, and the *margin of error* (+ *or* − *m*) is in the conclusion but not in the premise.

> *Guideline.* Structure an inductive generalization, when it would be loyal to do so, so that the conclusion drops the term *sampled* and adds a margin of error.

The Logical Constant Sampled

The term *sampled* appears in the premise but disappears in the conclusion. This is what makes this form of argument a generalization—the premise is strictly about those individuals in the population that have been sampled, while the conclusion is generally about the population as a whole. We will treat *sampled* as a logical constant, like *if–then*, *or*, and *not*. Stylistic variants include *visited*, *seen*, *observed*, *tested*, *polled*, and *experienced*. When you can see that an argument is an inductive generalization, translate all of these stylistic variants to *sampled*.

> *Guideline.* In the premise of an inductive generalization, translate stylistic variations into the logical constant *sampled*.

EXERCISES Chapter 14, set (a)

Identify the term that is being used as a stylistic variant for *sampled* in each of these sentences, then paraphrase each sentence so that it displays correct form for the premise of an inductive generalization.

Sample exercise. Of the 100 people I asked, 53 said they are better off now than they were four years ago.

Sample solution. *Asked* is the stylistic variant. 53 percent of the sampled people say they are better off now than they were four years ago.

1. I've never had a piece of pie at the Country Kitchen that I didn't think was delicious.

2. Half of the Web sites that I checked had counters on them.
3. There has never been a documented case of a human attacked by a healthy wolf.
4. We began our study by randomly selecting 1,000 students enrolled in the college and interviewing them. It turned out that 820 of them said "yes" to the question, "Does it annoy you to be asked questions as part of a randomly selected sample?"
5. Sixty percent of the ex-football players that were X-rayed had spinal damage.
6. Only 5 of the 25 cars we saw driving on the beach today had off-road permits displayed in their windows.

EXERCISES Chapter 14, set (b)

List five stylistic variants for *sampled* that have not yet been introduced in the text, and make up an ordinary-language frequency statement (not necessarily in standard format) that uses it.

Sample answer: Rode on. All of the Metro buses I *rode on* had a bumpy ride.

The Margin of Error

The second difference between premise and conclusion is the + *or* − *m* of the conclusion, which represents the **margin of error.** Consider the following inductive generalization:

1. Fifty percent of the sampled voters favor Jones.

∴ C. Fifty percent (+/− 3 percent) of the voters favor Jones.

The 3 percent margin of error simply means that between 47 percent and 53 percent—inclusive—of the voters favor Jones. Professionals term *47 percent to 53 percent* the confidence interval. That is, the conclusion would mean the same thing if it were stated in this way:

∴ C. The percentage of voters who favor Jones is somewhere in the range from 47 percent to 53 percent.

Notice that the margin of error strengthens the argument enormously. Without the margin of error, the conclusion would have been the much more precise *50 percent of the voters favor Jones.* And this would have been false if the actual frequency of voters favoring Jones had turned out to be .53 or even .501. By including the margin of error in the conclusion, the conclusion turns out to be true with either result.

The margin of error is sometimes expressed more colloquially. When the premise in a casually expressed argument is, for example, *Half of the sampled F are G*, one way of including a margin of error in the conclusion is to say *About half of F are G*. Or when the premise is, for example, *All sampled F are G*, a margin of error is being incorporated when the conclusion is expressed as *Almost all F are G*. As you can see, *about half* and *almost all* are much more likely to generate a true conclusion than *half* and *all*.

Why, then, shouldn't an arguer include the largest possible margin of error in every inductive generalization? For the simple reason that *we need some degree of precision* in the answers to most of the questions that inductive generalizations answer. A pollster would certainly be much more likely to have a true conclusion with the following argument:

1. Fifty percent of the sampled voters favor Jones.

∴ *C*. Fifty percent (+ or − 50 percent) of the voters favor Jones.

As long as anywhere from 0 percent to 100 percent of the voters turn out to be in favor of Jones, the pollster's results are accurate. But the pollster would also quickly be unemployed; we don't need professionals to tell us that between none and all of the voters favor a particular candidate. Even narrow margins of error can sometimes render an inductive generalization useless. One recent poll of citizens of Quebec concluded that 49.5 percent (+/−3 percent) favored secession from Canada while 50.5 percent (+/− 3 percent) opposed it. The overlap produced by the 3 percent margin of error leaves us with an inconclusive result;[2] the margin would have to be reduced to less than one-half of a percent for this particular poll to be useful. The necessity of including even a 3 percent margin of error, in this case, renders the results useless.

This also applies to everyday life. Suppose one of my children is scared of monsters in the night. I turn on the light, check a few places in the room, find no monsters in the sampled places, and, remembering to include a margin of error, I say to my child, "I have concluded that almost no places in the room have monsters." This would clearly not be satisfactory, for the situation requires a conclusion with much greater precision—namely, the very precise "No places in the room have monsters."

[2] As statisticians would put it, the overlap in the margins of error means that the difference in the two results is not *statistically significant*.

It can be charitable to include a margin of error in your paraphrase, but only when loyalty allows it. If someone argues, "I've never witnessed a single rainy day in southern California, so I conclude that it absolutely never rains in southern California," it would be disloyal to paraphrase the conclusion with a margin of error, even though it would make it more likely to be true:

1. No sampled days in southern California are rainy.

∴ C. *Almost no* days in southern California are rainy.

On the other hand, if someone says, "Half of my students tell me that they are planning to pursue an advanced degree, and I take that as a reliable indicator of the plans of students throughout the country," then it seems proper to provide this charitable paraphrase:

1. Half of the sampled American college students are planning to pursue an advanced degree.

∴ C. *About half* of the American college students are planning to pursue an advanced degree.

Many inductive generalizations, for better or for worse, are like the rainy day argument above—they cannot be loyally paraphrased with any margin of error in the conclusion. This does *not* mean that such an argument fails to satisfy the correct form condition; rather, it simply means that it should be understood as including a margin of error of 0 percent.

Guideline. When the principle of loyalty allows, paraphrase inductive generalizations so as to include a non-zero margin of error in the conclusion.

Correct Form for Inductive Generalization

1. *n* of sampled *F* and *G*. (Where *n* is *any* frequency, including 0 and 1.)

∴ C. *n* (+ or − *m*) of *F* are *G*.

EXERCISES Chapter 14, set (c)

Provide a conclusion, in correct form for inductive generalization, for each of the premises in set (a) of the exercises for this chapter. Include a non-zero margin of error; don't worry for now about whether the margin of error is too large or too small. (And don't forget to drop the term *sampled.*)

Sample exercise. 53 percent of the sampled people are better off now than they were four years ago.

Sample answer. 53 percent (+ or − 10 percent) of the people are better off now than they were four years ago.

THE TOTAL EVIDENCE CONDITION (1): SAMPLE SIZE

As we have established, if an inductive argument is to be logical it is not enough that it satisfies the correct form condition. Correct inductive form makes the argument a *candidate* for logical success, but it can tell you nothing about how inductively strong the argument is. This is where the total evidence condition makes its entrance. Once we see that the conclusion fits the premises, we must then see how well it fits the total available evidence.

For an inductive generalization, when considering the total evidence condition the central question to ask is this: *Is the sample representative of the population?* Does the part of the elephant touched by the blind man feel like the rest of the elephant? Does the tasted spoonful of soup taste like the rest of the pot? Do the polled voters accurately reflect the views of the entire electorate? There is only one way to be completely sure—namely by sampling the remainder of the population. But this is generally not practicable; if you taste the rest of the soup, there's none left for the dinner guests.

There are two things to look at when assessing whether the sample accurately represents the population: the *size* of the sample—it must be large enough—and the *randomness* of the selection process—every member of the population must have an equal chance to be included in the sample. Inductive generalizations that fail in one or both of these areas are sometimes said to commit the ***fallacy of hasty generalization.*** It is worth mentioning this fallacy, however, only because it reminds us of how easy it is to be satisfied with a sample that is not representative. The fallacy tells us nothing about the specific way in which the argument fails; for that reason, it is best to avoid the term and focus your evaluation on specific failures in measuring up to standards for size of sample and randomness of selection.

Total Evidence Condition for Inductive Generalizations

WHAT MAKES THE SAMPLE REPRESENTATIVE

1. The sample must be large enough.
2. The sample must be randomly selected.

The Sample Must Be Large Enough

The first total-evidence question to ask is this: *Is the sample large enough?* No single size is right for every sample. Sometimes a sample of one should be enough. How many spoonfuls do you have to taste to decide if there is enough salt in the soup? But in other cases, 1,000 might be closer to the right number. Most market research and public opinion firms seem to interview roughly that number of people. And sometimes the really ambitious researchers go for gigantic samples (though, as we will see, this is almost always unnecessary). Dr. Alfred Kinsey, for example, who published the enormously influential volumes *Sexual Behavior in the Human Male* and *Sexual Behavior in the Human Female* in the mid-20th century, was convinced that he needed to collect 100,000 histories to have a representative sample of the population.

Guideline. In considering whether an inductive generalization has satisfied the total evidence condition, first ask, *Is the sample large enough?*

When a Sample of One Is Enough

We will proceed from here via a few simple rules of thumb; these tips will give you all that you need for most practical purposes to evaluate most inductive generalizations. (If you are thirsty for more, you may wish to read a book or take a course in statistics.) The first rule of thumb is this: *for most inductive generalizations, you need a sample of either one or 1,000.*

The way to decide whether it should be one or 1,000 is to ask the question, *Is this an all-or-none property?* With some properties, it is fairly clear that either all or none of the entire population has it. Saltiness of soup—assuming the pot has been stirred—is a good example; before you take a taste, it is reasonable to believe that if the taste is too salty, then the *entire* pot is too salty; but if it is not salty enough, then the *entire* pot is not salty enough. The properties *too salty* and *not salty enough* are in this case all-or-none properties.

We can look around us and discover many more everyday examples of all-or-none properties. Are you curious about what the morning edition of the *Chicago Tribune* reports about the snow conditions on the slopes of Vail? When you buy a copy and see that it reports excellent snow conditions, it is reasonable for you to conclude that this is what is reported by all the papers in that entire edition. That is, it is reasonable for you to reason as follows:

1. All sampled copies of the morning edition of the *Chicago Tribune* report excellent snow conditions at Vail.

∴ C. All copies of the morning edition of the *Chicago Tribune* report excellent snow conditions at Vail.

Reporting excellent snow conditions at Vail is likely to be an all-or-none sort of property for copies of the same edition of a newspaper; so a sample size of one is sufficient. You could buy a thousand copies from newsstands and newspaper boxes throughout Chicago and check them, just to be sure the sample is large enough to support your conclusion. Doing so would strengthen your argument a bit, since it would help rule out the remote possibility that the first copy was the result of some bizarre error or trick. But that possibility is typically so remote that the added strength of the 999 extra copies would be negligible.[3]

Calvin Coolidge, it is said, was once visiting a farm with some friends. When they came to a flock of sheep, one of the friends said, "I see these sheep have just been shorn." Coolidge, famous for his caution, replied, "Looks like it from this side." Coolidge was reluctant to generalize from the visible part—the sampled part—of each sheep to the whole sheep. But he didn't really have to be so cautious. Given what most of us know, it is reasonable to believe that whether a sheep is shorn is an all-or-none sort of property; thus, even if we have sampled only one part of the sheep, if that part is shorn we can generalize to the whole sheep.

Inductive generalizations, however, are often criticized quite legitimately for relying on samples of one, or samples larger than one that are nevertheless too small. You would not, for example, interview merely one voter to find out which presidential candidate is preferred by the electorate, since *favors candidate A* is not typically an all-or-none property; we expect to find variety in the population with respect to this property. (The story is very different if you wish to find out which presidential candidate is favored by the

[3]A property that is *normally* an all-or-none property is, nevertheless, not *necessarily* such a property. If you have reason to think that the soup has not been stirred, or that this copy of the newspaper is a dummy, then a sample of one is not sufficient.

electoral college of a single state; since they all vote the same way, depending on which candidate won the plurality of the state's votes, you can generalize to them all if you know the vote of one.) Likewise, you should not—and if you are careful, you would not—make a decision about, say, someone's honesty based on a single interchange with that person. Someone's honest behavior in your first brief conversation may or may not be representative of that person's behavior in general. A sample much larger than a single meeting is necessary for a logical argument about general behavior—this is one of the reasons we typically date before marriage.

If the inductive generalization is conducted scientifically—by a public opinion poll, say, or an experiment on rats or human subjects—then typically you will find that the property is *not* all-or-none. If the scientists had believed it to be an all-or-none property, they would not have gone to the trouble and expense required to construct a large sample so carefully.

Guideline. If the property is likely to be all-or-none, then a sample of one is typically enough. It is almost certainly not an all-or-none property if there has been an effort to scientifically construct the sample.

EXERCISES Chapter 14, set (d)

For each of the simple arguments below, clarify it in standard format, identify the relevant property, and state whether it is probably, for this population, an all-or-none property.

Sample exercise. One camper to another, taking a thermometer out of a pot of water boiling over the fire: "See, the thermometer shows 99 degrees Centigrade. So that's the temperature at which water boils at an altitude of 5,000 feet."

Sample answer.

1. All sampled water at an altitude of 5,000 feet boils at 99 degrees Centigrade.

∴ *C.* All water at an altitude of 5,000 feet boils at 99 degrees Centigrade.

Property is *boils at 99 degrees Centigrade.* It is probably an all-or-none property, thus a sample of one should be enough.

1. One 7-Eleven shopper to another, holding up a can of coffee: "I can see from this can that 13-ounce cans of Folger's coffee cost $3.99 here."
2. That driver almost ran me off the road. It's obvious that people who live in this city are terrible drivers.
3. You have trouble doing long division? Then you're not very intelligent, are you? (Hint—make the population *opportunities to show intelligence.*)
4. How do I know that any copy of her brand new book that you pick up will be long? I just read all 750 pages.
5. I've known two other people from Syracuse, and they were both of Norwegian descent. So I guess most people from Syracuse are Norwegian.
6. That ant bit me and left an angry red welt on my leg. I'm not going near the rest of them.

When a Sample of 1,000 Is Enough

When the *one-or-1,000* rule of thumb is applied and the property is *not* all-or-none, you can assume for most purposes that a sample of 1,000 is sufficient for a logically strong argument—assuming the sample is randomly selected. This is well illustrated by public opinion polls and marketing surveys, which almost always have samples of roughly that size. But there is nothing magical about the number 1,000; its sufficiency depends on several things—most notably the margin of error. Whether a random sample of 1,000 is big enough depends on whether the margin of error is at least 3 percent. If it is impossible to collect a sample of 1,000, then the arguer must settle for a larger margin of error or for a logically weaker argument.

Let us look at this in a more general way. We have already seen two things that can increase the logical strength of an inductive generalization. The larger the margin of error, the stronger the logic of the argument. And the larger the sample size—assuming it is randomly selected—the stronger the logic of the argument (though, as we have already seen, increases in sample size after a certain point are only marginally helpful). This suggests another rule of thumb: *if the margin of error increases appropriately as the sample size decreases, the logical strength of the argument remains steady.* The bigger the margin of error, the smaller the necessary sample size. The reverse is likewise true: the smaller the margin of error, the larger the necessary sample size.

Statisticians can establish for any sample size (assuming the sample is randomly selected) the margin of error that can be confidently assumed. Here are some useful points along the continuum:

SAMPLE SIZE	MARGIN OF ERROR
10	+/− 30 percent
100	+/− 10 percent
500	+/− 4 percent
1,000	+/− 3 percent
2,000	+/− 2 percent

This means that a voter opinion survey of 1,000 people can provide the basis for a strong inductive generalization *so long as the conclusion allows for a margin of error of at least 3 percent.* Suppose this is the premise:

1. Fifty percent of the sampled voters favor Jones.

A random sample of 1,000 is large enough to support this conclusion:

∴ *C.* Fifty percent (+/− 3 percent) of the voters favor Jones.

But if the random sample were only 100, the logic of the induction would be equally strong only if the argument concluded that from 40 percent to 60 percent favored Jones. If the random sample were 10, then the conclusion would have to be that from 20 percent to 80 percent favored Jones. If, however, it were as large as if 2,000, then the conclusion could be narrowed to the assertion that 48 percent to 52 percent favored Jones.

Some arguments do not need a high level of precision. Suppose I am interested in providing venture capital to fund a specialty candy store in the local shopping mall, and I determine that at least 10 percent of the shoppers will have to buy something in the store if it is to succeed. I randomly (*really* randomly) interview 10 shoppers and find that 6 of them would have bought candy from my store. From this I can conclude that 60 percent (+/− 30 percent) of the shoppers would buy candy from the store (I take this directly from the preceding table of sample sizes), that is, anywhere from 30 percent to 90 percent. This is well above my cutoff point of 10 percent, so greater precision is not necessary. Again, in general, the less precision needed in the conclusion, the smaller the sample that is needed.

Guideline. For properties that are not all-or-none, if the margin of error increases appropriately as the sample size decreases, then the logical strength of the argument remains steady.

Rules of Thumb for Judging Sample Size When the Sample Is Randomly Selected

1. *One* is enough when the property is all-or-none.
2. *1,000* are enough when the property is not all-or-none and the margin of error is at least 3 percent.

EXERCISES Chapter 14, set (e)

For each sample that is described write a conclusion with an appropriate margin of error.

Sample exercise. A random sample of 500 pairs of socks put into clothes dryers showed that one-fourth of the pairs lost one member by the end of the cycle.

Sample answer. Twenty-five percent (+/– 4 percent) of pairs of socks put into clothes dryers lose a member by the end of the cycle.

1. In a random sample of 10 owners of Acuras in the model year 1999, 5 of them were "extremely pleased" with their car.
2. Four percent of 2,000 randomly sampled American homeowners said they preferred renting.
3. In a random sample of 100 days in Atlanta, on 7 of them unhealthful levels of ozone were in the air.
4. One-tenth of a random sample of 1,000 mosquitoes captured in a Florida swamp were carrying the virus that causes encephalitis.
5. In a random sample of 1,000 Texas adults, 483 believe the state sport should be rodeo.
6. In a random sample of 500 television episodes from 50 years of television history, one-third of them depicted at least one murder.

7. Eighteen percent of the 500 streetlights sampled at random in Manhattan were out of order.
8. Of 2,000 randomly sampled American Express cardholders, 1,609 were pleased with their customer service.

Population Size

Although the size of the sample is very important, the size of the *population* has very little to do with the logical strength of the argument. This may initially strike you as contrary to common sense. But note that common sense does not tell you that you must take a bigger taste if you have a bigger pot of soup, assuming it is properly stirred.

If the population is very small, population size can matter. Suppose you have 1,000 trees in your apple orchard and you want to sample them to learn how many trees are diseased. *Being diseased* is not likely to be an all-or-none property in an apple orchard, so our *one-or-1,000* rule tells us to sample 1,000 trees. Suppose you do that and find that 160 of them are diseased. You no longer need to generalize; you have sampled the entire population, you have found 16 percent to be diseased, and no inference from sample to population is necessary. Small populations matter because they make inductive generalizations unnecessary.

Suppose, however, that owing to the cost and difficulty of testing the trees, you cannot randomly check more than 500 of them; you do so and find that 71 of the sampled trees are diseased. At this point the best thing you can do is refer to the preceding sample size table. If you want a logically strong argument, you must conclude that 14.2 percent, plus or minus 4 percent, are diseased—the same as if your sample of 500 had been from an orchard 10 times larger. We find the same phenomenon in polling practices. If there are 100 voters in our hamlet, we can interview every voter and avoid the generalization. If there are 10 million voters, which is roughly the case in Canada, pollsters require a random sample of 1,000 to conclude that half the voters, with a margin of error of 3 percent, favor Jones. And if there are 100 million voters, which is roughly the case in America, they still require a random sample of 1,000 to conclude that half the voters, with a margin of error of 3 percent, favor Jones.

Why does this work? If 16 percent of the trees are diseased, then for each randomly selected tree there is a 16 percent chance, or a .16 probability, that it is diseased. This is true whether we are talking about 16 percent of 1,000 or 16 percent of 10,000. And if exactly half of the voters favor Jones, then—

whether we are talking about half of 10 million or half of 100 million—there is a 50 percent chance, or a .50 probability, that each randomly selected voter favors Jones. It is this property of each member of the sample that governs the behavior of the sample as a whole.

For practical reasons it may be more difficult to get a random sample when the population is far larger. Ten thousand trees or 100 million voters may be spread over a huge geographical area, making it impossible to give every member of the population an equal chance of being included in the sample. Thus, sample size or margin of error may be strategically increased to offset these practical difficulties (as we will see in the next section). But these adjustments are directly due to lack of randomness, and only indirectly due to population size.

Guideline. When the population is large, variation in population size has no bearing on the size of the random sample that is needed, although it may have a bearing on how easy it is to get a random sample.

Logical Strength and Confidence Level

Exactly how logically strong is the inductive generalization that begins *50 percent of the sampled voters favor Jones*, assuming that it is based on a random sample of 1,000 and a margin of error of 3 percent? How much support does the premise provide the conclusion? This can be answered quite precisely: the probability of the conclusion, based on this premise and the relevant background evidence, is .95.

Suppose the population of voters in the Jones poll numbers 10 million, and suppose that exactly 5 million—that is, 50 percent—favor Jones. Statisticians tell us that if we took 20 different random samples of 1,000 from that population of 10 million, 19 of those 20 times the number in the sample that favored Jones would be in the range of 47 percent to 53 percent (that is, 50 percent +/−3 percent). Since the true conclusion, namely, *50 percent (+/− 3 percent) of the voters favor Jones*, would occur 19 out of the 20 times, or in 95 percent of the cases, its probability of success is .95. We may have gotten it wrong this time, but that would mean that this is the 1 time in 20 it would happen.

If, on the other hand, we took 20 different random samples of only 10 from that population, 19 out of 20 times the number in the sample that favored Jones would be in the range of 20 percent to 80 percent. To get the same .95 probability of success with such a small sample, the conclusion must be *50 percent (+/− 30 percent) of the voters favor Jones.*

Professional researchers would typically term this a ***confidence level*** of .95. Confidence level, however, is just another expression for the probability of the conclusion, given the truth of the premise and given the relevant background information. That is, it is just another expression for logical strength. (It is not the level of confidence that you do have, but the level of confidence that you rationally ought to have.) Professional researchers tend to aim for arguments with a .95 probability, and we will typically refer to arguments that achieve this level of probability as *very strong*.

No rule says that when the probability is .95 you should *believe* the conclusion. We are only talking about the argument's logic. There must also be a very high probability that the premises are true before you accept the argument as sound. Nor does any rule say that when you do accept such an argument as sound and when you do believe the conclusion that you should act with confidence on it. If the argument's conclusion has to do with whether a rope bridge over a treacherous waterfall is able to support you, you may quite reasonably turn around and go home unless you can be given much better than a 19 out of 20 chance of survival. But if the conclusion has to do with whether a black speck on the table is a fly or an imperfection in the surface, you may quite reasonably attempt to brush it away even if the confidence level is considerably lower than .95.

The vocabulary of logical strength, probability, and confidence level can also be applied to the other sorts of arguments we have covered. In deductively valid arguments, for example, the conclusion would be true *every* time you considered the premises; thus, they confer a probability of 1.00 on their conclusions—that is, they have a confidence level of 1.00. And consider frequency arguments, such as this one:

1. Sixty-seven percent of the marbles in the clay pot are red.
2. The marble I've just taken in my hand is a marble in the clay pot.

∴ *C.* The marble I've just taken in my hand is red.

Assuming I have no relevant background evidence except for the frequency expressed in the first premise, we can say that the conclusion will be true 67 percent of the times that I take a marble in my hand. Thus, the conclusion, given those premises and that background evidence, has a probability of .67—and the argument has a confidence level of .67.

> *Guideline.* Judge as *very strong* the logic of any inductive generalization that renders its conclusion .95 probable.

EXERCISES Chapter 14, set (f)

Create a brief argument of the sort described and with the degree of logical success described. Explain.

Sample exercise. Inductive generalization, no support at all.

Sample answer. Half of the Corvettes I have seen have been red, so it follows that half of all red cars are Corvettes. (No support because does not satisfy the correct form condition.)

1. Inductive generalization, .95 probability (very strong).
2. Frequency argument, .55 probability (very weak).
3. Singular affirming the antecedent, 1.00 probability (valid).
4. Frequency argument, .50 probability (no support).
5. Singular denying the antecedent, .50 probability (no support—note that a probability below .50 would support the falsity of the conclusion).

THE TOTAL EVIDENCE CONDITION (2): RANDOM SELECTION

Random Selection

To review, we are considering how to evaluate the logic of inductive generalizations. We are assuming that the correct form condition is satisfied and we are focusing on the total evidence condition. For the total evidence condition to be satisfied, recall, the key question is whether the sample accurately represents the population. This can be divided into two questions: whether the sample is large enough, and whether the sample has been randomly collected. We now turn to the second question.

To say that sample selection is ***random***, for the practical purposes of this text, is to say that every member of the population has had an equal opportunity to be included in the sample, so that exactly the relevant variations of the population might be proportionately represented. This is an important definition, for it differs from the way we ordinarily use the term. There would be nothing unusual about my saying, "I randomly interviewed 30 people at the bus station to find out what people in the city think of rapid transit." This, however, is not the sort of randomness that we are looking for in evaluating inductive generalizations. In this relaxed use of the term, *random* simply means *indiscriminate*, or *without any special principle of selection.* But notice that not everyone in the city had an equal opportunity to be included in the sample—only those who happened to be at the bus station. This means that relevant variations of the population have almost certainly been omitted from the sample; for example, people who never ride the bus, and so are excluded from the sample, probably tend to have views on this subject that differ from those who ride it. In short, the randomness that we are looking for is not indiscriminate randomness; it requires carefully considered principles of selection.

An ideal way to get a perfectly random sample would be to list all the members of the population, run the names through a computerized randomizing program (or shake them thoroughly in a giant hat, or put each name on a surface of a huge many-sided fair die), and sample the first 1,000 that are selected. But this is almost never something that works in real life. It would be prohibitively expensive to do this if, say, you were generalizing about voter preferences across the entire American population. And it would simply make no sense if you were, say, generalizing about pollution throughout an entire river. (How would you list all the potential beakers of water that make up the river?)

Professionals usually find it simpler to achieve randomness by a technique called ***stratification.*** They make an informed judgment regarding which subpopulations are likely to differ from the larger population in the frequency with which they exhibit the property in question. They divide the population proportionately into these smaller populations, or strata, and sample at random from each stratum. Suppose, for example, the population is *registered voters in the state of North Carolina* and the property is *prefers the Republican candidate in the North Carolina gubernatorial election.* Voter preference is likely to vary according to factors such as party affiliation, ethnicity, economic status, and gender. So the pollsters must ensure that they have randomly selected, for example, Republicans, African-Americans, welfare recipients, and women in sufficient numbers so that their share of the sample matches their share of the population of North Carolina's registered voters. Voter preference is not likely to vary, however, according to astrological sign, so there is no need to be sure that a Scorpio stratum is included in the sample.

Guideline. Do not judge an inductive generalization to be logically strong unless its sample is randomly selected—that is, unless the sample includes the relevant variations in the appropriate frequency. Remember that not all variations are relevant.

EXERCISES Chapter 14, set (g)

For each statement in set (e), list *(i)* the population, *(ii)* the property, *(iii)* two relevant variations in the population, and *(iv)* one irrelevant variation.

Sample exercise. A random sample of 500 pairs of socks put into clothes dryers showed that one-fourth of the pairs lost one member by the end of the cycle.

Sample answer. Population: pairs socks put into clothes dryers. Property: lost one member by the end of the cycle. Relevant variations: size of load, time of cycle. Irrelevant variation: brand of socks.

Random Mistakes

Our purpose in this textbook is not to design samples but to evaluate arguments. This section will help you in detecting ways in which a sample might fail to be randomly selected and thereby contribute to an unsound argument.

Sometimes you can see that a relevant variation has been omitted without knowing the exact sampling process that was used. If you knew that 75 percent of those in the sample were men, and the question was whether Americans thought that women were treated equally in the workforce, then you would know there was a problem with the sample; attitudes on this vary with gender, so the genders must be equally represented. If, on the other hand, the question were whether baseball fans favored the designated hitter rule, you probably would not know whether there was a problem with the sample. It may well be that 75 percent of all baseball fans are men, in which case they would turn up with this frequency in a random sample.

Often you simply have no details about the sample, in which case your approval of the argument's logic may depend on whether you trust the person or organization that collected it. The Chapter 9 guidelines for appeals to authority are directly pertinent here. Was the research done by a credible organization? Is there no sign of sponsorship by a business that has an interest in a certain outcome? Is the prior probability of the outcome reasonably high? Yes answers to all of these questions count in favor of the argument.

There are, however, a few tips that can reliably tell you when a sample is *not* randomly selected. ***Grab sampling,*** for example, is the process of including in your sample whatever members of the population happen to come your way. This is the method used in the bus station case; it is easy to do, but it rarely provides a representative sample. In *The De-Valuing of*

America, William Bennett recounts the use of such a technique by a department chair at a prestigious university, who remarked the day after the 1980 presidential election: "I voted for Carter. Most of my colleagues voted for Carter. And a few voted for Anderson. But Reagan got elected. Who the hell voted for Reagan?"

The following *Los Angeles Times* story includes an obviously flawed grab sample:

> The Water Quality Control Board is considering imposing fines of $10,000 against the City of Los Angeles for each major discharge of raw sewage. But Harry Sizemore, assistant director of the city Bureau of Sanitation, insists that the water in the ocean does not cause disease. "I swim there," he said. "And several members of our bureau are avid surfers who use the area. None of us has ever caught any diseases from it."

This argument has several defects besides its dependence on a flawed sampling procedure. For example, there is some reason to distrust the reports of this particular group—and thus, reason to doubt the truth of the premise. Further, the sample is a very small one. And we would prefer an analysis of a random sample of the *water itself* rather than a random sample of those who have been in the water. But the relevant point here is that Sizemore has not provided us with a random sample of those who have been in the water. It is a grab sample, made up of whomever Sizemore happened to talk to at the office, and thus there is no reason to think that it is representative.

Snowball sampling, a close relative of grab sampling, is the process of adding new members to the sample on the basis of their close relationship with those already included (thus gathering members in the same way that a snowball gathers snow as it rolls along). I have already mentioned the highly publicized studies on sexual behavior conducted by Alfred Kinsey in the 1940s and 1950s. Kinsey frequently selected new interview subjects by asking his interview subjects to refer him to their friends and acquaintances. Given that he had a special interest in talking to those whose sexual practices were not considered mainstream, and given that friends and acquaintances of those who were not in the sexual mainstream were themselves somewhat likely to be out of the mainstream, this snowball sampling produced significant distortions in his sample. True, Kinsey collected an enormous sample. But, due to his snowball technique, the magnified sample size magnified the distortion.

Self-selected sampling is probably the most common, and most insidious, error. This occurs when members of the population decide for themselves whether to be included in the sample. Before we stray too far from Alfred Kinsey, note this *Psychology Today* review of a similar but more recent study:

> *Love, Sex, and Aging* is a report of a survey of 4,246 Americans aged 50 and older—the largest sample of older persons about whom detailed sexual data exist. It is composed entirely of volunteers who responded to an ad in *Consumer Reports.* The authors of the book say, "We are confident that many or most of our findings apply to a very broad segment of Americans over 50," and present their findings in that spirit. Item: two-thirds of the women and four-fifths of the men 70 or older are still sexually active. Grandma, Grandpa, you couldn't! You don't!

Let's begin by treating the argument a bit more fully. For simplicity, let's clarify only the argument about men:

1. Eighty percent of the sampled men aged 70 or older are still sexually active.

∴ *C.* About 80 percent of men aged 70 or older are still sexually active.

The frequency is 80 percent, the population is *men aged 70 or older,* and the property is *still sexually active.* I've charitably included an informal margin of error (*about* 80 percent) in the conclusion, which seems warranted by the imprecise way the authors express their conclusion ("most of our findings apply to a very broad segment of Americans"). I will take the premise to be *probably true,* since I have no reason to doubt the truthfulness of the authors and no compelling reason to doubt the word of those who submitted the survey (though it is possible that those who submitted the surveys either overstated or understated the extent of their sexual activities).

This brings us to an evaluation of the argument's logic. It clearly satisfies the correct form condition, so we can move on to the total evidence condition. Is the sample large enough? It is hard to say, since the excerpt merely states that 4,246 people over the age of 50 responded to the survey; but the argument we are considering is based only on the surveys submitted by men over the age of 70. Let's suppose there are a few hundred in this category, thus probably the sample is large enough to support the vague "about 80 percent" of the conclusion.

But is the sample randomly selected? Certainly not. As the passage states, the sample is made up of those who voluntarily responded to a survey in *Consumer Reports.* This filters out all of those who read *Consumer Reports* but are not interested enough in sex to be interested in filling out a survey on the topic. It also filters out a large group of elderly people who ignore *Consumer Reports* because they can't afford most of the items described in the magazine. These people are also unable to afford top medical care and for that reason they are probably less healthy and less interested in sex. In short, the sample is self-selected and thus grossly unrepresentative.

For that reason alone, the logic of the argument is very weak. There is no problem with the argument's premise or with its conversational relevance, but because of its weak logic it is clearly unsound.

The Internet provides countless opportunities for this sort of error. One common feature of Web sites is a little survey that asks you to check one of several choices—which director deserves to win the Academy Award, which city is the most desirable place to raise a family, which pitcher should win the Cy Young Award, which tax reform proposal is preferable. You submit your vote, there follows a quick calculation, and you immediately see how many people have voted and the frequency of each selection. These surveys are entertaining, but should never be used as the premise in an inductive generalization. The self-selected nature of the sample means that it does not include those who aren't very interested in the topic, who are not able to afford Web access, who do not have sufficient education to use the Web, or who for some good reason haven't found that particular Web site.

Web surveys perpetuate the flaws of 1-900 phone number surveys. Dial this number to vote yes, that one to vote no. Those who do not have as much at stake are less likely to vote, as are those who cannot afford the 50 cents or those who have less ready access to a telephone. Thus, the sample is unlikely to be representative of the population and should not be taken as the basis for any generalization.

Finally, ***dirty sampling*** is the contamination of the sample—usually unintentional—by the sampling process itself. If you are examining your newly laundered shirts with muddy hands, your sample shirts will be muddy. Even if you have made no other sample-selection mistakes, this sample cannot support the general conclusion that all your newly laundered shirts are muddy. This is a failure of randomness, since in a randomly selected sample, exactly the relevant variations of the population are proportionately represented. Introducing mud is introducing a relevant variation that is not in the population.

Dirty sampling does not necessarily introduce dirt, but it does introduce a change in the sample that makes the sample relevantly different from the population. Suppose you are a somewhat absent-minded naturalist and wish to learn more about the eyesight of a tiny species of shrew that is nearing extinction. You use a strong light to see their eyes better, and find that all shrews in your sample have extremely small pupils relative to the size of their eyes. Your sampling procedure, of course, is dirty, since in mammals strong light typically causes the pupils to contract. The sampling process cannot be considered random, and the premise can provide no support to the conclusion.

Guideline. Be alert for ways in which an argument may fail to include a relevant variation in its sample. Typically, arguments that depend on grab sampling, snowball sampling, self-selected sampling, or dirty sampling do not have randomly selected samples and are thus logically very weak (and thus unsound).

EXERCISES Chapter 14, set (h)

For each of these passages, clarify the inductive generalization and then answer, with a brief explanation, the two total evidence questions.

Sample exercise. "The people, it seems, have declared Ronald Reagan the winner of the Reagan–Carter debate. Nearly 700,000 people paid 50 cents each to take part in an instant ABC News telephone survey following the presidential debate, and by a 2-to-1 margin they said Ronald Reagan had gained more from the encounter than President Carter. ABC said that of the callers who reached one of the two special 900-prefix numbers during the 100 minutes following Tuesday night's debate, 469,412 people or 67 percent dialed the number designated for Reagan and 227,017 or 33 percent dialed the one assigned to Carter. The network said an especially heavy volume of calls was recorded from 'Western states' but had no more precise breakdown immediately."—from the Associated Press

Sample answer.

1. Sixty-seven percent of the sampled Americans considered Reagan the winner of the debate.

∴ *C.* About 67 percent of Americans considered Reagan the winner of the debate.

The sample is easily big enough (by 700 times). But it is not randomly selected. It was self-selected, with more Democrats (who would have favored Carter) filtered out because they are not as able to afford the 50 cents and with more non-Westerners (who would have been less likely to favor the Californian Reagan) filtered out because they were in a later time zone and had gone to bed.

1. 21 of 30 students in an English 101 course at the local community college expressed doubt that the degree they were working toward would actually get them a good job. From this it seems reasonable to conclude that the majority of the students at the school don't have much faith in the practical value of their education.
2. Only 25 percent of 1,000 residents of Manhattan polled at a free concert in Central Park said they would support privatizing the park and instituting a mandatory fee for entrance. The sample would seem to reflect the attitude of New Yorkers in general.
3. You are in charge of quality control for a pharmaceutical company, and part of your job is to run a laboratory that collects random samples of your company's drugs each month and examines them carefully for purity. One month your lab obtains a startling result: 60 percent of the sampled drugs are impure. You alert the company president (and, of course, the public relations officer) that over half of that month's product is tainted. (Meanwhile, one of your lab technicians inspects the beakers used for pre-examination sample storage and discovers that due to a change in laboratory cleaning protocol this month, a microscopic chemical residue is left on the beakers after cleaning. Minute amounts of this residue have commingled with many of the drugs, causing the impurity.)
4. In 1936, in the midst of the Great Depression, the *Literary Digest* randomly selected 10 million names from phone books across the country and mailed them sample ballots for the upcoming presidential election between Republican Alf Landon and Democrat Franklin Delano Roosevelt. About 2 million of the ballots were returned and, based on the results of that sample, the magazine predicted confidently that Landon would win by a clear majority. (Postscript: Roosevelt won with 60 percent of the popular vote, and the *Literary Digest*, having lost all credibility, ceased publication soon after.)
5. An elderly woman overheard speaking to her friend: "Recently I drove through a small 'art-colony' village in Pennsylvania, which is normally frequented by tourists. I got the shock of my life when I saw about 75 young people all dressed exactly alike—in blue denim! I wondered if there had been a prison break, or an invasion of the Union Army. What

is it with our young people? They have about as much individuality as connected sausage links. They all look alike. Same dress, same jeans, same long straight hair—it's hard to tell one from the other."

6. Most of the kids in this remote, rural high school in Grants, New Mexico, have only television to provide them with their images of big cities. Paul Sanchez confesses that he hates what he has seen of New York on television. As part of a class assignment, he writes: "New York seems like a corrupt place. Crime seems to rule. I am not a person who is easily intimidated but TV did it."—*TV Guide*
7. Americans support the idea of letting children attend public schools of their choice. The public favored by a margin of 62 percent to 33 percent allowing students and parents to choose which public schools in their community the students attend. Officials said the Gallup-Phi Delta Kappa poll is the most comprehensive survey of American attitudes on educational issues since the series began in 1969. This year, Gallup interviewers asked a selected sample of 1,500 American adults 80 questions. The margin of error was 3 percentage points.—Associated Press
8. I have a master's degree in mathematics and was well thought of by my professors. I am working as a computer programmer, and my coworkers, supervisors, and users admire my abilities. I scored in the upper 2 percentile on college entrance tests, usually in the upper percentile for mathematics and biology. However, I would probably score poorly on the Kaufmans' test because I have a poor short-term memory. If I call up the operator for a telephone number, I have to keep repeating it to myself until I dial it, or I will forget the number. It sometimes takes me several months to learn my telephone number and address when I move. I find it hard to believe there is a strong correlation between short-term memory and the ability to think logically.—Letter to the editor, *Science News*

Four Ways Samples Can Fail to Be Randomly Selected

1. Grab sampling
2. Snowball sampling
3. Self-selected sampling
4. Dirty sampling

EVALUATING THE TRUTH OF PREMISES ABOUT SAMPLING

Everything we said in Chapter 9 about the truth of premises applies to the premise of an inductive generalization. Of all the points covered there, the most important for present purposes is the point about dependence on authority. Usually, whether you accept the premise of an inductive generalization is a matter of whether you believe the sampler. Did the person really sample that population and find that property with that frequency? Make this decision in the same way you make any other decision about whether to rely on an authority.

Misunderstood Samples

In ***misunderstood samples,*** the method used for collecting information about the sample is not entirely reliable. This results in a misunderstanding of the sample's properties, rendering the premise false. A. C. Nielsen, who established the Nielsen ratings system for television shows, began his career doing market research for retailers. One of his early accounts was Procter & Gamble, for whom he did a survey on soap. He carefully constructed his sample, did his survey, and returned with results that were drastically at odds with the Procter & Gamble sales data. The main discrepancy was that sales of Lux bar soap were lagging badly, even though huge numbers of those surveyed said they used Lux regularly. Nielsen was perplexed until he realized that Lux had the image of a soap for the well-to-do; people wanted to impress the interviewer, and thus said they used Lux whether they did or not. His sample was representative—it was large enough and it was randomly selected. The problem was with the premise, which stated that the sampled consumers used Lux with a certain frequency. They did not; the premise was false. The lesson for Nielsen was to find a more reliable way of determining what people really think.

In an old Frank Capra movie called *Magic Town,* James Stewart plays a public opinion pollster who doesn't have the resources to compete with the major organizations like Gallup and Harris. He happens upon a small town that perfectly reflects the variations found in the American public in general. He regularly solicits their opinions by disguising the interviews as casual conversation and produces astonishingly accurate results. But his love interest, a journalist played by Jane Wyman, finds out about his technique. Choosing truth over love, she writes a widely distributed feature article about the town. With the appearance of the article, one town councilman snorts, "In one week's time I wouldn't give the wart off my nose for anybody's opinion in this town." And he is right. Soon the townspeople are setting up booths for the dispensing of their opinions and affecting pompous airs. Aware of their importance, they take themselves too seriously, and the next poll is a disaster. Their views haven't ceased to be representative; rather, they are now expressing views that they think they ought to have instead of their real views.

There are things that can be done to encourage a misunderstanding of the sample. In Chapter 4 we saw the power of slanted language; two questions might have the same cognitive content, but, cloaked in very different language, might generate very different reactions. Jerry Falwell, leader of the ultraconservative Moral Majority, once took out a full-page advertisement asking readers to return their answers to several questions. One of the questions was this:

> Are you willing to trust the survival of America to a nuclear freeze agreement with Russia, a nation that rejects on-site inspection of military facilities to ensure compliance?

It is very hard to say "yes" to the question. But if 90 percent of the respondents said "no" and Falwell reported, say, that *90 percent of the sampled Americans oppose a nuclear freeze agreement with Russia*, it is likely that the premise would be false. Even if 90 percent *said* they opposed it, many would not have been expressing their true views.

At the same time, creative researchers often find ways of overcoming obstacles to understanding the sample. One study by a market research firm asked people to name their favorite magazine, knowing that they were likely to cite magazines that might impress the interviewer, such as *Harper's* or the *New Yorker.* The surveyors, out of gratitude for the interview, then offered each person a free copy of any magazine of the person's choice. The frequency with which they chose *People* and *TV Guide* was much higher than the frequency with which they admitted it was their favorite. You can imagine which data the researchers used as the basis of their report.

Because people's attitudes are easily hidden they are easy to misunderstand. Misunderstanding of samples is not necessarily limited, however, to people's attitudes. In principle, any sample can be misunderstood; but the more hidden the property, the greater the opportunity for misunderstanding. I am less likely to misunderstand if I am sampling the weather in my backyard or the number of autos on the freeway. But I may start to slip if I am sampling the weather in China or the number of microparticles in auto emissions on the freeway.

There is no special reason to think that a misunderstood sample is also a dirty sample. As you scrutinize the auto emissions through your microscope, dirt on the lens may lead you to misunderstand the sample and so to offer a false premise about it. But it is not a dirty sample—and thus not unrepresentative—until the dirt falls from the lens and into the microparticles.

Guideline. Be especially alert for ways in which the sample may have been misunderstood, thus producing a false premise. The more hidden the property, the greater the opportunity for misunderstanding.

EXERCISES Chapter 14, set (i)

For each of these passages, clarify the inductive generalization and then evaluate the truth of the premise, with a special view to whether and how the sample has been misunderstood.

Sample exercise. One study showed that, based on their own report, 80 percent of the population is above average in intelligence.

Sample answer.

1. Eighty percent of the sampled population is above average in intelligence.

∴ C. About 80 percent of the population is above average in intelligence.

The premise is probably false. (Not certainly, since we are not told the sampling process, and it is possible that the sampling was not random, but was done, say, at a reunion of college graduates.) If people are asked if they are above average in intelligence, they will usually say they are (and probably believe that they are) even if they are not. So there is no reason to accept the premise.

1. In the first 1972 Democratic presidential primaries, polls conducted by reputable organizations predicted that segregationist candidate George Wallace would receive about 20 percent of the votes. When the results came in, however, he consistently received around 40 percent.
2. According to her, the whole world is rosy. You'd expect her to think that, since she's always looking at it through rose-colored glasses.
3. A study by the fitness club study showed that 95 percent of its customers looked better after two months in its program. Subjects were asked to decide whether the customers looked better before or after

based on "before" and "after" photographs supplied by the fitness club. (Scrutiny of the photographs indicates that in the "after" pictures the lighting was better and the customer had on more makeup, better clothes, and a bigger smile.)

4. Two University of Texas at Austin sociologists, David A. Snow and Cynthia L. Phillips, tested 1,125 students to see whether they were primarily concerned with themselves or society—with "impulse" or "institution," as the researchers put it. Eighty percent saw themselves guided by their own "feeling, thought, and experience." Only 20 percent saw themselves guided by "institutionalized roles and statuses."—*Psychology Today*

COMPLEX ARGUMENTS

Complex arguments, as we have seen, are nothing more than chains of simple arguments. If you can clarify and evaluate simple ones, you can do the same for complex ones. There is one fairly common sort of chain, however, that includes an inductive generalization and is worth considering here.

Sometimes, especially in informal arguments, we move from a statement about a sampled portion of a population to a conclusion about another member of the same population. I might argue, for example, "Every Japanese car I've ever owned has been well-built, so that Nissan is probably well-built." Some would create a special category for such an argument; some logicians, for example, term it a *singular predictive inference*. Others might quite naturally take it to be an argument from analogy, in which *that Nissan* is argued to be analogous to *every Japanese car I've ever owned*. (See the next chapter for more detail on arguments from analogy.) But, as we saw briefly in Chapter 11, it is probably most useful to clarify it as a complex argument, made up of an inductive generalization followed by a singular categorical argument (or, in related cases, followed by a frequency argument). The clarification, then, would look something like this:

    1. All sampled Japanese cars are well-built.
∴ [2. All Japanese cars are well-built.]
   [3. That Nissan is a Japanese car.]
∴ *C*. That Nissan is well-built.

The inference to 2 is an inductive generalization, while the inference from 2 and 3 to *C* is a singular categorical argument.

Using reasoning of this sort, the FBI makes detailed profiles of criminals, interpreting evidence left at the scene in the light of their extensive records of similar crimes. In one sensational case a white female murder victim, naked and mutilated, was found in the Bronx. Agents at the FBI concluded that the killer was white, because in the overwhelming majority of mutilation murders, the killer is the same race as his victim. They further concluded that the murderer was in his mid-20s to early 30s, because the crime scene demonstrated a kind of methodical organization and such organization made an impulsive teenager or someone in his early 20s an unlikely suspect. An older man would likely have been jailed already, as the urge to commit brutal sex murders tends to surface at an early age, and the chances that a person could commit a number of such murders over a span of years without being captured would be slim. In this way, the FBI put together a detailed portrait of the killer and quickly found and convicted him.

This reasoning includes the sampling of hundreds of cases of mutilation murders; it also includes the application of that experience to a specific case. The following clarification captures one of the many similar complex arguments contained in the passage:

1. Almost all sampled mutilation murderers are the same race as their victims.

∴ 2. Almost all mutilation murderers are the same race as their victims.

3. The Bronx murderer is a mutilation murderer.

∴ *C.* The Bronx murderer is the same race as his victim.

It can now be evaluated in two parts—the first as an inductive generalization, the second as a frequency argument.

> *Guideline.* When an argument moves from a sample to a specific instance, clarify and evaluate it as an inductive generalization followed by a singular categorical argument or frequency argument.

EXERCISES Chapter 14, set (j)

For each of these passages, clarify and evaluate the complex argument.

Sample exercise. "'My name is McGlue, sir—William McGlue. I am a brother of the late Alexander McGlue. I picked up your paper this morning, and perceived in it an outrageous insult to my deceased relative, and I have come around to demand, sir, WHAT YOU MEAN by the following infamous language: "The death-angel smote Alexander McGlue, and gave him protracted repose; he wore a checked shirt and a number nine shoe, and he had a pink wart on his nose. No doubt he is happier dwelling in space over there on the evergreen shore. His friends are informed that his funeral takes place precisely at quarter-past-four."

"This is simply diabolical. My late brother had no wart on his nose, sir. He had upon his nose neither a pink wart nor a green wart, nor a cream-colored wart, nor a wart of any other color. It is a slander! It is a gratuitous insult to my family, and I distinctly want you to say what do you mean by such conduct?

"'. . . How could I know,' murmured Mr. Slimmer, '. . . that the corpse hadn't a pink wart? I used to know a man named McGlue and he had one, and I thought all McGlues had. This comes of irregularities in families.'"—Max Adeler, "The Obituary Poet"

Sample answer.

1. All sampled McGlues have pink warts on their noses.

∴ 2. All McGlues have pink warts on their noses.

3. Alexander McGlue is a McGlue.

∴ *C.* Alexander McGlue has a pink wart on his nose.

EVALUATION OF ARGUMENT TO 2

TRUTH

Premise 1 is probably true (in the story—given the silly nature of the story); no special reason to doubt Slimmer's report.

LOGIC

Extremely weak. Satisfies correct form condition for inductive generalization. But a sample of one is insufficient, since *having a pink wart on one's nose* is not an all-or-none property for families.

SOUNDNESS

Unsound due to weak logic.

EVALUATION OF ARGUMENT TO *C*

TRUTH

Premise 2 is certainly false; not only is it not supported by the argument provided, but the story gives evidence that Alexander is a counter example.

Premise 3 is probably true—given context of story—no reason to doubt it.

LOGIC
Valid singular categorical argument.
SOUNDNESS
Unsound due to falsity of premise 2.

1. A recent survey of 500 owners of golden retrievers indicated that 95 percent of them considered their dog to be well behaved with children. I think I'll get this golden retriever, then—since it should be good with my kids.
2. Two educational psychologists at Temple University analyzed the instructor evaluation ratings done by 5,878 students at Temple, matching the ratings with the grades that the students had predicted for themselves. They found that in most courses, evaluations seem to be based on a variety of factors that generally outweigh the matter of just getting a good grade—that teachers can't significantly affect their scores by leading students to believe that they will get good grades. So, your professor in this class shouldn't expect assurances of good grades to inflate your instructor evaluation.

EXERCISES Chapter 14, set (k)

Clarify and evaluate the following arguments.

1. Most teenage girls now aspire to professional occupations, such as doctor or lawyer, according to a report by Helen Farmer, a psychologist at the University of Illinois. Farmer queried 1,234 9th and 12th graders from nine Illinois schools. By way of contrast, less than half of the boys had similar aspirations.—Associated Press.
2. Video arcades are dominated by teenage boys. We counted 200 people playing the games across two Saturdays in the video arcade at our local mall, and only 25 of them were girls—often just watching their boyfriends. (Take *video arcades* as the population.)
3. "I'm grateful that CBS still carries the 'Bugs Bunny/Road Runner' show, that collection of Warner Bros. animated classics. The only catch is that occasional bits of cartoon 'violence' have been trimmed away by the network. This strikes me as unnecessary and downright silly. After all, I watched these cartoons without cuts when I was a kid, and I turned out fine. Or at least OK."—*TV Guide*
4. "I watched 'The MacNeil-Lehrer News Hour' one night last week and I watched the 'ABC Evening News' an hour later. With about 28.5

minutes more than the 21 actually delivered by ABC, PBS did an inferior job. I know that ABC's commercials reap a good deal more cash from the network's news operation in a month than the alms givers contribute to PBS stations in a year. But I also know that thorough reportage and editing costs no more than sloppy work. The network product is much better, and that's not what the beggars are claiming." (Take *PBS newscasts* as the population.)—George Higgins, *Wall Street Journal*

5. Yankelovich Clancy Shulman, a market research company based in Westport, Conn., asked 2,500 consumers whether they agreed or disagreed with the statement: "I feel somewhat guilty when buying non-American made products generally." The figure was 51 percent, with a margin of error of 2 percentage points. "Something in the back of Americans' heads is saying that they do or ought to feel guilty," said Susan Hayward, senior vice president of Yankelovich.—*Washington Post*
6. I confess in advance that I saw only a few gusts-worth of "The Winds of War. Not the least amazing thing about the series is that so many had so many evenings free to give it. It is absolutely true that I am, metaphorically speaking, judging the roll by the caraway seed, but caraway seeds aren't nothing. It seemed to me on brief acquaintance that the acting, to put it in a kindly way, was serviceable rather than inspired.—Charles Champlin, *Los Angeles Times*

SUMMARY OF CHAPTER FOURTEEN

Inductive generalizations are typically represented as arguments with a single premise, in which both the premise and the conclusion are frequency statements. When an argument satisfies the correct form condition for an inductive generalization, the premise states that a *sampled portion* of a population has a certain property with a certain frequency, while the conclusion says that the *entire* population has the same property with the same frequency. Thus, these arguments *generalize* from a sample to a whole. In addition, the conclusion typically allows for a margin of error; this makes the argument logically stronger by making it more probable that the conclusion is true. Large margins of error, though logically helpful, can undermine the practical value of the argument.

The total evidence condition is usually a matter of whether the sample is representative of the population as a whole. Testing for representativeness requires asking two questions. The first question is whether the sample is large enough.

As a rough-and-ready rule of thumb, samples should be made up of either one or 1,000 members of the population, regardless of the size of the population itself. A sample of one is enough if the property in question is an all-or-none sort of property. Otherwise, a random sample of 1,000 is typically enough, assuming a margin of error of 3 percent is satisfactory; a larger random sample is required for a smaller margin of error, while a smaller sample requires a larger margin of error. Samples set up in this way can result in arguments with very strong inductive logic; their confidence level is .95, simply meaning that the premises support the conclusion with a .95 level of probability.

The second question is whether the sample is randomly selected. For the practical purposes of this text, this means that every member of the population has had an equal opportunity to be included in the sample, so that exactly the relevant variations of the population might be proportionately represented. If there is no obvious problem with the sample and it is the result of research by a reputable organization, then that may be enough to support the judgment that the sample is randomly selected. There can be many easy-to-detect flaws with samples, however, including grab sampling, snowball sampling, self-selected sampling, and dirty sampling.

Inductive generalizations that are logically strong may nevertheless have false premises. A special problem for such arguments is the misunderstanding of samples; the more hidden the property, the easier it is to misunderstand the sample.

Samples are sometimes used as the basis for conclusions about unsampled single members of the population, without any specific mention of an intermediate general subconclusion. These arguments are best taken as complex enthymemes, made up of an inductive generalization followed by a singular categorical argument or frequency argument.

GUIDELINES FOR CHAPTER FOURTEEN

- Structure an inductive generalization, when it would be loyal to do so, so that the conclusion drops the term *sampled* and adds a margin of error.
- In the premise of an inductive generalization, translate stylistic variations into the logical constant *sampled.*
- When the principle of loyalty allows, paraphrase inductive generalizations so as to include a non-zero margin of error in the conclusion.
- In considering whether an inductive generalization has satisfied the total evidence condition, first ask, *Is the sample large enough?*

- If the property is likely to be all-or-none, then a sample of one is typically enough. It is almost certainly not an all-or-none property if there has been an effort to scientifically construct the sample.
- For properties that are not all-or-none, if the margin of error increases appropriately as the sample size decreases, then the logical strength of the argument remains steady.
- When the population is large, variation in population size has no bearing on the size of the random sample that is needed, although it may have a bearing on how easy it is to get a random sample.
- Judge as *very strong* the logic of any inductive generalization that renders its conclusion .95 probable.
- Do not judge an inductive generalization to be strong unless its sample is randomly selected—that is, unless the sample includes the relevant variations in the appropriate frequency. Remember that not all variations are relevant.
- Be alert for ways in which an argument may fail to include a relevant variation in its sample. Typically, arguments that depend on grab sampling, snowball sampling, self-selected sampling, or dirty sampling do not have randomly selected samples and are thus logically very weak (and, thus, unsound).
- Be especially alert for ways in which the sample might have been misunderstood, thus producing a false premise. The more hidden the property, the greater the opportunity for misunderstanding.
- When an argument moves from a sample to a specific instance, clarify and evaluate it as an inductive generalization followed by a singular categorical argument or frequency argument.

GLOSSARY FOR CHAPTER FOURTEEN

Confidence level—the logical strength of the argument; the frequency with which the conclusion would be true if the premise(s) were true.

Dirty sampling—the contamination—usually unintentional—of a sample by the sampling process itself. This is a failure of randomness. In a randomly selected sample, exactly the relevant variations of the population are proportionately represented. Introducing contamination is introducing a relevant variation that is not in the population.

Fallacy of hasty generalization—the mistake of arguing from a sample that is not representative—that is not large enough or randomly selected. It is normally more illuminating if you avoid this term and focus your evaluation on the more specific mistakes made by the argument.

Grab sampling—the process of including in your sample whatever members of the population happen to come your way. This is a failure of randomness.

Inductive generalization—argument that draws general conclusions about an entire population from samples taken of members of the population. Form is:

1. *n* of sampled *F* are *G*. (Where n is *any* frequency, including 0 and 1.)

∴ *C*. *n* (+ or − *m*) of *F* are *G*.

Margin of error—in the conclusion to an inductive generalization, the range of frequencies within which the property is stated to occur. Also called the confidence interval.

Misunderstood sample—when the method used for collecting information about the sample is not entirely reliable it results in a misunderstanding of the sample's properties, rendering the premise false. The more hidden the property (people's attitudes, for example, are easily hidden), the more likely the misunderstanding.

Random selection—the process of selecting a sample such that every member of the population has had an equal opportunity to be included, so that exactly the relevant variations of the population might be proportionately represented.

Self-selected sampling—when members of the population decide for themselves whether to be included in the sample. This is a failure of randomness.

Snowball sampling—the process of adding new members to the sample on the basis of their close relationship with those already included (thus gathering members in the same way that a snowball gathers snow as it rolls along). This is a failure of randomness.

Stratification—the construction of a random sample, for practical purposes, by identifying groups within the population that tend to be relatively uniform and including strata, or groups, of the sample in numbers that proportionally represent their membership in the entire population.

CHAPTER FIFTEEN

Arguments from Analogy

Arguments that make their point by means of similarities are impostors, and, unless you are on your guard against them, will quite readily deceive you.

—Plato

Analogies decide nothing, that is true, but they can make one feel more at home.

—Sigmund Freud, *New Introductory Lectures on Psychoanalysis*

TOPICS

Arguments from analogy declare that because two items are the same in one respect they are the same in another. As Freud notes, they can make you feel at home—and for that reason they can be especially persuasive.

During World War I, the Socialist Party distributed leaflets to recent draftees, urging them to oppose the draft. The draft, they contended, violated the constitutional amendment against involuntary servitude. Oliver Wendell Holmes, chief justice of the Supreme Court, argued that they did not have the right to circulate the leaflets during wartime. The right to free speech, he asserted, "would not protect a man in falsely shouting fire in a theater and causing a panic." Since in both cases "the words used . . . create a clear and present danger," he concluded, the right to free speech did not protect the Socialists in expressing ideas that might harm the war effort. The argument begins with something familiar—of course we don't have the right to falsely shout fire in a theater—and invites us to conclude the same about something less familiar—under certain circumstances we don't even have the right to explain to others our interpretation of the U.S. Constitution. (Holmes is often quoted as calling it "a crowded theater." He didn't, though it is probably what he had in mind.)

Arguments from analogy are almost always enticing because, by their very nature, they use two of the quick-and-dirty shortcuts in reasoning described in Chapter 1. By beginning with the familiar, they exploit our dependence on the vividness shortcut; and by presenting similarities between the familiar and the unfamiliar, they take advantage of our dependence on the similarity shortcut. They are custom-made for the way our minds naturally operate. This makes us especially susceptible to them and heightens the importance of being able to evaluate them effectively.

CORRECT FORM FOR ARGUMENTS FROM ANALOGY

Analogies are often used merely for rhetorical effect. Acel Moore of the *Philadelphia Inquirer*, for example, writes: "Writing editorials is a lot like wearing a navy blue suit and standing in a rainstorm on a cold day and wetting your pants; it may give you a warm feeling for a minute, but no one else is going to notice." Moore doesn't attempt to establish any conclusion based on the similarity—he simply makes note of it. Don't jump to the conclusion that an analogy introduces an argument unless there really is—at least implicitly—a conclusion.

When there is an ***argument from analogy,*** as in the preceding free speech argument, it can typically be clarified according to the following form:

1. *A* is *F* and *G*.
2. *B* is *F*.

∴ *C*. *B* is *G*.

A and *B*, as always, are used here as name letters. They name the two ***analogs***[1]—that is, the two things (or classes of things) that are said to be analogous. *A*, the ***basic analog,*** is the one that we are presumed to be more familiar with; in the free speech argument it is *falsely shouting fire in a theater.* *B*, the ***inferred analog,*** is the thing in question, the one that the argument draws a conclusion about; in the free speech argument it is *expressing ideas that might harm the war effort.*

We will continue to use *F* and *G* as property letters. *F* is the ***basic similarity,*** the property that the two analogs share, presumably without controversy. In the free speech argument, the basic similarity is that they *create a clear and present danger.* And *G* is the ***inferred similarity,*** the property that the inferred analog is purported to have on the grounds that the basic analog has it. *Is not protected by the right to free speech* is the inferred similarity in the free speech argument. Here is one good way to clarify the argument:

1. Falsely shouting fire in a theater creates a clear and present danger and is not protected by the right to free speech.
2. Expressing ideas that might harm the war effort creates a clear and present danger.

∴ *C*. Expressing ideas that might harm the war effort is not protected by the right to free speech.

Variations on this model are common. The basic or inferred analog, for example, will sometimes include more than one item, as in this example:

> Manatees must be mammals, since whales and dolphins, like manatees, are sea creatures that give live birth, and whales and dolphins are definitely mammals.

In this case, the basic analog—the content of *A*—is *whales and dolphins.*

[1]The British usually spell it *analogue*. Historically, the term was *analogon*.

Likewise, either the basic similarity or the inferred similarity may include more than one property, as in this example:

> Manatees must be mammals, since whales, like manatees, are sea creatures that give live birth and that nourish their young on the mother's milk, and whales are definitely mammals.

In this example, the basic similarity—the content of *F*—is *sea creatures that give live birth and nourish their young on the mother's milk.*

Correct Form for Arguments from Analogy

1. *A* is *F* and *G*.
2. *B* is *F*.

∴ C. *B* is *G*.

Clarifying an argument from analogy is usually a straightforward matter. It is easiest to begin by identifying the analogs—the two items that the arguer is comparing; insert the one that is not in question into the *A* position as the basic analog, and the one that is in question into the *B* position, as the inferred analog. Then insert the basic similarity—the property the two analogs uncontroversially share—into both premises as *F.* Finally, insert the inferred similarity into the first premise and the conclusion, as *G*.

Arguments from analogy are sometimes enthymemes. When there is an implicit statement, it is usually the second premise, the one that establishes the basic similarity. This is because arguers often assume, rightly, that the similarity between two analogs is so obvious that it goes without saying. Suppose I say to a friend of mine, whose son is about to enter first grade, "Since John behaves respectfully towards his parents, he will surely treat his teachers with respect." The basic analog is *John's parents*, the inferred analog is *John's teachers*, and the inferred similarity is *are treated with respect by John*. But what is the basic similarity? We must identify a relevant trait that parents and teachers have in common, namely, that they are *authority figures to John*. Here is the clarified argument. (Brackets, as usual, indicate that premise 2 is implicit, but we also must supply to premise 1 the part about authority figures.)

1. John's parents are authority figures to him and are treated with respect by him.
[2. John's teachers will be authority figures to him.]
∴ *C.* John's teachers will be treated with respect by him.

Guideline. Structure arguments from analogy, when it would be loyal to do so, by identifying four things—the basic and inferred analogs and the basic and inferred similarities— then inserting each into its proper place in the form. Remember that the second premise, which declares the inferred similarity, is often implicit.

EXERCISES Chapter 15, set (a)

For each of these arguments from analogy, identify the basic analog, the inferred analog, the basic similarity, and the inferred similarity. Then clarify it in standard clarifying format.

Sample exercise. "Expressions of shock and sadness came from other coaches and administrators following the announcement by Tulane President Eamon Kelly that the school planned to drop its basketball program in the wake of the alleged gambling scheme and newly discovered NCAA violations. Coach Jim Killingsworth of TCU said: 'I think they should deal with the problem, not do away with it. If they had something like that happen in the English department, would they do away with that? I feel like they should have tried to solve their problems.'" —Associated Press

Sample answer. Basic analog: English department. Inferred analog: basketball program. Basic similarity: is a college program (implicit). Inferred similarity: should not be eliminated if experiencing problems.

1. The English department is a college program and should not be eliminated if it is experiencing problems.
[2. The basketball program is a college program.]
∴ *C.* The basketball program should not be eliminated if it is experiencing problems.

1. In a good marriage, partners often seek counseling to help them resolve their difficulties. You're having trouble with your boss—why

should a conflict in an employer–employee relationship be treated any differently?

2. So you got tickets to the Metropolitan Opera's production of the "Flying Dutchman"? You should try to smuggle in a flashlight and a good book. I made the mistake of going to Wagner's "Parsifal"—that night was one of the most boring years of my life.
3. Etiquette arbiter Emily Post contended that men need not remove their hats in elevators when there are women present. She reasoned that an elevator is a means of transportation, just like a streetcar, bus, subway, or train. The only difference is that an elevator travels vertically, rather than horizontally. A man is not expected to remove his hat in other vehicles, so there is no need for him to do so in an elevator.
4. View expressed in a mid-20th century article by a professional sociologist: One attribute with which women are naturally and uniquely gifted is the care of children. Since the ill and infirm resemble children in many ways, being not merely physically weak and helpless but also psychologically dependent, it is fairly easy to conclude that women are also especially qualified to care for the sick.
5. "Suppose you had a son, a fine writer who had brought national recognition for his college newspaper and a scholarship for himself. Suppose that, in his junior year, a big-city newspaper offered him a reporter's job with a three-year guarantee at an unheard-of salary. Would you advise him to turn down the offer of a professional newspaper job? We know the answer. And we would not think twice before urging him, *begging* him, to hire on with the newspaper. After all, we'd say, the reason he was in college was to start to prepare himself for a decent career in the field of his choosing. So, why all the fulmination about a star athlete's taking the chance to make himself a cool $5 million by doing for pay what he's been doing for free (presumably) for three years?" —William Raspberry, *Los Angeles Times*
6. "We feel instinctive sympathy for the defendant who pleads, 'I tried to get a job and nobody would hire me. Only in desperation did I turn to robbery.' Now consider the logically parallel defense: 'I tried to seduce a woman legitimately and nobody would sleep with me. Only in desperation did I turn to rape.' Nobody would buy that from a rapist, and nobody should buy it from a robber." —Steven Landsburg, *Forbes*

THE TOTAL EVIDENCE CONDITION (1): RELEVANT SIMILARITIES

If an argument from analogy can be loyally paraphrased in the form described above, then it satisfies the correct form condition. But for an inductive argument to be logically strong it must not only satisfy the correct form condition; it must also satisfy the total evidence condition. As with frequency arguments and inductive generalizations, there are two parts to the total evidence condition for arguments from analogy: the basic similarity must be relevant, and any dissimilarities must be irrelevant. If an argument does poorly on either one of these conditions, it should be judged no better than logically weak.

Although analogical arguments are sometimes accused of committing the ***fallacy of false analogy*** (or the *fallacy of faulty analogy*), this fallacy is very much like the fallacy of hasty generalization. The existence of the named fallacy highlights the ease with which we can make mistakes in this sort of reasoning. But to accuse an argument from analogy of committing this fallacy says nothing about what has gone wrong with the argument. It is far better to explain more specifically how it is that some necessary condition for soundness has not been satisfied.

Total Evidence Condition for Arguments from Analogy

1. *The basic similarity must be relevant*—it must count in favor of the inferred similarity.
2. *The dissimilarities must be irrelevant*—any dissimilarity between the two analogs must not make the basic analog a better candidate for the inferred property.

The argument is logically weaker to the extent that it fails in either area.

The Relevance of the Basic Similarity

Begin your deliberations about the total evidence question by asking, *Is the basic similarity relevant?* The more relevant it is, the stronger the logic of the argument might be. When you consider this question, forget about the two analogs and simply consider *to what extent the basic similarity counts in favor of the inferred similarity.* A television advertising campaign by a dairy company shows old but cheerful citizens of the Republic of Georgia eating yogurt; they have eaten yogurt all their lives, we are told, and they are now well past the century mark—one woman is now 134! Eating yogurt, we are encouraged to believe, could do the same for us. The first step in evaluating how well this argument satisfies the total evidence condition is to ignore the two analogs (citizens of Georgia and us) and ask whether the basic similarity—eating yogurt—counts in favor of the inferred similarity—a long life. There is no special reason to think so, and the argument doesn't help by providing one. So the logic of the argument is very weak.

More commonly an argument from analogy satisfies the condition at least to some degree. One large state university published the following story in its alumni magazine:

> A preliminary appraisal of the results of a major assessment of faculty and graduate programs conducted by the Conference Board of Associated Research Councils placed our institution second in the nation among public research universities and in the top five overall. "It is gratifying to see our faculty receive this national recognition of their superior research and teaching," said the Chancellor. Even though the study focused on graduate programs, he pointed out that the results could also be applied to the undergraduate program as well, since the two programs share the same faculty.

The university's graduate program is the basic analog and its undergraduate program the inferred analog. The basic similarity is that the university's excellent faculty staffs them. And the inferred similarity is that the academic programs are excellent. Is the basic similarity relevant? That is, does having an excellent faculty count toward the excellent academic programs? Of course it does. So this argument easily clears the first hurdle of the total evidence condition. But it is too soon to conclude that the argument is logically strong; there is still a second total evidence hurdle to clear.

> *Guideline.* In considering whether an argument from analogy has satisfied the total evidence condition, first ask, *Is the basic similarity relevant?* To answer this question, look at the extent to which the basic similarity counts in favor of the inferred similarity.

Relevant Similarities and the Fallacy of Equivocation

Suppose I say, "Einstein was smart, and he was able to revolutionize physics. The physics teacher I had in high school is smart, too, so he should be able to revolutionize physics." The basic similarity is relevant to the inferred similarity—smart is better than stupid when it comes to revolutionizing physics. But there is smart, and then there is smart. Surely my high school physics teacher is not as smart as Einstein. Doesn't that weaken the argument? Let's clarify it and see:

1. Einstein was *smart* and was able to revolutionize physics.
2. My high school physics teacher is *smart*.

∴ C. My high school physics teacher is able to revolutionize physics.

Smart shows up in both premises. To ask whether my high school physics teacher is as smart as Einstein is to ask, in effect, whether the word means the same thing in each case. It is a *general* expression. Recalling our coverage of generality in Chapter 5, this means that it is an expression that allows for degrees (examples were *fine*, *bald*, *brown*, *living together*, *incompatible*, *wrong*, and *evil*). As we saw, generality is usually unproblematic. It becomes problematic, however, when the meaning of the expression shifts from one use to the next, and when the apparent success of the argument depends on that shift. In that case, the argument commits the fallacy of equivocation; the lesson from Chapter 5 is to eliminate the ambiguity.

Let's eliminate the ambiguity by using the reasonable-premises approach in revising premise 2; in that case it is as follows:

2. My high school physics teacher *is smart, though not as smart as Einstein.*

While this is probably true, we now have a major problem with the logic of the argument—namely, it no longer satisfies the correct form condition, since the basic similarity, established in premise 1, is not asserted in premise 2. (The form is now something like this: 1. A is F and G; 2. B is sort of like F; ∴ C. B is G.) Let's try revising it again, this time using the reasonable-logic approach. This gives us the following:

2. My high school physics teacher is *just as smart as Einstein.*

This nicely fixes the logical problem, but at the cost of what is pretty obviously a false premise. Either way, the argument is unsound.

The Oliver Wendell Holmes free speech argument, presented at the beginning of the chapter, provides a weightier example of the same problem. The basic similarity, *creating a clear and present danger,* certainly counts in favor of the inferred similarity of *not being protected by the right to free speech.* But is the danger caused by the wartime expression of potentially subversive ideas *as* clear and *as* present as the danger caused by the false shout of fire in a theater? If not, doesn't this weaken the argument? Let's take another look at Holmes's clarified argument.

1. Falsely shouting fire in a theater creates *a clear and present danger* and is not protected by the right to free speech.
2. Expressing ideas that might harm the war effort creates *a clear and present danger.*

∴ *C.* Expressing ideas that might harm the war effort is not protected by the right to free speech.

The phrase *clear and present danger,* like the term *smart* in the Einstein example, is a general term that seems to apply to a greater degree in premise 1 than in premise 2. It is plausible to suppose that this shift contributes to the apparent success of the argument, and thus that the argument commits the fallacy of equivocation. So we should revise our paraphrase of premise 2 to eliminate the ambiguity. On the one hand, we could paraphrase it to say that those who scattered the leaflets created *a clear and present danger, though less clear and present than falsely shouting fire in a theater.* The premise would probably be true, but we would have created the same logical difficulty described in the Einstein argument—the basic similarity is not the same in each premise. On the other hand, we could paraphrase it to say that they created *a clear and present danger that is just as clear and present as falsely shouting fire in a theater.* We have now satisfied the correct form condition but probably have a false premise.

The problem is one to look for whenever you are clarifying an argument from analogy.

Guideline. When the basic similarity is described by a general term, consider whether its meaning shifts from one use to the next. If it shifts enough to affect the soundness of the argument, revise your clarification to eliminate the ambiguity.

EXERCISES Chapter 15, set (b)

For each of the arguments in set (a), answer whether the basic similarity is relevant.

Sample exercise. See sample in set (a).

Sample answer. The basic similarity (that something is a college program) has some relevance to the inferred similarity (that it shouldn't be eliminated if it is experiencing problems), but only to a limited extent. It is relevant only insofar as there is some weak presumption in any sort of institution that a program that has been set up was set up for a good reason.

THE TOTAL EVIDENCE CONDITION (2): IRRELEVANT DISSIMILARITIES

The Irrelevance of the Dissimilarities

The second total evidence question is *Are there relevant dissimilarities?* Preferably they are irrelevant, for the more relevant the dissimilarities, the weaker the logic of the argument. When you consider this question, forget about the basic similarity and concentrate on the two analogs. There are always innumerable ways in which they are dissimilar, but most or all of them will be irrelevant. What matters is *to what extent any dissimilarity makes the basic analog a better candidate for the inferred property.*

Consider, for example, the free speech argument. There are many dissimilarities. One of the activities happens in a theater, for example, while the other could happen anywhere; but this is irrelevant, since there is no reason to think that things said in a theater are less deserving of protection by the right to free speech than things said anywhere else. Or, for example, one of them is spoken aloud, while the other could be written down; but again, this is irrelevant, for there is no general reason to think that the spoken word is more worthy of free speech protection than the written word.

Some of the dissimilarities, however, are relevant. In the theater case, what is expressed is intentionally deceptive, while in the leaflet case, what is expressed seems to have been utterly sincere. This, taken by itself, certainly makes the theater case a better candidate for exemption from free speech protection, and thus it counts as a relevant dissimilarity. Furthermore, in the theater case, the action is sure to have a harmful result; but in the leaflet case, there is no assurance that anyone will pay any attention or, if they do, that they will be influenced (in fact, it was established that no one had been persuaded by the leaflet). This, too, makes the theater case a better candidate for lack of protection by the right to free speech.

In short, even if we forget that the phrase *clear and present danger* may be equivocal, the argument does not score well on the second portion of the total evidence condition. Its logic can be judged, at best, as fairly weak. Brilliant jurist that he was, I should note that Oliver Wendell Holmes relied, as he should have, on a good deal more than just this argument in support of his conclusion.

Let's now return to the academic excellence argument. Here is the clarification:

1. The university's graduate program is staffed by the university's faculty and is academically excellent.
2. The university's undergraduate program is staffed by the university's faculty.

∴ *C.* The university's undergraduate program is academically excellent.

There are many dissimilarities between the graduate and undergraduate programs of any large state university. Graduate courses, for example, are usually assigned higher catalog numbers than are undergraduate courses. But this is irrelevant; catalog numbers are not like scores flashed by Olympic judges, with higher numbers going to better courses. Another difference is that in large state universities the graduate students tend to have much more exposure to the faculty than do the undergraduate students—their classes are much smaller and are more frequently taught by the regular faculty members. This is relevant, since student exposure to faculty can contribute powerfully to academic excellence. The conclusion may still be true. But even though this argument does well on the first condition, it performs badly on the second and so its logic must be considered weak.

Guideline. In considering whether an argument from analogy has satisfied the total evidence condition, ask next, *Are any of the dissimilarities relevant?* To answer this question, look at the extent to which any dissimilarity makes the basic analog a better candidate than the inferred analog for the inferred property.

EXERCISES Chapter 15, set (c)

For each of the arguments in set (a), do three things: (*i*) state an irrelevant dissimilarity, and explain, (*ii*) explain any relevant dissimilarities, and (*iii*) state your evaluation of the argument's logic based on this and the previous exercise.

Sample exercise. See sample in set (a).

Sample answer. (*i*) The basketball program probably has a higher proportion of students on full scholarship than does the English department. This doesn't seem relevant, since it doesn't make English a better candidate for preservation in the face of difficulties. (*ii*) The most important dissimilarity is that the English department is not only an academic program, but also one that is central to the mission of the institution, while the basketball program is an athletic program and thus more peripheral to its mission. This means there is a far stronger impetus to work out English department difficulties before disbanding it. (*iii*) Though the argument is OK on the first part of the total evidence condition, it fails the second part and is logically very weak.

THE SPECIAL CHARACTER OF ARGUMENTS FROM ANALOGY

Arguments from Analogy as Logical Borrowers

As you may have noticed, every example of an argument from analogy worked out in this chapter has been declared logically weak and thus unsound. This is not an aberration. Although not all arguments from analogy are unsound, they do establish their conclusions far less often than any other sort of argument. Plato, in the lead quotation for this chapter, calls them "impostors." Analogical arguments, unlike any other arguments we look at in this book, have a built-in logical shortcoming.

Let's take another look at the logical form of arguments from analogy:

1. *A* (basic analog) is *F* (basic similarity) and *G* (inferred similarity).
2. *B* (inferred analog) is *F* (basic similarity).

∴ C. *B* (inferred analog) is *G* (inferred similarity).

What is the source of logical strength for such an argument? Not the correct form condition; as with every other inductive argument, satisfying this condition merely qualifies the argument for any strength that might be conferred by the total evidence condition. Not the second part of the total evidence condition; the absence of relevant dissimilarities simply means there is no evidence to undermine whatever strength it has.[2] This leaves the first part of the total evidence condition as the sole positive source of logical strength.

How does the first part of the total evidence condition provide logical strength? By virtue of the fact that the *basic similarity counts in favor of the inferred similarity*. But what does *count in favor of* mean here? The only meaning I know is *a sound argument can be offered for it*. So we can now see that logically strong analogical arguments derive their logical strength from another argument—the argument that can be offered from the inferred similarity to the basic similarity. We will call such an argument (an argument from *F* to *G*—see premise 1 of the form clarified above) a ***background argument.*** Stated simply: an analogical argument's only logical strength is borrowed from a background argument.

Any other sort of argument can, in principle, lend its strength to an argument from analogy. For example, in the preceding chapter we looked briefly at the argument *Every Japanese car I've ever owned has been well built, so that Nissan is probably well built*. It could easily be clarified as an argument from analogy, clarified as follows:

1. Every Japanese car I've ever owned has been a Japanese car and has been well built.

[2. That Nissan is a Japanese car.]

∴ *C*. That Nissan is well built.

If the similarity is relevant in this case, it is because the background argument is a logically strong inductive generalization that goes from my experience of Japanese cars (the basic similarity) to the conclusion that Japanese cars in general are well built (the inferred similarity). The argument from analogy is logical only if this generalization works. So it borrows its logical strength from an inductive generalization.

The next passage, from *Science News*, provides a second example of borrowed logic in an argument from analogy.

[2]The second part of the total evidence condition for frequency arguments operates the same way.

> The concept of "vintage year" took on a new meaning this week when two scientists presented the first chemical evidence that wine existed as far back as about 3500 BC. They had noticed a red stain while piecing together jars excavated from an Iranian site. They compared the stain with a similar stain in an ancient Egyptian vessel known to have contained wine. The researchers scraped the reddish residue from the jars and analyzed the samples with infrared spectroscopy. Residues from the Iranian and Egyptian jars looked alike and were full of tartaric acid, a chemical naturally abundant only in grapes. "Those crystals are a signature for wine," says one researcher.

The argument can be clarified thus:

1. The Egyptian jar had a certain red stain and contained wine.
2. The Iranian jar had the same red stain.

∴ *C.* That Iranian jar contained wine.

In this case, if the similarity is relevant it is because the background argument is a sound explanatory argument (of a sort we will cover thoroughly in the next chapter) that establishes that the red stains (the basic similarity) have properties that are best explained as caused by wine (the inferred similarity). This argument's logical strength is borrowed from an explanatory argument.

As a final example, arguments from analogy can even borrow their logical strength from deductive arguments. Consider the validity counterexamples of Chapter 10. In that chapter we started with an inverted—and invalid—Socrates argument:

1. All men are mortal.
2. Socrates is mortal.

∴ *C.* Socrates is a man.

We then offered as a validity counterexample this obviously invalid (because of true premises and false conclusion) Atlantic argument:

1. All ponds are bodies of water.
2. The Atlantic Ocean is a body of water.

∴ *C.* The Atlantic Ocean is a pond.

In this way we saw that the Socrates argument was invalid. Like any validity counterexample, the reasoning can be represented as an argument from analogy, clarified as follows:

1. The Atlantic argument has a certain form and is invalid.
2. The Socrates argument has the same form.

∴ *C.* The Socrates argument is invalid.

Here the relevance of the similarity depends on a deductive background argument; for the way to argue that a certain form (the basic similarity) is invalid (the inferred similarity) is by use of this valid affirming the antecedent argument, which has a self-evidently true first premise:

1. If the form of an argument is such that it is possible for the premises to be true and the conclusion false, then the argument is invalid.
2. This particular form is such that it is possible for the premises to be true and the conclusion false.

∴ *C.* The argument is invalid.

In this case, the logical strength of the analogical argument is borrowed from a sound deduction.

By its very nature, then, when an analogical argument works it works on borrowed logic. The two analogs mainly serve to get in the way by providing a basis for relevant dissimilarities. It is the background argument, which ignores the analogs and is concerned solely with the basic and inferred similarities, that serves as the argument's motor. In the end, the background argument cannot itself be some other argument from analogy, since the background argument would depend on a background argument (and so on).

There are two practical lessons here. First, if you can see what the background argument is, bring it to the foreground when you clarify the argument, abandoning the analogical form. The Nissan argument, for example, would be much easier to evaluate properly if clarified as a complex argument composed of an inductive generalization and a frequency argument (as illustrated in Chapter 14); and the Iranian jar argument, likewise, if paraphrased as an explanatory argument. Second, if you cannot see what the background argument is, you should normally resist the temptation to judge it as logically strong until you better understand the background argument. As noted at the beginning of the chapter, analogical arguments are custom-made for the way our minds work, which makes them extraordinarily persuasive. But their inherent reliance on logical borrowing also makes them very good at concealing logical defects. When a persuasive car salesman won't let you open the hood to inspect the motor, it may be prudent to shop elsewhere.

Guideline. When you can clearly see the background argument, clarify it rather than the argument from analogy. When you cannot see the background argument, you should normally reserve final judgment about the strength of the argument's logic.

Arguments from Analogy as Psychological Lenders

From a logical point of view, analogical arguments are borrowers. But from a psychological point of view, they often put other arguments deeply into their debt. They can hint as well as hide.

Look, for example, at the Iranian jar argument. The analogy between the two stains is what suggested to the researchers that the jar had once contained wine. This set in motion a research effort in which samples scraped from both jars were examined by infrared spectroscopy, revealing crystals that were "a signature for wine." One *could* perhaps say that this new evidence converts the initial analogical argument from a merely suggestive one into a logically strong one, by showing just how relevant the basic similarity (same red stain) is to the inferred similarity (that it contained wine). But it would be much clearer to simply say that the background argument *displaces* the argument from analogy. Analogical reasoning has *lent* a powerful psychological boost to the research program by producing the suggestive idea. Still, any logical strength it gains from that research program is borrowed from the background argument—that is, from the explanatory argument about crystals developed by the researchers. Clarity is increased if the initial analogy drops out of any account of the logical support for the conclusion—as long as it remains as a central feature of the history of the discovery.[3]

Analogical arguments can lend a valuable psychological boost to inquiry of every sort. Consider the free speech argument. Even if you are not persuaded by the proposed analogy between shouting fire and distributing leaflets, it is certainly suggestive. In particular, it suggests that you are wrong if you think that all expressions are protected. Further, it suggests a way of reasoning about which ones are not protected—namely, by thinking

[3]To use terminology mentioned elsewhere in the text, it is important in the context of discovery, but not in the context of justification.

about the possible dangers caused by the speech in question. If that way of reasoning succeeds, the argument from analogy gets psychological credit for suggesting it, even if it gets no logical credit for supporting it.

Nineteenth-century philosopher John Stuart Mill aptly declared that good reasoners will consider any analogical argument as a "guidepost, pointing out the direction in which more rigorous investigations should be prosecuted." Arguments from analogy brilliantly serve a necessary function in reasoning. We would be lost without good guideposts. But we should not confuse them with destinations.

EXERCISES Chapter 15, set (d)

Fully clarify and evaluate each of the arguments from analogy. In cases where you can see the background argument, you may clarify and evaluate either the analogical argument or the background argument.

1. I've only seen one Hitchcock movie—*Psycho*. It was scary. Let's try *The Birds*. I bet it will be scary too.
2. To solve our drug problems, instead of outlawing drugs we must make them as safe and risk-free and—yes—as healthy as possible. It's like sex. We recognize that people will continue to have sex for nonreproductive reasons, whatever the laws, and with that in mind we try to make sexual practices as safe as possible in order to minimize the spread of the AIDS virus.
3. *Question* (investigator, to a university president): "Your administration will undertake reviews or investigations of members of your faculty without their being informed of the fact?"

   A: "I believe it's very possible. I believe it happened in this case."

   Q: "Do you consider that proper and appropriate?"

   A: "Personal opinion? Yes."

   Q: "Can you tell me why?"

   A: "I don't know. Why not? I guess in an analogy, I don't think J. Edgar Hoover, for example, ever advised everybody he was investigating that they were being investigated."

   Q: "But he, J. Edgar Hoover, wasn't running a university."—*Lingua Franca*

4. Breceda and lifeguards up and down the beach stressed the dangers of sleeping on the beach at night. "The people who get hurt are pretty much innocent," Breceda said. "They take a walk on the beach at Puerto Vallarta at 3 A.M. and nothing happens, and so they assume it's OK to do it here. But a whole different situation occurs here." In addition to the dangers posed by muggers and rapists, people sleeping on the beach also could get run over by sweepers. —*Los Angeles Times* (Consider the argument attributed to the people who sleep on the beach.)
5. "*Question:* Surely society has a right to rid itself of a man like Ted Bundy? *Answer*: My main opposition to the death penalty is what it does to society. Our society kills people in cages. It is like going hunting in a zoo. In the cage they are not dangerous, but executing them is very dangerous—for us." —I. Gray and M. Stanley, eds., *A Punishment in Search of a Crime: Americans Speak Out Against the Death Penalty*
6. "At their August 1945 Potsdam meeting, Truman remarked to an aide, 'Stalin is as near like Tom Pendergast as any man I know.' Pendergast was a Missouri machine boss who helped get Truman elected to the Senate. For some superficial reason Truman concluded that, like Pendergast, Stalin was a man one could deal with, a man of his word. 'It led Truman to believe that Stalin would hold free elections in Eastern Europe,' says Deborah Larson, a UCLA political scientist." —*Associated Press*
7. Gerry Spence is serving as the pro bono defense attorney for an "environmental terrorist" who embedded metal plates in trees so that the bulldozers would be wrecked (and, potentially, the drivers injured). He is asked if "monkeywrenching" trees is ever justified. Spence's sleight-of-hand answer reveals why he wins so many cases: "In most circumstances, breaking the law is improper. Now, suppose a tractor is about to run over a child. Is it improper to demolish the tractor? Suppose the tractor was going to run over something inanimate, a painting by Van Gogh that cost $32 million. Now, what about a tractor running down a tree? A 400-year-old original growth tree?" —*Forbes*
8. "Thoughtful and right-minded men place their homage and consideration for woman upon an instinctive consciousness that her unmasculine qualities, whether called weaknesses, frailties, or what we will, are the sources of her characteristic and a special strength within the area of her legitimate endeavor. In actual war, it is the men who go to battle, enduring hardship and privation and suffering disease and death for the cause they follow. It is the mothers, wives, and

maids betrothed, who neither following the camp nor fighting in battle, constitute at home an army of woman's constancy and love whose yearning hearts make men brave and patriotic. So, in political warfare, it is perfectly fitting that actual strife and battle would be apportioned to men, and that the influence of woman, radiating from the homes of our land, should inspire to lofty aims and purposes those who struggle for the right." —Grover Cleveland, *Ladies Home Journal*, 1905

9. One philosopher, arguing that the rights of a rape victim to make decisions about her body can be more important than the right to life of a fetus, develops the following analogy: "Let me ask you to imagine this. You wake up in the morning and find yourself back to back in bed with an unconscious violinist. A famous unconscious violinist. He has been found to have a fatal kidney ailment, and the Society of Music Lovers has canvassed all the available medical records and found that you alone have the right blood type to help. They have therefore kidnapped you, and last night the violinist's circulatory system was plugged into yours, so that your kidneys can be used to extract poisons from his blood as well as your own. The director of the hospital now tells you, 'Look, we're sorry the Society of Music Lovers did this to you—we would never have permitted it if we had known. But still, they did it, and the violinist now is plugged into you. To unplug you would be to kill him. But never mind, it's only for nine months. By then he will have recovered from his ailment, and can safely be unplugged from you.' Is it morally incumbent on you to accede to this situation?" —Judith Jarvis Thompson, *Philosophy and Public Affairs*

10. "Look round the world. Contemplate the whole and every part of it. You will find it to be like one great machine, subdivided into an infinite number of lesser machines, which again admit of subdivisions to a degree beyond what human senses and faculties can trace and explain. All these various machines and their parts are adjusted to each other with an accuracy which ravishes into admiration all men who have ever contemplated them. From this we can see that the curious adapting of means to ends throughout all nature resembles exactly, though it much exceeds, the adapting of means to ends in the things made by human beings. Since, therefore, the effects resemble each other, we are led to infer, by all the rules of analogy, that the causes also resemble, and that there is an Author of Nature who is somewhat

similar to the mind of man, though possessed of much larger faculties, proportioned to the grandeur of the work which he has executed. Therefore we prove at once the existence of God and his similarity to human mind and intelligence." —David Hume, *Dialogues Concerning Natural Religion*

SUMMARY OF CHAPTER FIFTEEN

Arguments from analogy typically contend that because two items are the same in one respect, they are the same in another respect. The basic analog is compared to the inferred analog; because they have the basic similarity in common, it is concluded that the inferred analog also has the inferred similarity.

The total evidence condition has two parts. First, the basic similarity must be relevant—that is, it must count toward the presence of the inferred similarity. Second, there must not be any dissimilarities that are relevant—that is, any dissimilarity between the two analogs must not make the basic analog a better candidate for the inferred property. The argument is logically weaker to the extent that it fails in either of these two areas.

Their only positive logical strength comes from the background argument that establishes that the inferred similarity follows from the basic similarity; thus, whatever logical success analogical arguments have is borrowed. This makes it especially important to pay close attention to the first part of the total evidence condition. On the other hand, analogical arguments play an important psychological role in suggesting lines of reasoning, and so should be cultivated for that purpose.

GUIDELINES FOR CHAPTER FIFTEEN

- Structure arguments from analogy, when it would be loyal to do so, by identifying four things—the basic and inferred analogs and the basic and inferred similarities—then inserting each into its proper place in the form. Remember that the second premise, which declares the inferred similarity, is often implicit.

- In considering whether an argument from analogy has satisfied the total evidence condition, first ask, *Is the basic similarity relevant?* To answer this question, look at the extent to which the basic similarity counts in favor of the inferred similarity.
- When the basic similarity is described by a general term, consider whether its meaning shifts from one use to the next. If it shifts enough to affect the soundness of the argument, revise your clarification to eliminate the ambiguity.
- In considering whether an argument from analogy has satisfied the total evidence condition, ask next, *Are any of the dissimilarities relevant?* To answer this question, look at the extent to which any dissimilarity makes the basic analog a better candidate than the inferred analog for the inferred property.
- When you can clearly see the background argument, clarify it rather than the argument from analogy. When you cannot see the background argument, you should normally reserve final judgment about the strength of the argument's logic.

GLOSSARY FOR CHAPTER FIFTEEN

Analogs—the two things (or classes of things) that are said to be similar in an argument from analogy.

Argument from analogy—an argument that asserts that because two items are the same in one respect, they are the same in another respect. They can be represented by this form:

1. *A* is *F* and *G*.
2. *B* is *F*.

∴ C. *B* is *G*.

Background argument—an argument that shows that the inferred similarity (of an analogical argument) follows from the basic similarity—that is, an argument that shows that the basic similarity is relevant.

Basic analog—in an argument from analogy, the item that we are presumably more familiar with, which is presumably known to have both the basic and the inferred similarities.

Basic similarity—in an argument from analogy, the property that the two analogs share, presumably without controversy.

Fallacy of false analogy—the mistake of using an argument from analogy in which the basic similarity is not relevant or in which there are relevant dissimilarities between the basic and inferred analogs. Because this term says nothing about what precisely has gone wrong with the argument, it is better to explain more specifically how it is that some necessary condition for soundness has not been satisfied. Also called the *fallacy of faulty analogy*.

Inferred analog—in an argument from analogy, the item in question, about which the argument is drawing its conclusion.

Inferred similarity—in an argument from analogy, the property that the inferred analog is alleged to have because the basic analog has it.

CHAPTER SIXTEEN

Explanatory Arguments

Sit down before fact as a little child, be prepared to give up every preconceived notion, follow humbly wherever and to whatever abysses nature leads or you shall learn nothing.

—T. H. Huxley, letter, September 23, 1860

Hypotheses and theories are not *derived* from observed facts, but *invented* in order to account for them.

—Carl Hempel, *The Philosophy of Natural Science*

TOPICS

Correct Form for Explanatory Arguments
The Total Evidence Condition (1): the Improbability of the Outcome
The Total Evidence Condition (2): the Probability of the Explanation

Explanatory arguments are probably the most fundamental and frequently used of all arguments, both in science and in everyday life. Like their close cousins, inductive generalizations, explanatory arguments aim to expand our knowledge. But they differ from inductive generalizations in an important way. Both the premise and the conclusion of an inductive generalization are concerned with the same subject matter. Suppose, for example, that on a camping trip to the mountains you say to your friend, "This pot of water boiled quickly at this altitude; so all water boils quickly at this altitude." The premise and conclusion are both about the boiling of water at this altitude. Explanatory arguments typically expand our knowledge by offering a different subject matter in the conclusion. Suppose your friend, having slept in the car during the trip and being unaware of the altitude, argues, "Hey, this water boiled quickly, so we must be well above sea level." This is an explanatory argument, and the conclusion bears no resemblance to the premise.

Explanatory arguments require humble attention to the facts of our experience, as Huxley notes above. But, as Hempel suggests, that is not all they require—they require imagination. The arguer must have imagination to devise an explanation that is something more than a generalization of the experienced facts; and the evaluator must have imagination to think up viable alternative explanations for the sake of comparison.

As with the other argument forms introduced in this text, there are a variety of alternative terms for explanatory arguments, none of which seems to have taken the lead. The most common alternative is the term *theoretical argument*—in which, it is said, a theory is supported by appeal to facts. This terminology is acceptable but can be misleading, since many theories are quite factual and many facts are highly theoretical.[1]

CORRECT FORM FOR EXPLANATORY ARGUMENTS

Explanations, to recall Chapter 2, are not necessarily arguments. Suppose on the camping trip your friend wonders why the water boiled so quickly, and you reply, "Because we are at a higher altitude." This is not an argument. It is not offered as a reason to believe that the water boiled quickly.

[1]Several other terms account for roughly the same thing. Gilbert Harman is associated with the phrase *inference to the best explanation*, Carl Hempel with *hypothetico-deductive* arguments, Charles Peirce with *abductive* reasoning, and David Hume with *transcendental* reasoning. More recently, Larry Wright has called this sort of argument *diagnostic* reasoning.

Why would you try to persuade your friend of something you have both just agreed is true? It is just an explanation, designed to make the unexpected experience easier to understand.

But when, having slept in the car, your friend says, "This water boiled quickly, so we must be well above sea level," this is offered as a reason to believe that we are well above sea level. It is an argument. And it contains the two essential components of an explanatory argument. First, its conclusion—that we are above sea level—is an explanation. An ***explanation***—also termed a *theory* or an *explanatory hypothesis*—is, for our purposes, loosely defined as a statement that enables us both to predict and to better understand the cause of that which it explains. Second, its explicit premise—*this water boiled quickly*—is the observable outcome of the explanation. The ***observable outcome***—also termed the *data*, the *prediction*, or the *facts*—follows from the explanation and can in a certain way, at a certain time, and under certain conditions, be seen, heard, smelled, tasted, or touched.

The correct form for an ***explanatory argument,*** assuming that *P* is the explanation and *Q* is the observable outcome, is this:

1. If *P* then *Q*.
2. *Q*

∴ C. *P*

The first premise, often implicit, states that the explanation enables you to predict the observable outcome—that it really is an *outcome*. The second premise states that the observable outcome is known to have happened—that it has been *observed*. The argument concludes with the assertion of the explanation. The mountain argument can be clarified roughly as follows:

[1. If we are well above sea level, then water boils quickly.]
2. Water boils quickly.

∴ C. We are well above sea level.

For a more substantial example, let's look at a famous explanatory argument from science.[2] In 1687, Isaac Newton published his monumental *Principia*. It included an account of the physical laws that govern the interactions of the planets, stars, and other heavenly bodies. The physics of

[2]For a fuller—and fascinating—account of Halley's reasoning, see Ronald Giere, *Understanding Scientific Reasoning*, 3rd ed. (New York: Harcourt Brace Jovanovich, 1991). A longer, but quite accessible, narrative can be found in *The New York Times Guide to the Return of Halley's Comet* by Richard Flaste, Holcombe Noble, Walter Sullivan, and John Wilford (New York: Times Books, 1985).

Descartes still dominated science, and it would be several decades before Newton's views completely won out. In 1695, Edmund Halley began to ponder whether Newton's account of celestial mechanics was correct and, in particular, whether it applied to the motion of comets. To simplify, Halley wondered about the following statement

> Newton's account of celestial mechanics is correct and, in particular, applies to the motion of comets.

So far as anyone at the end of the 17th century had been able to tell, the motion of comets was utterly irregular. But if Halley was right about Newton's views, there would be detectable regularities—certain comets would be found to follow fixed elliptical orbits around the sun.

Halley was especially interested in a comet he had observed in 1682. After much research, he found that comets with similar orbits had also been observed in 1530 and in 1606. Applying Newton's laws to these data, he boldly made the following prediction:

> A comet with an orbit similar to the 1530 and 1606 comets will appear in December 1758.

It was a remarkably precise prediction—preposterous, really, given the rarity of comets, unless one made the assumption of Newton's celestial mechanics. As the decades passed it was not forgotten, and the comet appeared on Christmas Day, 1758. Some historians mark this as the day of the final triumph of the Newtonian over the Cartesian theoretical tradition.

The sentence *Newton's account of celestial mechanics is correct* . . . serves here as an explanation of the otherwise unpredictable appearance of the comet on Christmas Day of 1758. The sentence *A comet with an orbit similar to the 1530 and 1606 comets will appear in December 1758* is the observable outcome, that which the explanation enables us to predict and to better understand. The comet argument can be clarified as follows:

1. If Newton's account of celestial mechanics is correct and applies to the motion of comets, then a comet with an orbit similar to the 1530 and 1606 comets will appear in December 1758.
2. A comet with an orbit similar to the 1530 and 1606 comets did appear in December 1758.

∴ *C.* Newton's account of celestial mechanics is correct and applies to the motion of comets.

Guideline. Structure an explanatory argument, when it would be loyal to do so, as follows: the first premise states that if the explanation is correct, then a specified outcome of it will be observable; the second premise states that the outcome has been observed; and the conclusion states that the explanation is thus correct.

Correct Form for Explanatory Arguments

1. If P then Q.
2. Q

∴ C. P

P is the explanation.
Q is the observable outcome.

The Fallacy of Affirming the Consequent

The correct form for an explanatory argument should look familiar—it is also the form of the fallacy of affirming the consequent, introduced in Chapter 11. Does this mean that explanatory arguments are always fallacious? No. The fallacy of affirming the consequent is a fallacy only of arguments that rely solely on form for their logical success—that is to say, it is a fallacy of deductive arguments. But explanatory arguments are inductive arguments. They must satisfy the correct form condition, but, like every other inductive argument, they would be logical failures were that their only success; they must also satisfy the total evidence condition. This condition is the logical requirement on any inductive argument that its conclusion fit appropriately with the total available evidence.

In practice, it is usually easy to tell the difference between an explanatory argument and a deductive argument. Is the if-clause intended to provide a better causal understanding of the then-clause? Is the if-clause offered as superior to alternative explanations of the then-clause? Then it is an explanatory argument. On the other hand, does the arguer seem to expect the form alone to provide the logical support for the conclusion? Then it is a deductive argument and commits the fallacy of affirming the consequent.

Suppose I say to you, "If he is from Chicago, then he is from Illinois—and he is indeed from Illinois, so he must be from Chicago." You can't be absolutely sure without some wider context, but it normally wouldn't make sense for me to explain someone's residency in Illinois by pointing to his residence in Chicago. If I were trying to give you a better causal understanding of it, you would probably expect me to tell you something about the chain of events—the family history or career decisions—that led him to Illinois. So an argument of this sort is probably just a logical mistake, not an explanatory argument.

It can also be helpful to know that when explanatory arguments occur in ordinary language, the if–then premise is more often than not implicit (which tends not to be the case with the fallacy of affirming the consequent). And, though you may not find the if–then premise, there are two things you can always expect to find if the argument is explanatory: reference to the explanation, often with a discussion of why it is better than alternative explanations; and reference to the observable outcome, often with a discussion of how unlikely that outcome would otherwise have been.

That a deductive failure and an inductive success can share the same form reminds us of an important lesson: deductive arguments rely only on the correct form condition, while inductive arguments also have recourse to the total evidence condition. A form that cannot pull any of the load in a deductive argument may nevertheless pull a share of the load in an inductive one.

Guideline. Be careful not to confuse explanatory arguments with deductive arguments that commit the fallacy of affirming the consequent.

Signs that an Argument Is Explanatory Rather Than Fallacy of Affirming the Consequent

1. If-clause is intended to provide better understanding of then-clause.
2. If-clause is compared favorably to alternative explanations.
3. Then-clause is said to be unlikely without if-clause.
4. If–then premise is implicit.
5. Argument doesn't seem to depend on form alone.

EXERCISES Chapter 16, set (a)

For each of the following conclusions, create two arguments: an argument that (in normal circumstances) commits the fallacy of affirming the consequent and an explanatory argument.

Sample exercise. He's her father.

Sample answer. Fallacy of affirming the consequent.

1. If he's her father, then he's an adult.
2. He's an adult.

∴ *C.* He's her father.

Explanatory argument.

1. If he's her father, then he will go to great lengths to take care of her.
2. He goes to great lengths to take care of her.

∴ *C.* He's her father.

1. The roof is leaking.
2. I'm out of money.
3. My watch stopped.
4. The concert is sold out.

The Variety of Explanatory Arguments

Explanatory arguments come in several varieties. Two ways of distinguishing them—according to chronology and to generality—can be especially helpful.

The first point of distinction is chronological. In many cases, an explanation is formulated *before* the observable outcome has been observed. Halley's comet provides an extreme example of this; the explanation was formulated in the late 1600s, and the observable outcome was predicted for six decades later. Often, however, the chronological order is reversed; the observable outcome is observed, then the explanation fashioned in response to it. If you find a dead body, for example, with assorted fingerprints on the candlestick, you are beginning with the observable outcome; only later does the detective invent the explanation that the butler did it. Here is an example from Arthur Conan Doyle's *A Study in Scarlet;* Dr. Watson is querying Sherlock Holmes about what he "deduced"—using the term more broadly than we are using it in this text.

> "How in the world did you deduce that?" I asked. "Deduce what?" said he, petulantly. "Why, that he was a retired sergeant of Marines." ". . . Even across the street I could see a great blue anchor tattooed on the back of the fellow's hand. That smacked of the sea. He had a military carriage, however, and regulation side-whiskers. There we have the marine. He was a man with some amount of self-importance and a certain air of command. You must have observed the way in which he held his head and swung his cane. A steady, respectable, middle-aged man, too, on the face of him—all facts which led me to believe that he had been a sergeant." "Wonderful!" I ejaculated.

Unlike the case of Halley's comet, the observable outcomes—a blue anchor on his hand, a military carriage, regulation side-whiskers, an air of command—are where the reasoning begins. The explanation—that he was a Marine sergeant—comes next. Nevertheless, we clarify and evaluate the argument just like the comet argument. Here is one good way of clarifying it:

1. If the man were a Marine sergeant, then he would have a maritime tattoo, a military carriage, regulation side-whiskers, and an air of command.
2. He had a maritime tattoo, a military carriage, regulation side-whiskers, and an air of command.

∴ *C.* The man was a Marine sergeant.

From a logical point of view, the chronological relationship between the two does not matter. We make our observations when we can and we fashion our explanations when they occur to us, and the same principles of evaluation apply regardless of which comes first. Practically speaking, however, explanations that do precede their observable outcomes are often logically stronger. It is easy to invent a convenient explanation for data you already have, but then to disregard failure to fully satisfy the total evidence condition. It is much harder to invent an explanation that successfully predicts future observations. You should be a bit more suspicious of explanatory arguments in which the observable outcome preceded the explanation—but for psychological, not logical, reasons.

A second way of distinguishing among explanatory arguments is in their level of generality. ***General explanations***—Newtonian celestial mechanics, for example—are intended to apply broadly; Newton's theories explain the motion of all heavenly bodies at all times. Such arguments are typical of science, though are not restricted to it. ***Singular explanations***—that the butler did it, or that the man was a Marine sergeant—are designed to apply to a very specific thing or event—to this particular murder or to that particular man's physical characteristics. Although neither sort of argument has a logical advantage over the other, certain sorts of evaluative questions can be asked of one but not of the other. For example, we can ask about the frequency of singular explanations—how frequently butlers leave their fingerprints on candlesticks or how frequently marines have tattoos—but it isn't helpful, probably not even meaningful, to ask about the frequency with which Newtonian mechanics is true.

> *Guideline.* Be more suspicious of explanatory arguments in which the explanation was invented after the observable outcome was observed.

Distinction among Explanatory Arguments

1. *Chronology*—the observed outcome can be observed either before or after the invention of the explanation (*after* being psychologically better).
2. *Generality*—the explanation can be either general or singular (each lending itself to different evaluative questions).

EXERCISES Chapter 16, set (b)

Clarify the explanatory argument in each of the following passages. Then state whether it is general or singular and whether the explanation or the observable outcome came first.

Sample exercise. "At the end of the summer term, the teachers at a New England school were informed that certain children had been identified as 'spurters' who could be expected to do well over the coming months. These youngsters had, in fact, been selected at random from among their classmates. . . . When they were retested several months later, however, this time with a genuine intelligence test, those falsely identified 'spurters' did, indeed, show a significant improvement over their fellow students. This result can be explained by the fact that because the teachers expected them to do well, their perceptions of each student's ability rose and those children's own self-image was enhanced." —David Lewis and James Greene, *Thinking Better*

Sample answer.

1. If higher expectations by teachers and by themselves causes students to perform better, then randomly selected students whom teachers believe—falsely—to have greater potential end up performing better.
2. Randomly selected students whom teachers believe—falsely—to have greater potential end up performing better.

∴ *C.* Higher expectations by teachers and by themselves causes students to perform better.

General explanation. Not clear from the passage which came first, though it was probably the explanation (apparently whoever set up the experiment already had the explanation in mind and was testing it).

1. It was a tiny dent, no larger than a nickel, on the main frame of one motorcycle moving along an assembly line that produces about 175 such vehicles every day. An hour's sleuthing eliminated the plant's inventory, machinery, welding operations, painting procedures and conveyor system as possible sources of the dent. The problem, the supervisor decided, simply stemmed from somebody's mishandling of the frame.
2. "And whatever happened to Satcom III, the telecommunications satellite that some say almost crippled the satellite insurance industry? 'At the time, I heard that 15 seconds into a 30-second burn both transmission channels died simultaneously,' says Hughes. 'That would tend to imply that the damned thing blew up.'" —*Science85*
3. Woman interviewed on TV: "At first I heard a funny roar. I thought it was the wind blowing up the canyon, like it does, you know, except it was real still. I saw the sagebrush and the grass wiggling and starting to shake, and I thought, 'Earthquake.'"
4. "I knew you came from Afghanistan. . . . The train of reasoning ran, 'Here is a gentleman of a medical type, but with the air of a military man. Clearly an army doctor, then. He has just come from the trop-

ics, for his face is dark, and that is not the natural tint of his skin, for his wrists are fair. He has undergone hardship and sickness, as his haggard face says clearly. His left arm has been injured. He holds it in a stiff and unnatural manner. Where in the tropics could an English army doctor have seen much hardship and got his arm wounded? Clearly in Afghanistan.'" —Arthur Conan Doyle, *A Study in Scarlet*

5. "There has recently been a startling decline in a large number of amphibian populations, apparently because UV radiation is harmful to them. Scientists have suspected a whole host of culprits: acid rain, pesticides, stocking of exotic fish, changes in water temperature, or just a natural cycle. But in an Oregon State University study that was replicated several times, wild frog eggs were placed in 72 cages, some with filters that let all sunlight inside except UV radiation. The cages were then placed in the same spot where the frogs laid the eggs. From 20 percent to 25 percent more eggs under the filters hatched successfully than those that were unshielded." — *Science News.*
6. "I can remember, not long ago, listening to a pal rail about a mutual friend's apparently overwhelming need to flirt with every man in a given room. I instinctively jumped to the tease's defense. 'Believe me, I know she's annoying,' I said. 'But don't you think she needs to flirt because she's so insecure?' 'Insecure?' my friend blasted back. 'Couldn't it be that she carries on like that because she has a huge and overweening *ego*?' Now *there* was a novel thought: Someone who acted obnoxiously because she was . . . obnoxious." —Sara Nelson, *Glamour*

THE TOTAL EVIDENCE CONDITION (1): THE IMPROBABILITY OF THE OUTCOME

As we have seen in the preceding chapters, the conclusion of a strong induction must fit both the premises *and* the available background evidence. For explanatory arguments there are two main parts to the total evidence condition: the outcome must be sufficiently improbable and the explanation must be sufficiently probable. In this section we will look at the improbability of the outcome.

The Total Evidence Condition for Explanatory Arguments

1. The observable outcome must be sufficiently improbable.
2. The explanation must be sufficiently probable.

The Outcome Must Be Sufficiently Improbable

No one would have expected a comet in December 1758 unless they were assuming the Newtonian explanation; such an event would have been extremely improbable. This is an important source of the comet argument's logical strength. If comets were common in December, then the premises of the argument would have still been true, but they would have given us no good reason to believe the conclusion. If the comet had been expected anyway, why should its appearance point toward Newtonian mechanics as opposed to whatever was the already accepted explanation? Similarly with our other cases. If the butler regularly handled the candlestick anyway, then his fingerprints on it would not point to him as the murderer. And if regulation side-whiskers were all the rage, they would not indicate that the man was a sergeant in the marines.

The first part of the total evidence condition is that the *observable outcome must have a low prior epistemic probability. Epistemic probability*, as explained in Chapter 9, refers to the probability of the statement's truth given all relevant available evidence. The term *prior*, in this case, means that the probability calculation must be done *prior to* your making any judgment about the explanation itself *and prior to* your making any observations pertinent to the observable outcome. In other words, it means that you cannot use *all* of the relevant available evidence in making this particular judgment—you must exclude the assumption that the explanation is true, and you must exclude observations that might have already been made in the attempt to verify premise 2.

This makes good sense. If you evaluate the probability of the appearance of the comet but *include* in your background evidence the assumption that Newton is correct, then (setting aside the problem this would probably be the fallacy of begging the question) the probability of the 1758 comet would be very high—it is, after all, *derived from* the Newtonian explanation as its outcome! Again, if you include the observations actually made in December of 1758, the probability would be very high—they saw it!

How to Think About Low Enough Prior Probability of Outcome

There would be no good reason to expect the outcome *prior to* these two steps:

1. Making any judgment about the explanation.
2. Making any judgment about the outcome.

Why is this criterion important? If the prior probability of the outcome is high, then we expect the outcome to happen anyway—even if the hypothesis is false. Suppose Halley had decided to look for confirmation of Newton's celestial mechanics by studying the sun rather than comets and, based on Newton, had confidently predicted that the sun would rise the next day. It is not likely that we would now call it *Halley's sun*. When the outcome already has a high prior probability, the hypothesis does no work. The work is being done by whatever independent reason we already have for expecting the outcome to occur.

Some writers refer to this as the *surprise criterion;* it tests to see if you would be surprised by the outcome were you *not* to assume the explanation. The more surprising the outcome would be, the lower the prior probability and the stronger the logic of the argument. This can be a useful standard, but remember that surprise is a psychological condition—thus, strictly speaking, it is an indicator of low subjective, rather than epistemic, probability. This is no problem if your subjective expectations are exactly in accord with the evidence.

Unfortunately, there is no formula for calculating the prior probability of the observable outcome. There are, however, several helpful strategies that you can follow in making your judgment.

Guideline. As a useful standard, apply the surprise test by asking whether the outcome would surprise you (assuming you reserved judgment about whether the explanation were true and whether the outcome had been observed). If so, then it probably has a low prior probability.

Strategies for Assessing the Probability of the Outcome

1. Reject unfalsifiable explanations.
2. Favor precise outcomes.
3. Favor outcomes for which no explanation already exists.
4. Favor outcomes that would falsify alternative explanations.

Reject Unfalsifiable Explanations

It isn't possible to say with precision how improbable the outcome must be to count as *sufficiently* improbable. But it is possible to specify the lowest hurdle that must be cleared. The explanation must, at a minimum, be falsifiable. ***Falsifiability*** applies when there is some possible observable outcome of the theory that *could* prove the explanation to be false. Suppose I am encouraging you in your fledgling acting career and argue, "You are so talented that all the critics who don't praise you are just jealous. I know that all the critics panned your opening performance last night. But that proves my point." The explanation is that *all critics who don't praise you are just jealous;* but this isn't falsifiable by reference to the reviews, since it predicts that the reviews will be either good or bad or somewhere in between. But it is highly probable, whether my theory is true or false, that the reviews will be good or bad or somewhere in between. So my jealousy explanation flunks the test for low prior probability.

Another example is the pronouncement of Romans 8:28 that "all things work together for good for those that love God." Some Christians will take any outcome at all to be, in some sense or other, good and thus to be evidence for the truth of this saying. When desperately needed money arrives mysteriously in the mail, that is support for Romans 8:28. When your entire family is wiped out in a car crash, that is support for Romans 8:28 too—after all, they are in heaven and you are going to have your character strengthened, so it is good. This interpretation of the saying is unfalsifiable and can receive no logical support from the nature of one's experience.

To put it more generally, to say that an explanation or an outcome is unfalsifiable is to say that *any observation at all* is consistent with the explanation. And it is highly probable that we will have "any observation at all." Any unfalsifiable explanation is in principle unable to satisfy the improbable-outcome criterion and can never be the conclusion of a sound explanatory argument. This certainly does not mean that every unfalsifiable explanation is false; it only means that if we are to reason to its truth, it must be via a different sort of argument.

Guideline. Reject explanatory arguments that have unfalsifiable explanations; they are in principle unable to satisfy the first part of the total evidence condition.

EXERCISES Chapter 16, set (c)

Each of these passages discusses an explanation that might be thought to be unfalsifiable. In a short paragraph, identify the explanation, discuss why it may be unfalsifiable, and explain how this results in a problem with the first part of the total evidence condition.

1. Some believers in the paranormal hold that skeptical attitudes can inhibit paranormal results. A professor at Bath University in England combines this rationalization with the idea that psychic powers work backward and forward in time; he suggests, in apparent seriousness, that the failure of attempted experiments to prove psychic forces is actually evidence in favor of parapsychology, since skeptics reading about successful experiments afterward actually project their skepticism back in time to inhibit the experiment!
2. Freud argued that repression and resistance are two important mechanisms of our minds. Repression is the mechanism by which we push out of awareness and into our unconscious memories of deeply traumatic childhood experiences. Resistance is the mechanism by which we refuse to allow these repressed memories to be brought back to the surface. When people insist that they have no repressed memories, then, Freud considers this to be evidence for the presence of resistance, which is itself evidence for the existence of repression.

Favor Precise Outcomes

Although there is no formula for deciding on the improbability of the outcome, there are some helpful strategies that you can follow in making your decision.

One good way to check for an improbable outcome is to ask this: *Is this outcome so vague that it might well be true anyway?* Recall, from Chapter 13, that larger margins of error make it much more probable that the conclusion of an inductive generalization is true; there is a much greater chance that between 50 percent and 60 percent of the voters favor Jones than there is that exactly 55 percent of them do. This point can be broadened: vague statements, in general, are more likely to be true than precise ones. Halley's job would have been much easier if, instead of predicting a comet precisely in December 1758, he had made the following vague prediction:

> At least one comet will appear somewhere in the sky at some time in the future.

This observable outcome easily follows from the Newtonian explanation—thus, it would provide us with an argument with true premises. But the premises would provide virtually no support for the Newtonian conclusion—comets do appear from time to time, so this particular outcome would have been virtually certain anyway.

In ancient Greece, when there was a difficult decision to be made, the wealthy Greeks would sometimes travel to Delphi and consult the oracle there—an oracle who, it was believed, had special powers to foresee the future. The oracle tended to utter solemn pronouncements of a very unspecific sort—for example, "I see grave misfortune in your future." It was almost inevitable that such a vague prediction would come true. For the Greek might count anything as grave misfortune, from a financial reversal to the death of an aged parent. When it did come true, it was often counted as reason to believe that the oracle had special powers. But the extremely high prior probability of the outcome renders the argument logically useless. For exactly the same reason, we can hardly consider astrology to be supported when someone finds that the day's horoscope has some truth in it; horoscopes are worded so vaguely that there are almost always events that can be interpreted as making them true.

The problem in all of these cases is that the explanation does no work. It is freeloading; so it deserves no credit when the outcome comes true.

> *Guideline.* Ask whether the outcome is too vague. Vague outcomes are likely to have a high prior probability and thus are likely to signal that the argument is logically weak.

EXERCISES Chapter 16, set (d)

For each of the brief explanatory arguments, identify the explanation and offer a more precise observable outcome that would lower its prior probability and thus make the argument logically stronger. Don't worry about whether the outcome has much likelihood of being true (since that has to do with the truth of premise 2, not with the logic of the argument).

Sample exercise. Astrology is reliable. Just watch—as my horoscope says, something will disappoint me today.

Sample answer. Explanation: Astrology is reliable. Observable outcome: As my horoscope says, at 3:00 today my bank will call and tell me that they have gone bankrupt and my life savings is lost.

1. My car will run out of gas within the next 300 miles; that should prove to you that it is running low.
2. He is a great quarterback. You'll see—his play will make a difference in the game.
3. I know of some people with cancer who smoke. Clearly, smoking causes cancer.
4. She must be a good driver, since she usually gets where she's going without running into anybody.
5. My employer values me. It will be proven when I get some sort of raise in the next few years.

Favor Outcomes for Which No Explanation Already Exists

Another good way to check for an improbable outcome is to ask this: *Does another explanation for this outcome already exist?* Included among your background evidence may be a belief that already serves as a perfectly good explanation for the outcome—in which case, you would expect the outcome anyway. This is why, for example, we are amused but not persuaded by the rooster who thinks that the sun is raised each morning by his mighty crowing. Another explanation for the sunrise already exists in our own background evidence—that the earth is rotating on its axis.

More subtle examples are easy to find. Wilson Bryan Key, whose most famous book was titled *Subliminal Seduction*, has argued that Madison Avenue strategically permeates its advertisements with camouflaged sexual images that are invisible unless you look very hard for them. For example, an unnoticed erotic image on a Ritz cracker, Key says, "makes the Ritz cracker taste even better, because all of the senses are interconnected in the brain." The problem with his argument is that another explanation for these "unnoticed images" already exists; we all know that we're capable of finding images if we look really hard for them, simply as the products of our imagination. His argument would gain some logical strength if, when we looked for them, we could find sexual images in advertisements more often than we find them in the clouds. Until then, the argument is no better than a product of Key's own imagination.

An even subtler example can be found in academic discussions of the theory that punishment motivates learning better than does reward. The experience of flight instructors was at one time taken to be good evidence for the theory. Instructors found that when a student pilot was scolded for a poor landing, the student usually did better the next time. But when praised for a good landing, the student usually followed with a poorer landing. The argument might be clarified as follows:

1. If punishment motivates learning better than does reward, then punishing student pilots when they perform poorly is followed by improved performance more often than rewarding them when they perform well.
2. Punishing student pilots when they perform poorly is followed by improved performance more often than rewarding them when they perform well.

∴ *C.* Punishment motivates learning better than does reward.

Then someone realized that this sort of evidence provided no logical support for the conclusion. For the observable outcome of premise 2 is something that we would fully expect, even if the explanation were false. Why? At any given time, each pilot has achieved a certain level of competence—call it the pilot's current *mean* level of competence. Any performance significantly better or worse than the student's current mean level of competence would be largely a matter of chance. After significantly departing from the mean level of competence, we would expect that the next attempt would be *closer* to the current mean. This means that an unusually good performance would typically be followed by a poorer one—returning *downward* to the mean—and that an unusually bad performance would typically be followed by a better one—again returning to the mean, but this time *upward.* The scolding and praise are no better than a fifth wheel in the argument, since the outcome is highly probable anyway. Because the explanation does no work in making the outcome probable, it should get none of the credit when the outcome is observed.

Guideline. Ask whether an explanation for the outcome already exists. If an explanation does already exist, then the outcome has a high prior probability and the argument is logically weak.

EXERCISES Chapter 16, set (e)

For each of the arguments below, offer an alternative explanation that already exists, which thus renders the outcome probable and the argument logically weak.

Sample exercise. New evidence shows that optimists live longer. Healthy elderly people who rated their health as "poor" were two to six times more likely to die within the next four years than those who said their health was "excellent." —*Bottom Line,* citing the work of Professor Ellen Idler of Rutgers University

Sample answer. Alternative explanation that already exists. Healthy people who rate their health as "poor" know enough about their health to know that they are not *as* healthy as healthy people who rate their health as "excellent." Given that they are elderly and in the low end of the healthy group, they will die sooner.

1. The lights in this old house keep flickering. When I bought the house—despite its terrible condition—the sellers let slip that someone had died here. I think it might be haunted.
2. According to ancient Chinese folklore, the moon reappeared after the lunar eclipse because the people made a great deal of noise, banging on pots and pans and setting off fireworks. It always does reappear after an eclipse when much noise occurs.
3. In Billy Graham's *Peace with God,* Graham refers to the failure of an international peace conference and asks, "Could men of education, intelligence, and honest intent gather around a world conference table and fail so completely to understand each other's needs and goals if

their thinking was not being deliberately clouded and corrupted?" Such failures, he continues, show that there is a devil, who is "a creature of vastly superior intelligence, a mighty and gifted spirit of infinite resourcefulness."

4. Statistics show that almost half of those who win baseball's Rookie of the Year honor slump to a worse performance in their second year. This is solid evidence for the existence of the so-called sophomore jinx.

Favor Outcomes that Would Falsify Alternative Explanations

Another good way to check for an improbable outcome is to ask this: *Does this outcome rule out the leading alternative explanations?* The philosopher Francis Bacon wrote four centuries ago of this experience:

> When they showed him hanging in a temple a picture of those who had paid their vows as having escaped shipwreck, and would have him say whether he did not now acknowledge the power of the gods, —"Aye," asked he again, "but where are they painted that were drowned after their vows?"

The explanation here is *The gods are powerful* and the observable outcome is *Many who worship the gods have escaped from shipwrecks.* But there is a viable alternative explanation for this outcome—namely, *Escaping from a shipwreck is largely a matter of luck, shipwrecks having little regard for passengers' religious beliefs.* The logic of the gods argument would benefit if its observable outcome ruled out the luck alternative—if, for example, the outcome were revised, as Bacon hints, to this: *Nobody who worships the gods has drowned in a shipwreck.* Partly because this revised outcome would be false, it has not been offered; so the argument is handicapped by an outcome that leaves the luck alternative still standing. So the outcome probably would be true even if the gods explanation were false, and the argument is logically extremely weak.

Favoring outcomes that rule out alternative explanations is an especially powerful strategy. For, as researchers have shown, we have a natural tendency—termed a ***confirmation bias***—to look for outcomes that support our preferred explanation rather than those that might falsify the alternatives—to look, for example, for worshippers who escaped rather than thinking also about those who drowned.

To illustrate this bias, suppose I tell you that I have in mind a set of numbers that includes the numbers 2, 4, and 6, and I then ask you to guess what set of numbers I am thinking of. You probably already suspect that it's the set of all even numbers; but before I make you commit to that answer, I offer you the opportunity to test your answer by suggesting one more number that is either in or out of the set. If you are like most people you suggest, "Eight is in the set." And my reply is that yes, 8 is included, *because I am thinking of the set of all whole numbers*. You can now see that you squandered your one opportunity. Influenced by the confirmation bias, you proposed a number that would confirm your preferred answer. But you would have done far better to propose, "Seven is *not* in the set." If you had been right, you not only would have confirmed your preferred even-numbers answer, but also you would have ruled out the whole-numbers alternative—thereby improving the logical support for your answer. And if you had been wrong—and you would have been wrong—you would have had the chance to correct the error of your ways.

To illustrate how this strategy is related to the prior epistemic probability of the outcome, suppose I propose the following fanciful explanation:

> I am bewitched, so that gravity has no affect on me whatsoever; the only reason I am able to walk around on the ground is because of magical shoes that counteract the bewitchment when I wear them.

My evidence? I offer the observable outcome that *I walk around on the ground while I wear the shoes*. And so I do. But this outcome provides no support for the explanation. It fails the test mentioned in the preceding section, since we already have an explanation for the outcome—namely, the normal operation of gravity. The argument would be greatly improved if the outcome included an attempt to rule out this alternative explanation, namely, *I walk around on the ground while I wear the shoes, and I float in the air when I take them off*. If this turns out to be true, it provides much better support for the explanation since it rules out the gravity alternative. An observable outcome for which there are fewer possible explanations is that much more improbable—and, thus, is that much logically stronger.

This helps to explain why so-called anecdotal evidence can be problematic. Suppose I have heard that vitamin C prevents colds; I don't know whether to believe it but decide it's worth looking into. I presume:

1. If vitamin C helps prevent colds, then when I take a lot of vitamin C I get fewer colds than normal.

I do take a lot of vitamin C over the winter and get only one or two colds, though I usually get three or four. So I add the premise,

2. When I take a lot of vitamin C I do get fewer colds than normal.

I then conclude,

∴ *C.* Vitamin C prevents colds.

My argument may provide a small measure of logical support for its conclusion, but what it does not do is rule out the following alternative explanations:

- The reduction in my colds was simply a coincidence.
- I was being more careful about my health because I was engaged in the experiment.
- I subconsciously wanted the test to succeed, so I tended not to count less severe colds that I otherwise would have counted.

A more careful test of the same theory would rule out these alternatives by using two large groups—one group that receives Vitamin C and a control group that receives a placebo—in a double blind test. (It is called double blind because neither those receiving the pills nor those administering the study knows which group is getting the real Vitamin C and which is getting the bogus Vitamin C.) By using large groups, the coincidence alternative is ruled out. By using the control group, the alternative is ruled out that the effect is somehow induced by the test itself. And by using a double blind test, the alternative is ruled out that the data were being interpreted differently for each group.

This argument would have the same form as the first one, differing only in the nature of the observable outcome.

1. If vitamin C helps prevent colds, then the group taking vitamin C has substantially fewer colds than the group taking the placebo.
2. The group taking vitamin C has substantially fewer colds than the group taking the placebo.

∴ *C.* Vitamin C helps prevent colds.

Because the observable outcome rules out the leading alternative explanations, its prior probability is far lower than the anecdotal argument—and thus the argument is logically much stronger.

Guideline. Ask whether an outcome rules out the leading alternative explanations. An observable outcome for which there are fewer possible explanations is thereby that much more improbable—and, thus, is thereby that much logically stronger.

EXERCISES Chapter 16, set (f)

For each of the passages below, (*i*) state the observable outcome and (*ii*) offer a different observable outcome that would rule out alternative explanations and lower its probability, thus making the argument logically stronger. Do not worry for now whether the observable outcome is true.

Sample exercise. "Hundreds of people gathered for a second night Wednesday to see an image described as the outline of the Virgin Mary on a wall of an empty house in Hanover Township, Pa. Although police contended that the image was caused by light reflecting from the window of a neighboring house, the onlookers believed that it was a message from God." —*Ann Arbor News*

Sample answer: Observable outcome: An image looking like the outline of the Virgin Mary was seen on the wall of a house. Improved outcome: An image looking like the outline of the Virgin Mary was seen on the wall of a house, and it remained there when the window of the neighboring house was opened.

1. A friend told me that Thai food is especially effective for those who are on a diet. I found a Thai restaurant and now I go there for lunch every day. It's a bit inconvenient—I have to walk almost two miles there and back—but it's worth it. My friend was right. I've really slimmed down.
2. I never thought it would work, but I read somewhere that we should get a cat if we wanted to rid ourselves of the mice in the garage. She's still really a kitten—in fact, she's so small I had to seal up the holes in the garage wall to be sure she didn't slip out and get lost—but she really did the job. No more mice.

3. After one of our couple friends started going to a fertility clinic, they just relaxed and stopped consciously trying to conceive. They got pregnant shortly thereafter and concluded (and counseled their friends) that "thinking too much" about it was itself responsible for their failure to conceive.
4. "It has long been my suspicion that, especially in Washington, when people say that they have 'read' a book, they mean something other than attempting to glean meaning from each sentence. I recently organized a small test of this hypothesis. A colleague visited several Washington-area bookstores and slipped a small note into about 70 books . . . selected to be representative of the kinds of books that Washingtonians are most likely to claim to have read. The notes were placed about three-quarters of the way through each book, hard against the spine so that they could not be shaken out. The notes said: "If you find this note before May 1, call David Bell at the *New Republic* and get a $5 reward," with our phone number. We didn't get a single response." —Michael Kinsley (who, to his credit, adds "I don't claim much for this experiment," and then goes on to consider additional evidence).
5. "Delynn Carter learned that the dramatic episodes of wheezing, which incapacitated her almost daily for the last eight years, were due not to asthma but to a vocal cord dysfunction that mimicked the symptoms of asthma and can be treated by speech therapy. Specialists found the cause by taking motion pictures of the patients' vocal cords during an attack and during a normal period. During an episode of wheezing, they found that the vocal cords, which are located in the airway leading to the lungs, formed almost a complete barricade across the passage. This closure did not occur during a normal period. Also, the doctors reported, an extensive battery of pulmonary function tests failed to produce the kinds of findings that are characteristic of an asthmatic. Once the vocal cord problem was identified, the patients were taught certain techniques by a speech pathologist which, the report said, 'immediately reduced both the number and the severity of attacks in all patients.' For her part, Delynn Carter said she knows what triggered her attacks. "It was all those asthma medications that I didn't need," she said. 'They took me off all of them and since then I've had no attacks. It's like coming back from the dead.'" —*Los Angeles Times*

THE TOTAL EVIDENCE CONDITION (2): THE PROBABILITY OF THE EXPLANATION

The Explanation Must Be Sufficiently Probable

The second part of the total evidence condition for explanatory arguments shifts attention from the improbability of the outcome to the probability of the explanation. As with the outcome, the concern here is also with *prior* epistemic probability—in this case, the probability that you would assess to the explanation *prior to* your making any judgment about the observable outcome. This makes good sense, because the probability of the explanation *after* you make a judgment about the observable outcome would roughly be your assessment of the soundness of the argument and it is too soon to make that judgment. Further, it is not necessary for the prior probability of the explanation to be high; if the explanation were already highly probable, there would be no need for the argument! Rather, it is simply necessary that *it not be implausibly low and that it be higher than that of the leading alternative explanations.*

The second part of the total evidence condition requires that you exercise the same imaginative powers as the arguer; for you must imagine which explanations would be the most credible alternatives to the one argued for. We typically favor the explanations with the highest prior probability. A house fire victim, for example, is quoted in the newspaper as explaining, "I kept smelling something, and then I saw the smoke. I thought somebody must be barbecuing. I couldn't believe it was a fire. After a few seconds, I knew it was." Barbecues occur far more frequently than house fires, so they have a much higher prior probability; but when the observable outcome—way too much smoke—does not follow from the barbecue explanation, we are logically forced to the less probable explanation that it is a house fire.

How to Think about High Enough Prior Probability of Explanation

Before making any judgment about the outcome, you should determine these two things:

1. The probability of the explanation is not implausibly low.
2. The explanation is more probable than the leading alternatives.

But sometimes the more probable explanation does not occur to us—we need more imagination or, perhaps, a better education. When he was a young lawyer, Abe Lincoln had to defend a client against a case that seemed to be strongly supported by a list of undisputed facts. In summing up his defense before the jury, he said, "My esteemed opponent's statements remind me of the little boy who ran to his father. The lad said that Suzy and the hired man were up in the hayloft—that Suzy had her dress up and the hired man had lowered his trousers. 'Pa!' exclaimed the youngster, 'they are getting ready to pee on the hay!' 'Well, son,' replied the father, 'you've got the facts all right, but have reached the wrong conclusion.'" Lincoln's client, we are told, was acquitted. Part of the reason, presumably, was because the jury saw that if they carefully thought about alternative explanations, they might find one with a higher prior probability than the one Lincoln's opponent was arguing for.

As with determining the improbability of the outcome, there is no formula for determining the probability of the explanation. There are, however, several useful strategies that we will discuss next.

> *Guideline.* The second part of the total evidence condition for explanatory arguments is this: the probability of the explanation must not be implausibly low and must be higher than that of the leading alternative explanations. This requires imagination in coming up with alternative explanations for the sake of comparison.

Strategies for Assessing the Prior Probability of the Explanation

1. Favor frequency.
2. Favor explanations that make sense.
3. Favor simplicity.
4. Look for coincidence as an alternative explanation.
5. Look for deception as an alternative explanation.

Favor Frequency

For singular explanations—such as *The butler did it* or *This man was a Marine sergeant*—the best question to ask is this: *Is this sort of thing known to occur, and does it occur more frequently than do the leading alternatives?* Suppose the phone rings and you pick it up, only to hear the "click" of someone's hanging up on the other end. "Aha!" you say, "Someone is casing the joint and now knows not to burglarize us, since someone answered the phone!" This explanation is the sort of thing that is known to happen—burglars do sometimes call ahead to see if anyone is home—so it is not implausibly low. But the problem is that there is at least one alternative explanation that occurs much more frequently. Consider the alternative that someone has accidentally dialed a wrong number, only to hang up when hearing an unfamiliar voice on the other end. Which occurs more frequently—burglars or butterfingers? Butterfingers, of course. So the logic of the burglar argument is shown to be weak.[3]

This can be a powerful evaluative tool. Consider the following Dear Abby letter:[4]

> Dear Abby: I'm a traveling man who's on the road five days a week. I have a pretty young wife (my second) whom I've always trusted until last Friday night when I came home, put on my bathrobe and found a well-used pipe in the pocket! I don't smoke a pipe. Never have. And my wife has never smoked anything. She claims she has never seen that pipe before and doesn't know how it got there. OK, so she's not admitting to anything, but the next day when I went to get the pipe, it wasn't where I had put it! It just plain disappeared. I searched the apartment, but it was nowhere to be found. My wife claims she doesn't know what happened to it. We are the only two people in this apartment. From what I've told you, what conclusions would you draw? No names, please. My wife calls me—Papa Bear
>
> Dear Papa Bear: It's just a wild guess, but I think somebody's been sleeping in your bed. Pity, the evidence went up in smoke.

About a month later this letter appeared—really:

> Dear Abby: The letter from the traveling man who spends five days a week on the road interested me. He said he came home to discover a well-used pipe in the pocket of his bathrobe. . . . Well, Abby, this should clear up the mystery of MY missing pipe. Being a plumber, I was summoned to the home of an attractive woman to repair a faulty

[3]Thanks for the example to W. V. Quine and J.S. Ullian, *The Web of Belief* (New York: Random House, 1978).

[4]Taken from the DEAR ABBY column by Abigail Van Buren.

> shower nozzle that was spraying water all over her bathroom. While waiting for my clothes to dry, I slipped into a robe hanging on a hook in the bathroom, and I must have thoughtlessly put my pipe into the pocket. After searching for it high and low later, I suddenly remembered. When I went back to that house, the door was open and I could hear a loud argument coming from another room, so I sneaked in and quietly retrieved my pipe. I hope this explains it for all hands. Pete McG. P.S. Could you find out for me which five days that man is on the road?
>
> Dear Pete: Sorry, no help from this corner for a plumber who can't keep track of his pipes.

Abby's explanation is that the wife is having an affair; the observable outcome is that the pipe unexpectedly appears and then mysteriously disappears. But the second letter, using the same observable outcome, offers an alternative explanation—namely, that a plumber visited, left the pipe, then surreptitiously retrieved it.

How does Abby's conclusion fare in the face of this alternative explanation? Not too badly, if we compare the frequencies of each. The plumber explanation is burdened with improbabilities:

- How often do people call an expensive plumber over a faulty shower nozzle when it could be easily unscrewed and replaced with a $5 part?
- How often do people leave water spraying everywhere rather than simply turning it off?
- How often do plumbers leave water spraying everywhere rather than turning it off—if not at the faucet, then at the main?
- How often do plumbers waste time by doing things such as drying their clothes when they can make more money by going on to another job?
- How many plumbers smoke pipes?
- The husband said he put the pipe somewhere, and the plumber had no way of knowing where; how often is someone going to be able to sneak in and find something like that without being caught?
- The plumber says he went to a house, while the man says he lives in an apartment; how often does someone make that sort of mistake?
- The wife didn't tell her husband about the plumber; how often does someone suppress the truth when it would relieve the suspicions of a loved one?

- The plumber could've called the man or sent a note (enclosed, perhaps, with his bill) to straighten things out, but wrote Dear Abby where there was a good chance it wouldn't be published or the man wouldn't read it; how often does a well-intentioned person take such an ineffective action to right a wrong?

The answer in each case is *very infrequently*. When we compare frequencies we see that the prior probability of each portion of the plumber explanation is quite low; and the *conjunction* of all portions (recall Chapter 10—this requires that the probabilities of all the parts be multiplied) is far, far lower. Clearly, the plumber explanation has a much lower prior probability than does the affair explanation. Abby's argument remains moderately strong.

Guideline. For singular explanations, ask whether this sort of explanation is known to occur and, if so, if it occurs more frequently than do the leading alternative explanations. If the answer is yes, then the argument is at least moderately strong (assuming it has not failed the first part of the total evidence condition).

EXERCISES Chapter 16, set (g)

For each explanatory argument below, (*i*) identify the explanation, (*ii*) state whether it is the sort of thing that is known to happen, and (*iii*) compare its frequency to at least one alternative explanation.

Sample exercise. "C. B. Scott Jones, a staff member for U.S. Senator Claiborne Pell (D-RI), wrote an alarmed letter to the secretary of defense; he had discovered the word 'simone' (pronounced si-MO-nee) in the secretary's taped speeches, as well as in the speeches of the secretary of state and of the president—when the speeches were played backwards. Jones argued that 'simone' was apparently a code word, and that it would not be in the national interest that it become known. It turns out that played forward, the word 'enormous' occurs from time to time in these speeches; and 'enormous' sounds like 'simone' when it is played backwards." —*Los Angeles Times*

Sample answer. Explanation: "Simone" is a code word. So far as I know, officials have not used backward code words in their public speeches, so the prior probability of the explanation is exceedingly low. An alternative explanation is that Jones was hearing the word "enormous," which sounds like "simone" backwards and occurs frequently in the speeches (and probably does not pose any danger to national security).

1. Teacher to student: "I never received your research paper. Wait—don't tell me—your dog ate it, right?"
2. Judge to scofflaw: "So, my papers show that you failed to pay 48 separate parking tickets. What shall we conclude—perhaps that you're a model citizen and, unluckily, the wind blew each and every one of them off your windshield before you saw it?"
3. Several of the younger trees by Beaver Creek stream are now nothing more than two-foot posts sticking out of the ground; the treetops are nowhere around, and the top of each stump comes to a curious point. This is further proof that aliens from outer space have visited us.
4. Woman on a TV talk show with theme "Moms who keep secrets from daughters": "Mom, you always told me that my father was killed in the war right after I was born. But I'm not stupid. You never talked about him like he was a hero—never made any effort to keep his memory alive with letters and pictures. Admit it. I'm illegitimate."
5. A young man expecting a phone call from a woman he's been dating waits in vain—the phone doesn't ring all evening. Though the dial tone sounds normal when he lifts the receiver, he concludes that there must be a problem with the line.
6. A medical student has been reading intensively about various diseases of the nervous system. One morning he wakes up after a late night reading and finds his vision is somewhat blurred; he immediately diagnoses optic neuritis.
7. "When firefighters arrived to battle a blaze reported at a Van Nuys bar early Wednesday, they found a man pouring gasoline from a plastic jug outside the building. In a window on one side was a burning Molotov cocktail. Firefighters doused the flaming Molotov cocktail and then detained the man . . . until police arrived and took him into custody. An arson investigator said the man offered an explanation: 'The suspect said that he was using the gas to start his car and that he felt

the jug was too full so he poured out some of the gasoline near the building. He claims he has no knowledge of the Molotov cocktail.'"
—*Los Angeles Times*

Favor Explanations that Make Sense

General explanations—such as *Newtonian mechanics applies to the motion of celestial bodies* or *Vitamin C helps prevent colds*—do not lend themselves to the question about comparative frequencies because they are general. But you can still ask *whether such explanations make sense, and whether they make more sense than the alternative explanations.* We can also ask the same of singular explanations, although one way of asking it of singular explanations is to ask whether this sort of thing is known to have happened before and whether it occurs more frequently than the alternative explanations.

Another way to put this is to ask whether there is a *satisfactory conceptual framework* for the general explanation—and whether it is more satisfactory than the alternatives. Would it require the world to function in mysterious ways or in ways that differ dramatically from the ways that are well established by science? If so, it is probably better to judge the logic of the argument as, at best, undecidable and, at worst, extremely weak. It must be emphatically added that the world is in many ways mysterious, and that science *can* be mistaken, and often is. But explanatory arguments that rely heavily on mystery or that depend on the overthrow of science cannot be considered successful until they do the hard work of filling in the blanks. If there are too many blanks, then the explanation's prior probability is too low for the argument to be logically strong.

Examples of this abound, even in some of the most widely accepted explanatory theories. Many smart people refused at first to wholeheartedly endorse Newtonian mechanics because it lacked a satisfactory conceptual framework in one important respect. It assigned a central role to gravity, which is, in effect, action at a distance; but it did not offer any account of how gravitational forces can act across space without any intervening physical bodies. Due to this defect, it took an especially rich array of observable outcomes and an especially compelling theoretical simplicity for it to gain rational acceptance. In another example, continental drift initially was reasonably rejected as the explanation for the striking biological and geological similarities between continents that are widely separated by oceans because there was no known mechanism for the drift. But the theory of plate tectonics eventually provided a conceptual framework for continental drift, and the explanation no longer has an unacceptably low prior probability. Meteorites provide yet another example. Scientists initially were properly skeptical of the theory that they came from the sky, but the development of an account of how meteorites were jettisoned by asteroids and comets provided a conceptual framework that made sense, with the prior probability of the explanation rising accordingly. (The Vitamin C example is similar; one reason that researchers have not worked harder at collecting evidence for the theory is because it is unclear how it would work. Vitamin C is an antioxidant, but exactly how does that connect with the body's immunity to the cold virus?)

When established scientists reject offbeat theories, defenders of such views love to cite these cases. Scientists rejected Newton, they rejected continental drift, they rejected meteorites, and they were wrong! So the scientists are wrong when they reject the paranormal, ancient astronauts, and homeopathic medicine! Scientists were right to reject these formerly offbeat views until they could make good sense of them, and they will be right to reject the paranormal, ancient astronauts, and homeopathic medicine until they can also make good sense of them. Some explanations will eventually measure up to the standards of good reasoning; that is no reason to eliminate the standards.

> *Guideline.* For both general and singular explanations, ask whether this sort of explanation makes sense—that is, whether there is a satisfactory conceptual framework for it and whether it is more satisfactory than the alternatives. If the explanation leaves too much to mystery, or requires too much of established science to be replaced by less well-established views, then the argument can normally be no better than logically weak.

EXERCISES Chapter 16, set (h)

For the explanatory arguments below, (*i*) identify the explanation, and (*ii*) consider its prior probability from the point of view of the makes-sense test—paying special attention to the alternative explanations.

Sample exercise. A 17-pound meteorite of unknown origin was found in Antarctica. Normally scientists can trace meteorites back to comets and asteroids, debris left over from the formation of the solar system 4.6 billion years ago. Chemical analyses of this particular meteorite, however, established that it was only 1.3 billion years old and made of cooled lava. Where, then, could the extraterrestrial have come from? Searching for a once volcanic place of origin, researchers ruled out both Venus, because the atmosphere is too thick for such a rock to have escaped, and the moon, since it stopped erupting 3 billion years ago. Then NASA's Donald Bogard compared the meteorite's "fingerprint" of noble gases to those found on Mars by the Viking lander—and discovered that they matched closely. "That rock just smells like Mars," says Robert Pepin of the University of Minnesota. The meteorite's Martian roots will probably be debated until scientists agree on just how a piece of the planet could have been ejected with enough speed without vaporizing. —*Newsweek*

Sample answer: Explanation: the meteorite came from Mars. Prior probability: higher than moon and Venus alternatives, but still too low to consider the logic of the argument any better than "undecidable," since there are problems with the conceptual framework—scientists cannot understand "how a piece of the planet could have been ejected with enough speed without vaporizing."

1. "For many years, ship captains navigating the waters of Antarctica have been intrigued by rare sightings of emerald icebergs. Now it's been discovered that the icebergs are broken pieces of huge ice shelves that are hundreds of years old, according to a study reported in the *Journal of Geophysical Research*. The unusual coloring occurs when the icebergs capsize, revealing the underside where frozen sea water contains yellowish-brown organic material. Pure ice appears blue, and the presence of the organic material shifts the color to green." —*New York Times*
2. Death and disaster provide a convincing argument that, contrary to the persistent notion, women are not the weaker sex. Archeologist Donald Grayson of the University of Washington has found some evidence in the Donner Party catastrophe. It's a favorite of macabre schoolchildren. Delayed on the way west in 1846, 87 pioneers were stranded in late October by heavy snows in the Sierra. Nearly half the party died before an April rescue, the survivors cannibalizing the dead. Thirty of the 40 who died were men and, says Grayson, most of the male deaths occurred before that of a single woman. Even eliminating four violent deaths (all men, two of them murders), the 53 percent

death rate for men far exceeded the 29 percent rate for women. Men were exposed more frequently to the elements, since they did the hunting and tree cutting. But Grayson believes it's unlikely such factors fully explain the statistics. For instance, of 15 Donner Party members who attempted to snowshoe out in late December, all five women survived while eight of the ten men died. And chivalry didn't make the difference, the researchers say, since women got no more food than men. "It comes down to physiology," says Grayson. "Men are evolutionarily built for aggression. Women are built for giving birth, and the long haul that involves." *—In Health*

3. Scientists at the University of Manchester have discovered a distant planet where virtually no one would have expected it to be, orbiting a pulsar star, PSR1829, which was born during a supernova. The planet is too dim to be seen, but the scientists said they are convinced it is there because the pulsar emits radio signals that vary in a way that can best be explained by the gravitational tug of a nearby planet—the waves are a bit early for three months, then for three months arrive a bit late. One other possible explanation is that as the pulsar spins it might be wobbling due to some strange effect in the inside of the star, though such an effect is not understood and has never been observed before. *—Science News*

4. For years, scientifically trained observers dismissed voodoo death as primitive superstition. But eventually, confronted by many cases in which there seemed to be no medical reasons for deaths, anthropologists and psychiatrists came to accept it as a pathology in its own right, linked to the victim's belief in sorcery. But how can the mere belief that one is doomed be fatal? Two kinds of theories have been proposed. One emphasizes the power of suggestion as a psychological process; if faith can heal, despair can kill. The other roots the power of suggestion in physiology: extreme fright and despair disrupt the sympathetic nervous system and paralyze body functions. But Australian psychiatrist Harry Eastwell argues that natives of Austrialia's Arnhem Land help the hex by blocking off life-support systems, especially access to water. The victims and their families realize there is a hex; it becomes difficult to live a normal life, and the stress exacerbates any bodily problems. Relatives gather close to the victim, wailing, chanting, and covering the victim with a funeral cloth. Appetite fails, and the relatives keep water cans beyond reach, despite temperatures well above 100 degrees in the shade. With total restriction of

> fluids, death follows in 24 hours. In Arnhem Land, it seems, sorcery kills not by suggestion or paralyzing fear, but by dehydration. —*Psychology Today*

Favor Simplicity

Simplicity can be a significant contributor to the probability of an explanation. The point is not that the world is necessarily simple, any more than the world is necessarily filled only with frequently occurring or nonmysterious things. The point is that, other things being equal, simple explanations, like frequently occurring and nonmysterious explanations, have a higher prior probability. An explanation is in this way like a machine. Some machines require a large number of moving parts to work properly. But the more moving parts a machine has, the more likely it is that it will break down—so a well-designed machine includes no more parts than absolutely required.

This applies to both singular and general explanations. One good way to check for simplicity—a way typically more useful with singular than with general explanations—is to ask *whether the explanation offers only as many explanatory entities as needed.* When faced with the dead body and the candlestick bearing the butler's fingerprints, even if there were no evidence pointing toward the chambermaid, an alternative explanation might have been this:

> The butler and the chambermaid committed the murder together, but only the chambermaid was wearing gloves.

The observable outcome follows from this explanation just as well as it does from the explanation that it was merely the butler who did it, but the simpler butler explanation has a higher prior probability. Why? Suppose the prior probability that the butler did it was .10, likewise for the chambermaid. Then, recalling our discussion of evaluating the truth of both–and sentences in Chapter 10, the prior probability that it was both of them can be roughly understood as .10 times .10, or .01. Add a moving part to the machine, and the probability that every part will work drops dramatically.

This interlocks with the test, under the preceding improbable-outcome criterion, of asking whether an explanation for the outcome already exists.

When an explanation already exists, the arguer is free to respond in, for example, the case of the student pilots' performance, "OK, but this outcome is explained *both* by the efficacy of punishment and by the normal return to the current mean after an aberrant performance." But now it violates the second part of the total evidence condition as well!

Aspects of Simplicity

1. For singular explanations, the simplest one normally offers the fewest explanatory entities.
2. For general explanations, the simplest one normally predicts the smoothest curve.

For general explanations, a good way to check for simplicity is to ask *whether the explanation predicts the smoothest possible curve.*In the 17th century, the Italian mathematician Torricelli hypothesized that the Earth was surrounded by a sea of air, which decreased in pressure uniformly as the altitude increased. Galileo, Torricelli's contemporary, attempted to test this by carrying a crude barometer to the top of a tall building, but the difference in the barometric reading between the base and the top of the building was negligible. Another contemporary of his, French mathematician and philosopher Blaise Pascal, suspected that Torricelli was right but that a greater altitude was required to prove it. Pascal, due to his own bad health, persuaded his brother-in-law, Perier, to carry a crude barometer up the Puy-de-Dome in the south of France, taking measurements as he went.

Perier stopped and measured the barometer from time to time as he scaled the mountain, with results that were widely taken as impressive proof of Torricelli's hypothesis. The reading in Paris, at sea level, was 30 inches; at the base of the Puy-de-Dome, at 1,300 feet, it was about 28.7 inches; and at the mountain's peak, at 4,800 feet, it was about 25.2 inches. For the sake of illustration, I will slightly idealize the intermediate readings: say, it was 28.2 inches at 1,800 feet, then one inch lower at each of the next thousand-foot intervals.[5] A graph of these results, representing our evidence in this case, looks like this.

[5]An engaging and more detailed account of this experiment can be found in Keith Arnold's "Pascal's Great Experiment," *Dialogue* 28, (1989), pp. 401–15.

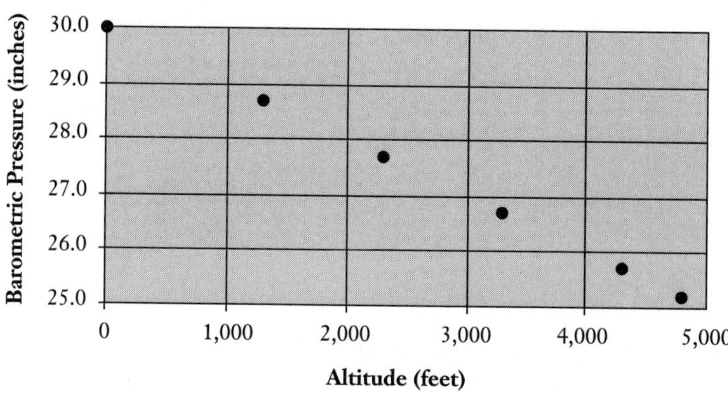

The argument might now be clarified as follows:

1. If the Earth is surrounded by a sea of air that decreases uniformly in pressure as the altitude increases, then Perier's barometer reads 30 inches at 0 feet, 28.7 inches at 1,300 feet, 28.2 inches at 1,800 feet, 27.2 inches at 2,800 feet, and 26.2 inches at 3,800 feet, and 25.2 inches at 4,800 feet.
2. Perier's barometer reads 30 inches at 0 feet, 28.7 inches at 1,300 feet, 28.2 inches at 1,800 feet, 27.2 inches at 2,800 feet, 26.2 inches at 3,800 feet, and 25.2 inches at 4,800 feet.

∴ *C.* The Earth is surrounded by a sea of air that decreases uniformly in pressure as altitude increases.

Given that the explanation calls for a *uniform* decrease in air pressure, it would then predict that if samples were taken at all other altitudes on the Puy-de-Dome, they would be plotted on the graph along a line described by the smoothest curve that can be drawn through the points already there, as follows.

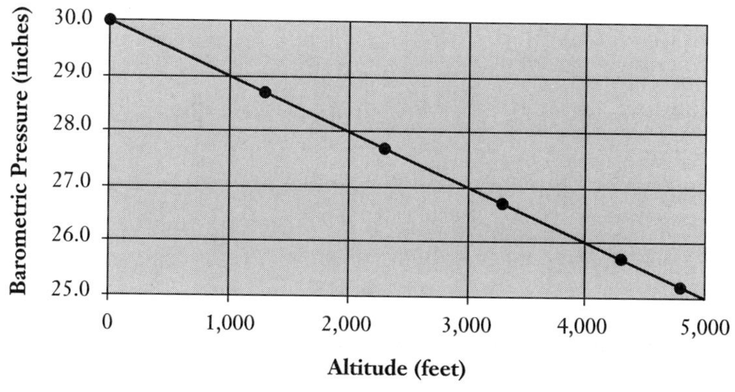

But suppose I offer the alternative explanation that air pressure is highly irregular but that it so happens that barometric pressure nevertheless would be 30 inches at 0 feet, 28.7 inches at 1,300 feet, 28.2 inches at 1,800 feet, 27.2 inches at 2,800 feet, 26.2 inches at 3,800 feet, and 25.2 inches at 4,800 feet. The line on the chart, I argue, does pass through the six plotted points but otherwise zigzags wildly, say, as follows.

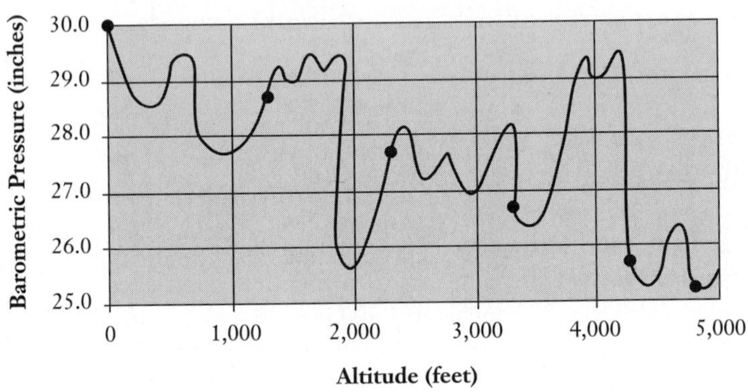

Both explanations do an equally good job of entailing Perier's results as their observable outcome. But the first one, Torricelli's, has a higher prior probability because it is simpler, due to its prediction of a smoother curve.

The simplicity test, as explained here, is related to the makes-sense test. As we have seen, explanations that make good sense are those for which we have an adequate conceptual framework—for which we have a reasonably good account of the causal mechanisms involved. Further, we suppose that causal mechanisms operate uniformly in the world—that under similar circumstances they operate similarly, and that slight dissimilarities in circumstances tend to produce slight dissimilarities in the way they operate. Slightly less oxygen means that we get tired a little sooner; slightly worn brakes stop the car a little more slowly; slightly less sunlight means the plant grows a little shorter. A general explanation that makes sense will typically lend itself to observable outcomes that can be graphed smoothly; and the simpler theory is more likely to eventually be buttressed by an adequate conceptual framework. This is what happened with Torricelli's hypothesis. The conceptual framework was eventually supplied: the most important causal mechanism behind it is gravity, and, according to the eventually well-established Newtonian laws, gravity's pull on the air molecules decreases regularly as distance from Earth increases.

Guideline. Simplicity contributes to epistemic probability, so ask whether the explanation is sufficiently simple. One test is to ask whether it offers only as many explanatory entities as needed. Another is to ask whether it predicts the smoothest curve.

Look for Coincidence as an Alternative Explanation

When you cannot think of another explanation, it can be tempting to accept an explanatory argument even when the prior probability of the explanation is exceedingly low. Resist the temptation, especially when you can see that coincidence has not been ruled out as an alternative explanation.

Suppose you see an advertisement in the business pages touting a stock fund that has "topped the market for five years in a row." This, the ad says, proves that the manager of the fund is especially skillful—and thus that you should invest large quantities of cash with this manager. The leading alternative explanation is that the manager has succeeded by sheer luck. What is the prior probability of this alternative? Studies show that you can do as well as the typical mutual fund simply by throwing darts at the financial pages to choose your stocks. Thus, the prior probability of beating the market in a single year is roughly .50.[6] The probability of two consecutive years of success is no higher than .50 times .50, or .25. Doing the math for five years, we find that the prior probability of the coincidence explanation is about .03—that is, about 1 in 30 could be expected to have this kind of success just by chance.

And what is the prior probability of the skill explanation? There are a few money managers who succeed on the basis of skill—multibillionaire Warren Buffet is the most famous example. Further, we have a conceptual framework for Buffet's skill—the causal mechanism makes sense—for his strategies have been widely publicized, and the small handful of others who have had the discipline to follow them have also succeeded over the long run. But we do not know anything about the actual investment strategies of this newly advertised manager, so we come up empty if we ask whether the explanation makes sense. The best we can do is look at frequencies; and research shows that the vast majority of money managers turn in performances that are no better than

[6]Roughly, since we are not allowing for the cost of commissions, for dividend income, and the like.

chance. It is doubtful that more than 1 in 30 is able to win five years in a row on the basis of skill—that is, the probability of succeeding for five years by skill is probably no better than the probability of doing it by chance. In short, coincidence has not been ruled out, so we cannot judge this to be a logically strong argument. Note that I am being careful *not* to say that coincidence is thus proven to be the correct explanation; the point, a more modest one, is that skill is *not* supported as the correct explanation. We do not have to establish the correct explanation to establish that the argument is a bad one.

This point is not lost on investment companies. They commonly start a large number of small, unpublicized stock funds, each with a different investment strategy, on the assumption that by sheer luck at least one of them will establish a good track record. The funds that fail are closed, and the manager of the one that succeeds is advertised widely. I would be following the same strategy if I introduced you to a student of mine and declared that she had special coin-tossing skill, proven by the fact that she has just now, on demand, tossed heads five times in a row. You might be impressed until you learn that I asked all 30 students in my class to stand up and try to toss heads. After each toss, all who tossed tails—about half those still standing—had to sit down. There were 15, then 8, then 4, then 2; then, after the fifth toss, this one student remained. The fact remains that she tossed heads, on demand, five times in a row, but you now realize that coincidence is at least as good an explanation as talent—after all, how many people can actually toss heads whenever they want?—and you are likely to lose interest.

This insight can be especially valuable when improbable events are explained by appeal to the paranormal. Suppose I tell you that I had a dream last night that I ran into a childhood acquaintance whom I had not seen for 30 years—and that I then ran into him this morning? Your first thought would probably be that this supports the explanation that we are sometimes able to see into the future via our dreams. But this explanation has an exceedingly low prior probability. No one can even begin to provide an account of the conceptual framework, of the causal mechanisms, that would make sense of it. This is the place to ask about coincidence as an alternative explanation. I have had many thousands of dreams—most of which I have immediately forgotten, in part because they have *not* come true. By sheer coincidence, a few of these thousands of dreams are going to seem to come true, and these are the ones that will stick most vividly in my memory (remember the vividness shortcut from Chapter 1). Just like the coin-toss and mutual fund cases, coincidence does make sense and is at least as likely here as the paranormal. So the argument's logic must be considered weak.

Guideline. If the prior probability of the explanation is extremely low and coincidence has not been ruled out as an alternative explanation, judge the logic of the argument to be weak.

Two Alternative Explanations to Bear in Mind

1. Coincidence
2. Deception

Look for Deception as an Alternative Explanation

When an explanation's prior probability is extremely low, another alternative explanation is deception. My heads-tossing student *may* have been skillful, or she *may* have gotten lucky . . . or she *may* have been secretly using a two-headed coin. Neither of the two alternatives has been ruled out, and either is more probable than that she is one of the very few people who has perfected special coin-tossing skill.

Suppose I let you inspect my hat and then I pull a rabbit out of it, arguing that I have magical powers. That explanation has a nearly nil prior probability, since it does not make any sense; there is no uncontroversial example of this sort of thing actually happening, and we haven't the slightest notion of the causal mechanisms that would be involved. We do know, however, that *deception* of this sort happens—that there are entertainers who work very hard at producing illusions like this, and they can make a lot of honest money at it. So, not only is the prior probability of magic negligible, but it is far lower than that of the leading alternative, illusion. The logic of the argument is accordingly weak.

This is not to say dogmatically that magic cannot happen. Rather, it is to say that an argument for magic must meet high standards, and this one does not yet do so. To return to an earlier case, no lesser a light than Thomas Jefferson, when he heard the reports of meteorites from Harvard and Brown professors, said, "I would rather believe that the Yankee professors lied than that stones fall from the heavens." This was probably reasonable as an initial reaction—though, in this case, the high standards were eventually met.

Nevertheless, smart people suffer lapses of rationality and allow themselves to be persuaded that a man like Uri Geller has special powers because he can perform feats that any practiced illusionist can perform—and can detect. The only difference is that Geller claims that he is not using deception. But this does not make the special-powers explanation more probable than the deception explanation; it simply enlarges the deception.

So-called crop circles in southern England's grain fields were widely reported in the media a few years ago. These were huge, precise patterns of bent stalks of wheat, corn, and barley that lent themselves to spectacular aerial photographs. Proponents of the paranormal seized on them as new evidence of visitations from other galaxies; said one Patrick Delgado, author of several profitable books on the subject: "No human being could have done this. These crops are laid down in these sensational patterns by an energy that is of a high level of intelligence." Alas, two British painters finally confessed that they had perpetrated the hoax over a 13-year period simply by pulling around flat, four-foot planks by hand with reins to topple over the stalks. Circles that had only later begun to appear elsewhere, they suggested, were created by copycats. Said author Delgado, "We have been conned. This is a dirty trick. Thousands of lives are going to be wrecked over this." At least one source of income was going to be wrecked.

Those desperate to discredit a good explanatory argument might misuse this guideline. Just as a good explanatory argument rules out coincidence, it also rules out deception. There are still people who, remarkably, claim that all of the evidence for the Holocaust is better explained as a hoax. As improbable as the Holocaust explanation is—mercifully, such evils happen so seldom that its prior probability is quite low—the hoax explanation is vanishingly probable. Far worse than the plumber explanation from Dear Abby, it requires a long list of independently improbable things all to be true—alternative ways, for example of accounting for the following: the vast documentation rescued from the German Archives; the elaborate sealed rooms set up for funneling the prisoners to their deaths; the movement of enormous quantities of asphyxiating Xyklon B gas to the death camps; the photographs of mounds of bodies; the vast body of eyewitness testimony by both victims and their murderers; and the otherwise mysterious disappearance from history of millions of Jews. The deception explanation should often be considered, but it is subject to the same high standards that apply to any other explanatory argument.

Guideline. If the prior probability of the explanation is extremely low and deception has not been ruled out as an alternative explanation, judge the logic of the argument to be weak.

EXERCISES Chapter 16, set (i)

Bring it all together by fully clarifying and evaluating the explanatory arguments in each of these passages.

Sample exercise. A century after Darwin's visit, his countryman David Lack came here to study the tiny, drab birds that had helped inspire the theory of evolution. Lack noticed that on an island shared by two species of finches, one's beak was markedly smaller than the other's. But where either species lived by itself on an island, it developed a beak in between these two extremes. Lack suggested that a finch species alone on an island evolved an intermediate beak for eating seeds of various sizes. But where the two species competed for seeds, one evolved a beak suited for the small seeds, while the other developed a beak for the large seeds. Skeptics have suggested another explanation: Perhaps this is because of peculiarities in each island's food. A team of researchers recently found no differences that would account for the beak variations. The researchers also monitored a drought that killed off 85 percent of the finches on an island one year. The survivors were the finches with beaks closest to either of the two extremes—a demonstration of how competition eliminates intermediate beaks and forces each species to specialize in seeds of one size. —*Science85*

Sample answer.

[1. If competition for food among finches on Galapagos is the main cause of extremes in beak sizes, then there are extremes in beak sizes on Galapagos finches, there is no relevant difference in food from island to island, and in conditions of scarcity the finches with extremes survive best.]

2. There are extremes in beak sizes on Galapagos finches, there is no relevant difference in food from island to island, and in conditions of scarcity the finches with extremes survive best.

∴ *C.* Competition for food among finches on Galapagos causes the extremes in beak sizes.

EVALUATION

TRUTH

Premise 1 is probably true. Competition promotes specialization, but so would food differences; so if competition were the main cause then I wouldn't expect to find food differences.

Premise 2 is probably true. The magazine reporting it is reliable, and there is no reason to distrust it in this case.

LOGIC

Fairly strong. Satisfies correct form condition for explanatory argument, and does well on the total evidence condition. First part: The prior probability of the prediction is extremely low—helped especially by the inclusion of predictions (i.e., no relevant difference in food from island to island) that succeed in falsifying alternative hypotheses (i.e., that the difference is because of difference in food). Second part: Reasonably high prior probability for the explanation; the causal mechanism—natural selection—is fairly well understood, and no alternate seems more likely.

SOUNDNESS

Probably fairly sound.

1. What prehistoric culture created the huge and magnificent likeness of George Bernard Shaw that is topographically sculpted on the southern tip of an island in the Leaf River in northern Quebec? The achievement is all the more remarkable when you consider that the mysterious sculptors created their masterpiece millennia before the existence of their subject. (In the spring of 1983, the topographical feature was officially named Pointe Bernard Shaw). —*Discover*
2. An estimated 10,000 computer disks were mailed from London to banks, hospitals, medical labs, and private citizens worldwide. Each was labeled "AIDS Information Diskette" and professed to carry "health information specially designed to help those concerned about AIDS." But once installed, the program destroyed previously stored data. Officials were left to wonder why the perpetrator would go to such trouble and expense. One theory is that the prank was intended as a lesson in how easy it is to get AIDS. But researchers and AIDS activists would seem unlikely targets for such an effort. It appears, in the end, that someone is simply very rich and very malicious. —*Time*
3. Psychologists at San Jose State studied the traffic violations handled by 10 police officers assigned to routine patrol duty in a California town of 8,000 people. Researchers found that during a three-year period, the percentage of tickets, compared to simple warnings, was considerably higher during the night shift: more than 71 percent of the drivers stopped at night got tickets, compared with 58 percent of those stopped during the day (the others got warnings). The researchers suggest that the ticket-happy cops may simply be suffering

from loss of sleep, which has been shown to increase irritability and aggressiveness. —*Psychology Today*

4. Why is Tylenol "the pain reliever hospitals use most?" The ads imply that it's better than other brands. But the editors at *Consumer Reports* learned that hospitals buy their drugs through competitive bidding, and that they usually only buy one brand of any drug, and that Tylenol is the cheapest of the painkillers. This may come as a surprise to you if you've recently bought a package—at retail it's among the priciest. But its maker, Johnson and Johnson, is the king of discounters when selling to hospitals. One doctor said, "One brand is as good as another. The company gives it to us dirt cheap, so how can we resist?"—*Consumer Reports* (Focus on the explanation that Tylenol is encouraging us to adopt.)
5. Dr. R. A. Rabinoff, professor of physics at Maharishi International University (MIU), presented a paper titled "Effect of Coherent Collective Consciousness on the Weather" reporting evidence that the weather could be modified by practicing transcendental meditation (TM). During the previous winter MIU had been involved in a major construction project (a domed structure for the practice of levitation). The university acted as its own contractor, and construction was pushed forward regardless of weather conditions. This disregard for weather extended even to the pouring of concrete. Concrete, according to the campus architect, was poured whenever the schedule required and the necessary materials were available. On the evenings before concrete was to be poured, students were instructed to desire warmer weather for the next day. Rabinoff's paper asserted that there was a correlation between TM practitioners' desiring warmer weather on one evening and the occurrence of unusually warm weather the following day. Rabinoff claimed that this was evidence for a cause–effect relationship between TM and the weather.

   A later investigation showed that there was indeed a correlation between TM and warmer weather, but an even stronger correlation between TM and the preceding afternoon's forecast of warmer weather for the next day. MIU had practiced TM on eight nonconsecutive days, without a miss, when the preceding day's forecast predicted mild or continuing mild weather. MIU's architect had said only that the decision to pour concrete was based on the construction schedule and the availability of certain materials. But it turned out that concrete was available only when mild weather had been predicted. The MIU supplier of concrete had required MIU to give one day's notice of the need for concrete, but never agreed to provide it for the next day until first referring to the National Weather Service. —Franklin D. Trumpy, *Skeptical Inquirer* (Concern yourself with the inference made by Dr. Rabinoff.)

SUMMARY OF CHAPTER SIXTEEN

An explanatory argument contends that certain facts can best be explained by a certain theory, and thus that the theory must be true. The first premise states that the theory, or the explanation, really does enable you to predict the facts, or the observable outcome. The second premise states that the observable outcome has happened—that it really has been observed. And the argument concludes that the explanation is thus true. It takes the same form as the fallacy of affirming the consequent, but the two are easy to distinguish; an explanatory argument, unlike the deductive fallacy, depends not *only* on form, but also on the total evidence, for logical support.

In some explanatory arguments, the explanatory theory is first invented, then the observable outcome is predicted and looked for. In others, the outcome is first observed, then the explanation is invented to account for it; although these are subject to exactly the same evaluative conditions as the first sort, we can more easily be fooled by them. In another type of distinction, some explanatory arguments are general, given that they have application to a wide range of possible observable outcomes; others are singular, in that they apply only to a specific outcome. Again, the two sorts are subject to the same logical standards, though we can shape our inquiry a bit differently in each case.

As with our other inductive arguments, the total evidence condition for logical success has two parts. The first part focuses on the importance of the improbability of the outcome. More precisely, the condition is that the prior probability of the observable outcome must be sufficiently low. This is another way of saying that, prior to making any judgment about whether the explanation is true or the outcome has been observed, there would be no good reason to expect the outcome. If there is good reason to expect it anyway, then the explanation is doing no work and receives no logical support. To test for this, there are several questions that can require "yes" answers. Is the explanation falsifiable? Is the outcome stated precisely? Is there no other explanation of the outcome that already exists? Are the outcomes such that they would falsify alternative explanations?

The second part of the total evidence condition focuses on the probability of the explanation. The explanation's prior probability—that is, its probability prior to judging whether the observable outcome is true—must not be implausibly low and it must be higher than that of the leading alternative explanations. As with the first part, there are various ways of testing for this. If it is a singular explanation, you can ask if it is the sort of thing that is known to happen, and if it tends to happen more frequently than do the alternatives. For any explanation you can ask whether it makes sense—that is, whether there is an adequate conceptual framework to account for the causal mechanisms required by the explanation. And, finally, you can ask if the explanation is sufficiently simple. In some cases, it can be tempting to accept an explanation with an extremely low prior probability simply because you cannot think of any plausible alternative. In these cases it is better to say that you simply cannot decide, especially if the argument has not ruled out coincidence or deception as alternative explanations.

GUIDELINES FOR CHAPTER SIXTEEN

- Structure an explanatory argument, when it would be loyal to do so, as follows: the first premise states that if the explanation is correct, then a specified outcome of it will be observable; the second premise states that the outcome has been observed; and the conclusion states that the explanation is thus correct.
- Be careful not to confuse explanatory arguments with deductive arguments that commit the fallacy of affirming the consequent.
- Be more suspicious of explanatory arguments in which the explanation was invented after the observable outcome was observed.
- As a useful standard, apply the surprise test by asking whether the outcome would surprise you (assuming you reserved judgment about whether the explanation were true and whether the outcome had been observed). If so, then it probably has a low prior probability.
- Reject explanatory arguments that have unfalsifiable explanations; they are in principle unable to satisfy the first part of the total evidence condition.
- Ask whether the outcome is too vague. Vague outcomes are likely to have a high prior probability and thus are likely to signal that the argument is logically weak.
- Ask whether an explanation for the outcome already exists. If an explanation does already exist, then the outcome has a high prior probability and the argument is logically weak.

- Ask whether an outcome rules out the leading alternative explanations. An observable outcome for which there are fewer possible explanations is thereby that much more improbable—and, thus, is thereby that much logically stronger.
- The second part of the total evidence condition for explanatory arguments is this: the probability of the explanation must not be implausibly low and must be higher than that of the leading alternative explanations. This requires imagination in coming up with alternative explanations for the sake of comparison.
- For singular explanations, ask whether this sort of explanation is known to occur and, if so, if it occurs more frequently than do the leading alternative explanations. If the answer is yes, then the argument is at least moderately strong (assuming it has not failed the first part of the total evidence condition).
- For both general and singular explanations, ask whether this sort of explanation makes sense—that is, whether there is a satisfactory conceptual framework for it and whether it is more satisfactory than the alternatives. If the explanation leaves too much to mystery, or requires too much of established science to be replaced by less well-established views, then the argument can normally be no better than logically weak.
- Simplicity contributes to epistemic probability, so ask whether the explanation is sufficiently simple. One test is to ask whether it offers only as many explanatory entities as needed. Another is to ask whether it predicts the smoothest curve.
- If the prior probability of the explanation is extremely low and coincidence has not been ruled out as an alternative explanation, judge the logic of the argument to be weak.
- If the prior probability of the explanation is extremely low and deception has not been ruled out as an alternative explanation, judge the logic of the argument to be weak.

GLOSSARY FOR CHAPTER SIXTEEN

Confirmation bias—our natural tendency to look for outcomes that support our preferred explanation rather than those that might also falsify the alternatives.

Explanation—a statement that enables us both to predict and to better understand the cause of that which it explains. Also termed a *theory* or an *explanatory hypothesis.*

Explanatory argument—an argument whose correct form, assuming that P is the explanation and Q is the observable outcome, is this:

1. If P then Q.
2. Q

$\therefore$ C. P

The first premise states that the explanation really does enable you to predict the observable outcome—that it really is an *outcome.* The second premise states that the observable outcome has happened—that it has been *observed.* And the argument concludes with the assertion of the explanation. Also called a *theoretical argument, inference to the best explanation, hypothetico-deductive argument, transcendental argument,* or *diagnostic argument.*

Falsifiability—the requirement that it be possible to specify some observable outcome of an explanation that *could* prove it to be false. This is a way of emphasizing the importance of an improbable outcome. To say that an explanation or an outcome is not falsifiable is to say that *any observation at all* is consistent with the explanation. And it is highly probable that we will have "any observation at all." So, an unfalsifiable explanation fails the improbable outcome test.

General explanation—an explanation that can apply to a wide range of observable outcomes. Newton's theories, for example, while applied here to Halley's comet, actually cover the motion of all objects at all times. General explanations are typical of science, though are not restricted to it.

Observable outcome—what is explained in an explanatory argument; the observable outcome follows from the explanation and can in a certain way, at a certain time, and under certain conditions, be seen, heard, smelled, tasted, or touched. Also termed the *data,* the *prediction,* or the *facts.*

Singular explanation—an explanation that is designed to apply only to a single thing or event. Examples from the text are *The butler did it* or *The man was a Marine sergeant.*

Epilogue

The wayfarer
Perceiving the pathway to truth,
Was struck with astonishment.
It was thickly grown with weeds.
"Ha," he said,
"I see that none has passed here
In a long time."
Later he saw that each weed
Was a singular knife.
"Well," he mumbled at last,
"Doubtless there are other roads."

—Stephen Crane

If you have performed well on the exercises in this book and on your exams, it shows that you understand the merits of arguments—that you know how to clarify an argument, check the truth of various kinds of statements, evaluate the logic of different argument forms, and tell whether an argument is connected to the conversation. One explanation for your success might be that you are a good reasoner. But a better explanation might be that you are a good student—good students being more common than good reasoners.

If, however, you are now incorporating this understanding into your life, then you consistently care about the quality of arguments; you accept answers to your questions only when the argument is clear, addresses your question, is logical, and has premises that are probably true. This means you are acquiring the virtue of critical reflection. If you are at the same time seeking out new evidence from the world around you when it is needed, then you are also acquiring the virtue of empirical inquiry.

The virtues of critical reflection and empirical inquiry are the observable outcomes of the virtue of intellectual honesty. Besides honesty, there is normally no other plausible explanation for their existence (brainwashing could produce them, but brains washed clean of all motives are rarer than brains with clean motives). And these virtues have a low prior probability—we would be surprised to find critical reflection and empirical inquiry in an intellectually dishonest person. So if you are becoming more reflective and inquisitive, the best explanation is that you actively *want* to be such a person—that you now want not merely to adopt convenient beliefs but *to know the truth* about the questions you care about. This explanatory argument can provide the best possible indication that you are becoming more intellectually honest. Because, in the end, intellectual honesty is the best possible guide to good reasoning.

INDEX